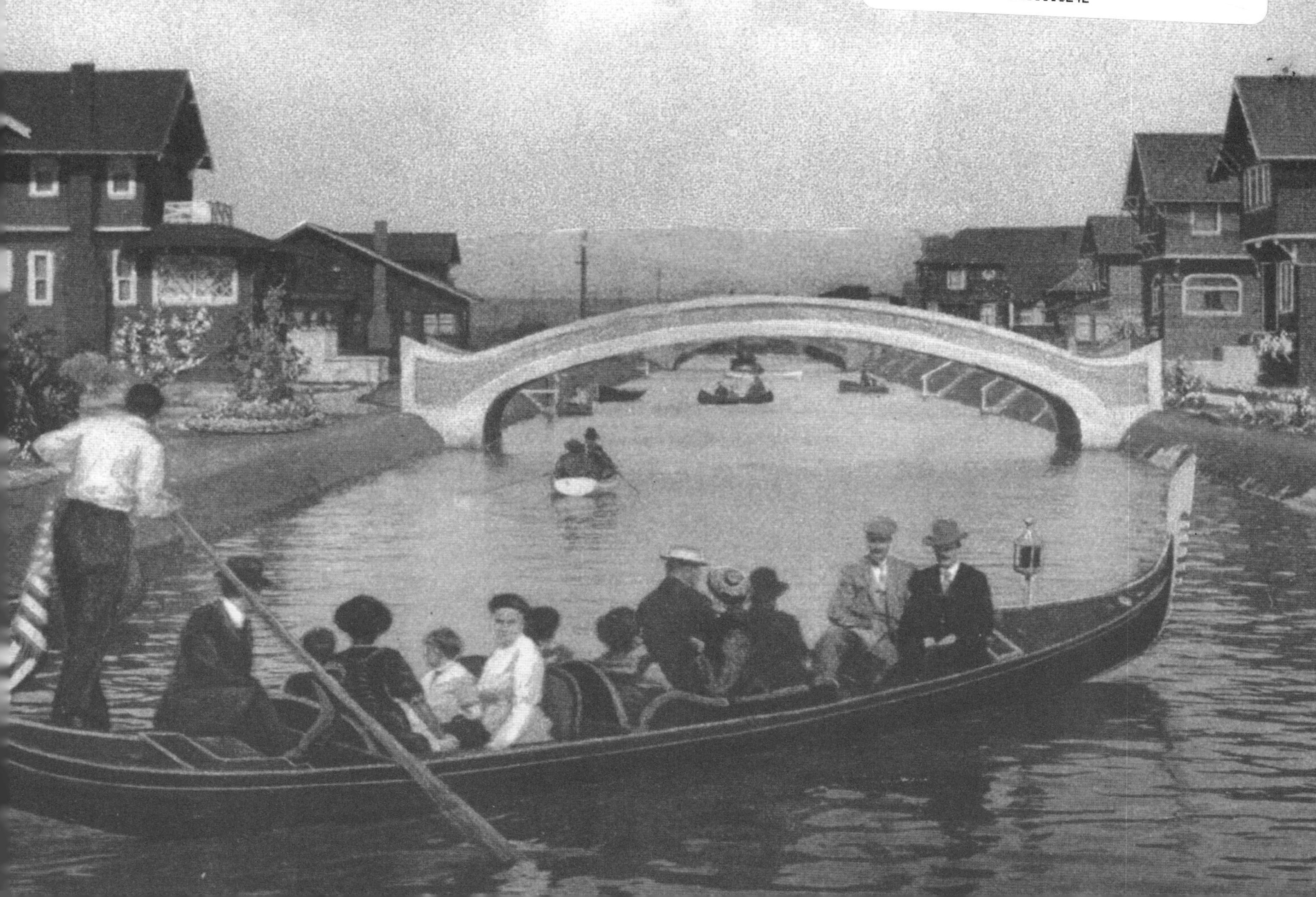
2404 – Residences on the Canal, Ve

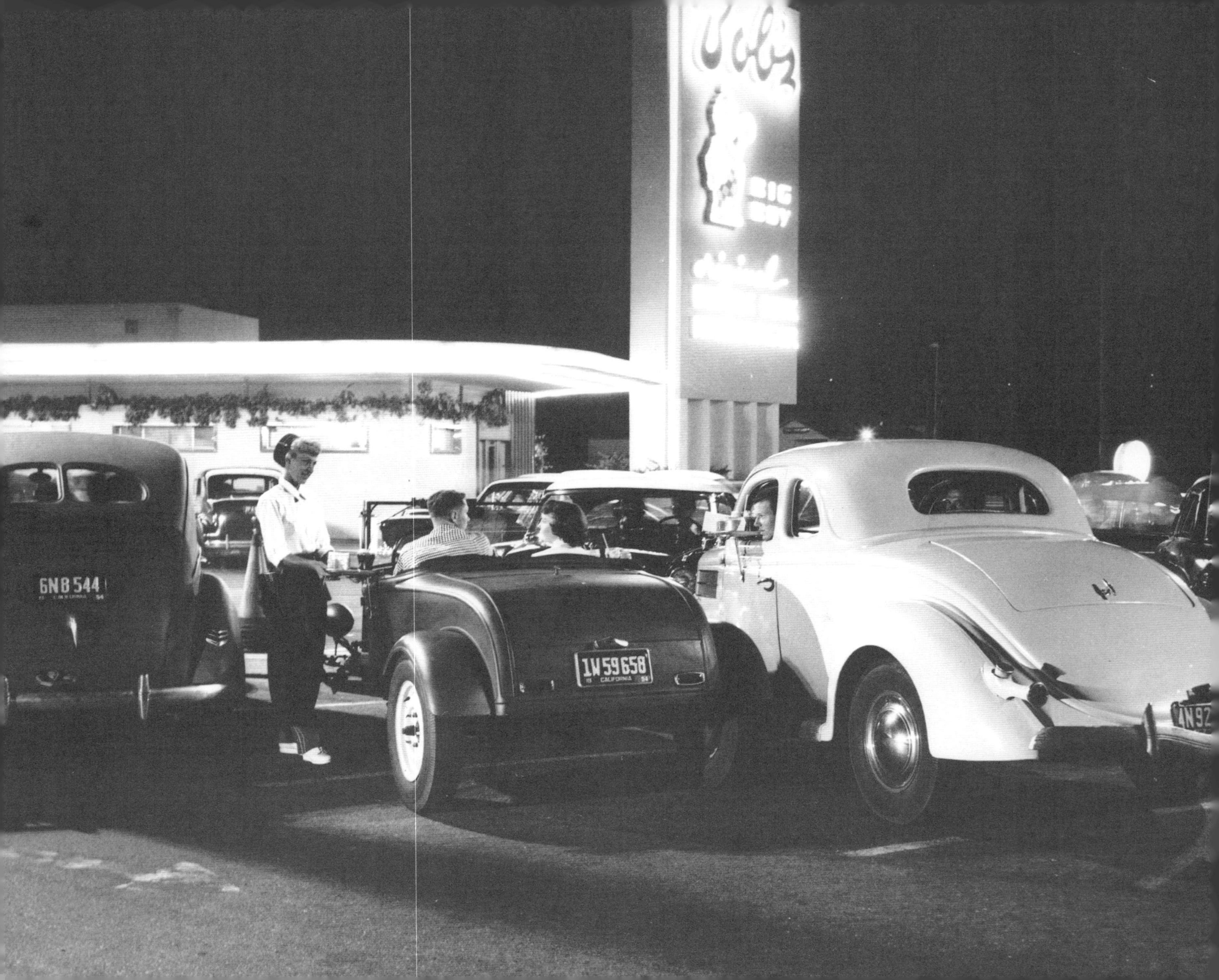
BIG BOY
6NB 544
CALIFORNIA
1W59658
CALIFORNIA

GREETINGS FROM

# Los Angeles

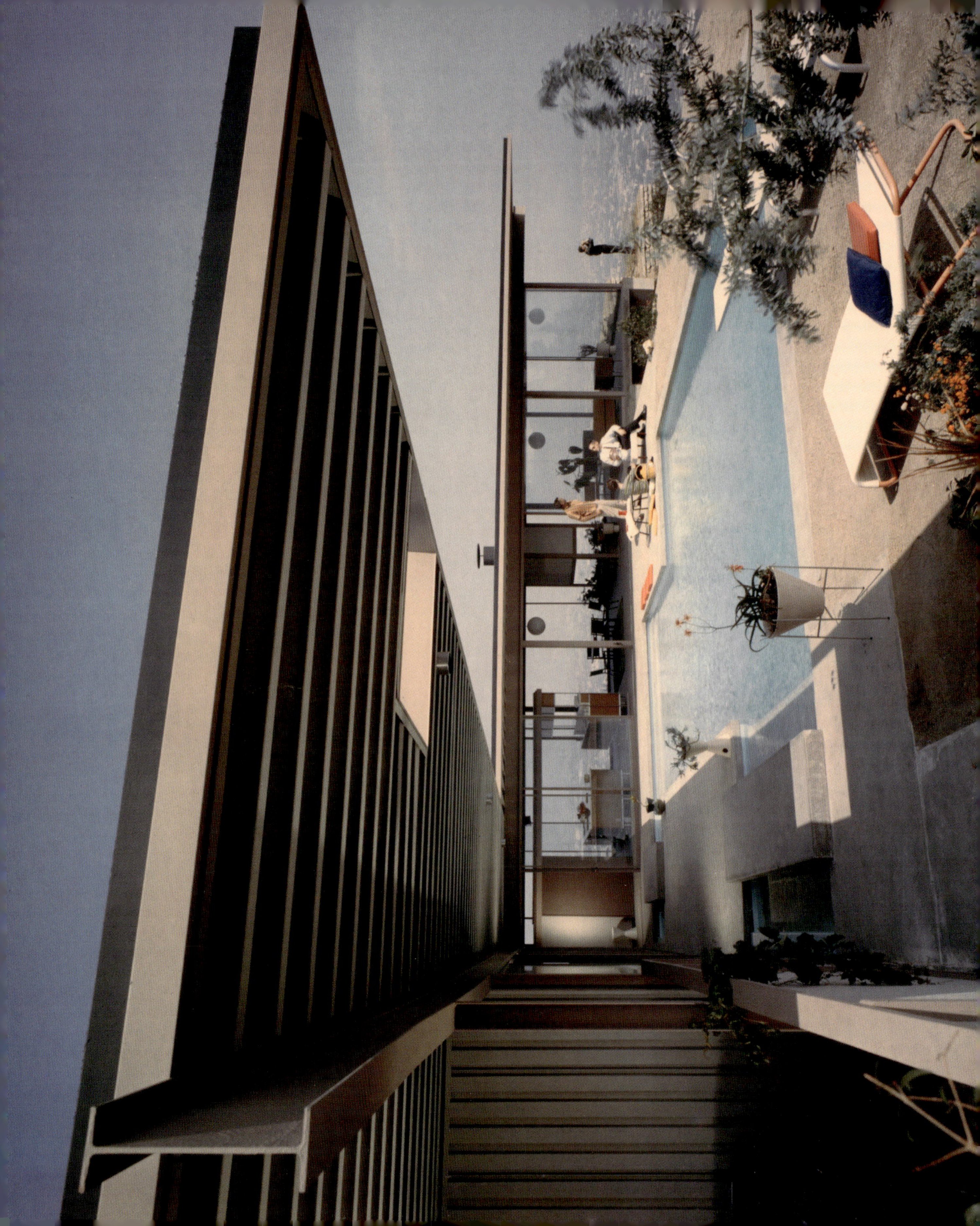

# Greetings from Los Angeles

PETER MORUZZI

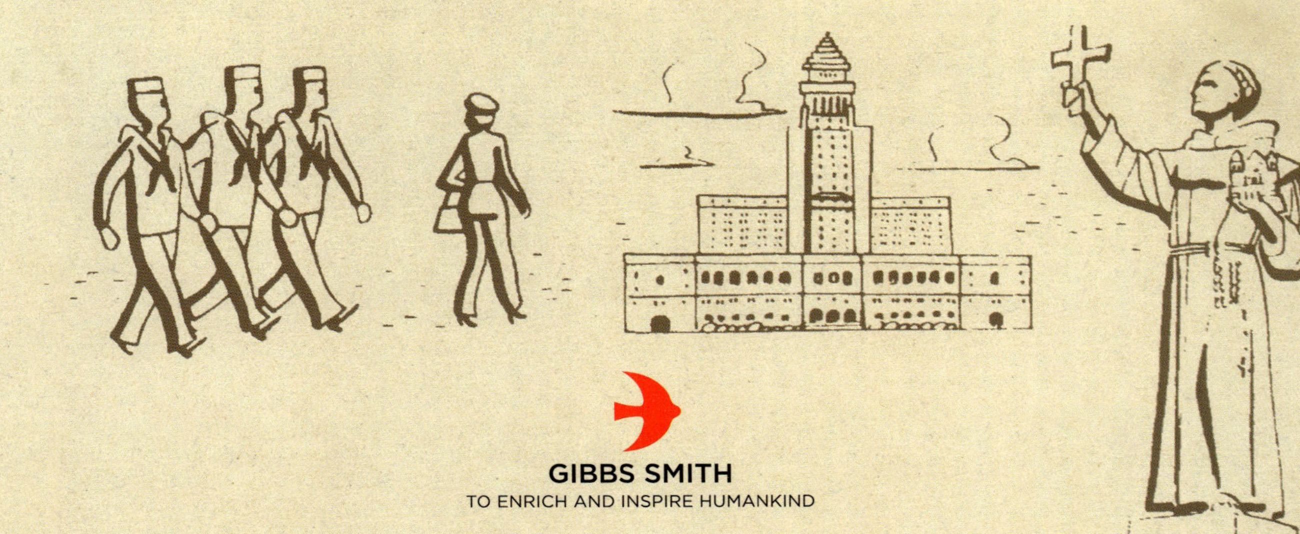

GIBBS SMITH
TO ENRICH AND INSPIRE HUMANKIND

First Edition
21 20 19 5 4 3



Published by
Gibbs Smith
P.O. Box 667
Layton, Utah 84041

1.800.835.4993 orders
www.gibbs-smith.com

Designed by Kurt Wahlner
Printed and bound in China

Gibbs Smith books are printed on either recycled, 100% post-consumer waste, FSC-certified papers or on paper produced from sustainable PEFC-certified forest/controlled wood source. Learn more at www.pefc.org.

Library of Congress Cataloging-in-Publication Data
Names: Moruzzi, Peter, author.
Title: Greetings from Los Angeles / Peter Moruzzi.
Description: First edition. | Layton, Utah : Gibbs Smith, 2017.
Identifiers: LCCN 2017000319 | ISBN 9781423647256 (jacketless hardcover)
Subjects: LCSH: Los Angeles (Calif.)--History--20th century--Pictorial works. | Neighborhoods--California--Los Angeles--History--20th century--Pictorial works. | Historic buildings--California--Los Angeles--Pictorial works. | Historic sites--California--Los Angeles--Pictorial works. |Los Angeles (Calif.)--Buildings, structures, etc.--Pictorial works.
Classification: LCC F869.L843 M68 2017 | DDC 979.4/94--dc23
LC record available at https://lccn.loc.gov/2017000319

# IMAGE CREDITS

All images from author Peter Moruzzi's collection except for the following:
Copyright © J. Paul Getty Trust. Getty Research Institute, Los Angeles (2004.R.10): Pages 2, 60, 61, 92 (bottom), 93, 106, 107, 114 (right)
Historic Site of the Original McDonald's Museum: Page 154 (left)
International Bowling Museum and Hall of Fame: Endsheets, page 142
Sven A. Kirsten: Page 176 (top right)
Los Angeles Department of Water and Power: Page 24
Los Angeles Public Library Photo Collection: Endsheets, Pages 63 (bottom), 79 (left and right), 80 (top left and bottom left), 85, 132, 133, 137, 140, 143 (top right and bottom right)
Los Angeles Times: Pages 70, 89
Chris Nichols Collection: Endsheets, Pages 8 (left), 47 (left), 65 (top right), 66 (right), 99 (bottom left), 104, 116 (left), 117 (top left and middle right), 118 (bottom), 120 (left), 126 (right), 158 (top right)
Gordon Powers Collection: Page 119 (top)
Kurt Wahlner Collection: Pages 50, 51 (bottom left)
Brent Walker Collection: Page 40 (top left)

# Contents

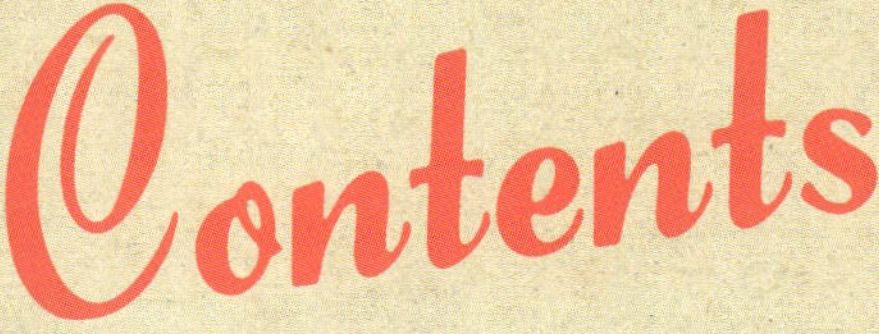
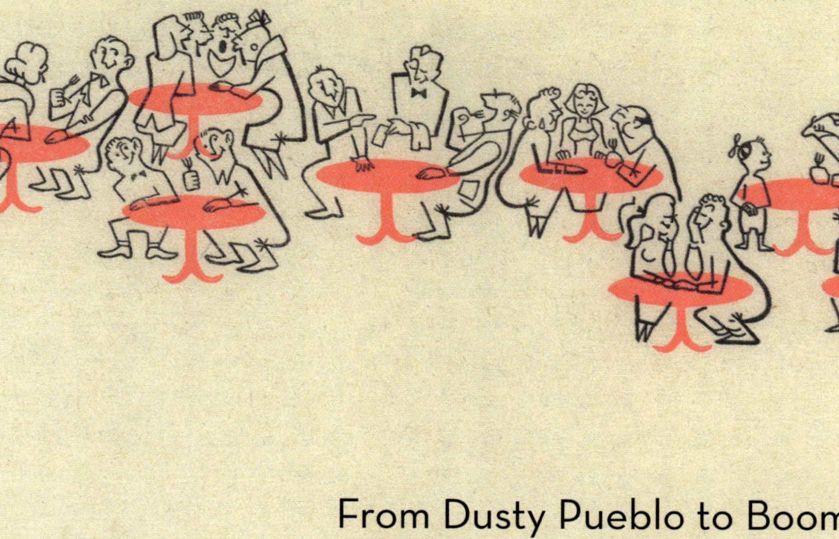

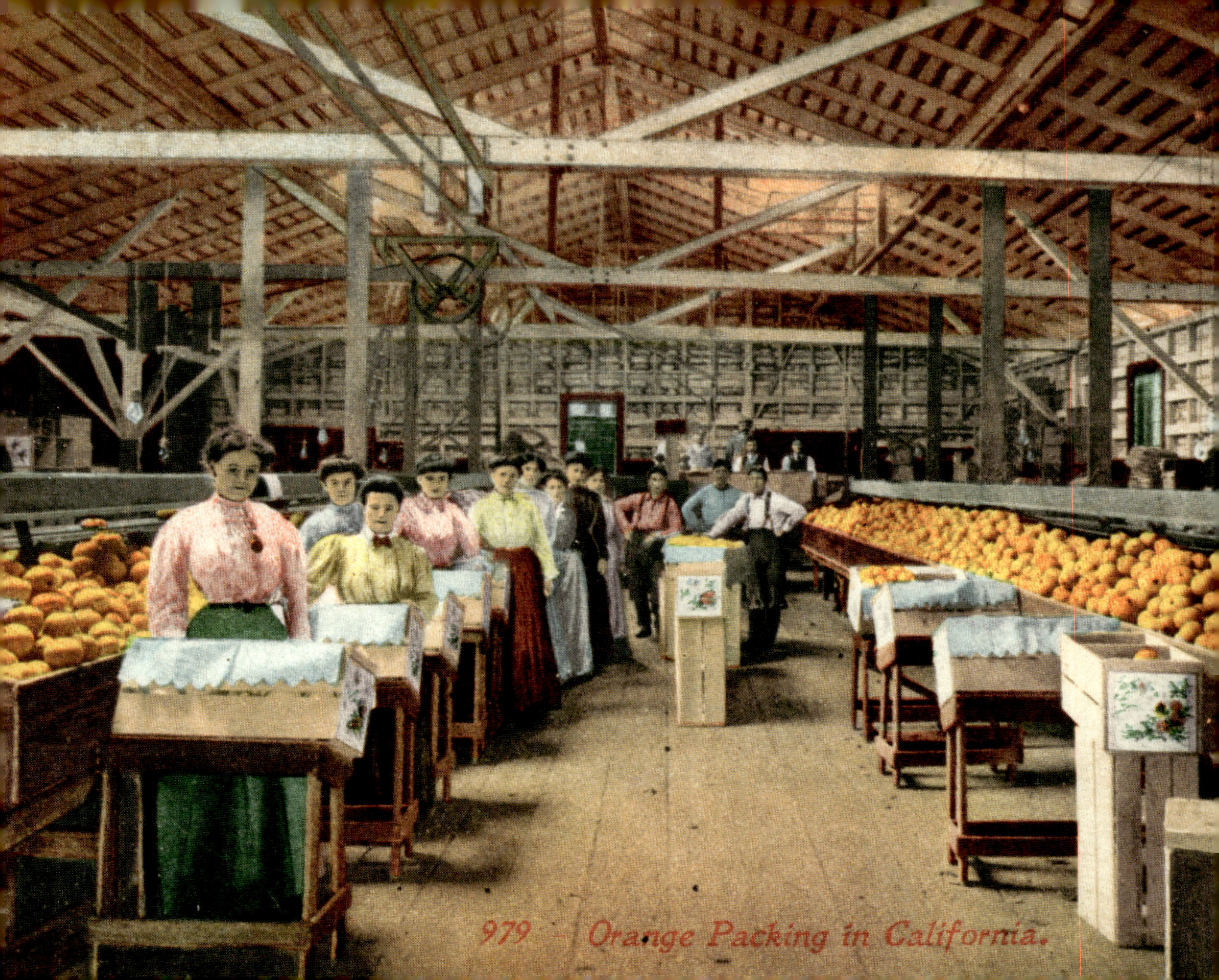
979 - Orange Packing in California.

# From Dusty Pueblo to Boomtown

## 1850–1900

The area that would become the city of Los Angeles began as a village established by the Native American Tongva (or Gabrieleño) people. In the 1760s, the Spanish Crown expanded its reach from Mexico north to Alta California, founding a pueblo in 1781 that they named El Pueblo de Nuestra Señora la Reina de los Ángeles (the Town of Our Lady the Queen of the Angels), or Los Angeles for short.

Starting in 1769, the government of New Spain established a series of Franciscan missions from San Diego to San Francisco, each separated by about a day's horse ride. New missions continued to be founded even after Alta California came under the jurisdiction of a newly independent Mexico in 1821. In the vicinity of Los Angeles were the San Gabriel and San Fernando missions, each of which was a self-sufficient compound of agriculture, livestock, and accommodations for the priests. Local Native Americans compelled into servitude provided most of the labor.

**FACING:** Women packing oranges for shipment east.

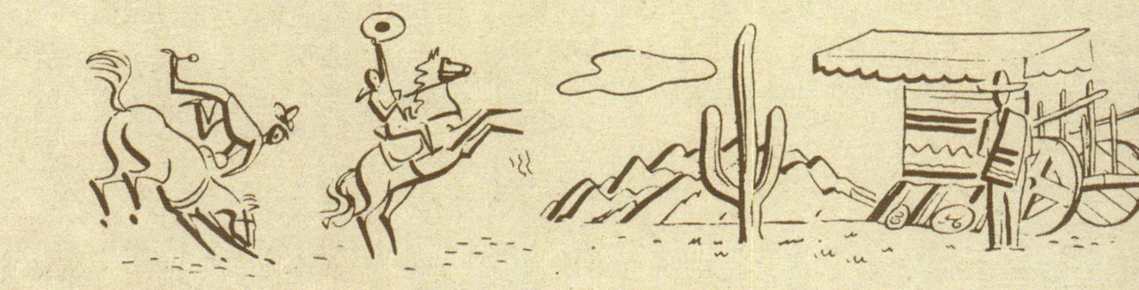

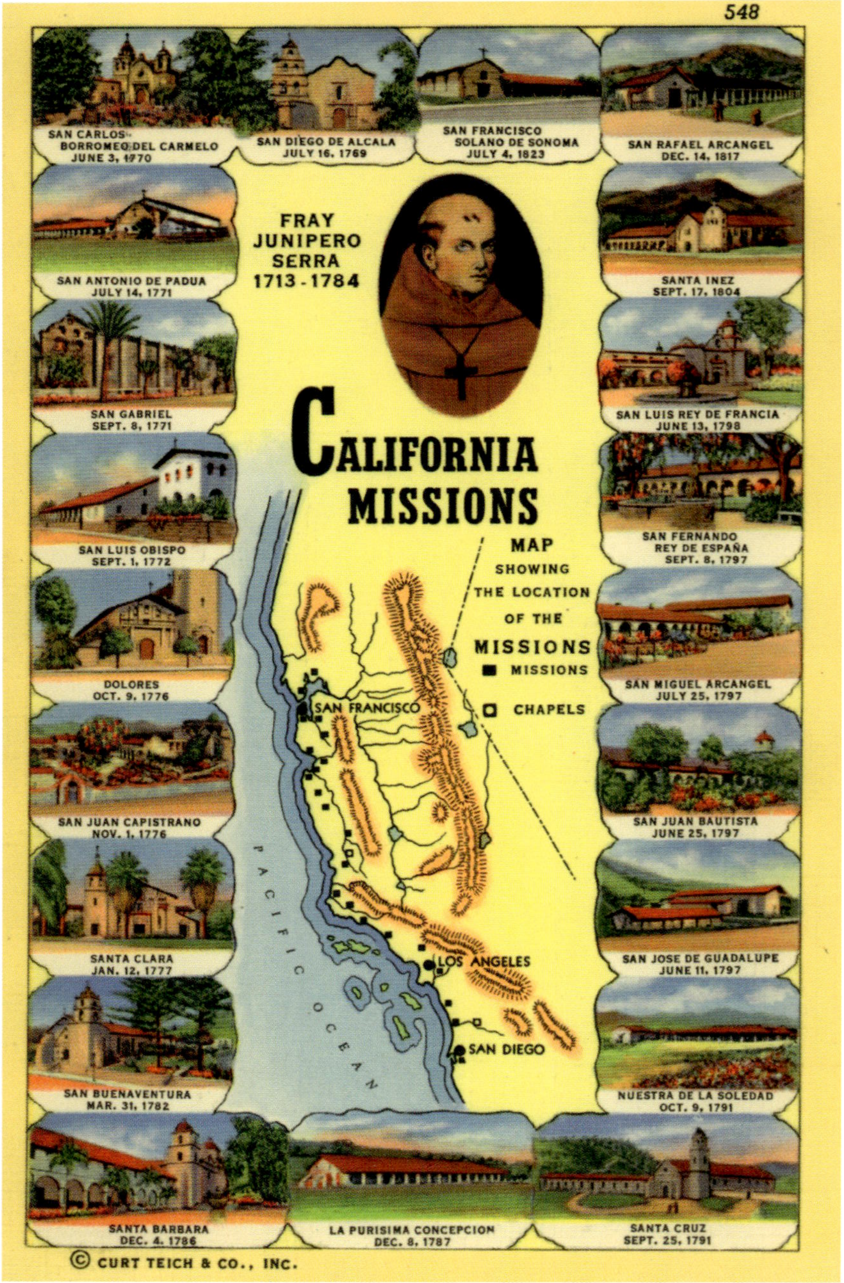

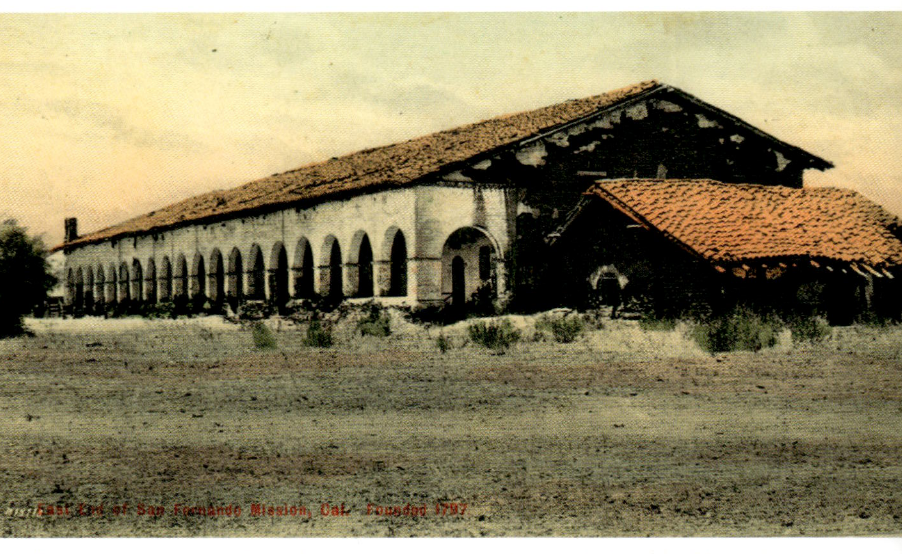


**LEFT:** Franciscan friar Junipero Serra established the first nine California missions.

**ABOVE:** The ruins of the San Fernando Mission, built in 1797.

**FACING:** A rare photo of La Plaza, the historic heart of Los Angeles, circa 1873. The actual plaza is in the center. The Pico House Hotel—which still stands—is on the upper right fronting Main Street.

Spanish and Mexican land grants became the famous ranchos of the Los Angeles region controlled by extended families of Californios. They included such familiar names as San Pedro, Los Feliz, Topanga Malibu, La Brea (Hollywood, West Hollywood), Boca de Santa Monica, Cahuenga (Burbank and Toluca Lake), and Los Encinos. In the years following the American takeover of Alta California in 1848 at the conclusion of the Mexican-American War, the ranchos eventually ended up in the hands of Yankees who either married into Californio families or purchased the land outright. These trends were hastened by the discovery of gold in Northern California in 1849 and the granting of statehood by the United States in 1850, when Southern California became a key source of beef cattle and agricultural products for the northern miners.

Los Angeles's original civic, social, and commercial heart was La Plaza, now a historic district where the Avila Adobe, La Placita parish church, and the elegant Pico House hotel from 1870 still stand.

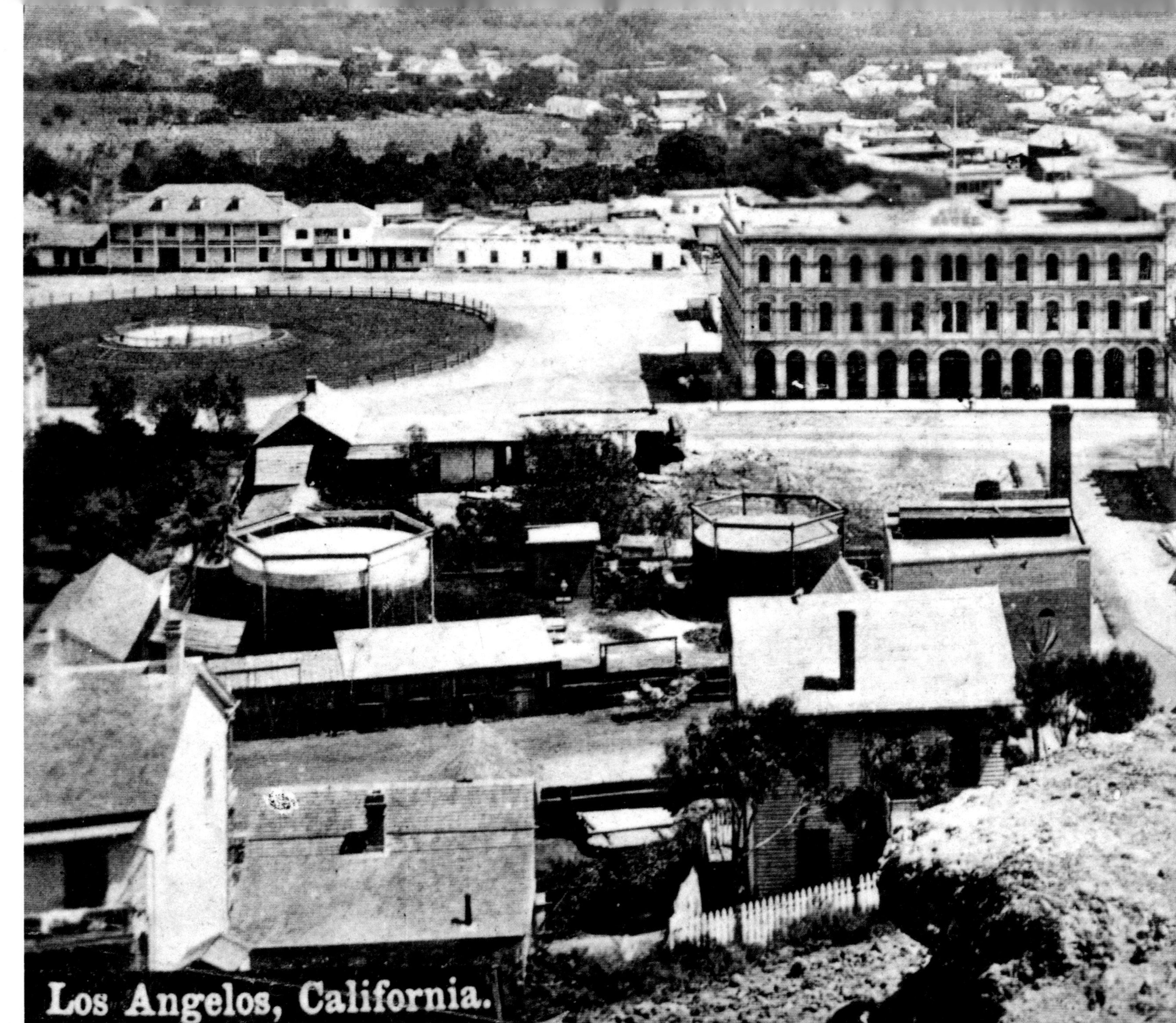
Los Angelos, California.

3732–Twin Palms.

With a population of around 1,600 in 1850, Los Angeles remained geographically isolated until the Southern Pacific Railroad extended their intercontinental line from San Francisco to the dusty frontier town in 1876. Then, in 1885, the competing Atchison, Topeka & Santa Fe Railway reached San Diego, and two years later Los Angeles, instigating a price war between the rail companies. For one day in 1887, the fare from St. Louis to Los Angeles was one dollar, touching off a real estate boom as investors rushed to Southern California. In 1887 alone, 36 cities or towns were established in the San Gabriel Valley as middle-class midwesterners and easterners purchased lots for speculation without any intention of actually building homes there. Monrovia, Pomona, South Pasadena, and Azusa were a few of the towns born in the boom that survived the real estate bust of 1888 and the resulting economic depression that descended upon the region. Dozens of other townsites disappeared entirely.

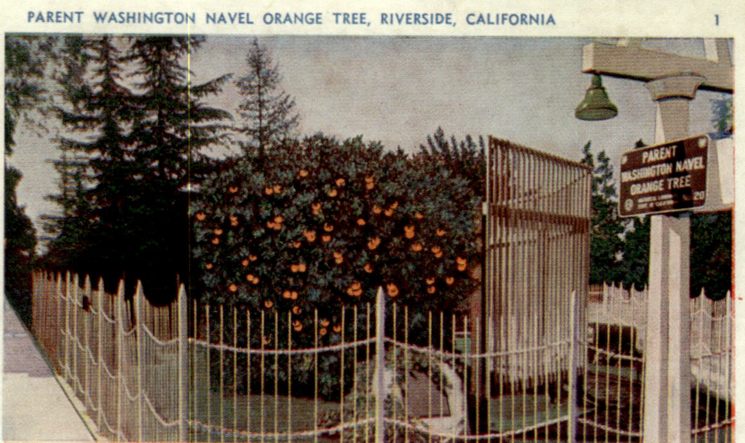


Meanwhile, a fortuitous event occurred in the inland city of Riverside, located 60 miles east of Los Angeles. There, 50-year-old suffragette Eliza Tibbets was nurturing a Brazilian citrus tree sapling that had been sent to her in 1873 by a friend at the U.S. Department of Agriculture. When the tree finally produced fruit a few years later, the oranges were plump, sweet, juicy, and most importantly seedless.

Dubbed Washington navel oranges, the trees were ideally suited to Southern California's semiarid climate, and because of their naturally thick skins could be successfully packed and shipped. By the 1890s, vast tracts of Washington navel orange groves had been planted across the region from budwood initially cut from Mrs. Tibbets's tree. Consequently, an entire agricultural empire—the Southern California citrus industry—which would come to define the region through the 1940s, was the result of a social activist's interest in horticulture.

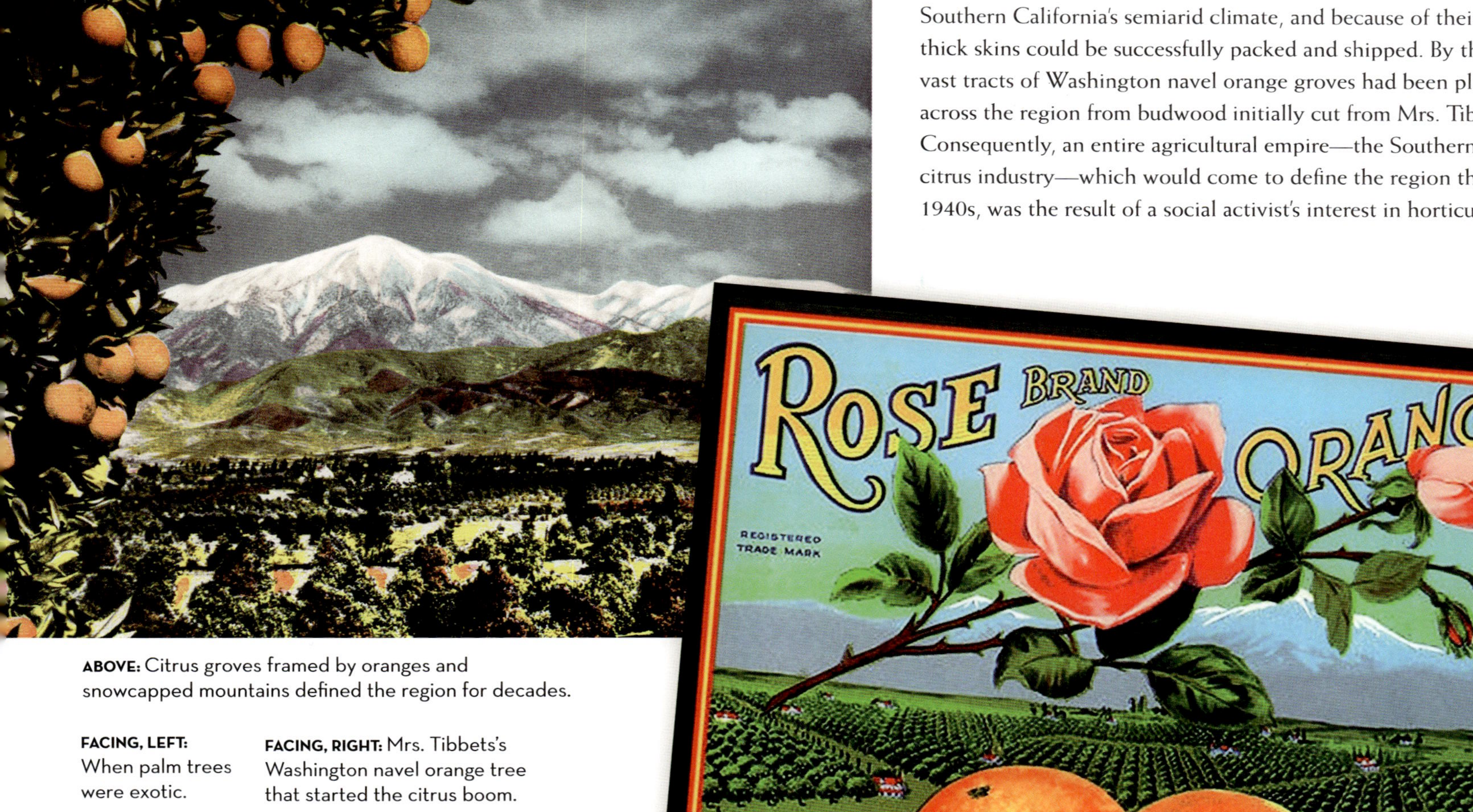


**ABOVE:** Citrus groves framed by oranges and snowcapped mountains defined the region for decades.

**FACING, LEFT:** When palm trees were exotic.

**FACING, RIGHT:** Mrs. Tibbets's Washington navel orange tree that started the citrus boom.

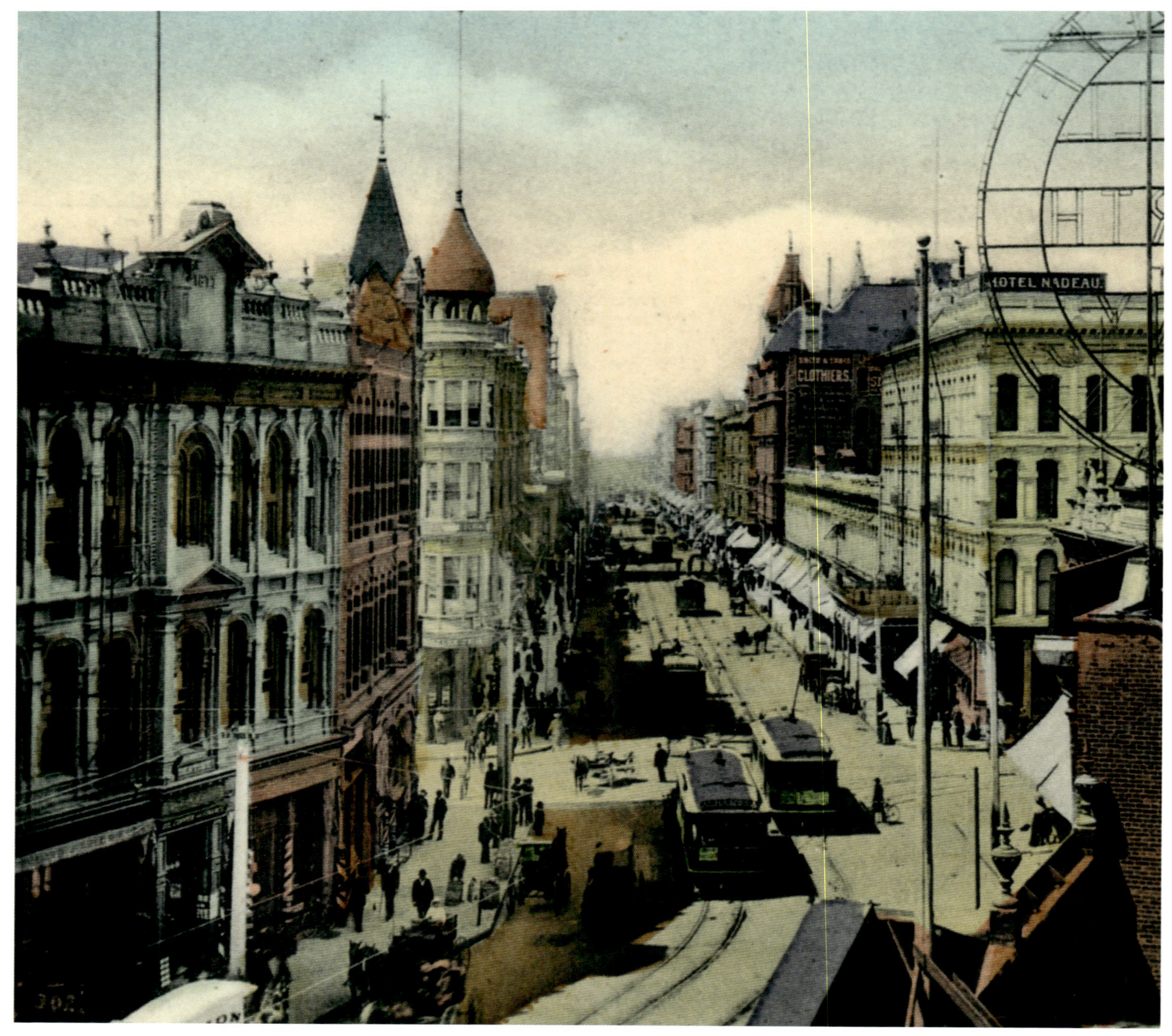
HOTEL NADEAU
CLOTHIERS

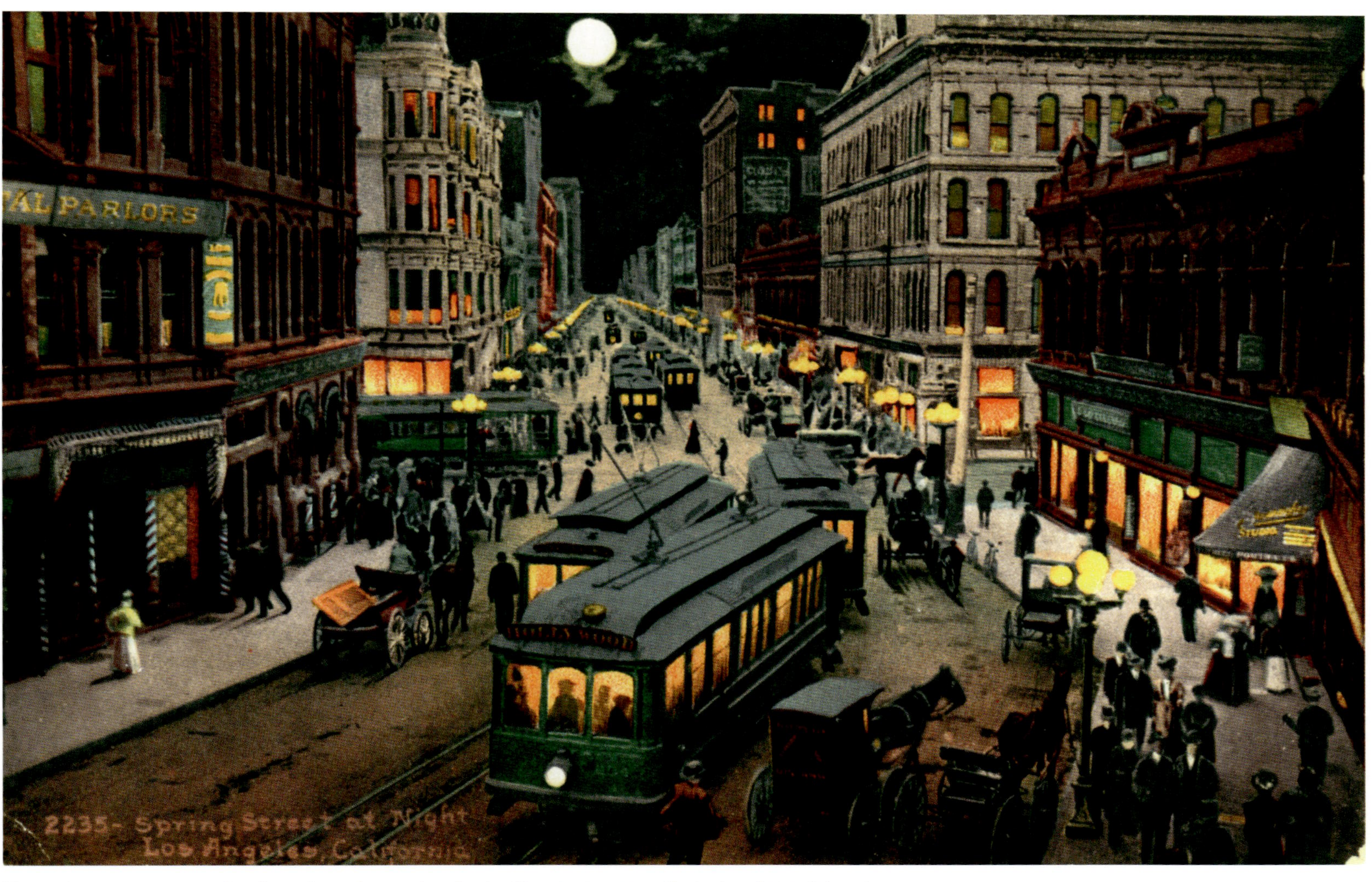


Horse-drawn carriages and trolleys share the road on Spring Street, circa 1890 (facing) and 1895 (above).

By 1890, Los Angeles was a city of 50,000, having grown fivefold in population in just 10 years. Large, bustling commercial blocks along Main Street, Broadway, and Spring Street were served by horse-drawn streetcars, then cable cars, and finally electric streetcars. Wealthier residents built elaborate Victorian mansions on Bunker Hill and in Angelino Heights overlooking downtown.

One of the city's first suburbs was Boyle Heights on the east side of the Los Angeles River, where from the 1890s through the 1940s, waves of immigrants would initially settle—Anglos, Mexicans, African Americans, Russians, Japanese, Jews. After World War II, Boyle Heights would become the center of the Mexican American (Chicano) community in Los Angeles.

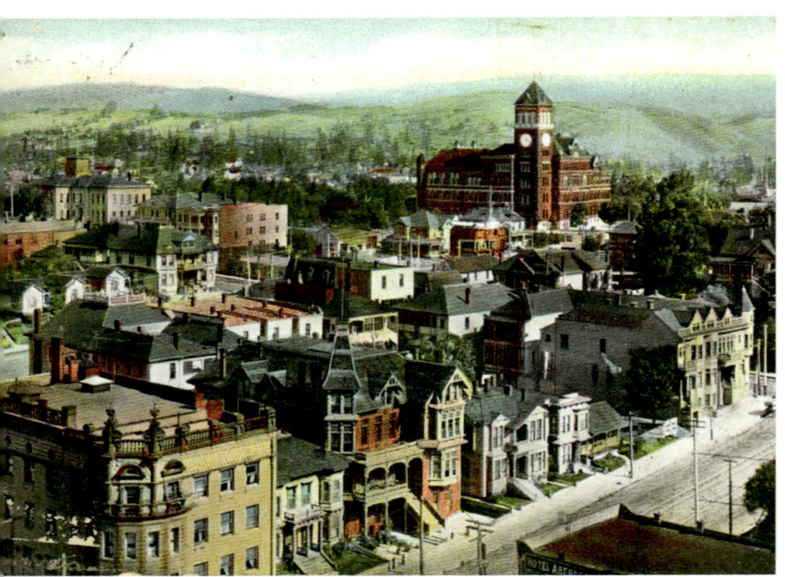

**ABOVE:** Bunker Hill mansions in the 1890s. Urban renewal would raze the entire area in the 1960s.

**RIGHT:** The old City Hall, built in 1888, would be replaced by the current City Hall in 1928.

**BELOW:** Highland Park was another early suburb of Los Angeles.

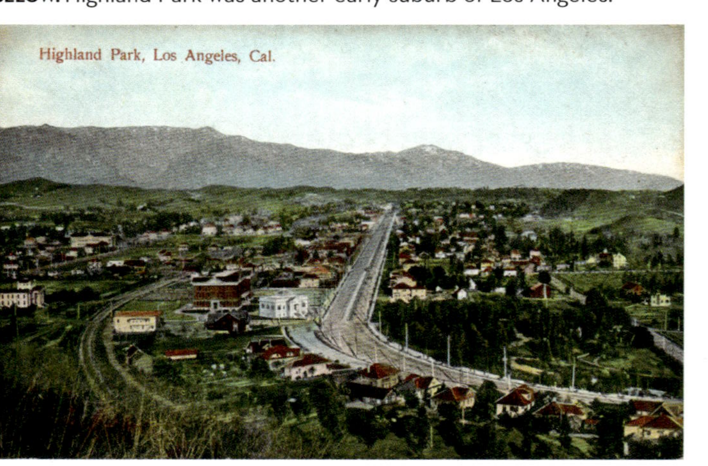

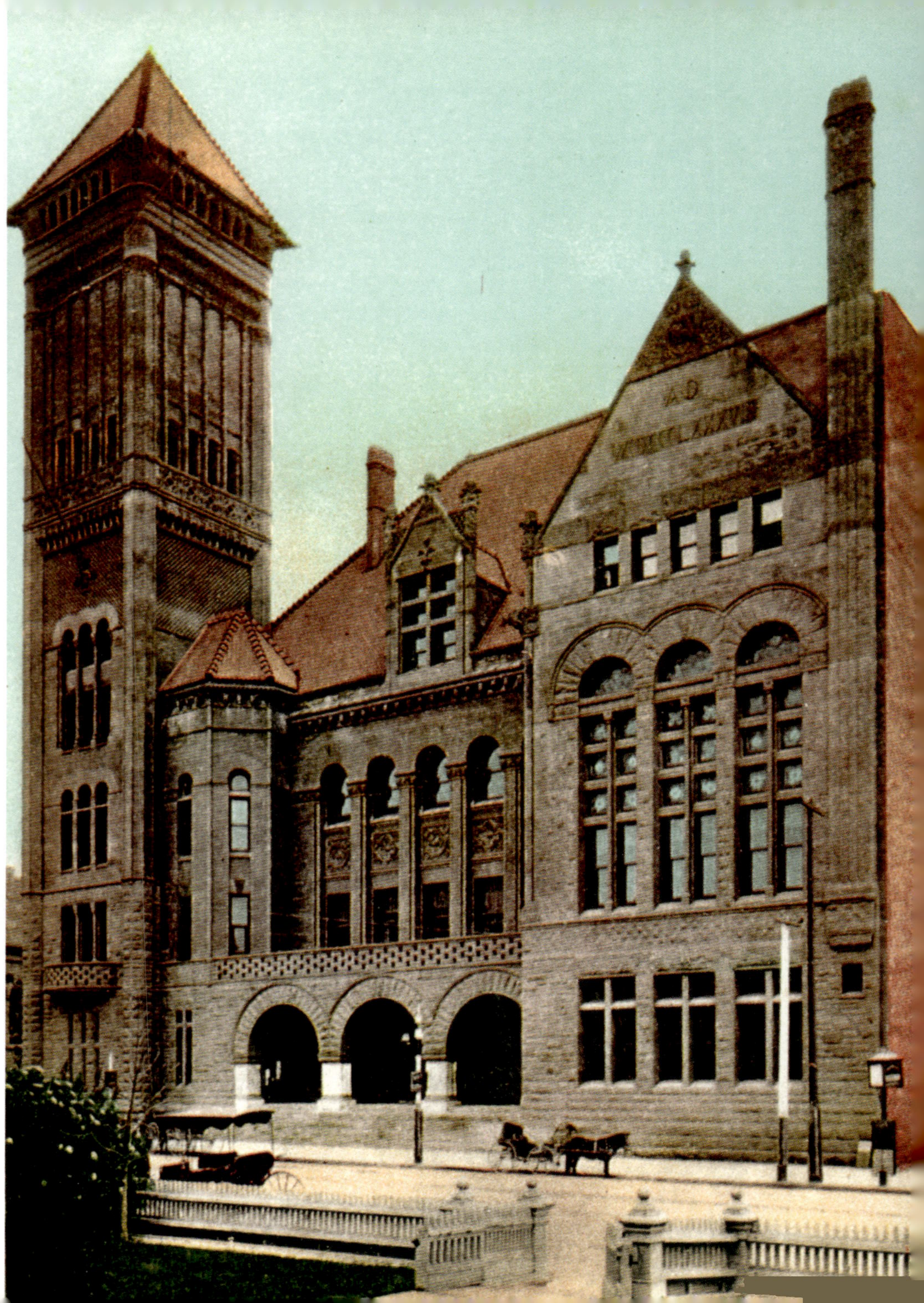

59 – COURT HOUSE, LOS ANGELES, CALIFORNIA.

**ABOVE:** The imposing Los Angeles Courthouse was built in 1891 and demolished in 1936.

**LEFT:** Effervescent sisters Judith and Lucy on the porch of their Victorian abode.

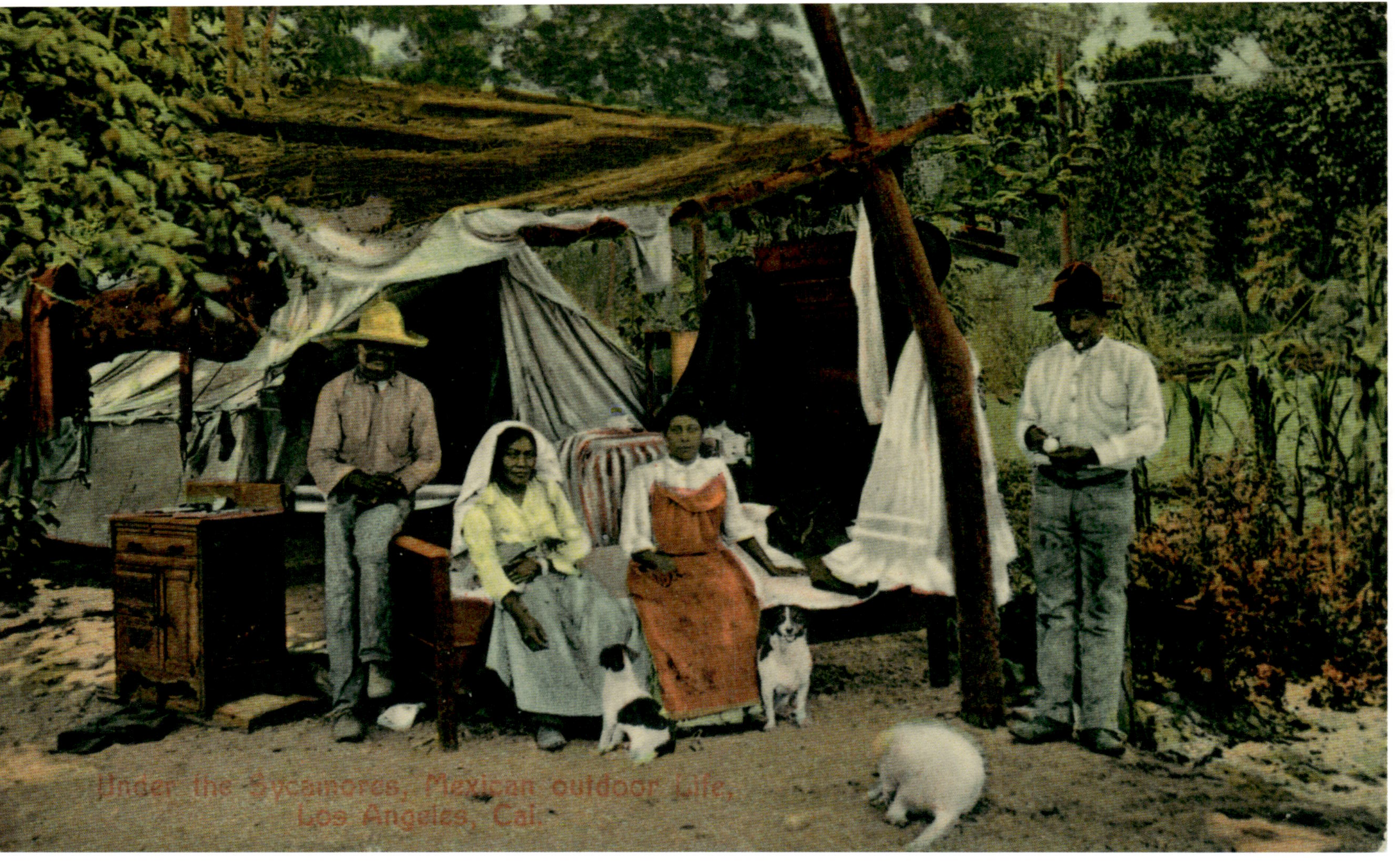


**ABOVE:** "Mexican outdoor life" in Los Angeles.

As development continued to move away from the original La Plaza it became contemptuously known as "Sonoratown," with the equally reviled Chinatown located just next door. Both were meant for those who were too poor or racially unwelcome in the dynamic new Anglo city growing to the south.

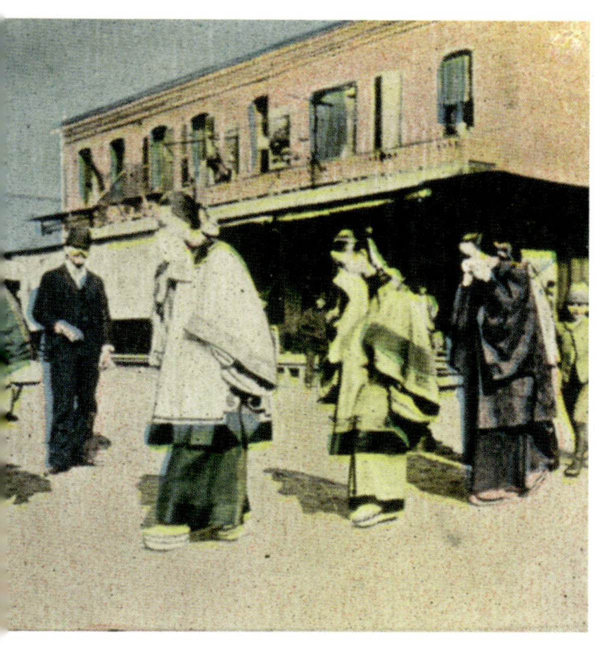

Rare photos of old Chinatown circa 1900, before its demolition to make way for Union Station in the 1930s.

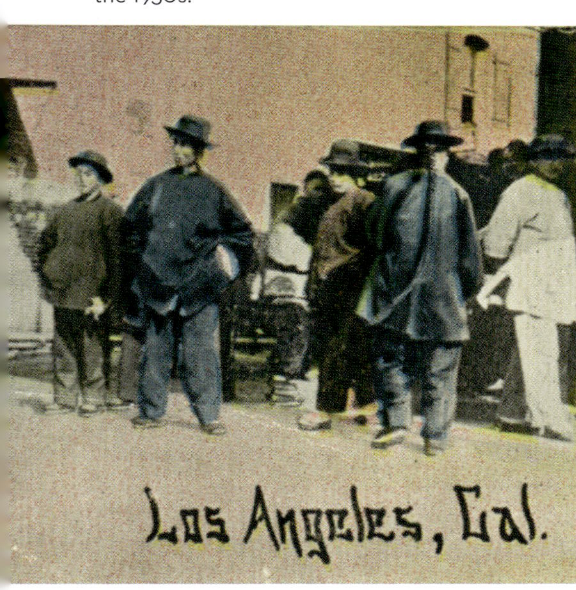

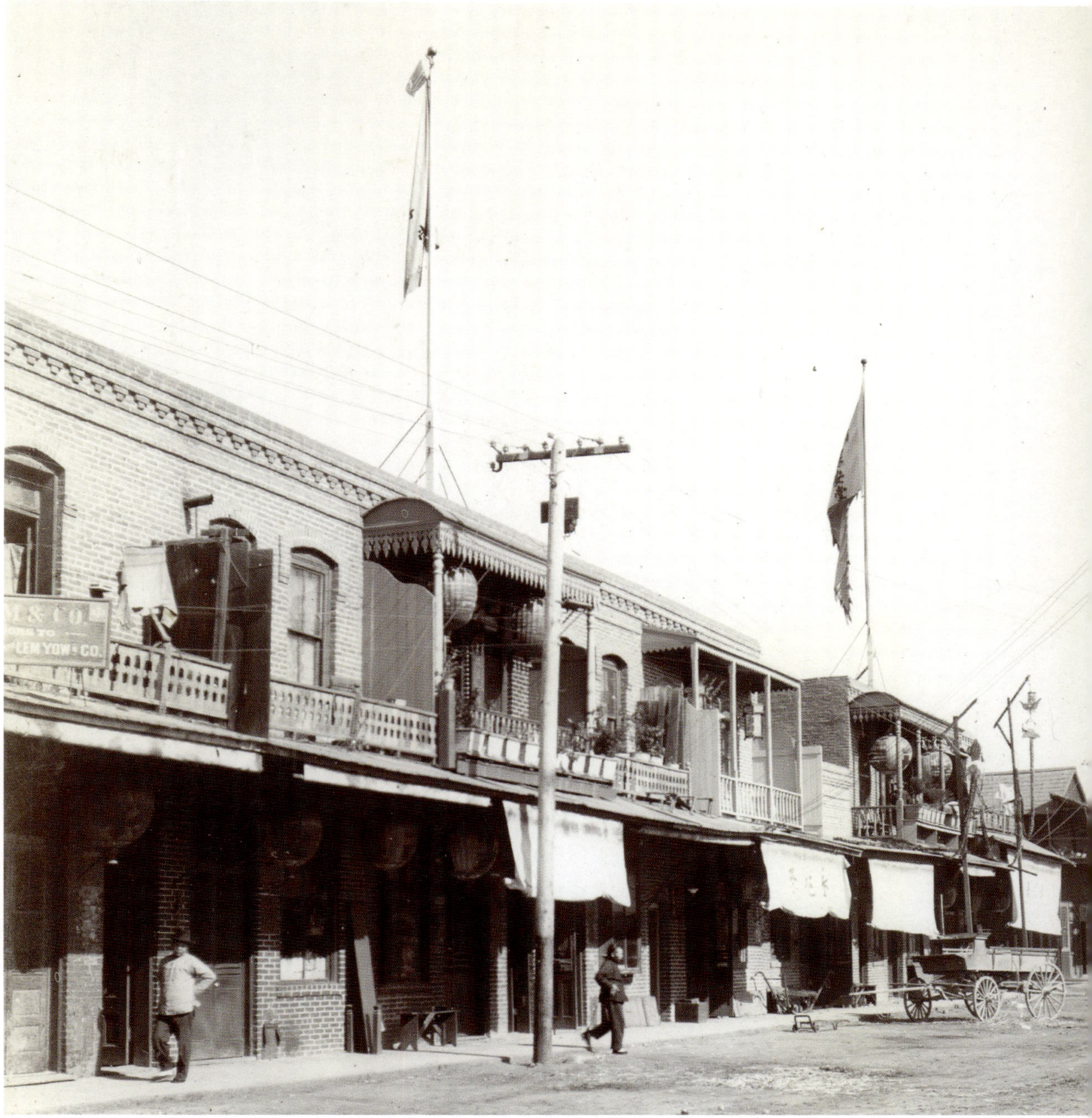

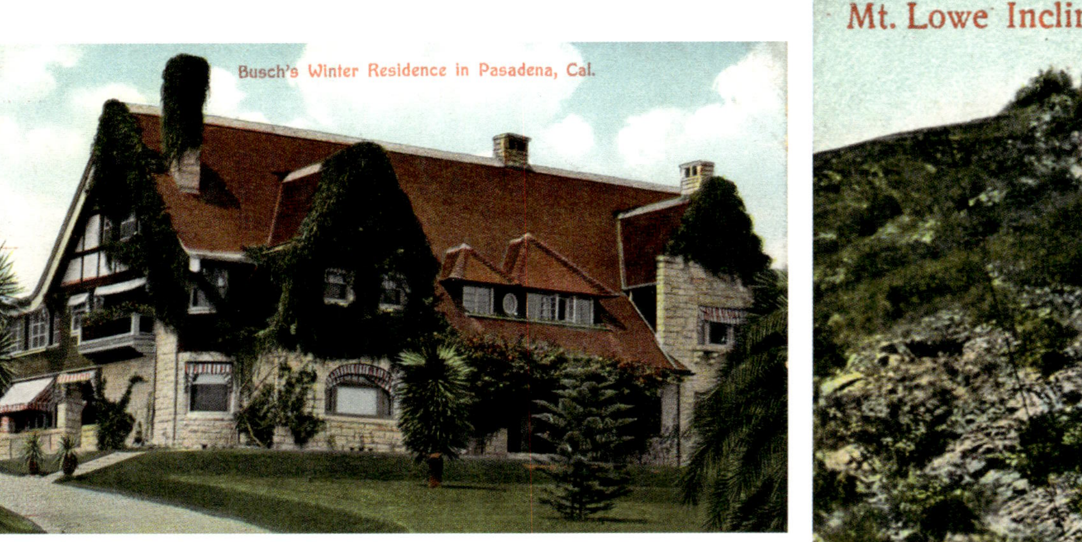


**ABOVE:** Ivy Wall, the winter home of Adolphus Busch (of Budweiser fame) on Pasadena's Millionaire's Row.

**RIGHT:** The start of the journey up Mount Lowe.

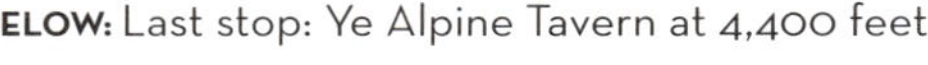

**BELOW:** Last stop: Ye Alpine Tavern at 4,400 feet.

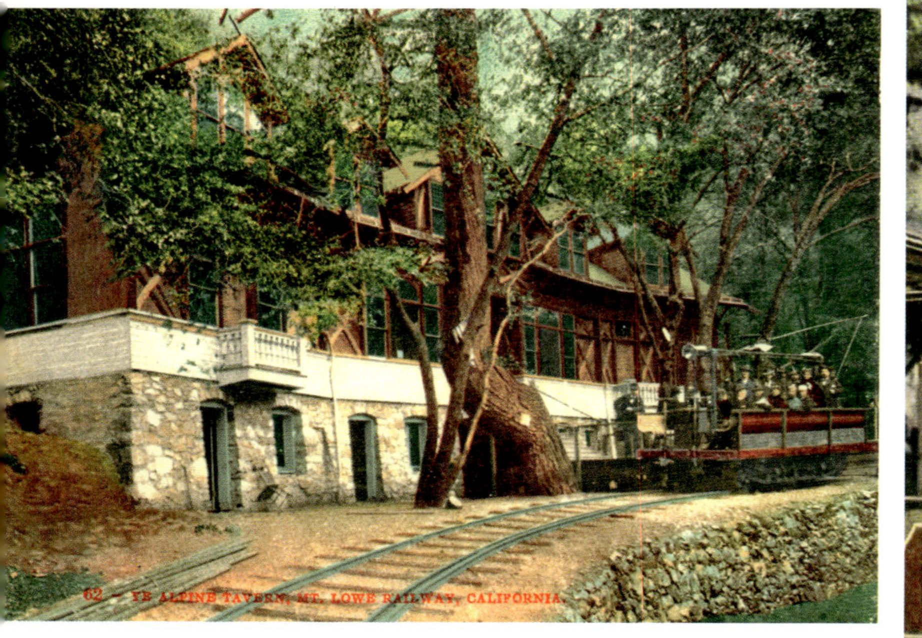

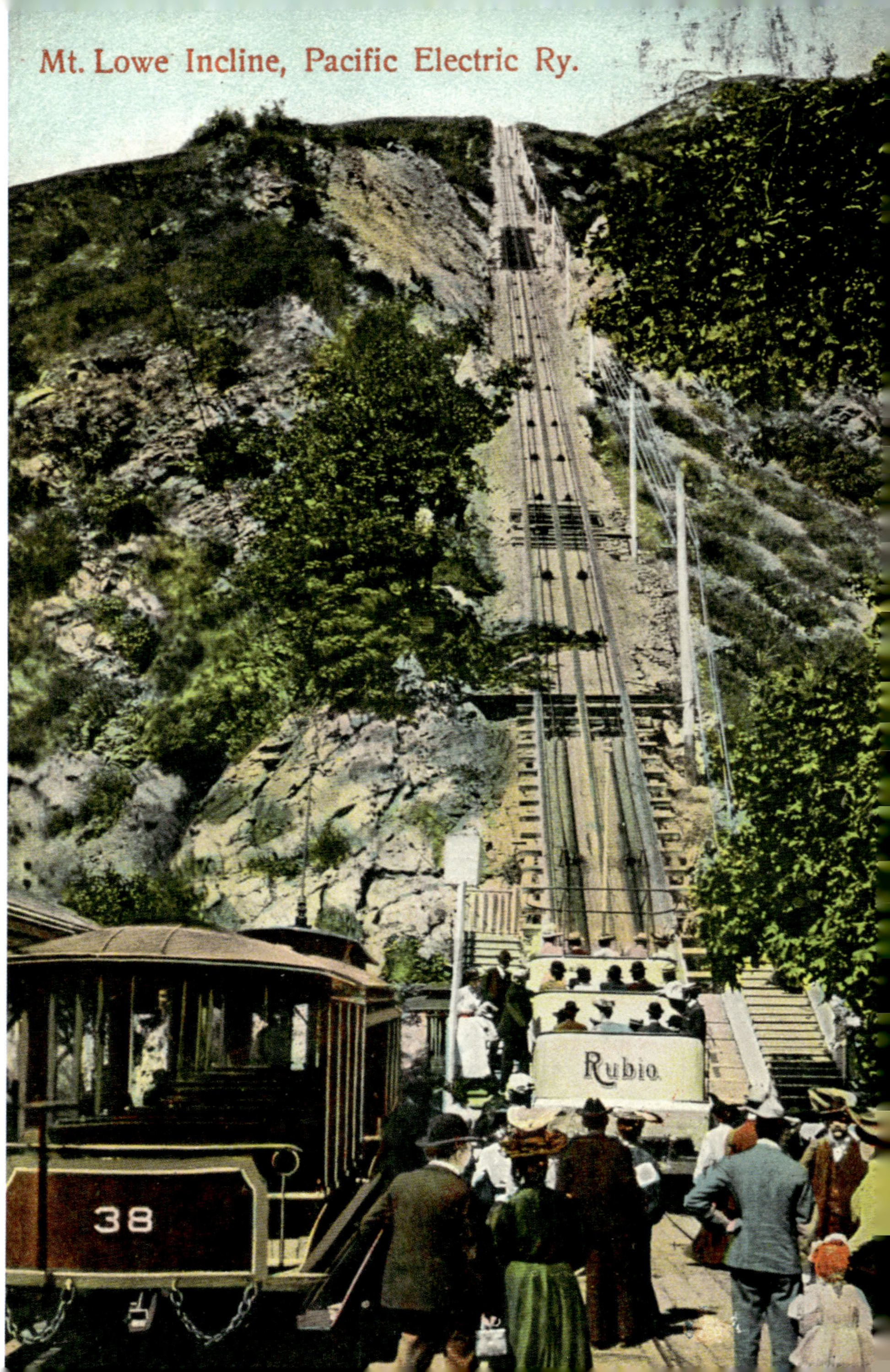

Mt. Lowe Incline, Pacific Electric Ry.

Rubio

38

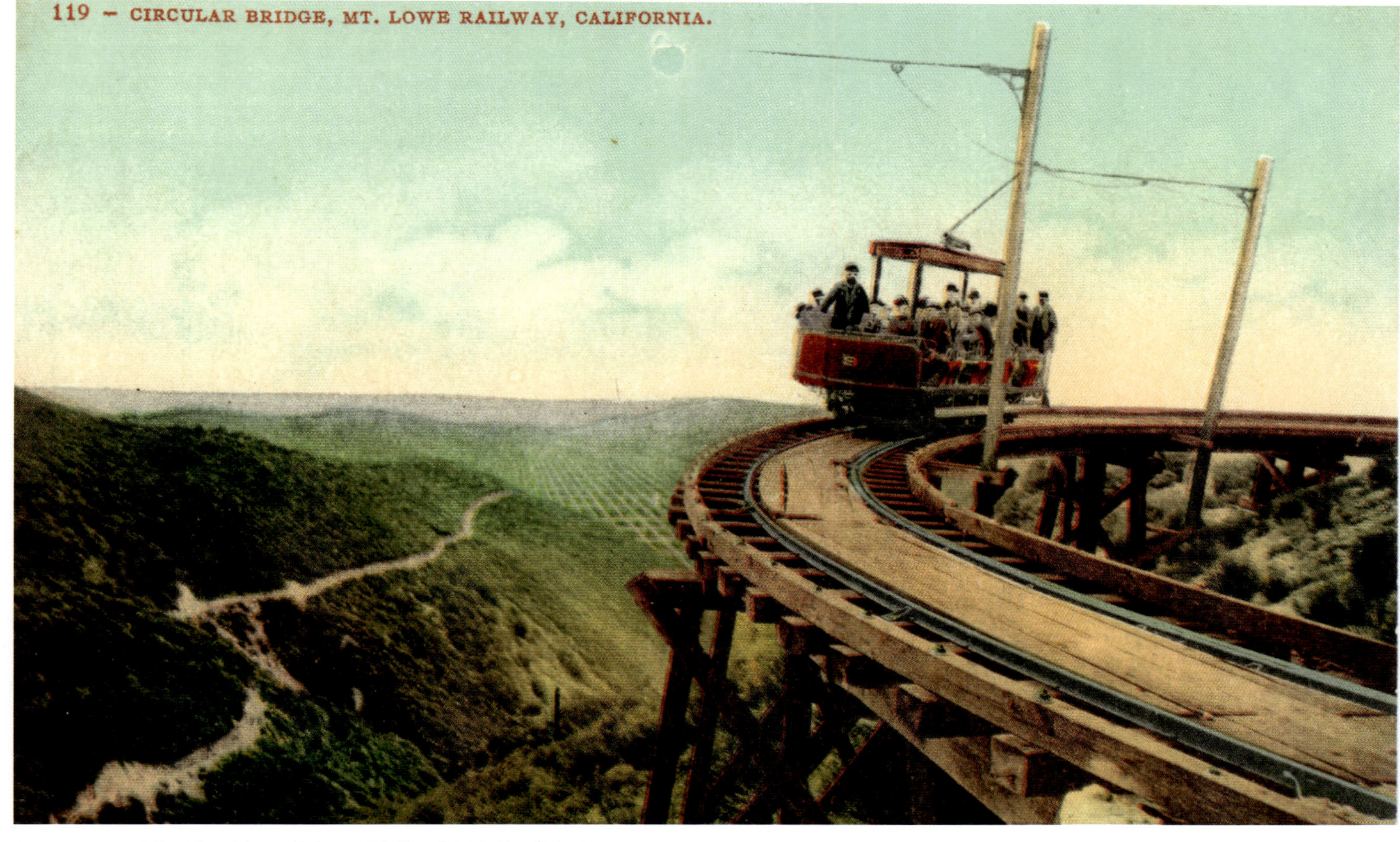


A scary curve on the Mount Lowe Railway with Pasadena in the distance.

Starting in the 1880s, wealthy midwesterners and easterners spent the winter season in cities such as Pasadena, just north of Los Angeles, to escape intolerable winters back home. The wealthiest lived on Orange Grove Boulevard, nicknamed Millionaire's Row. The region's sunshine and dry air also attracted those in search of relief from various respiratory ailments such as tuberculosis.

Just north of Pasadena in the San Gabriel Mountains was the Mount Lowe Railway, a scenic seven-mile electric trolley ride that rose to 4,420 feet above sea level. Opened in 1893, the railway route included the magnificent 70-room, Victorian-style Echo Mountain House, and at the end of the line, Ye Alpine Tavern, a 12-room chalet with views to the Pacific Ocean. Over three million visitors rode the trolley until the railway ceased operations in 1938.

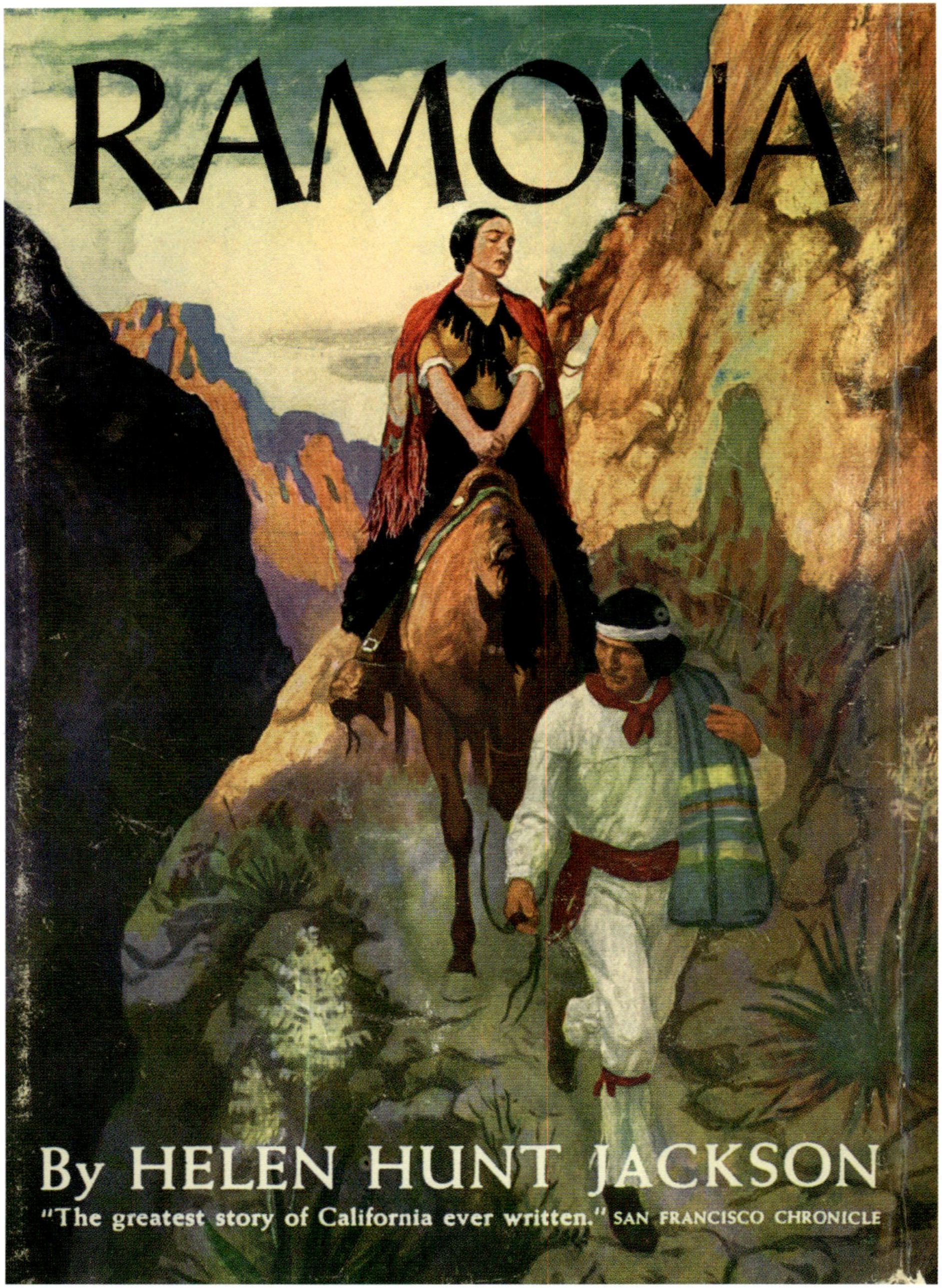

As part of the effort to encourage migration to the region, the railroads, real estate interests, and city boosters seized upon the idea of promoting Southern California's Spanish and Mexican past, particularly the time of missions and ranchos, fashioning a romantic age of gentle padres, docile natives, dashing caballeros, and elegant señoritas. One book in particular ignited this scheme—*Ramona*, the 1884 novel by Helen Hunt Jackson. Set during California's transition from Mexican to American rule, this heartbreaking love story featured a Scots–Native American orphan girl who suffers discrimination, hardship, and loss. This sentimental portrayal of Spanish-Mexican colonial life inspired thousands of eastern tourists to take advantage of the railroad fare wars in search of the fictional locations portrayed in the book. Many of these visitors would return to establish new lives in the Los Angeles region.

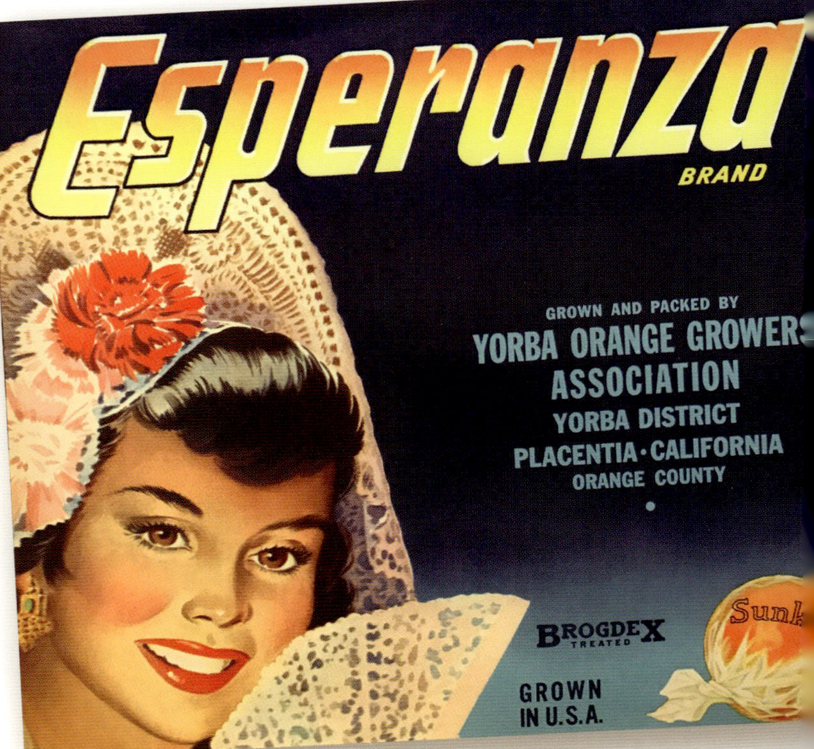

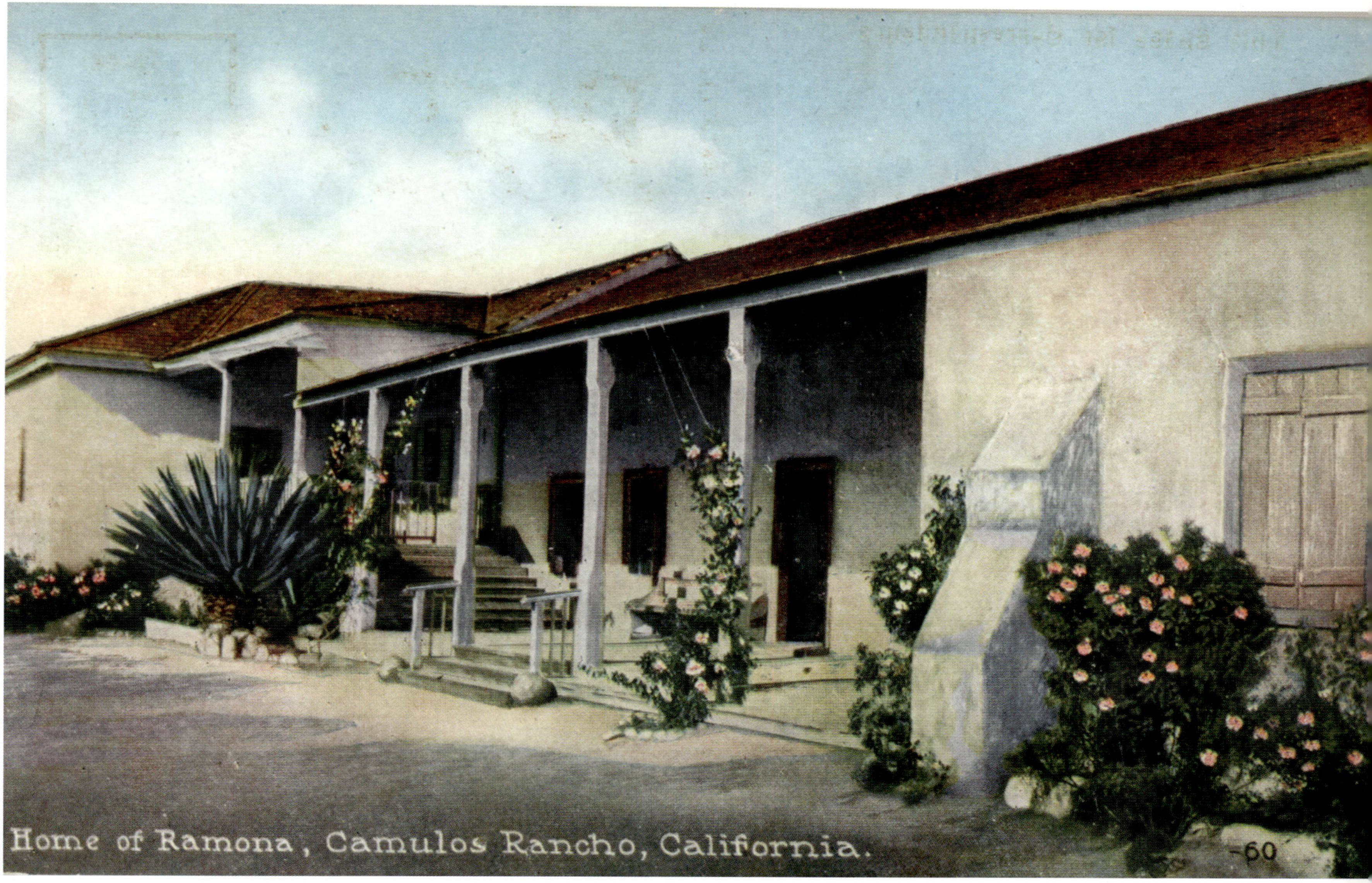

**FACING:** The novel *Ramona* (left) inspired the image of an alluring señorita for Esperanza brand oranges (right).

**ABOVE:** Supposedly the author's inspiration for the novel *Ramona*, Rancho Camulos became a major tourist destination.

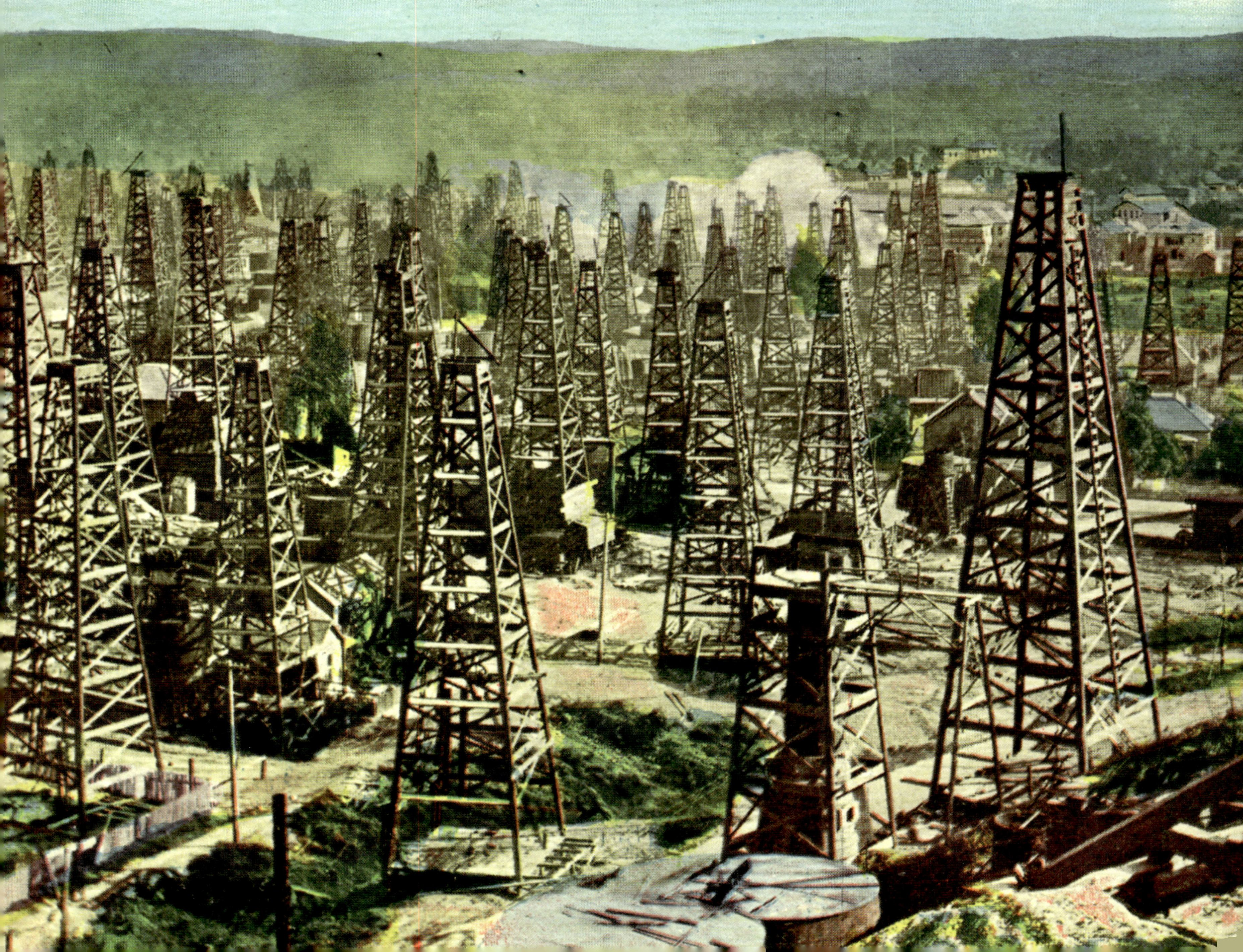
Oil Wells in the City of Los Angeles, Cal.

# Water and Power

## 1900–1920

By 1900, the population of Los Angeles had doubled in ten years to over 100,000. Only one thing stood in the way of the city's boundless growth—a lack of water. Because the Los Angeles River was dry much of the year and local groundwater almost depleted, a new source had to be found. The source selected was the Owens River, located 233 miles away in the eastern Sierra Nevada foothills. Chief engineer William Mulholland of the city's water department achieved the monumental task of bringing Owens River water to the city via an aqueduct of channels, tunnels, and enormous pipes that traversed mountains and the Mojave Desert before emerging in the San Fernando Valley. Completed in 1913, the Los Angeles Aqueduct was an engineering marvel with the capacity to support a population of two million using gravity alone to move water from source to terminus. The spellbinding 1974 movie *Chinatown* fictionalizes how insider knowledge of the coming aqueduct allowed nefarious businessmen to secretly purchase much of the then-agricultural San Fernando Valley before its value soared upon annexation by the newly water-rich City of Los Angeles.

**FACING:** The Los Angeles oil field encompassed the neighborhoods of Elysian Park, Chinatown, Echo Park, Westlake, and Mid-Wilshire (today's Koreatown).

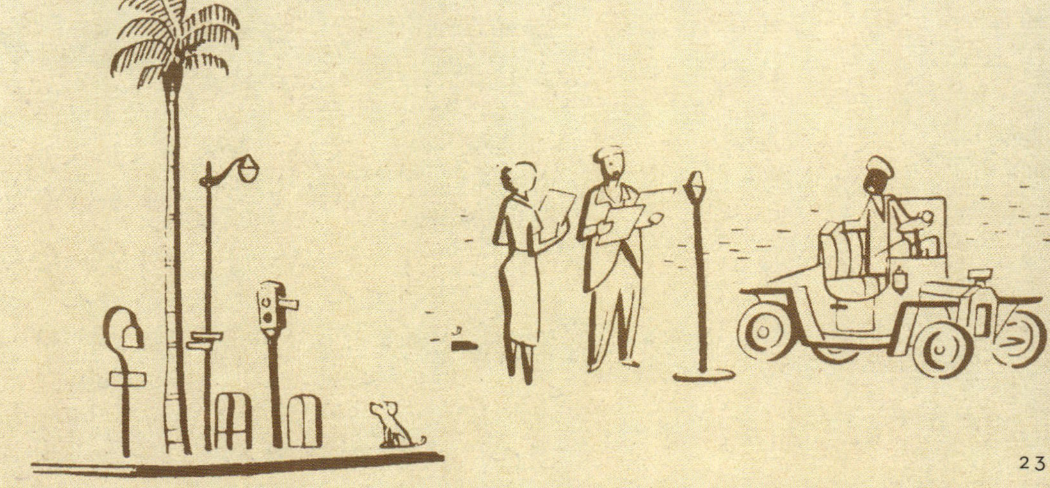

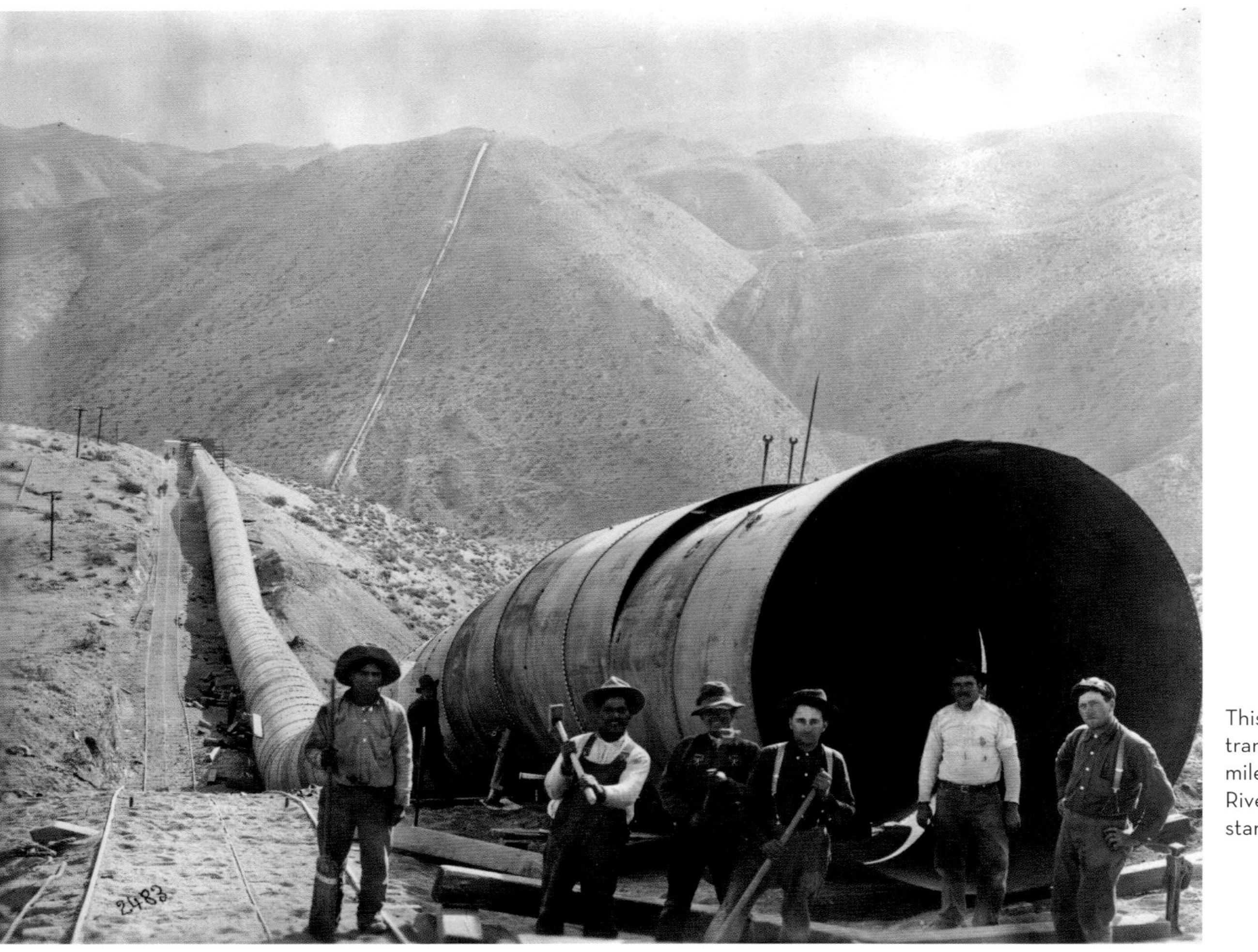


This enormous pipe transported water 233 miles from the Owens River to Los Angeles starting in 1913.

Water was also the weapon used to coerce surrounding communities to succumb to annexation. Between 1906 and 1927, five independent cities and numerous unincorporated areas with inadequate water sources agreed to annexation by its voracious neighbor chiefly because Los Angeles's city charter prohibited it from supplying surplus water outside of the city's boundaries. Among them were San Pedro (1909), Hollywood (1910), the San Fernando Valley (1915), West Adams (1918), Eagle Rock (1923), Venice (1925), Watts (1926), and Mar Vista (1927). The annexation of the San Fernando Valley alone added 169 square miles to Los Angeles. By 1927, Los Angeles had nearly attained its present size, having expanded from 43 to 441 square miles—a tenfold increase—since 1900.

Los Angeles's long-term economic viability was also contingent upon having a deep water port. With links to two intercontinental railroads, the newly dredged Los Angeles Harbor quickly became the most important on the West Coast, especially with the opening of the Panama Canal in 1914.

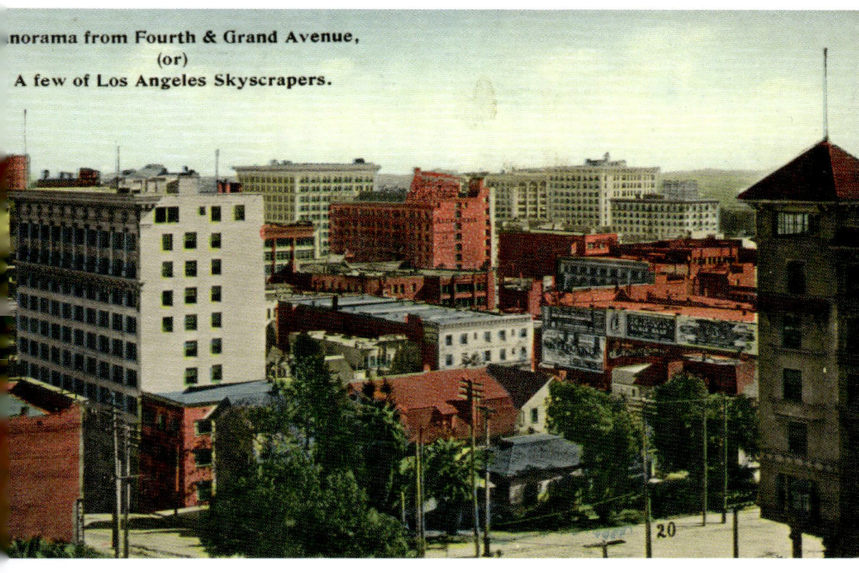


**ABOVE:** In the early 1900s, downtown Los Angeles was a mix of houses and "skyscrapers."

**BELOW:** Los Angeles Harbor circa 1914. Supersized container ships would come later.

**RIGHT:** Crowds packed Broadway at night in the 1910s. By 1920 there would be 161,846 cars registered in Los Angeles County, and 806,264 registered in 1930.

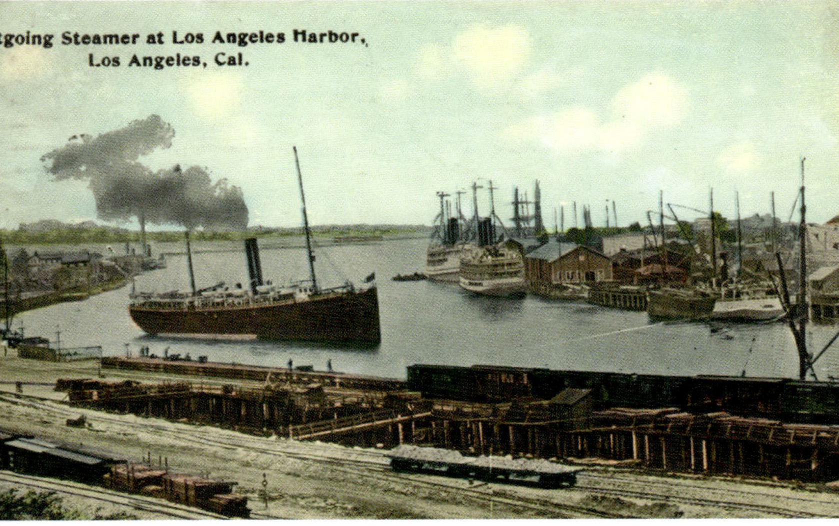

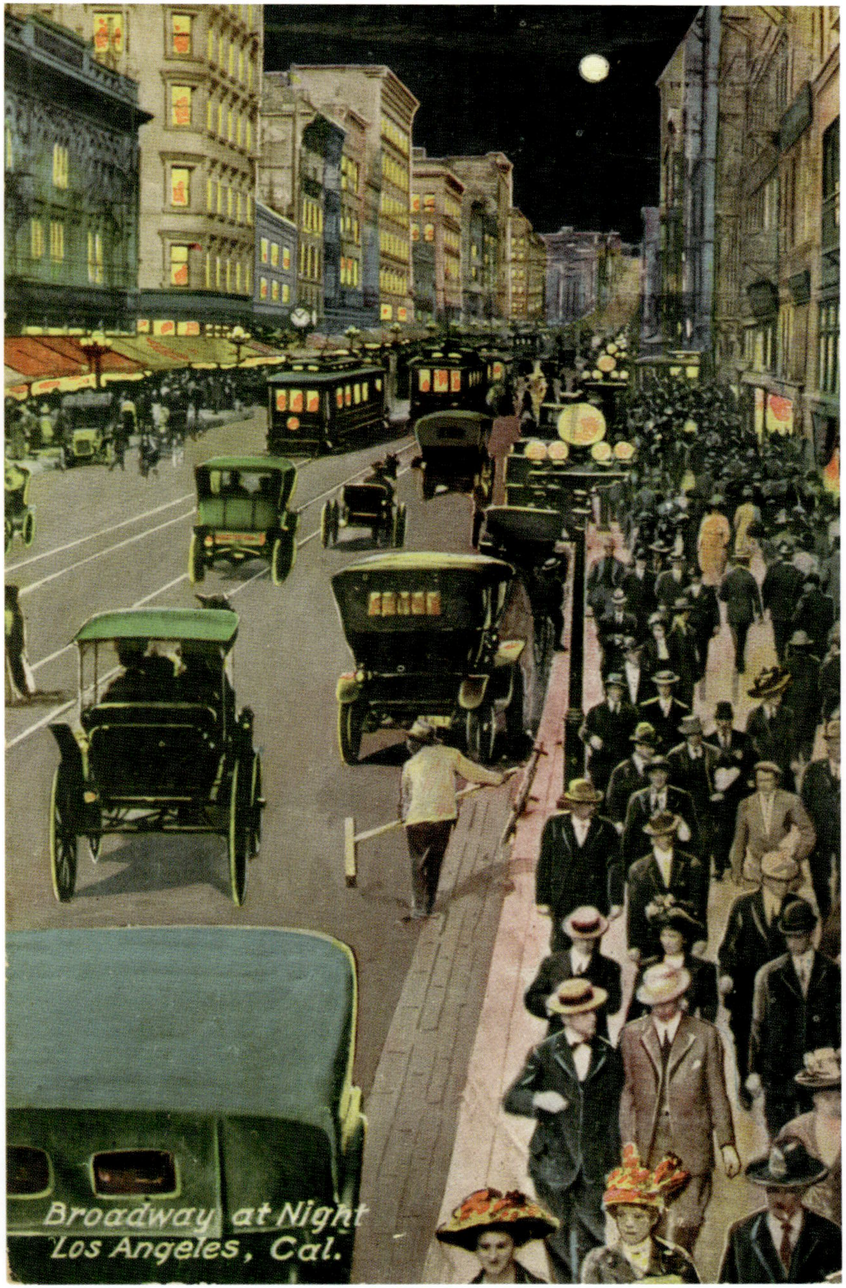

Broadway at Night
Los Angeles, Cal.

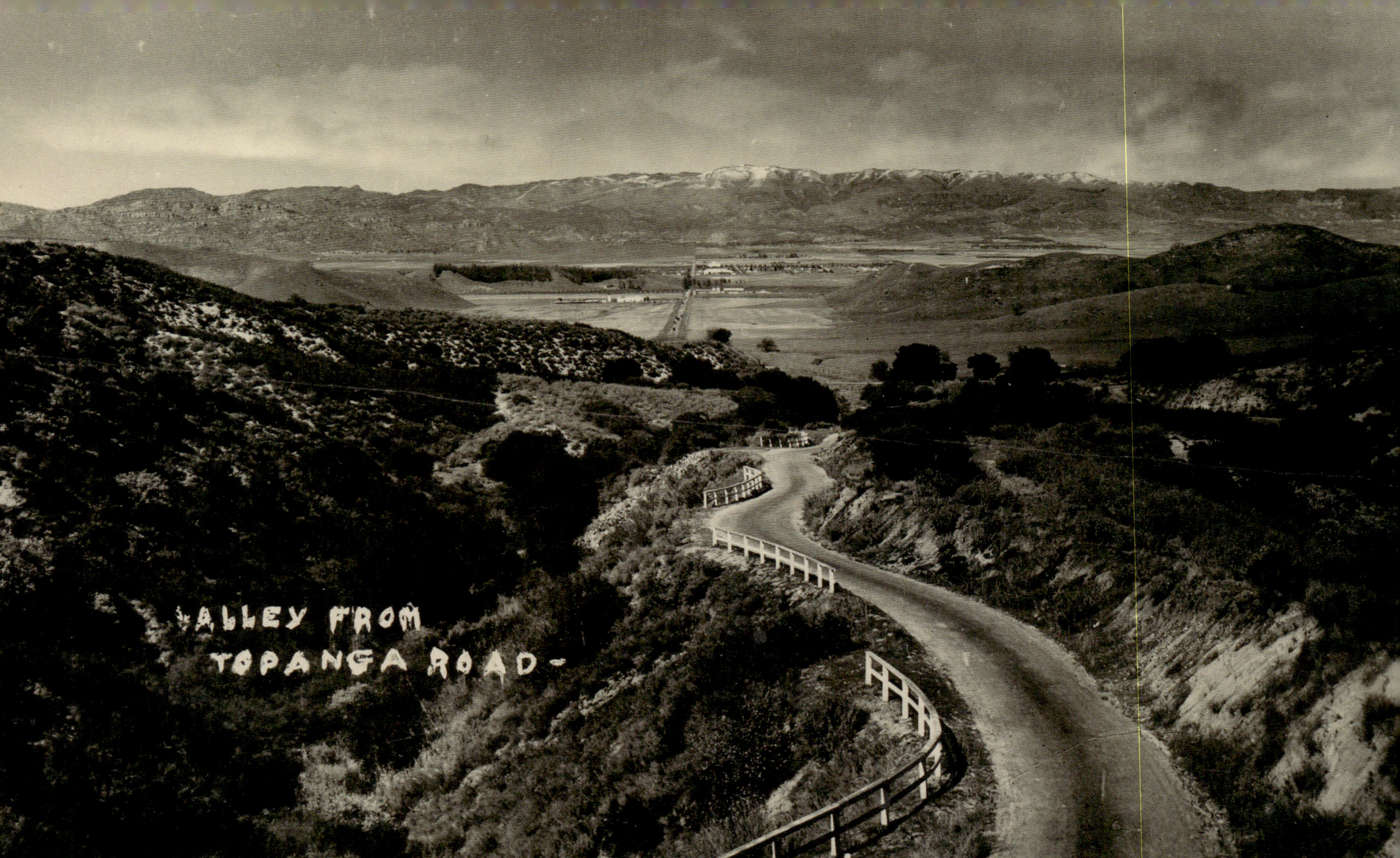


**ABOVE:** An empty San Fernando Valley in need of 100,000 tract homes.

In 1901, railroad executive Henry H. Huntington and banker Isaias W. Hellman became the primary investors in the establishment of a network of electrically powered streetcars that would soon link communities across Southern California. Their Pacific Electric (PE) Railway, or Red Car system, provided inexpensive passenger and freight transportation to areas outside of the Los Angeles city limits. The separate Los Angeles Railway, or Yellow Car system, operated within the municipality. The hub for both systems was downtown Los Angeles. Because the tracks shared the road with automobiles, traffic often slowed to a crawl, which was a major impetus for dismantling both railway systems after World War II.

For Huntington and his associates, the PE Railway was generally a money loser. But its primary purpose had never been mass transit, but rather real estate development. The Huntington syndicate had quietly purchased land along the routes that would soar in value once streetcar tracks were laid in their vicinity. A good example is the city of Huntington Beach, which was developed by, and named for, the railway magnate himself. In addition, small towns offered the syndicate low prices for local land to encourage the PE to extend tracks to their communities.

The PE system benefitted the San Fernando and San Gabriel Valleys, the South Bay, and the cities of Long Beach, Whittier, Santa Monica, Compton, Beverly Hills, and many others in Los Angeles County. Its reach out to San Bernardino, Riverside, and Orange Counties also helped these areas to grow. By 1915, with over 1,000 miles of track, the Pacific Electric was the largest electric railway system in the world.

There were two funicular lines (incline railways) in downtown Los Angeles: the still-existing Angels Flight (right), and the long-departed Court Flight (below), opposite the old Hall of Records. Note the boarding houses and hotels along the tracks.

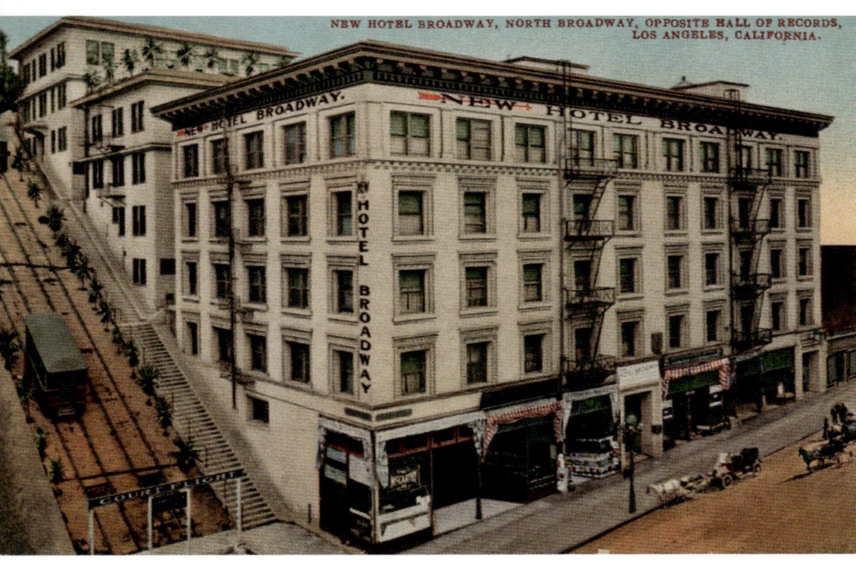

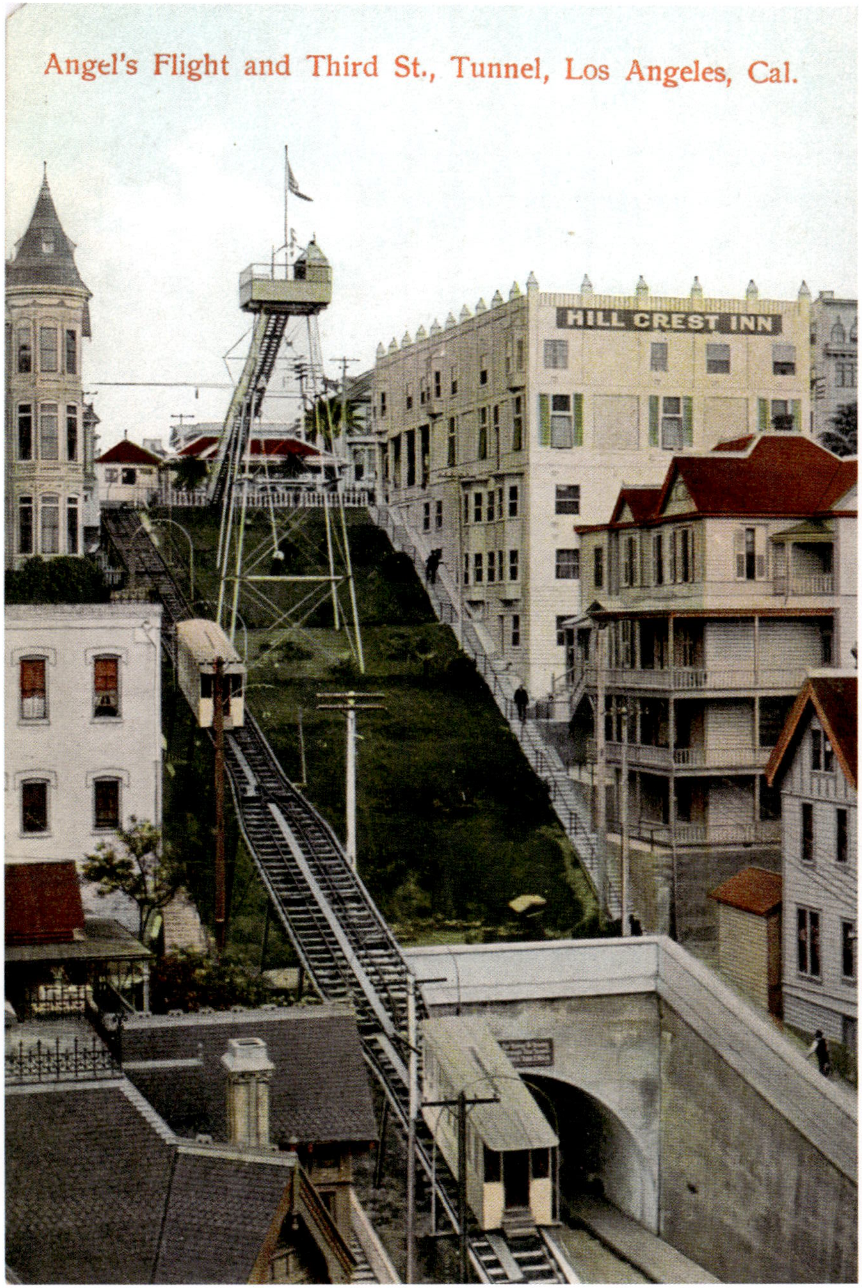

Angel's Flight and Third St., Tunnel, Los Angeles, Cal.

HILL CREST INN

# Balloon Route

Ten thousand tourists per month rode the Pacific Electric's Balloon Route excursion, so named because of its balloon-shaped route map. The one-dollar all-day trip started in downtown then passed through Sonoratown, the Los Angeles oil fields, Echo Park, Silver Lake's Sunset Junction, Hollywood, the citrus groves of Cahuenga Valley, Sherman (West Hollywood), Beverly Hills, Brentwood, Santa Monica, Ocean Park, Venice, Playa del Rey (for lunch), Manhattan Beach, Hermosa Beach, and Redondo Beach before returning to downtown by dusk.

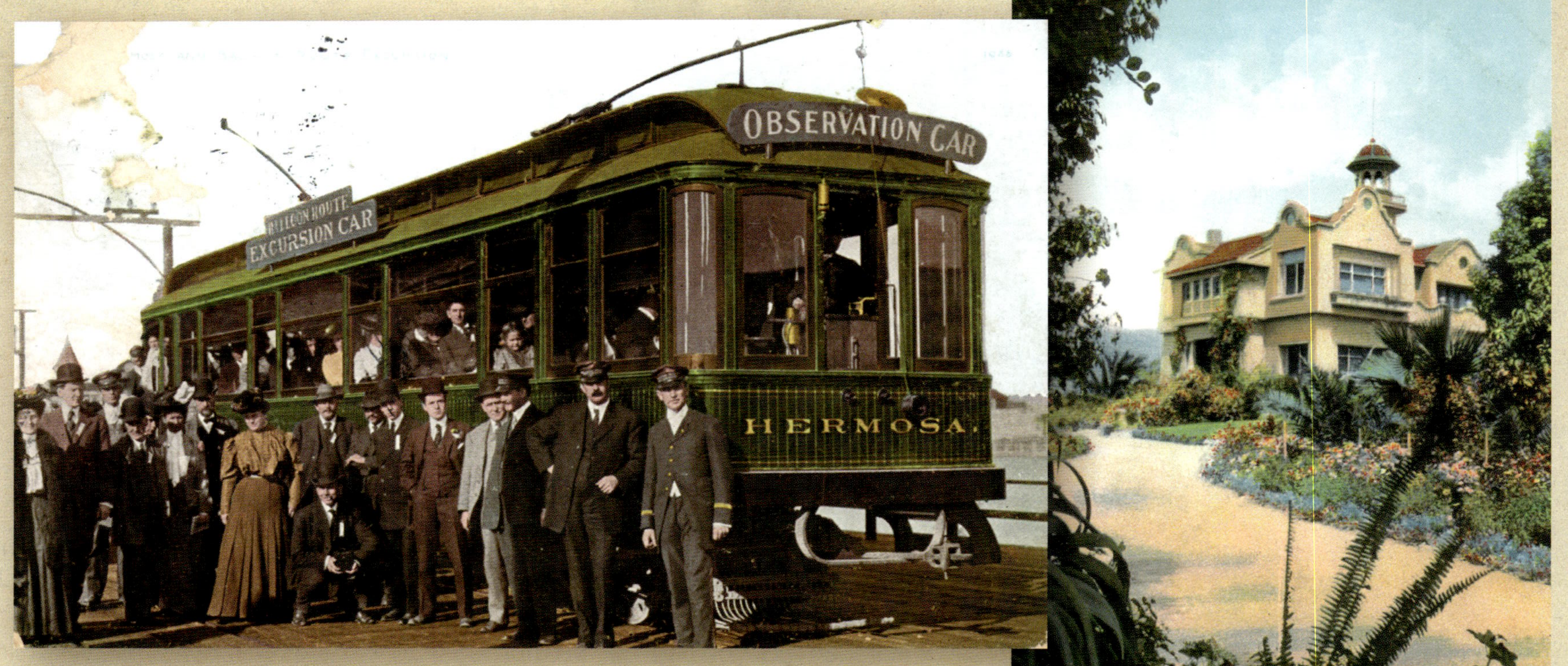


**ABOVE:** Aboard the Balloon Route's excursion car *Hermosa*. "100 miles and 100 sites for 100 cents."

**RIGHT:** A Balloon Route highlight was a stop at one of Southern California's top tourist attractions, the mansion and gardens of Hollywood's "King of Flower Painters," artist Paul de Longpré.

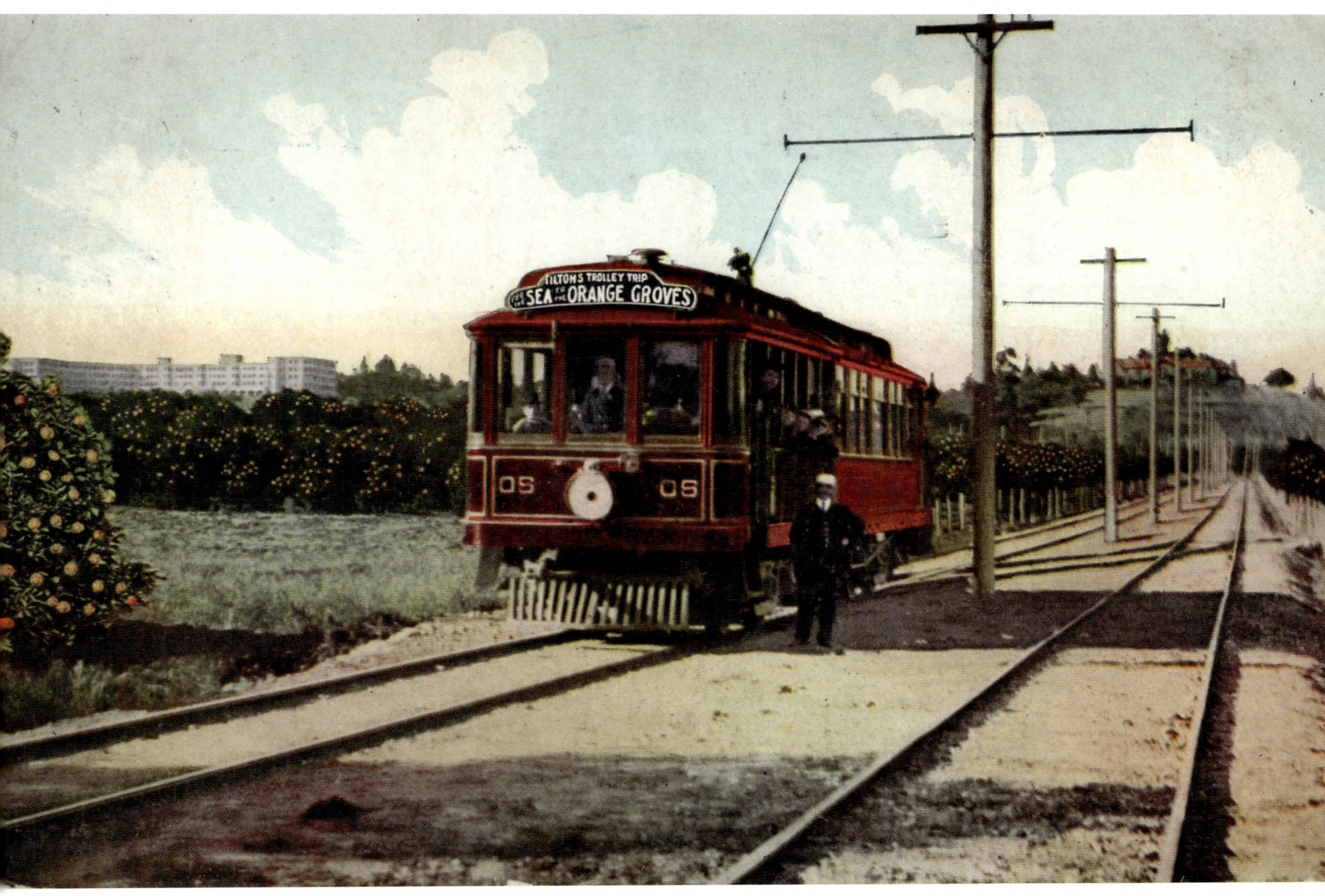


Tilton's Trolley Trip, whose slogan was "From the Sea to the Orange Groves," on its way through Pasadena in 1907. On the back of the card is written, "The oranges are so close that one can touch them from the car windows."

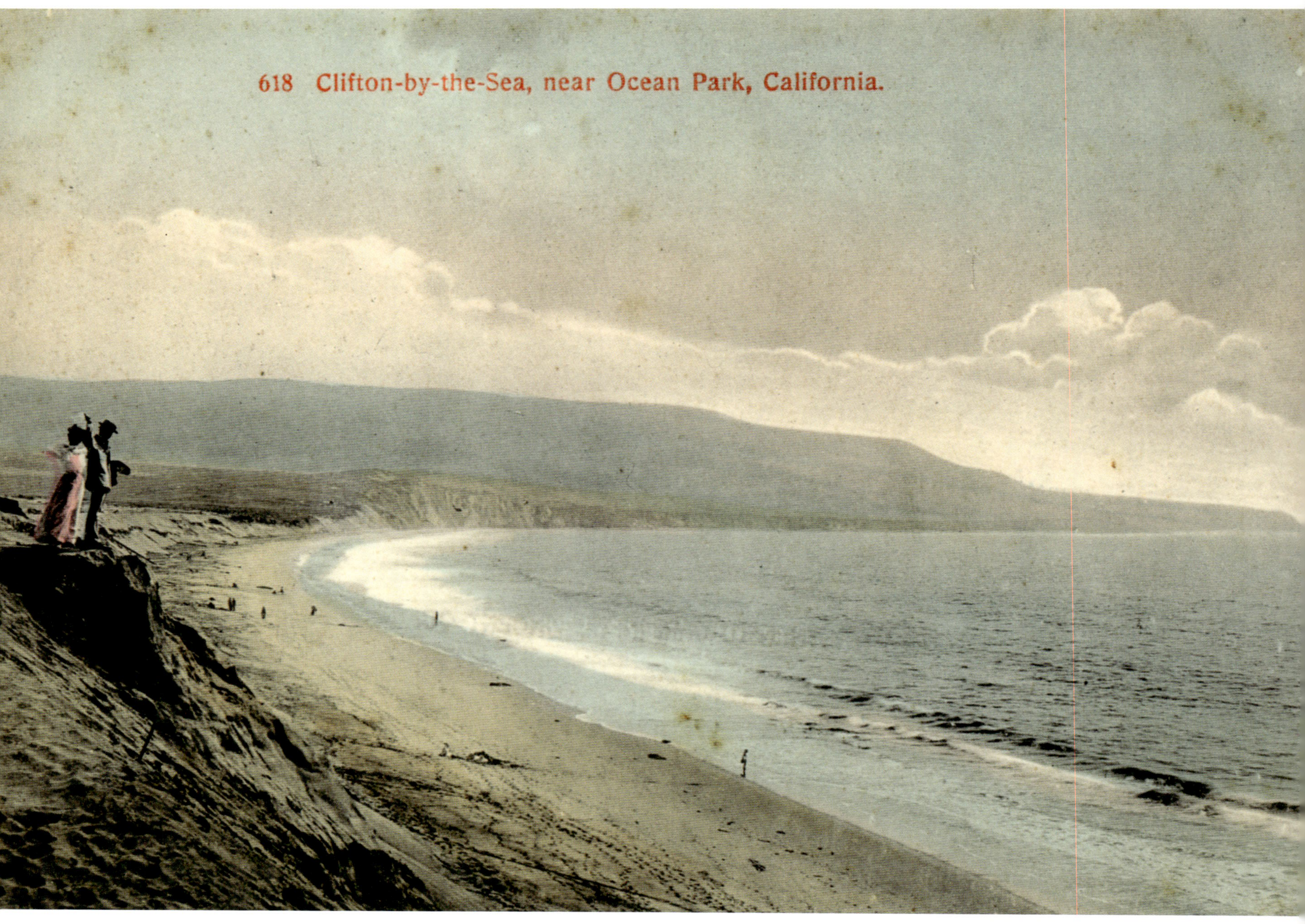
618 Clifton-by-the-Sea, near Ocean Park, California.

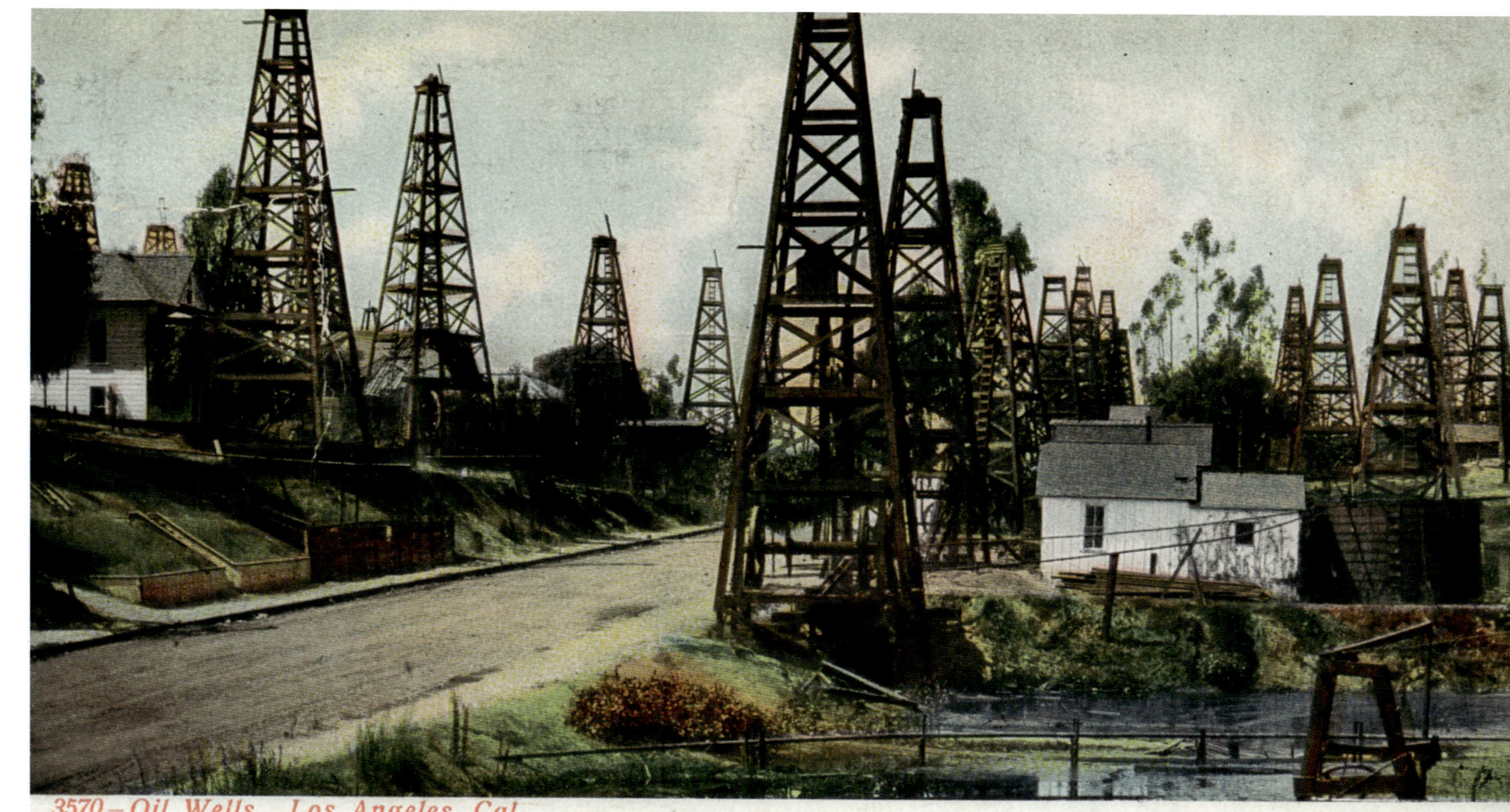


**ABOVE:** How about an oil derrick in your front yard?

**FACING:** Clifton-by-the-Sea encompassed the present-day beach cities of Manhattan, Hermosa, and Redondo. Not much activity from there to Palos Verdes in 1909.

Oil fever! It's hard to imagine today, but starting in 1892 until its peak in 1901, there were over 1,000 oil derricks near downtown Los Angeles crowding the skyline in a narrow four-mile band from Elysian Park (south of today's Dodger Stadium) west to Vermont Avenue. Derricks and oil storage tanks were mere feet from homes, churches, stores, and schools. Often there were two or three derricks on one 50 x 150 foot residential lot. By the time the oil field was mostly depleted nine years later, many investors and homeowners had become rich. As the derricks were taken down, others would soon appear in Signal Hill, Long Beach, Santa Fe Springs, Huntington Beach, and Venice, as major oil strikes in the 1920s and '30s made the region among America's top oil producers before World War II.

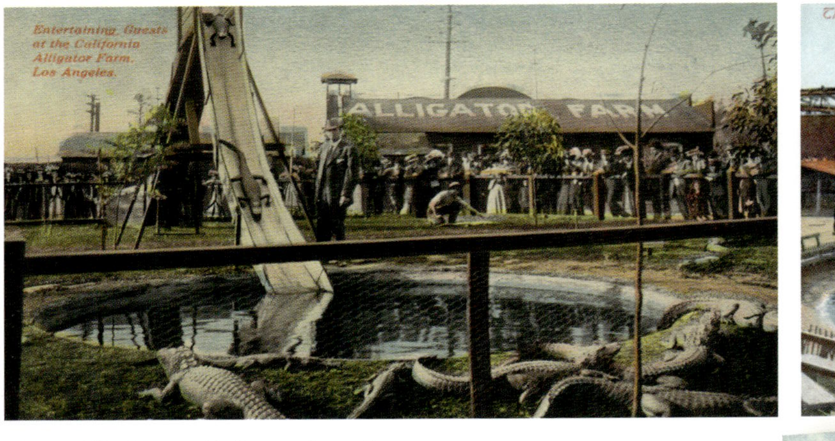


**ABOVE:** Alligators on their way down the alligator slide at the California Alligator Farm.

Alligator and ostrich farms, amusement parks, pleasure piers, beaches, bathhouses, rail excursions, public parks, museums, vaudeville, nickelodeons. These were some of the year-round attractions available to Angelenos before 1920. An annual special event was the Pasadena Tournament of Roses parade held on New Year's Day beginning in 1890 as a way of showcasing the region's mild winter weather.

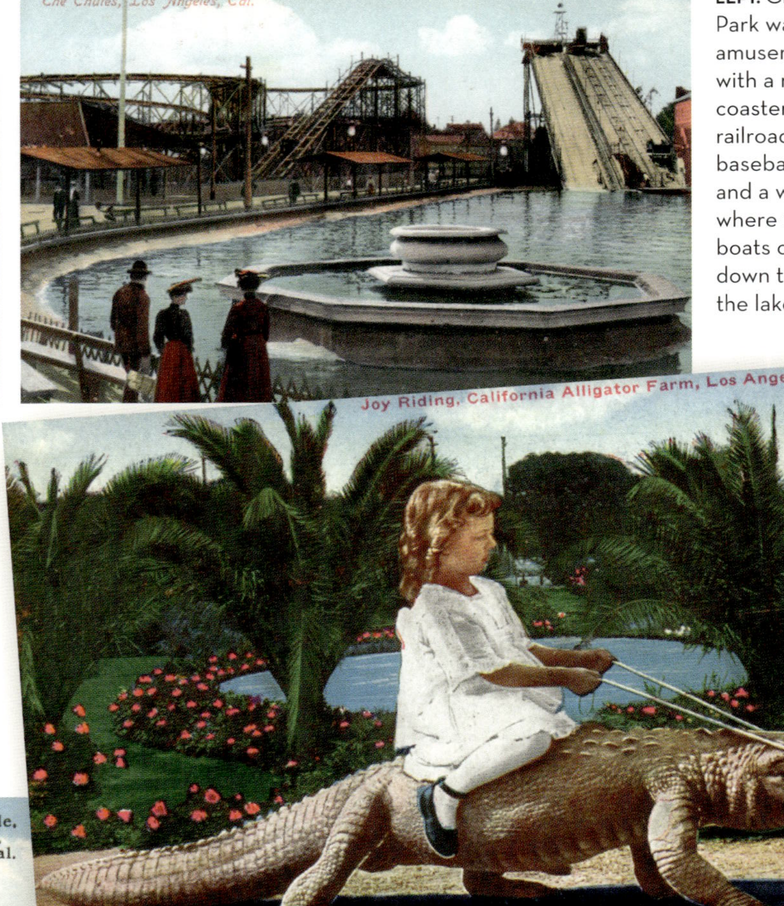


**LEFT:** Chutes Park was an amusement park with a roller coaster, miniature railroad, theater, baseball park, and a waterslide where riders in boats careened down tracks into the lake below.

**ABOVE:** "Joy riding" may not be the best description for this activity.



**LEFT:** This passed for entertainment in 1910.

**RIGHT:** The plunge in the festive Ocean Park Bath House (south Santa Monica) was fully enclosed despite being located on the beach. Note the rows of spectators ogling the virile bathers.

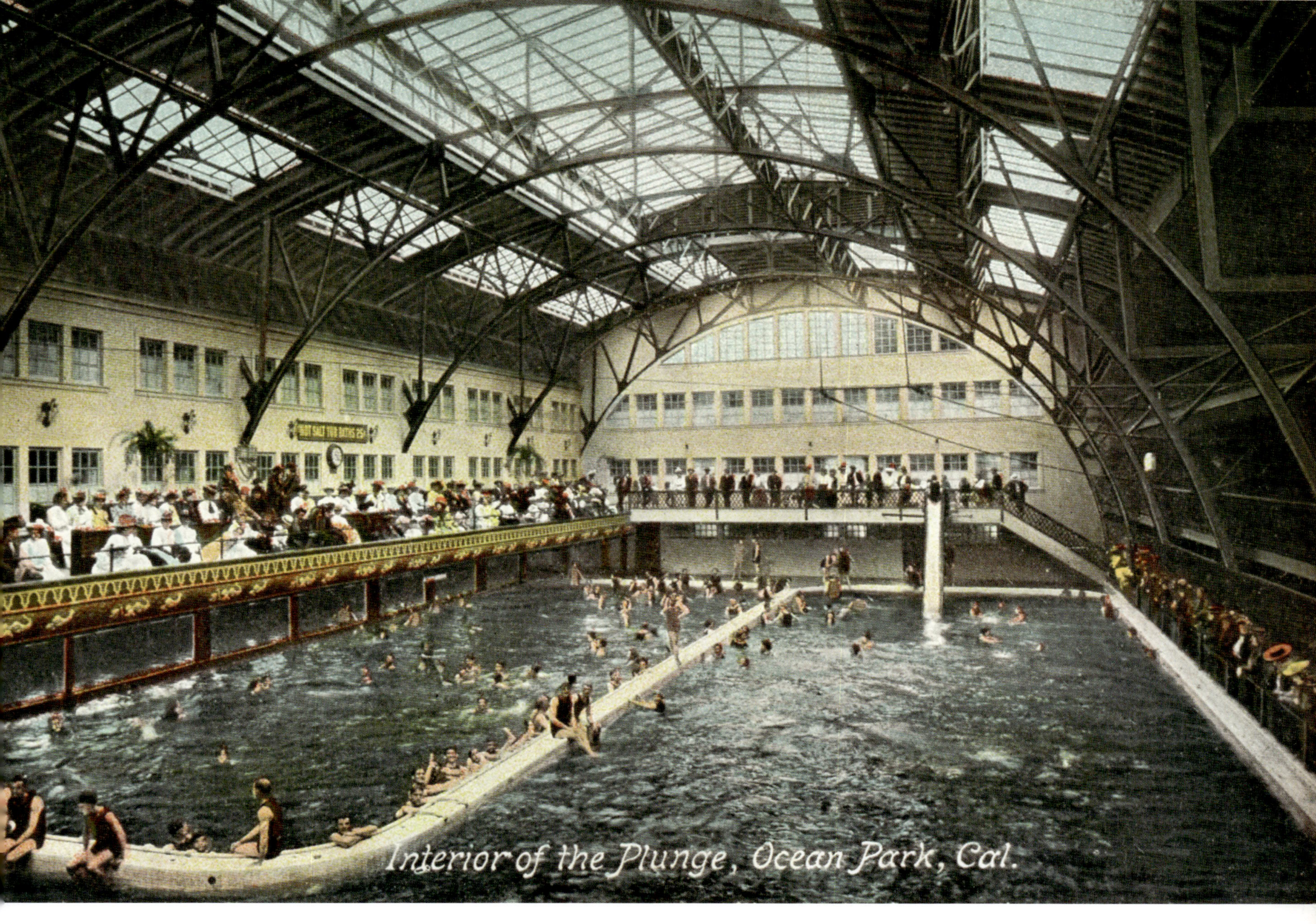
HOT SALT TUB BATHS 25¢
Interior of the Plunge, Ocean Park, Cal.

2404 – Residences on the Canal, Venice, California.

**LEFT:** Guiding a gondola in a Venice canal circa 1908. Abbott Kinney's Venice of America lasted until 1929, when the canals were filled and paved over with roads and the beach blighted by oil derricks (see page 53).

**RIGHT:** The "Scenic Railway" on Venice Beach.

**BELOW:** Scantily clad beachgoers at Playa del Rey (left) and Santa Monica circa 1910 (right).

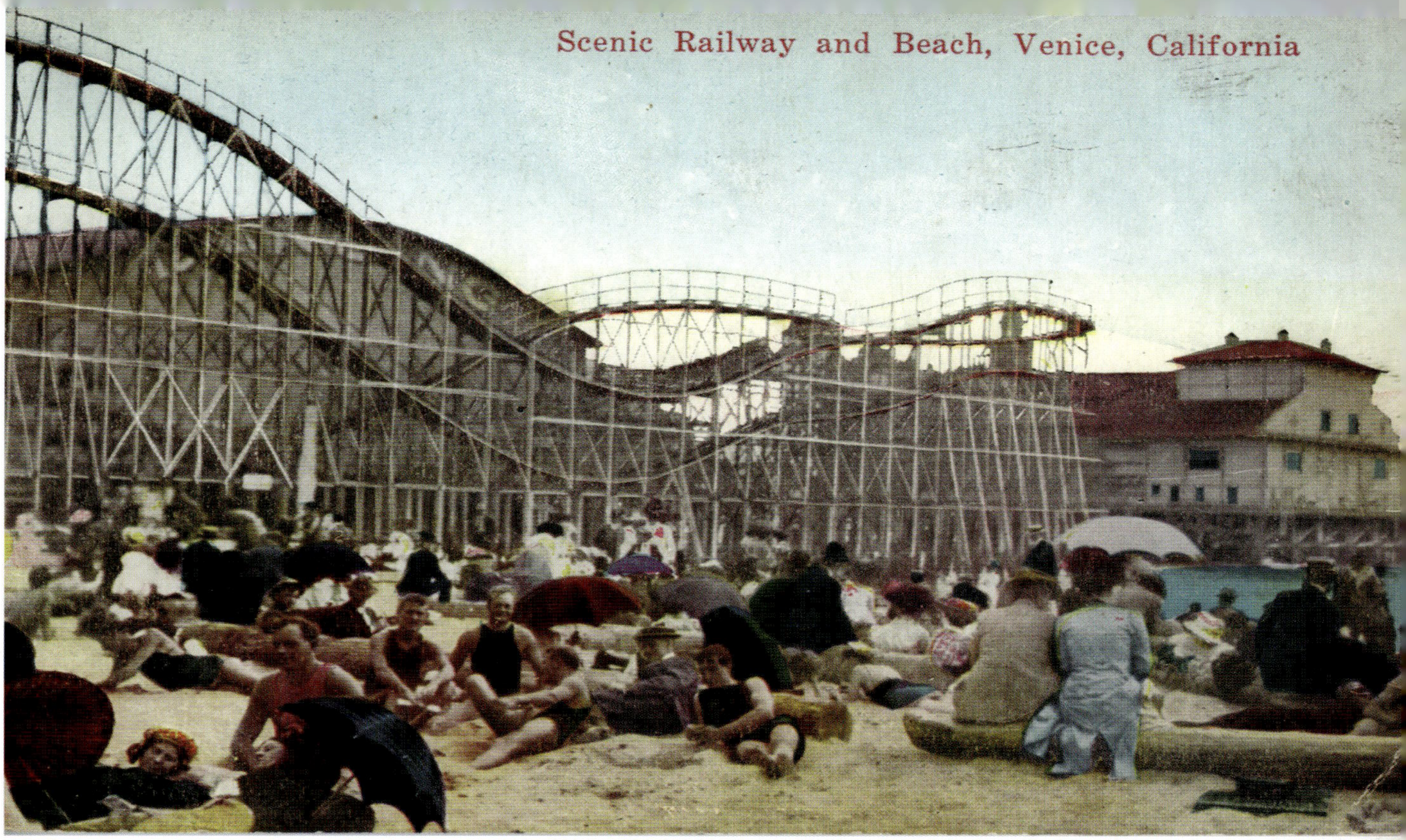

Scenic Railway and Beach, Venice, California

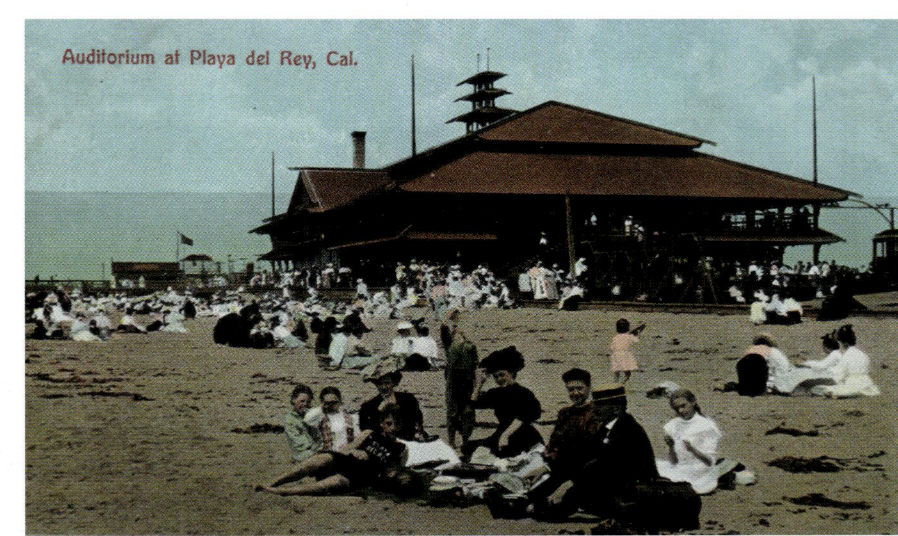


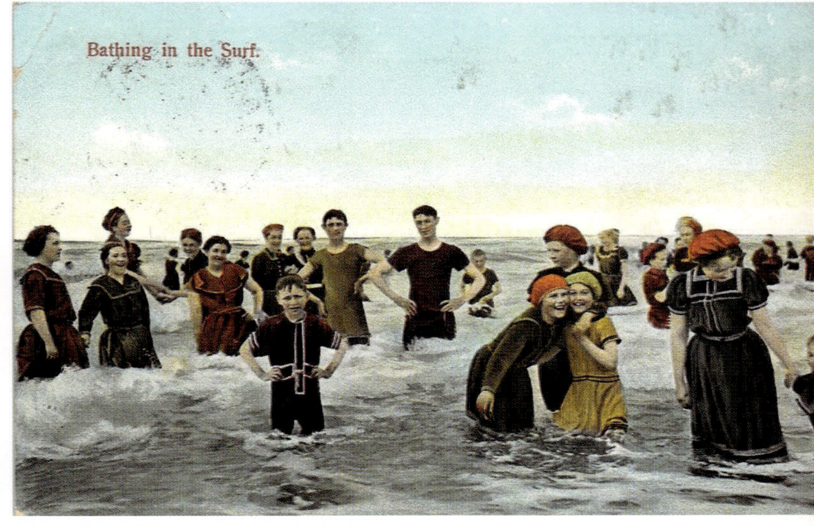

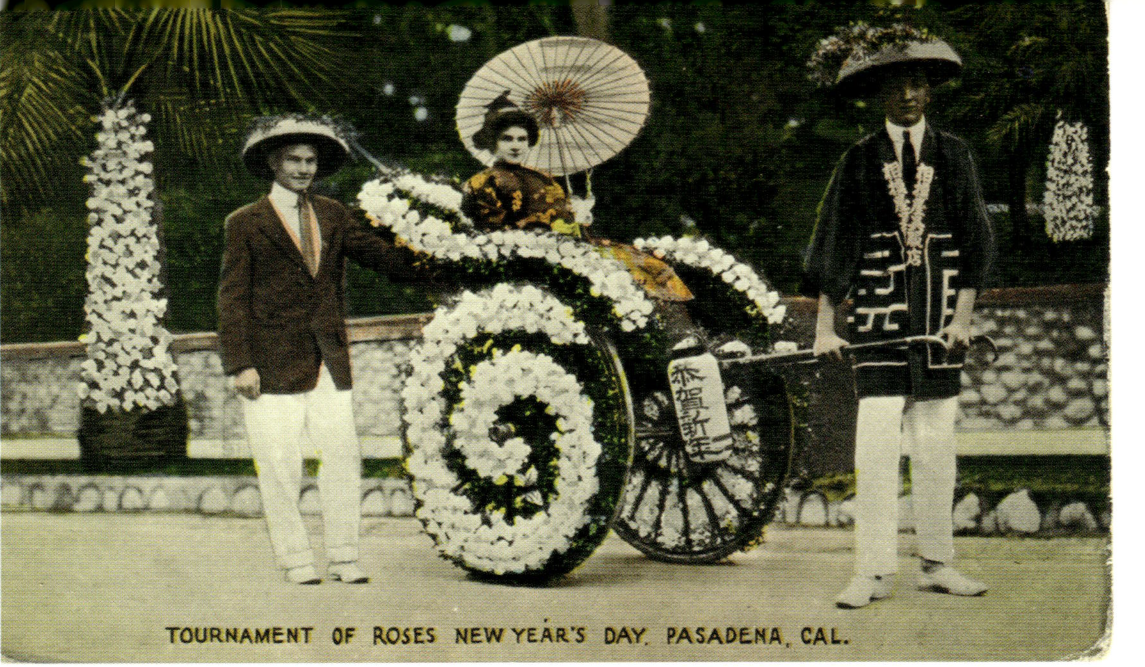


Floats in the Rose Parade. A low-budget entry featuring an Anglo in vaguely Asian garb pulling a "geisha" in a floral rickshaw (left). It's unclear why a small motorcar sits atop a mound of roses gliding down the street (below).

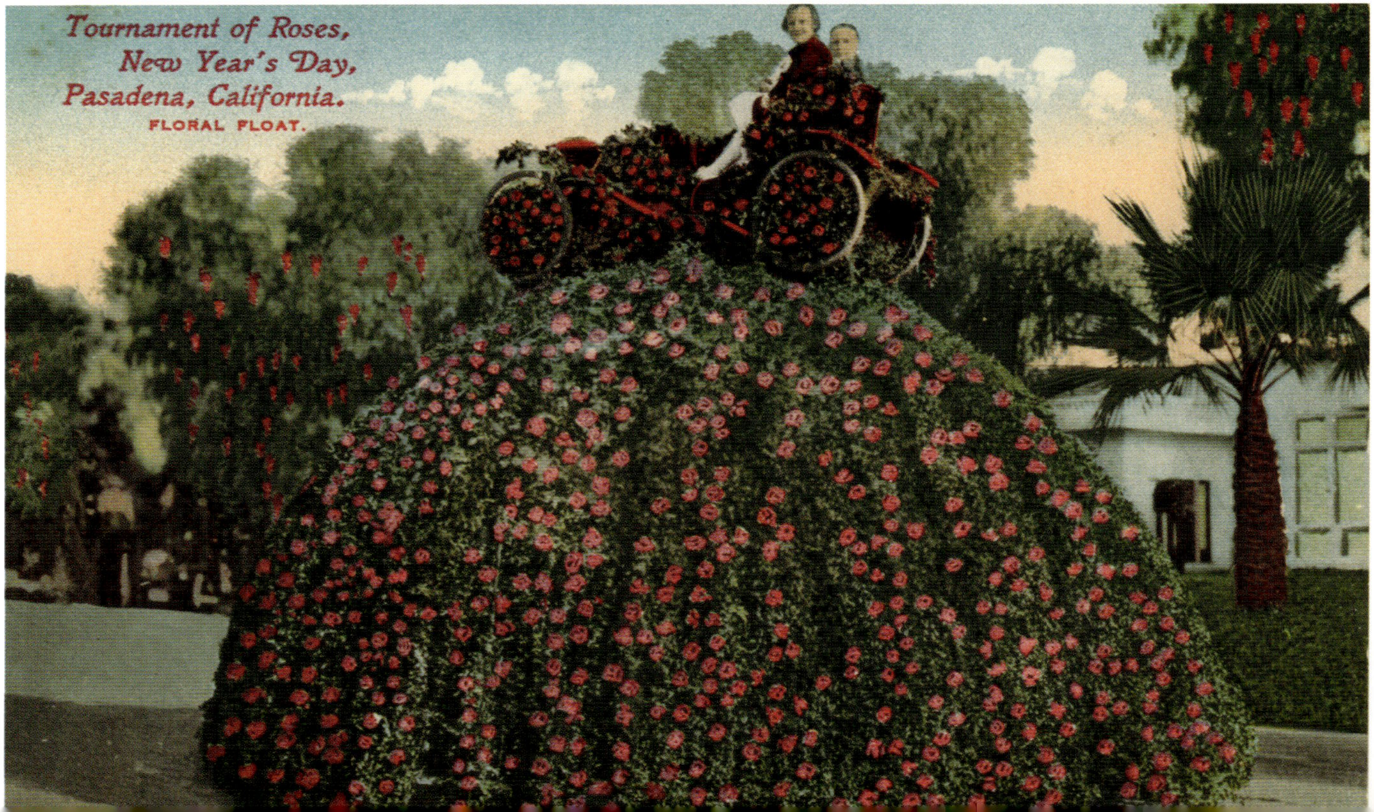

Tournament of Roses,
New Year's Day,
Pasadena, California.
FLORAL FLOAT.

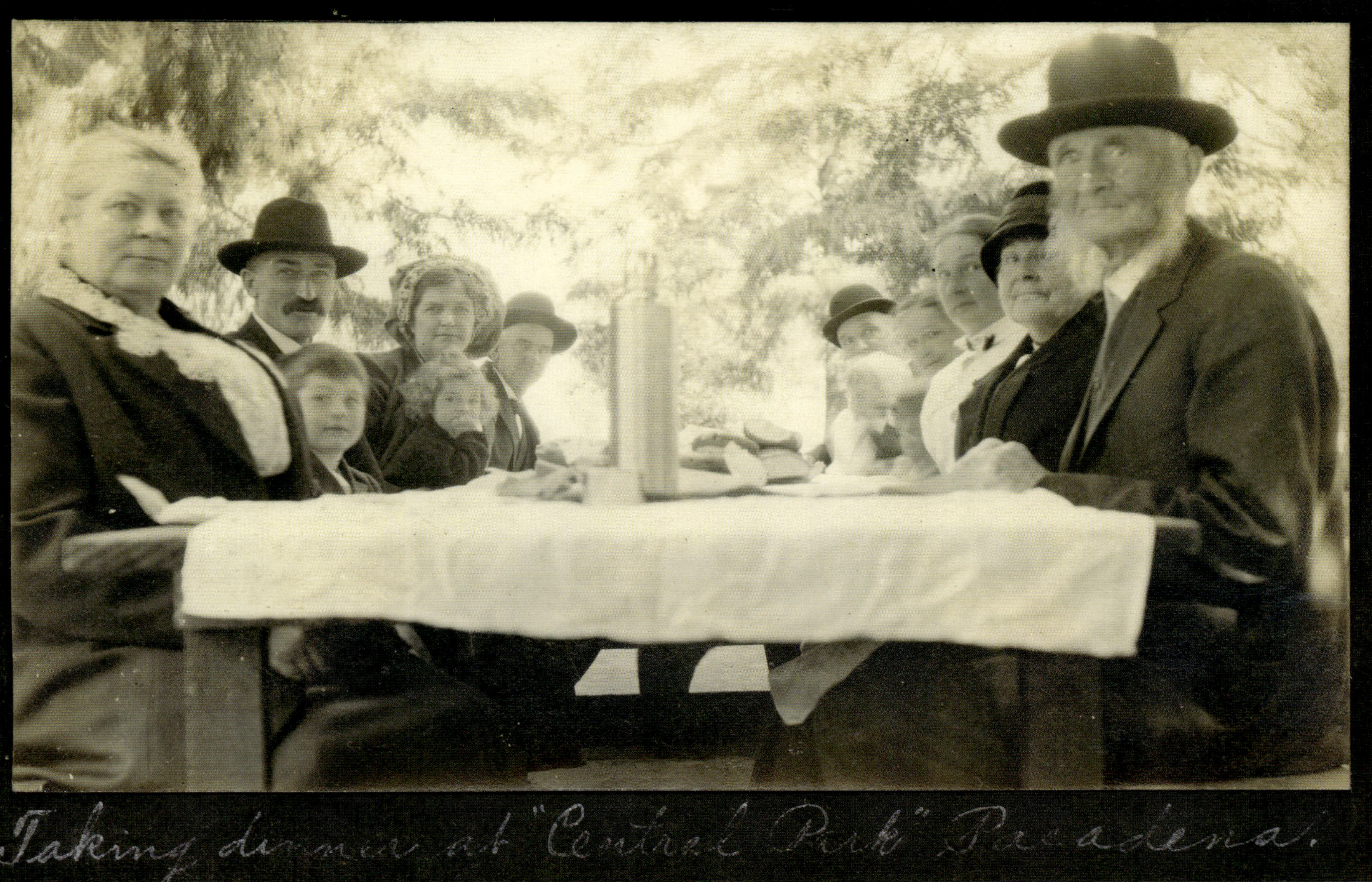


A jovial family "Taking dinner at 'Central Park' Pasadena" in 1915.

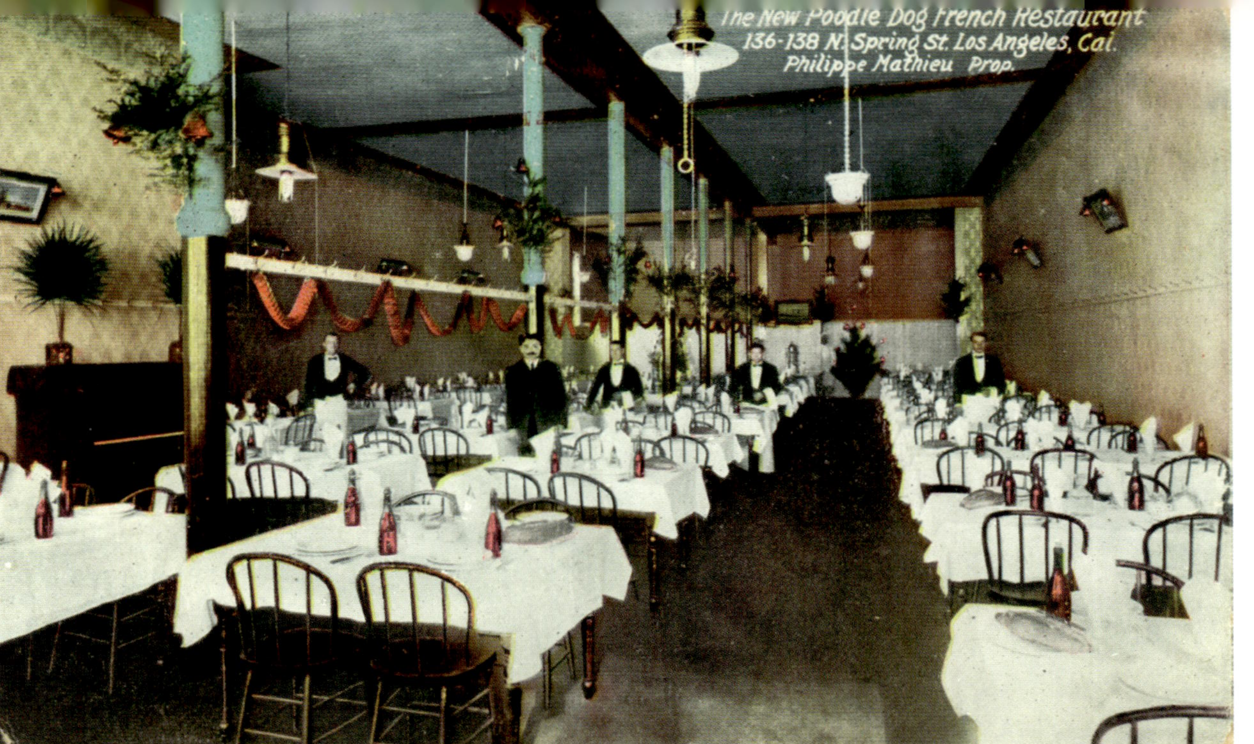


**RIGHT:** The New Poodle Dog French Restaurant featured snappy waiters, red wine, and piano entertainment. What it lacked was customers.

**BELOW, LEFT:** Big hats on parade at the upscale Café Bristol.

**BELOW, RIGHT:** Hamburger's Department Store had the "largest store aisle in the U.S.," extending from Broadway to Hill Street.

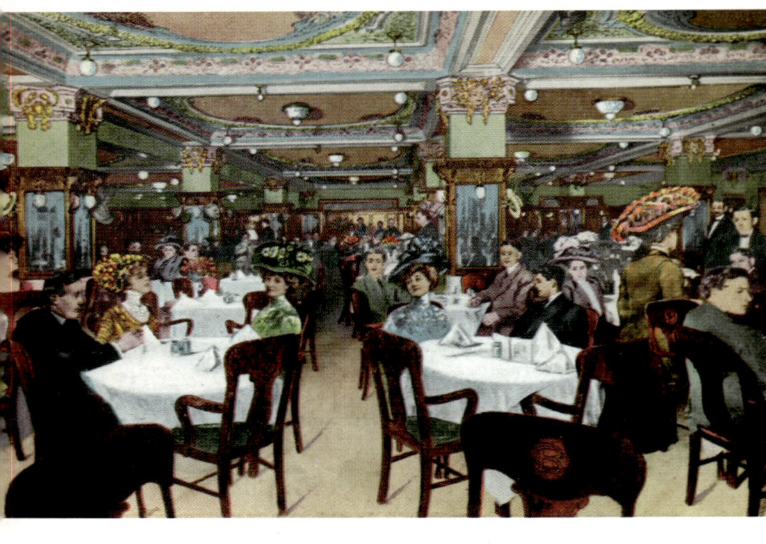

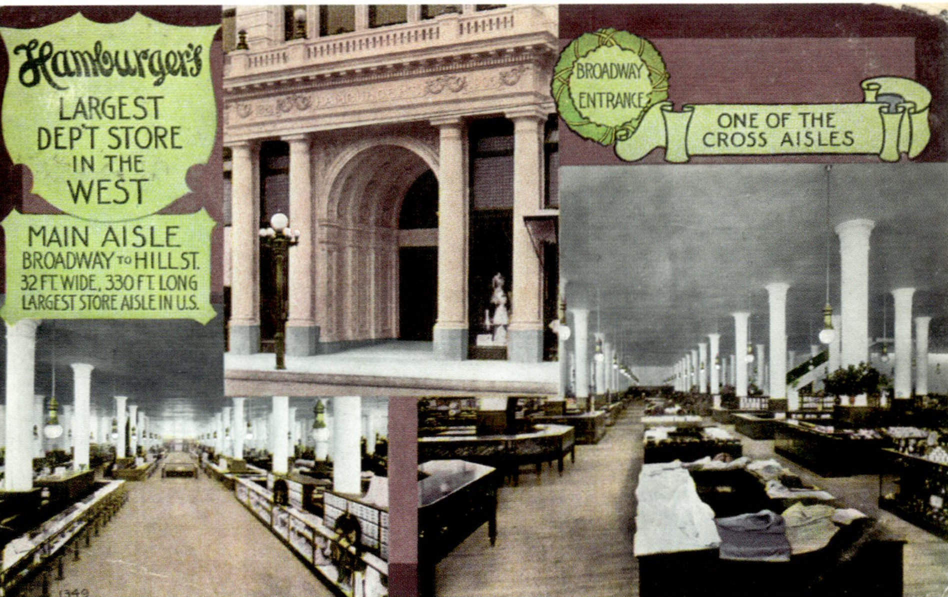

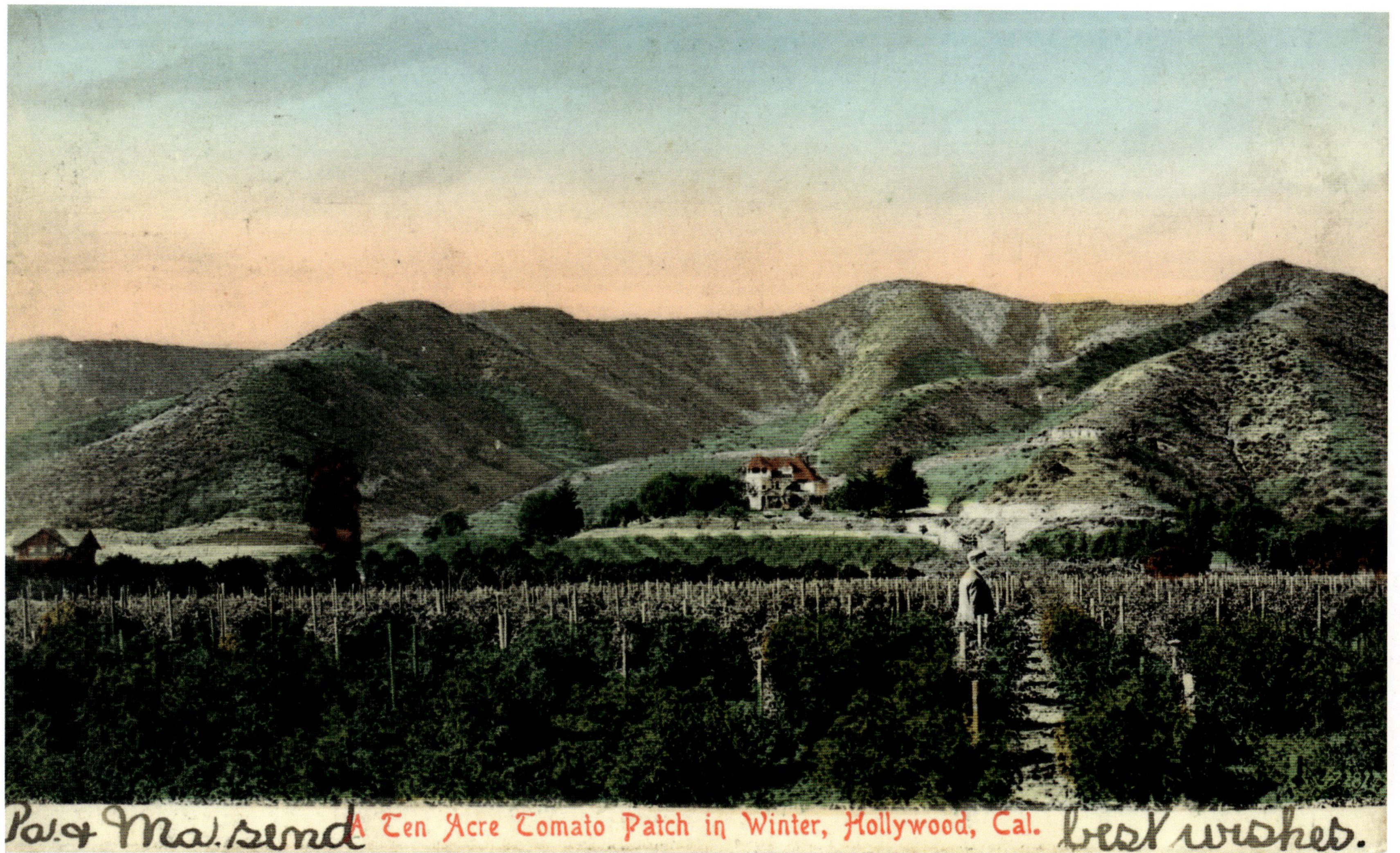


In 1907, Hollywood consisted of a tomato patch and a few farmhouses.

But it was the motion picture industry that would come to symbolize Los Angeles in the twentieth century. In the winter of 1907, a director and his cameraman with the Selig Polyscope Company came out from snowy Chicago to film exterior portions of *The Count of Monte Cristo* near Sycamore Grove Park (next to today's Arroyo Seco Parkway). In 1909, D. W. Griffith arrived from New York to shoot *Ramona* (remember her? see page 20). A few years later, in 1913, director Cecil B. DeMille and his filmmaking partners established a permanent movie studio in a rented barn in Hollywood, which had been an independent city before its annexation by Los Angeles in 1910. As more studios opened there, "Hollywood" became shorthand for the film industry.

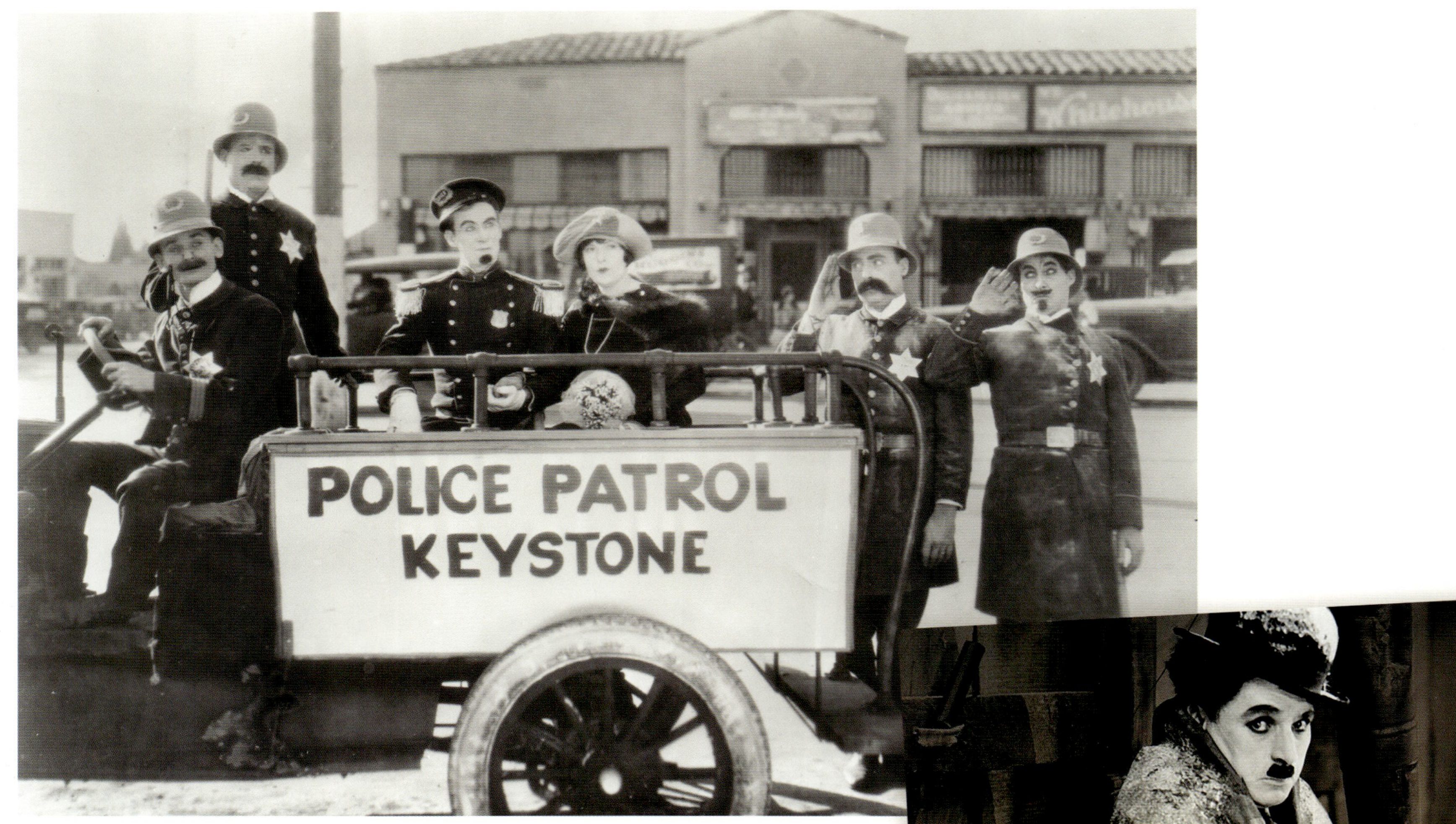


**ABOVE:** Keystone Cops hard at work. **RIGHT:** Charlie Chaplin as the Little Tramp.

Mack Sennett's famous Keystone Cop movies began in 1912, and for five years as the bumbling officers furiously chased criminals throughout Los Angeles, Sennett's film cameras unintentionally documented the fast-growing city. In 1913, Sennett cast Charles Chaplin in the English performer's first silent comedy, *Making a Living*. For his second film, Chaplin created the endearing tramp character that would define the comic actor for the rest of his life. Meanwhile, the 1910s saw the beginning of the Hollywood studio system with the establishment of Universal Pictures and United Artists.

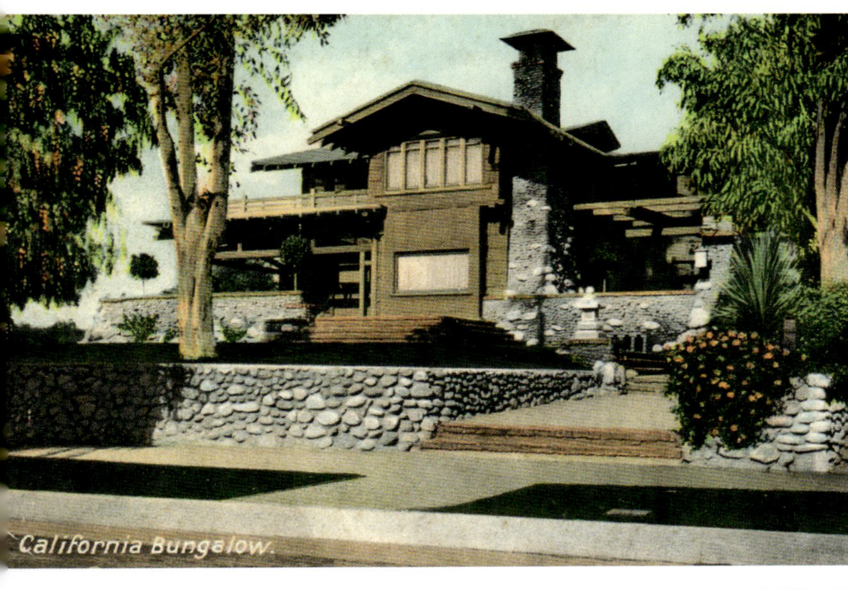


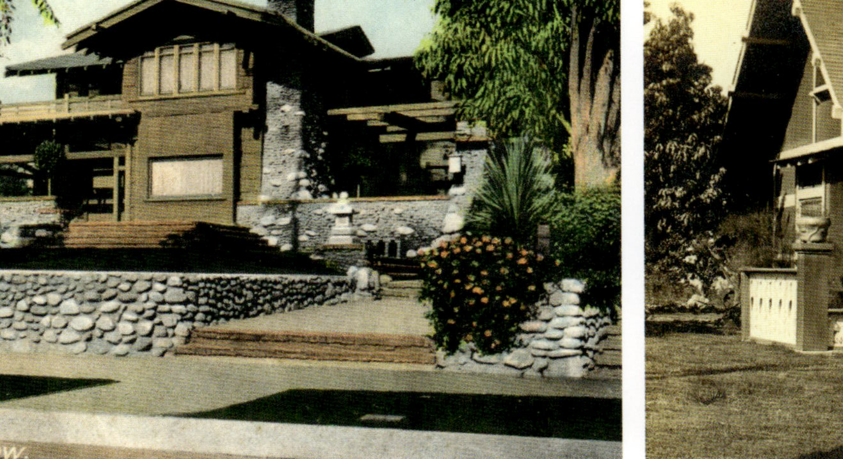

**ABOVE:** The 1908 Duncan-Irwin Residence remains a sublime Craftsman house in Pasadena designed by Greene and Greene, brothers who were masters of the style. The postcard misleadingly infers that this architectural gem is a "typical" California bungalow.

**ABOVE, RIGHT:** More typical was the 1908 Gracie's Bungalow, located at 3829 E. 15th Street.

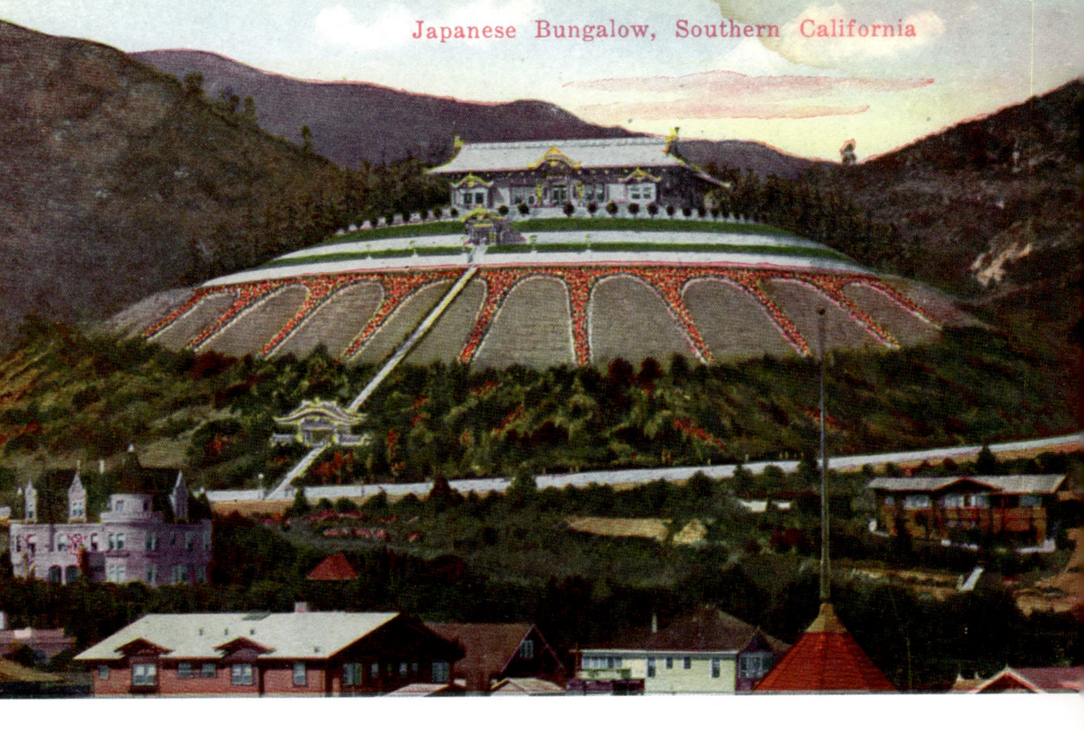


**RIGHT:** The Bernheimer brothers built this replica of a Japanese palace in 1914 to house their Asian art collection. Prominently located atop a hill in Hollywood, it later became the restaurant Yamashiro.

It was perhaps inevitable that Southern California would become America's movie capital, because it offered what no other region of the country could—a mild climate, year-round sunshine, cheap land, and perhaps most importantly a wide variety of exterior locations, from beaches, deserts, and mountains, to small towns, charming neighborhoods, and a bustling downtown.

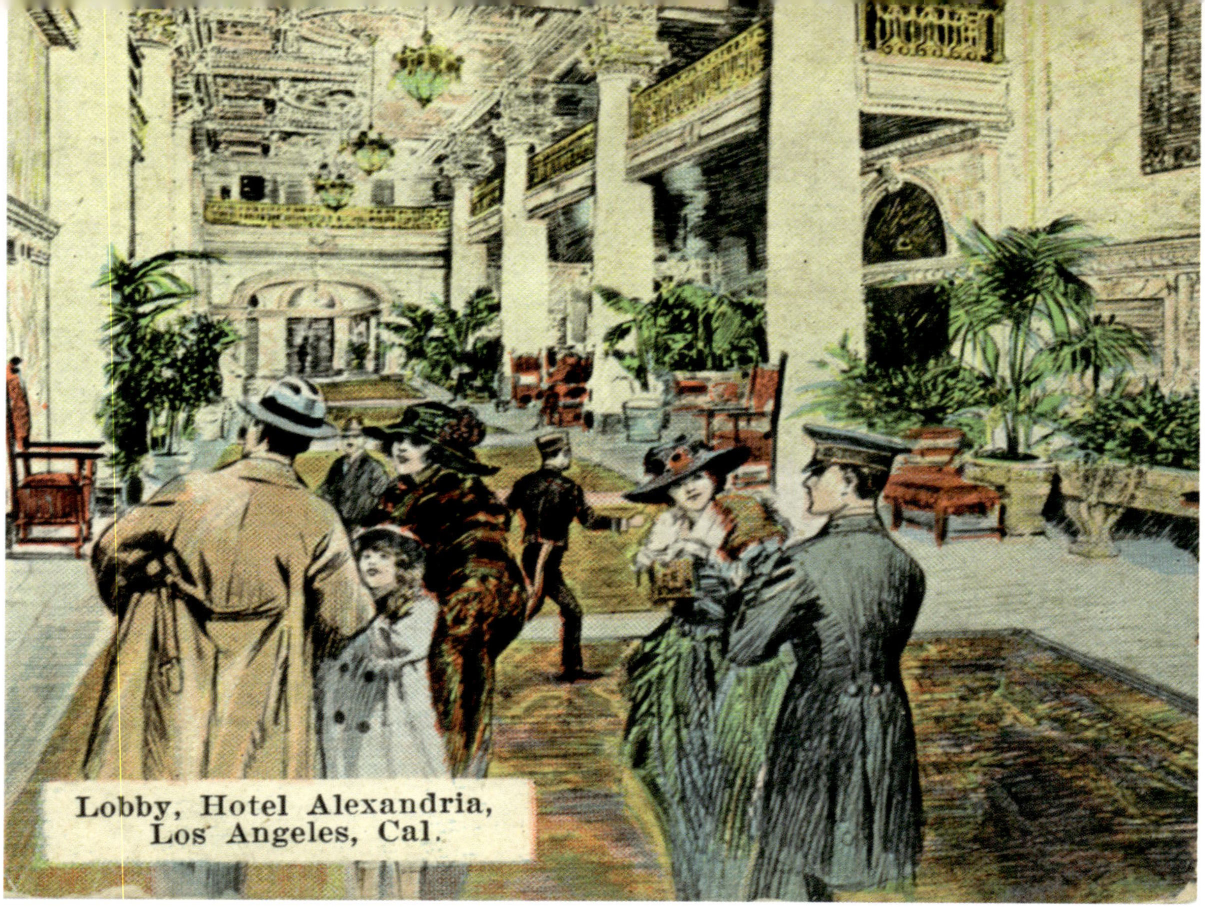

Lobby, Hotel Alexandria,
Los Angeles, Cal.

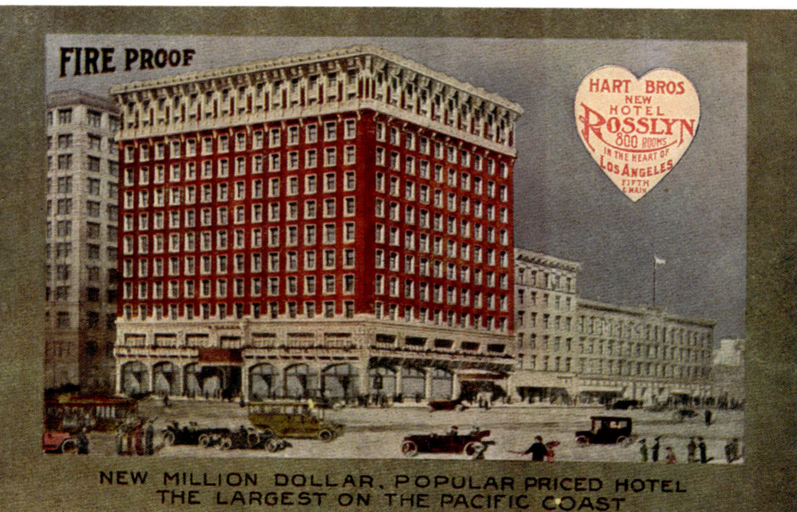


The Hotel Alexandria (above) on Spring Street was the city's most luxurious when it opened in 1906. The 1913 Million Dollar Rosslyn (right) had 800 fireproof rooms. Both hotels, which still exist, were designed by architect John Parkinson, who later codesigned City Hall, the Coliseum, and Union Station.

**FACING:** Downtown's Broadway was a very busy place, much of it photographed by Hollywood's motion-picture makers.

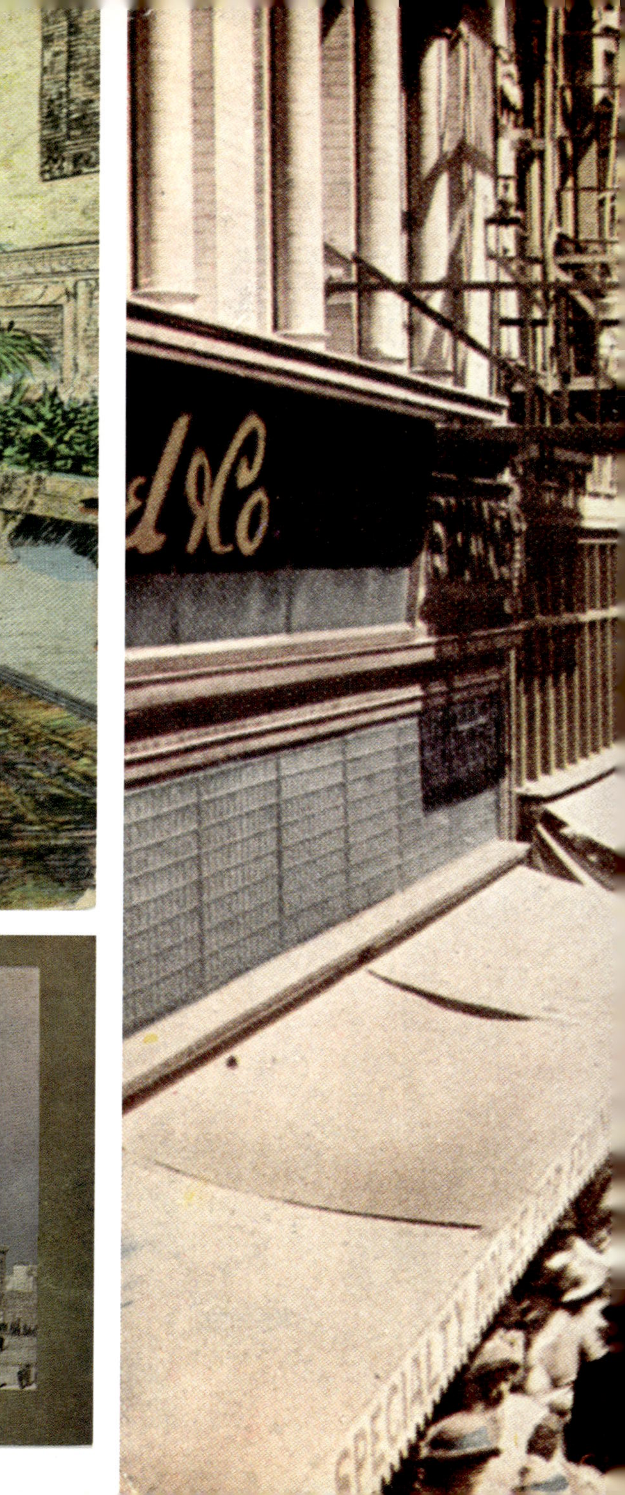

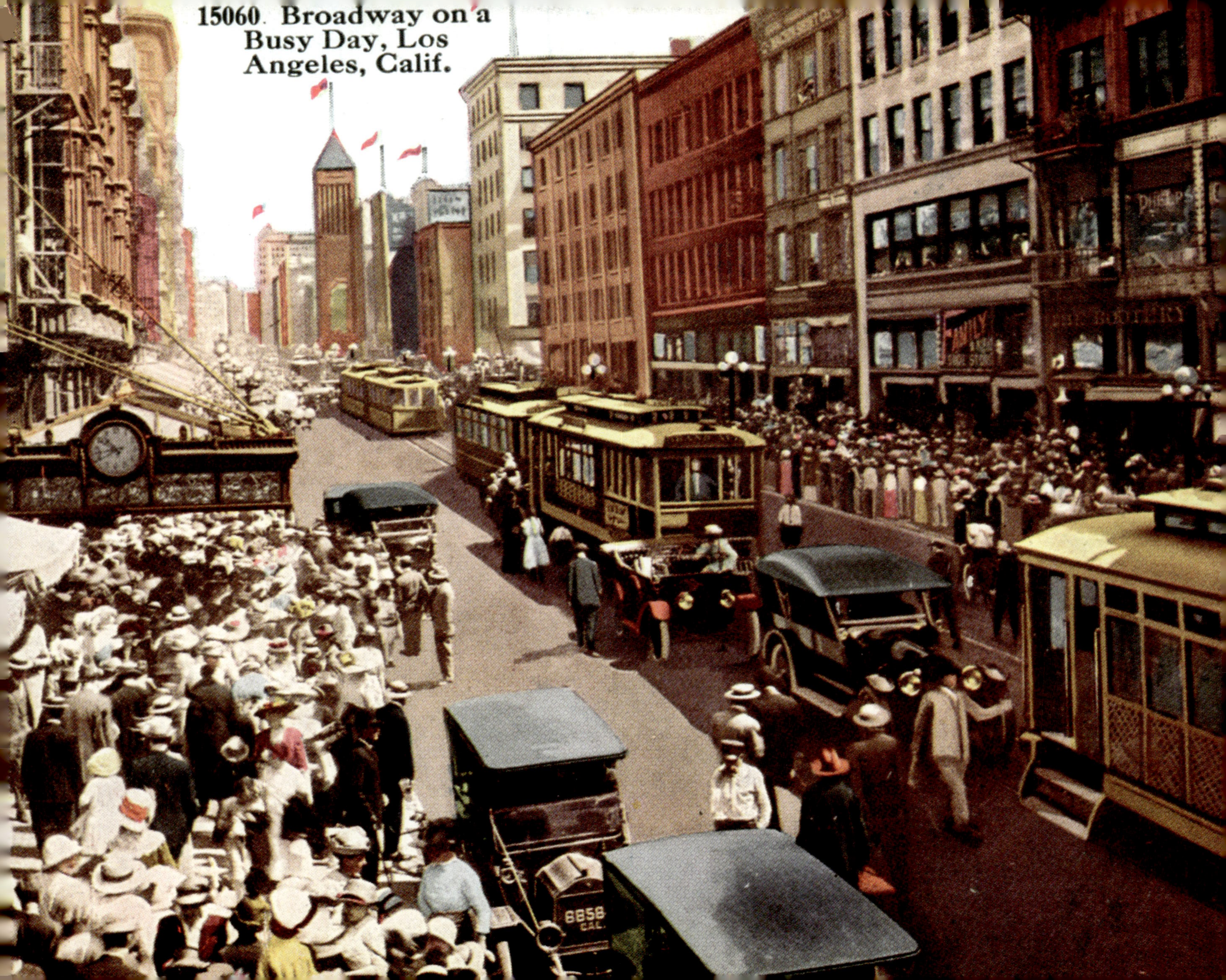

15060. Broadway on a Busy Day, Los Angeles, Calif.

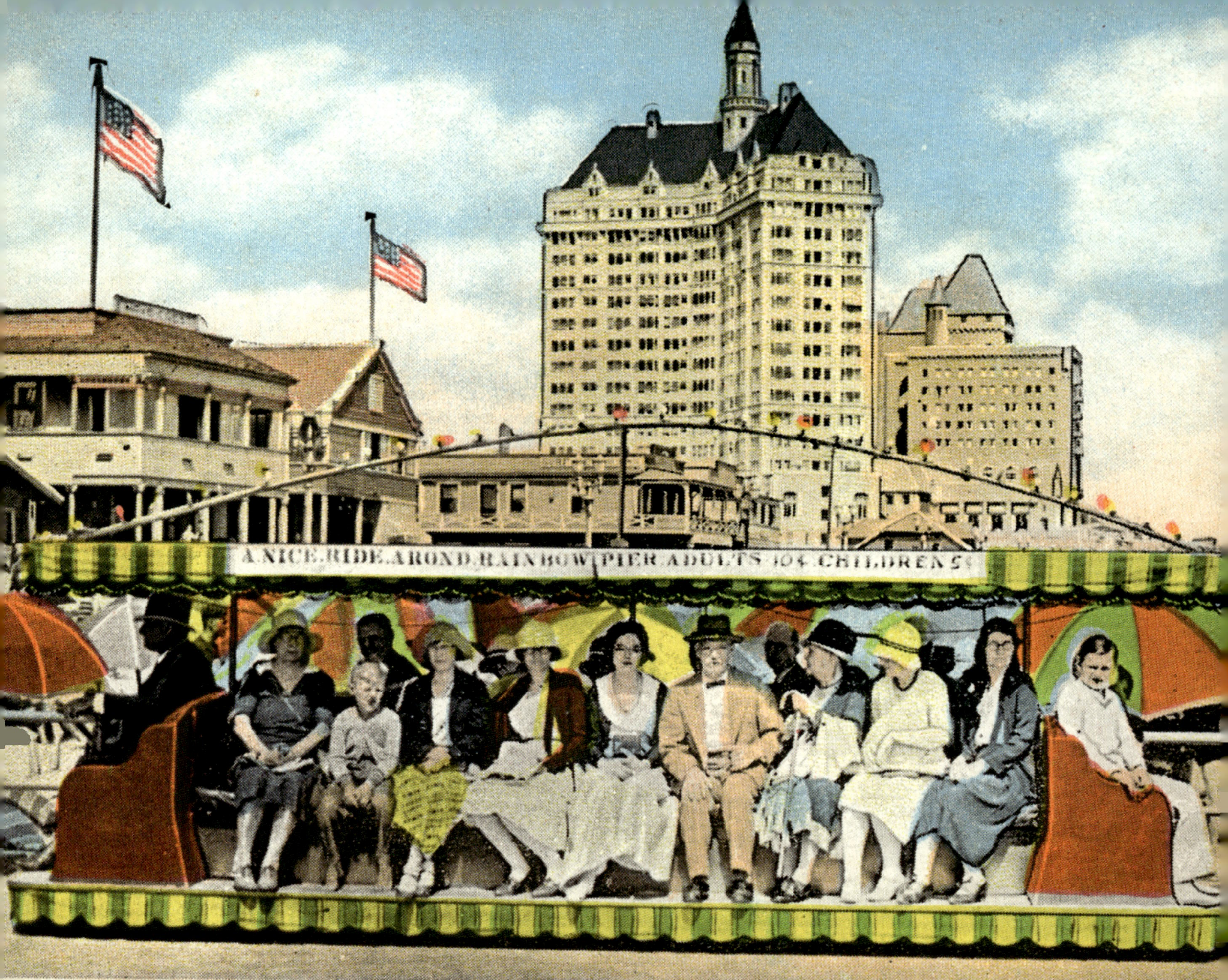
A.NICE.RIDE.AROND.RAINBOW.PIER.ADULTS 10¢ CHILDREN 5¢

# Invasion of the Midwestern Protestants

## 1920–1930

More than 650,000 people migrated to Los Angeles during the 1920s. By 1930, with a population of 1,200,000, it had become America's fifth largest city. Decades of promotion by the railroads, the Los Angeles Chamber of Commerce, and real estate interests had paid off as midwesterners sold their farms and moved from small towns to the promised land of sunshine and citrus. Compared with other large cities, the Roaring Twenties were not as roaring in the City of Angels because of the conservative Protestants that formed the majority of residents. Instead of flappers and speakeasies, Sunday church services and mass picnics organized by state—Nebraska and Iowa in particular—were civilized diversions. However, a major difference between Los Angeles and Omaha or Des Moines, in addition to the weather, was the glamour and excitement of Hollywood that mesmerized the awestruck newcomers.

**FACING:** Iowa by the Sea was the nickname for Long Beach due to the multitude of new residents from that state.

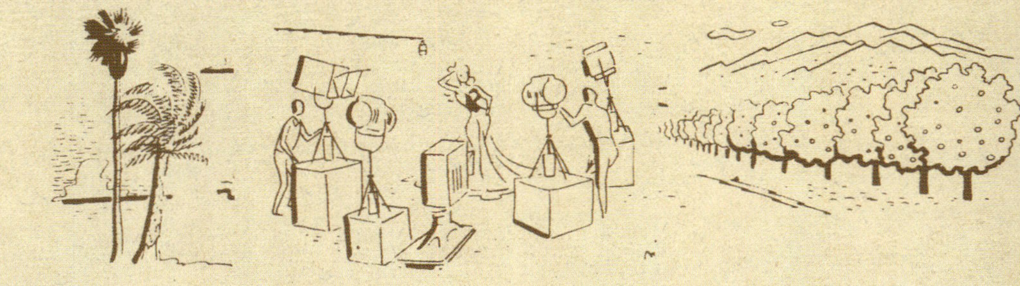

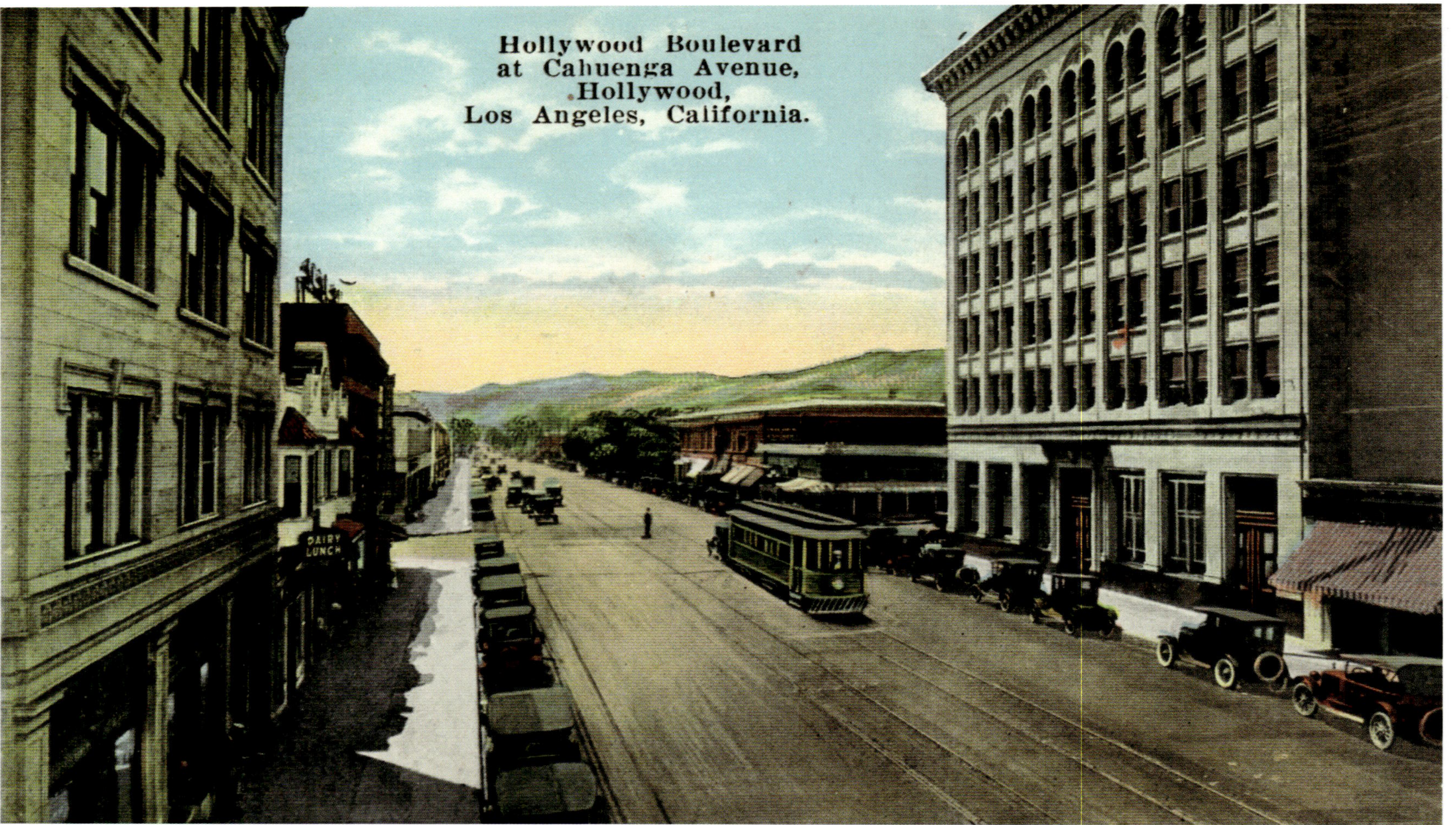


Sleepy Hollywood Boulevard at Cahuenga in the early 1920s.

Starting in the late 1910s and into the 1920s, the major motion picture studios we're familiar with today were formed—Universal, United Artists, Warner Brothers, Metro-Goldwyn-Mayer, Columbia, 20th Century Fox, and Paramount. Their stars became the most famous people in America, with millions of fans who went to the movies several times a week. Fabulous movie palaces were built to evoke the fantasy world depicted on-screen. In Hollywood, Sid Grauman opened his Egyptian Theatre in 1922 and the Chinese Theatre—arguably the most famous movie theater in the world—in 1927. That was also the year when talkies arrived. While movie stars became very rich with vast mansions in Beverly Hills, Brentwood, and Bel Air, their public and private lives were monitored and manipulated by the studios (not always successfully) so that reality did not displace carefully crafted myth. No form of entertainment had ever held such power over people. Hollywood movies were an addiction, an insatiable craving, and a big, big business.

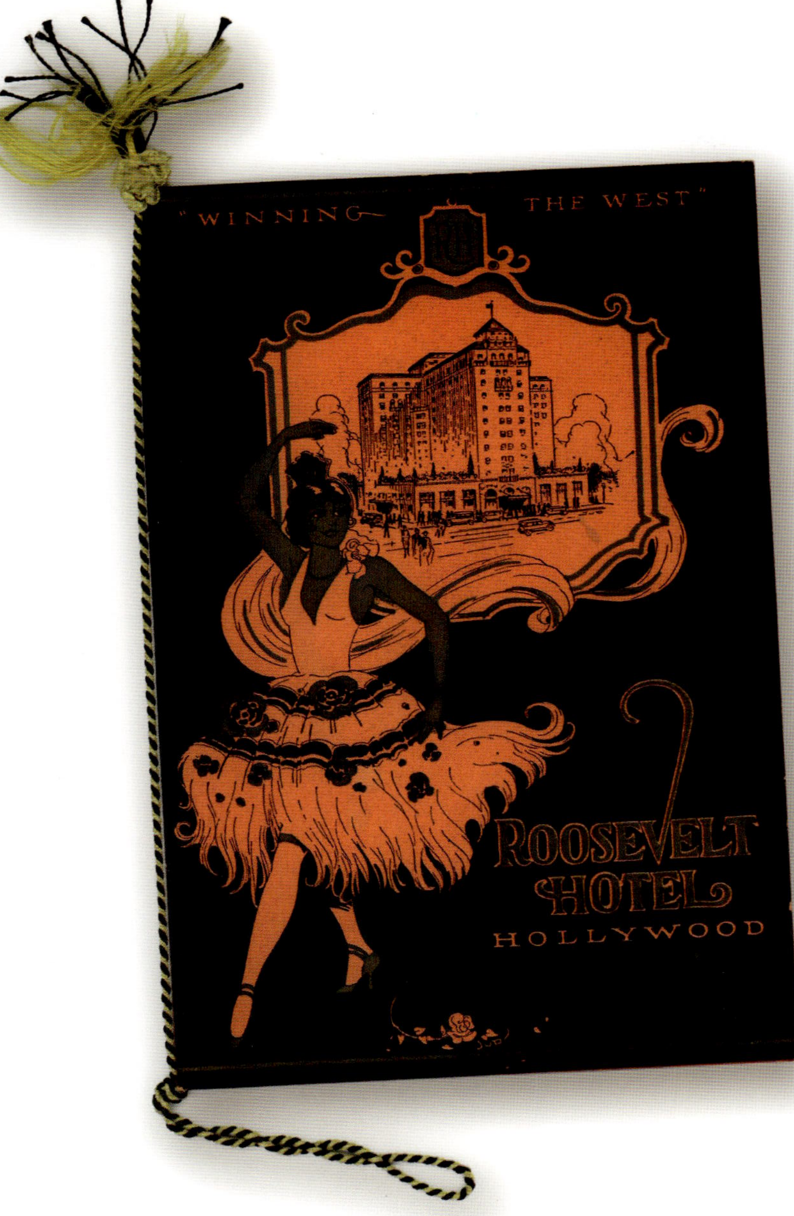

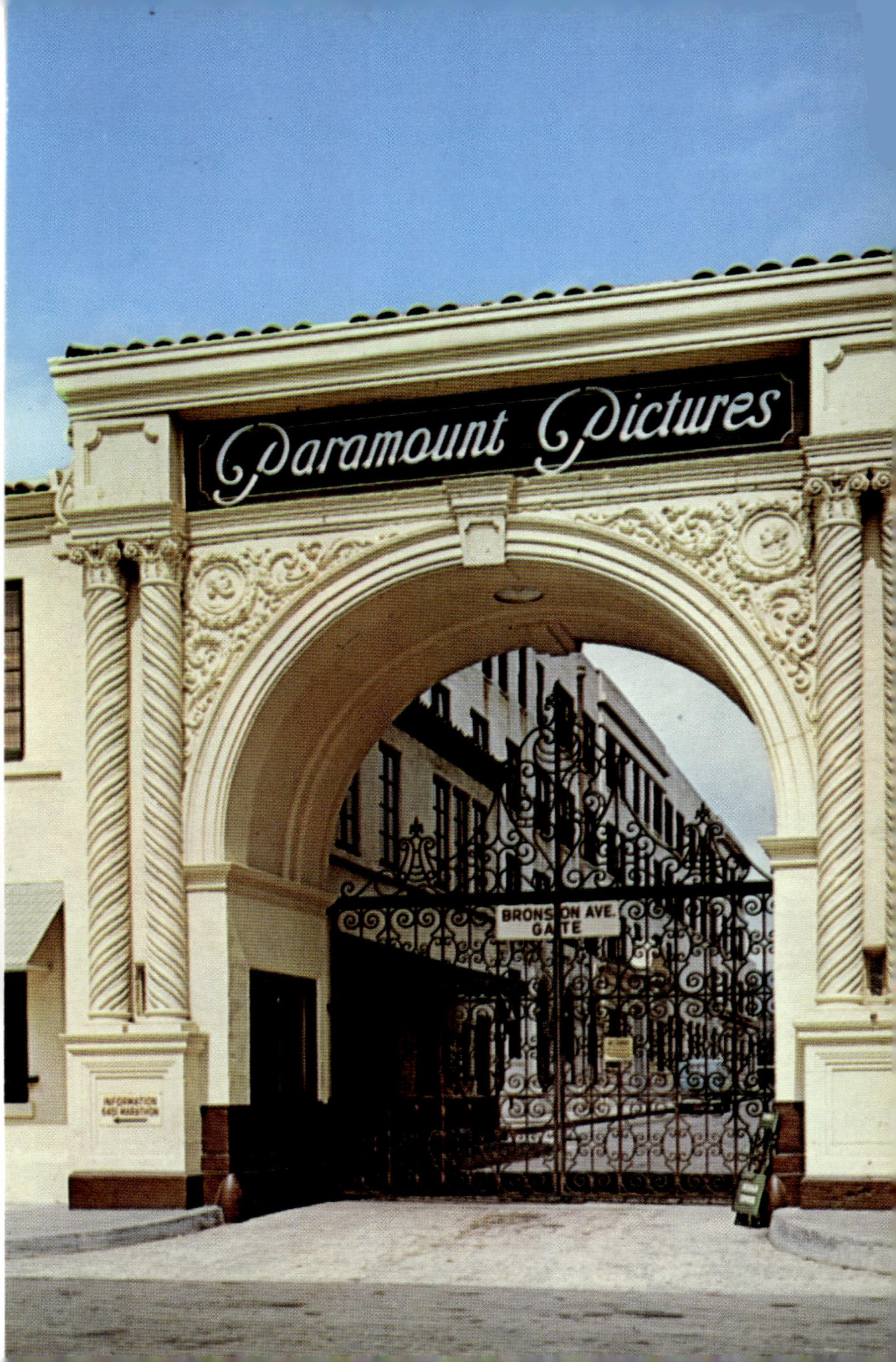

**ABOVE:** The Spanish Colonial Revival–style Roosevelt Hotel, across from Grauman's Chinese Theatre in Hollywood, opened in 1926. The first Academy Awards were held there in 1929.

**RIGHT:** The Bronson Gate at Paramount Pictures.

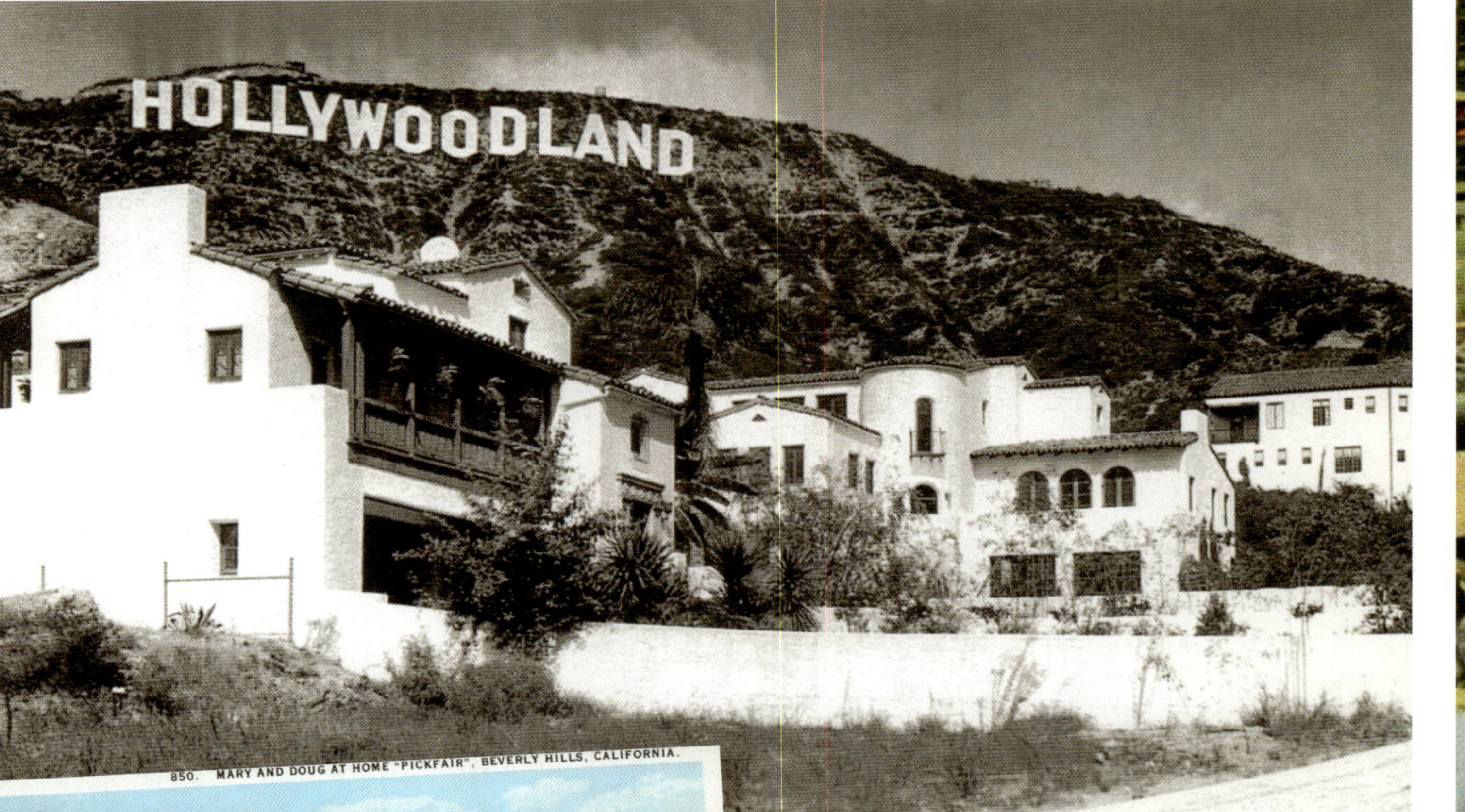


**ABOVE:** The Hollywood sign was originally erected in 1923 to advertise the new Hollywoodland housing development. Each letter is 45 feet tall. "Land" was removed in 1949 during the first of several preservation efforts.

**LEFT:** Silent film stars Mary Pickford and Douglas Fairbanks canoeing in their pool at Pickfair in Beverly Hills.

**RIGHT:** Directing via megaphone in 1922.

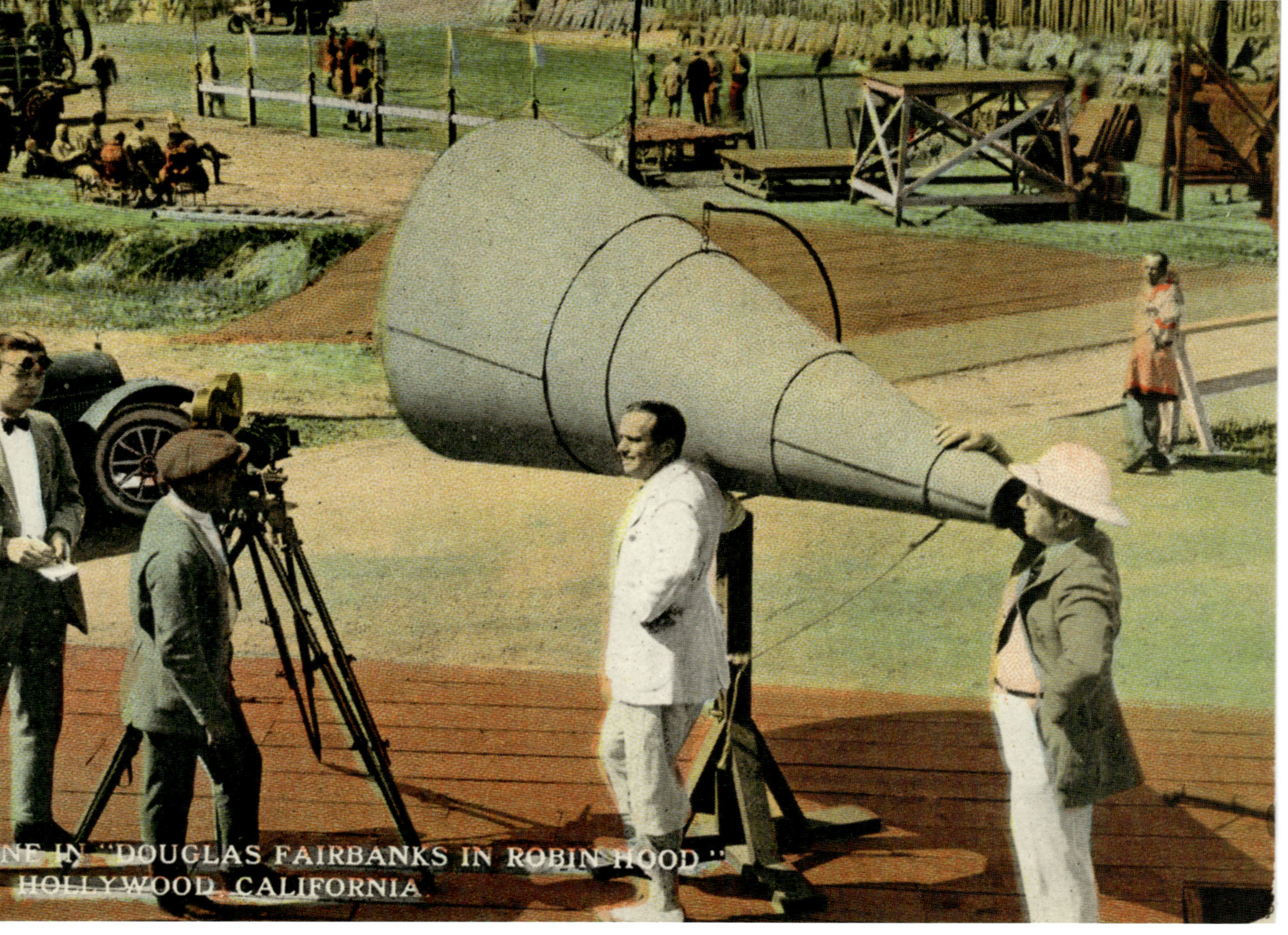
NE IN "DOUGLAS FAIRBANKS IN ROBIN HOOD."
HOLLYWOOD, CALIFORNIA

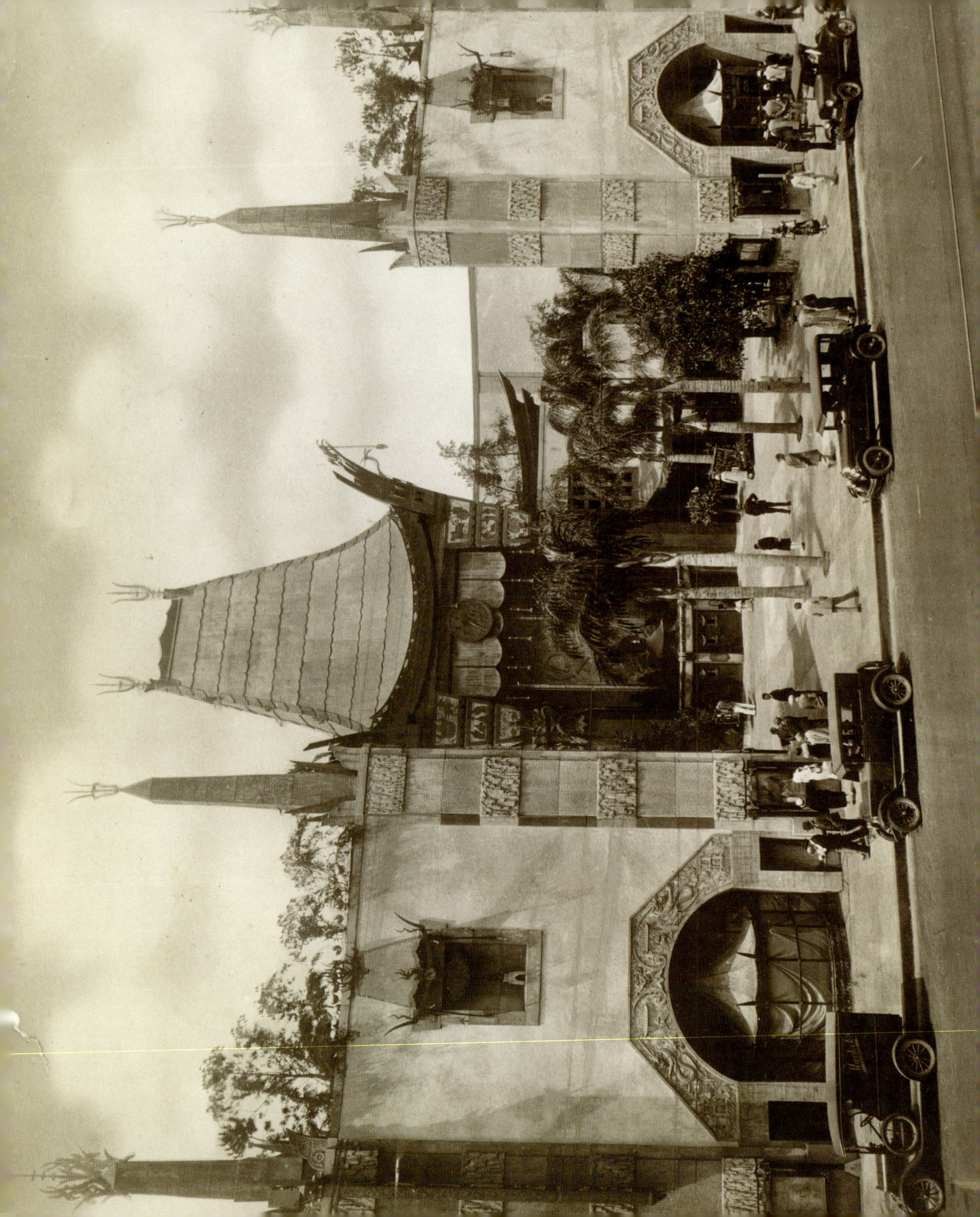

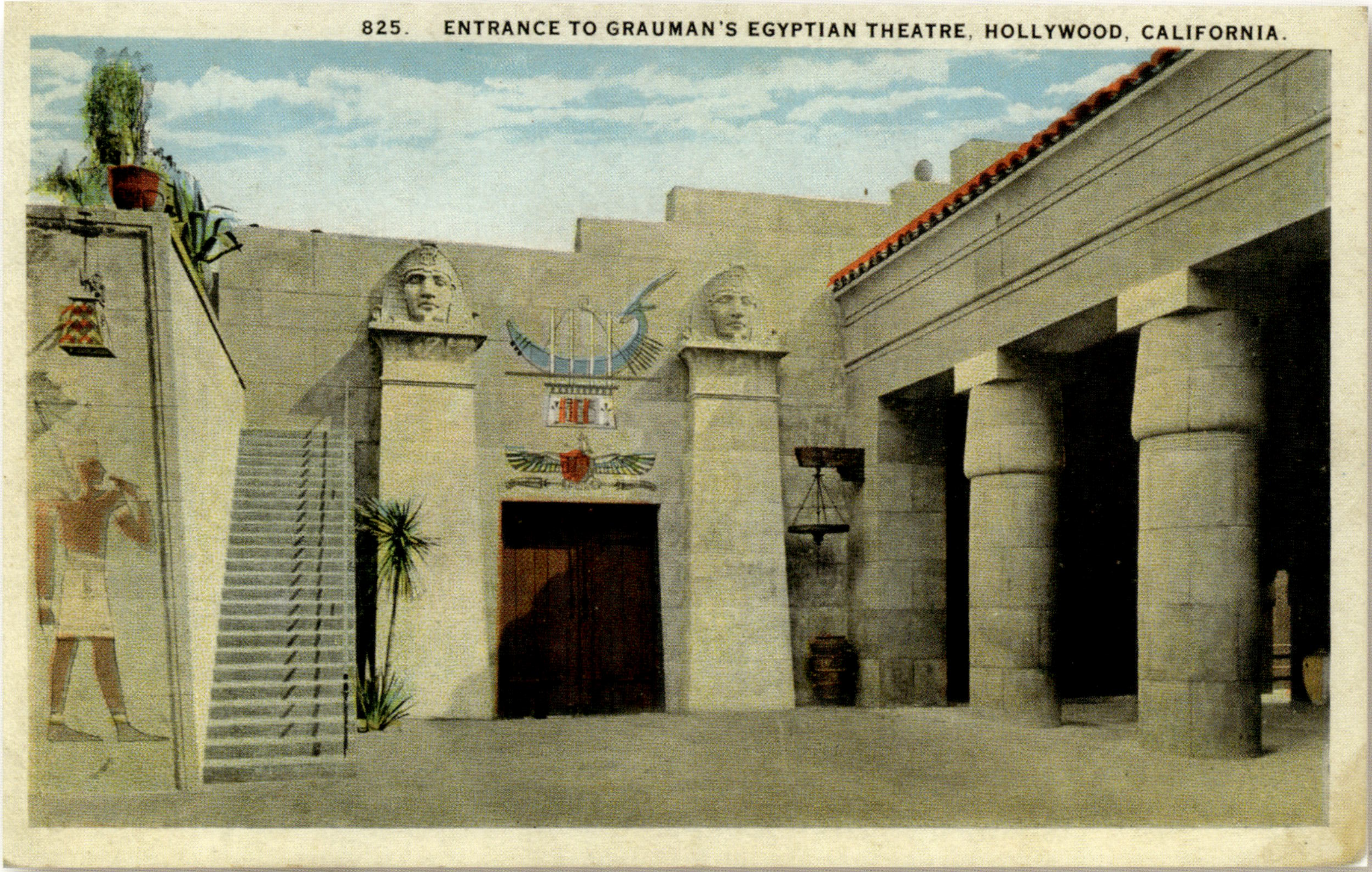

825. ENTRANCE TO GRAUMAN'S EGYPTIAN THEATRE, HOLLYWOOD, CALIFORNIA.

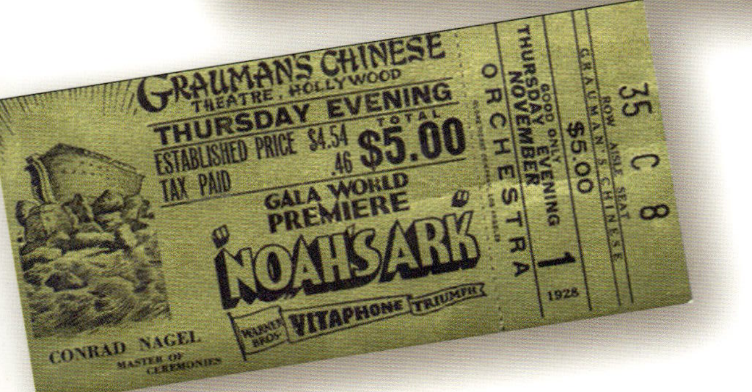


Showman Sid Grauman's 1922 Egyptian Theatre (above) and his Chinese Theatre of 1927 (facing) hosted countless movie premieres. But it was the Chinese, with its courtyard of celebrity handprints, that became world famous.

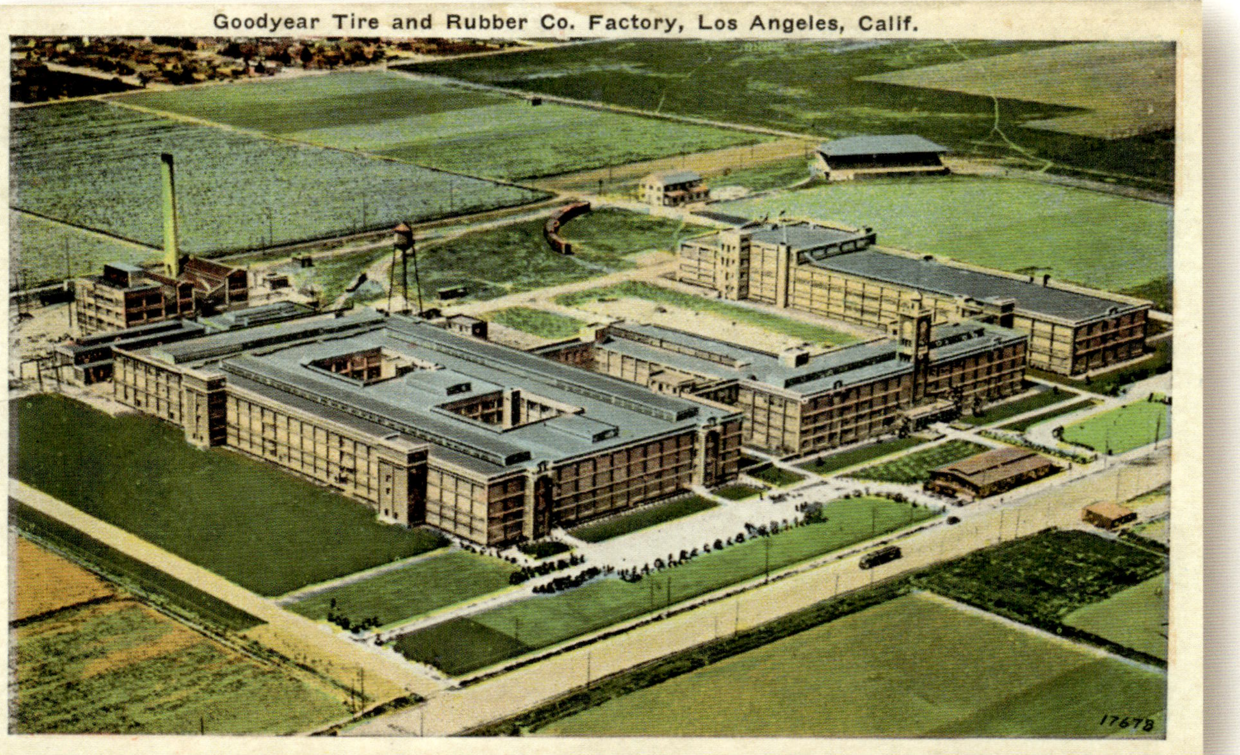


**LEFT:** Goodyear Tire and Rubber Company became the first tire manufacturer on the West Coast when it opened in 1920 south of downtown.

**FACING:** Abbott Kinney's charming Venice of America was wiped out by the tidal wave of oil discovered there in 1929. Witness this frightening forest of oil derricks despoiling Venice Beach.

The stereotype of Los Angeles as the land of automobiles got its start in the 1920s when half a million cars roamed the region (over 800,000 by 1930), more per capita than any city in the United States. Not surprisingly, the swarm of cars, pedestrians, and streetcars competing for space downtown led to gridlock. Because of the astounding local demand for cars, enormous new tire factories were constructed in the industrial districts south of the city. The combined output of the area's Firestone, U.S. Rubber, Goodyear, Goodrich, and Samson plants made Los Angeles the world's second-largest manufacturer of tires outside of Akron, Ohio. In the 1930s, local assembly plants for General Motors, Ford, and Chrysler were built to serve the middle-class consumers whose numbers had achieved critical mass sufficient to support the huge factories.

Powering these cars was the oil that Southern California had in abundance. In the 1920s, colossal gushers were discovered in Signal Hill near Long Beach, Santa Fe Springs east of Los Angeles, Huntington Beach in Orange County, and the beach town of Venice.

New factories meant new jobs. To house the necessary workers, thousands of modest working-class dwellings were built near the plants in the cities of Huntington Park, South Gate, Bell, Maywood, and others. Also employing large numbers of workers were the many aircraft factories that grew to be a major component of Southern California's economy by 1930, and which would rival Hollywood as a generator of employment in the region after World War II.

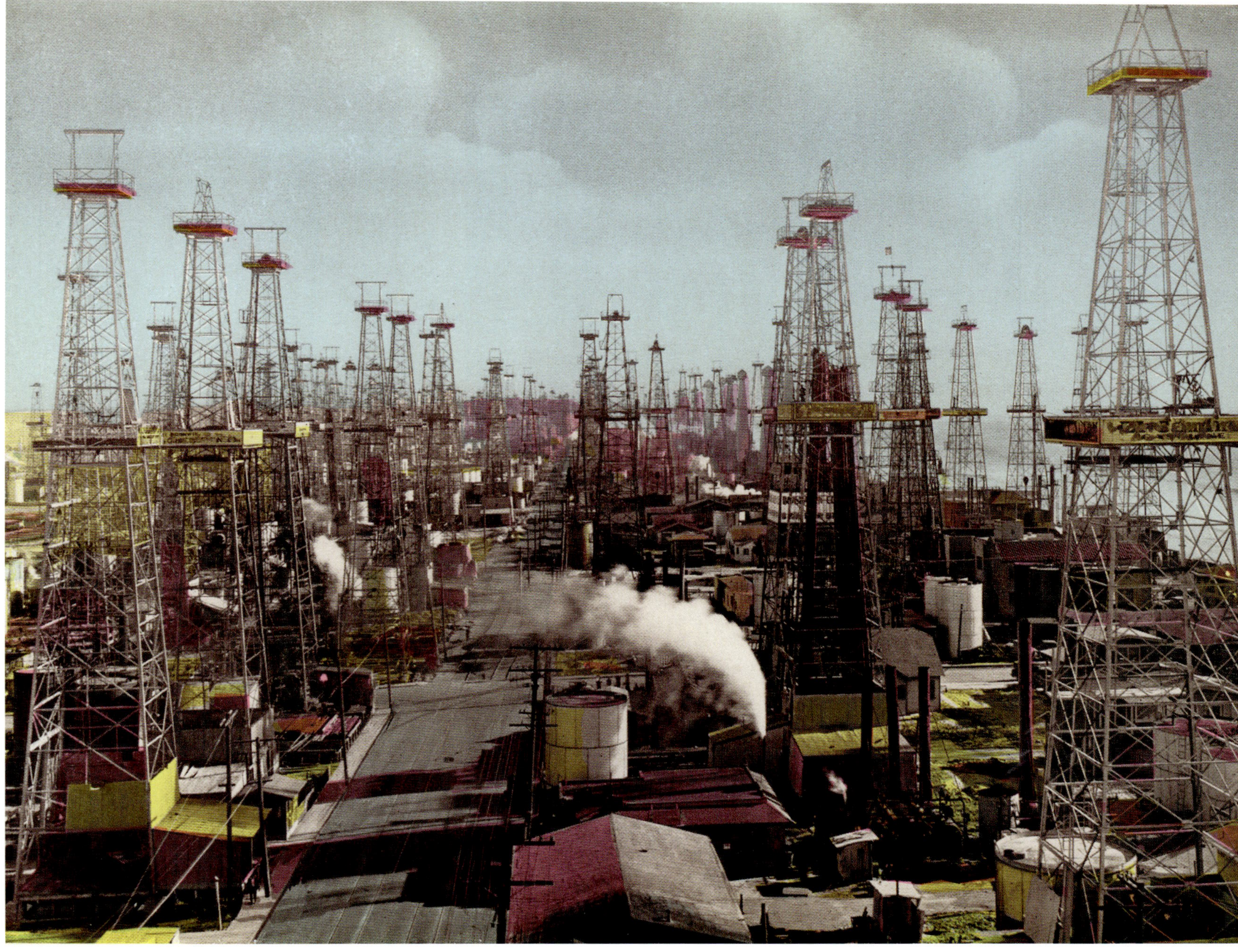

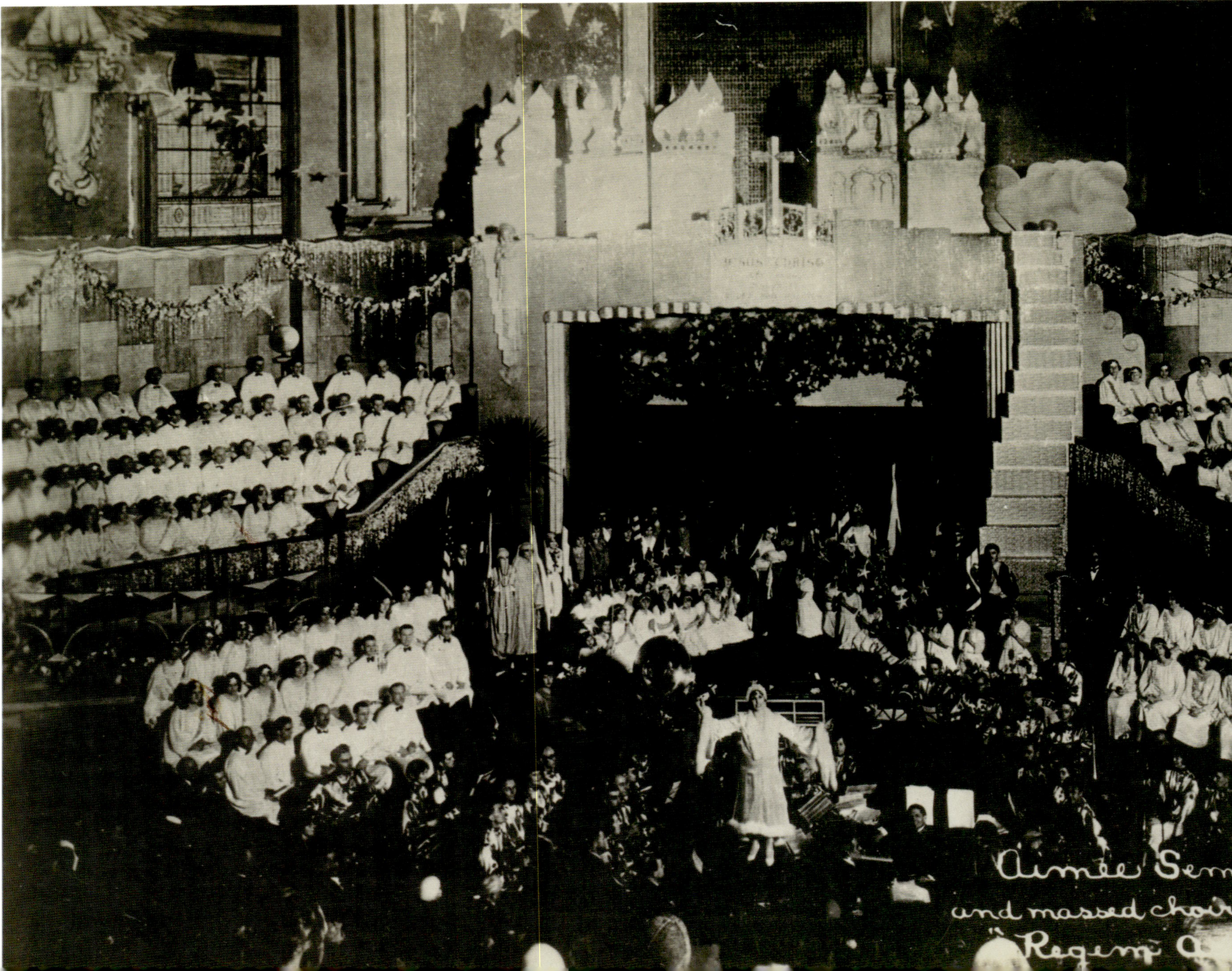
Aimee Sem
and massed choir

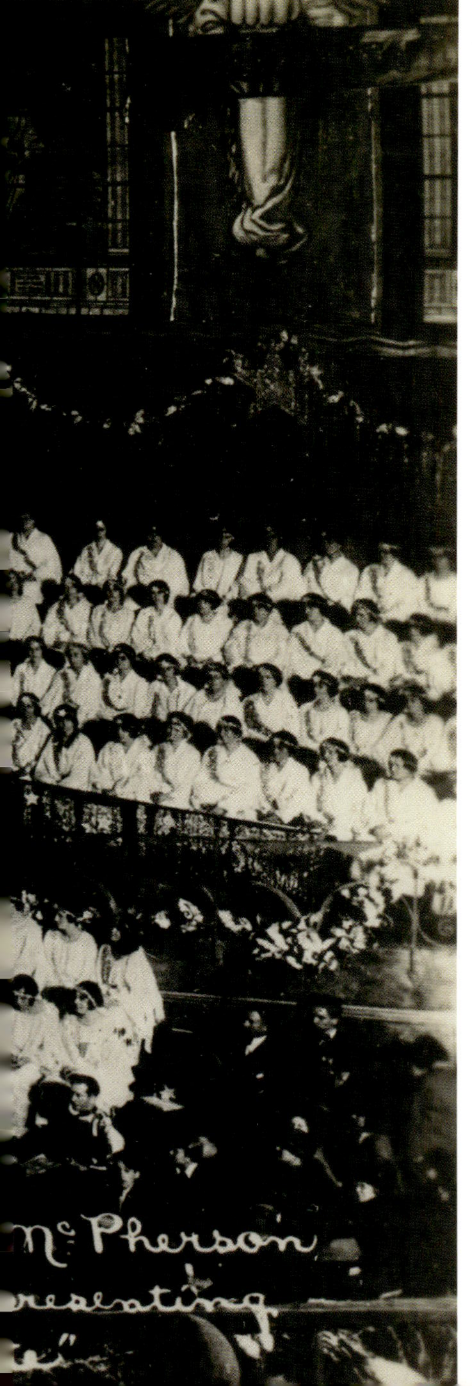


Yet some newcomers to Los Angeles found the bustling city to be disorienting and overwhelming in comparison with the small towns from which they had come. Many felt they had lost a sense of community, which annual state picnics could not mollify. Into this dispiriting void stepped a charismatic Pentecostal preacher who would use faith healing, pageantry, and radio to invigorate thousands as the foremost evangelical personality of her day.

Aimee Semple McPherson arrived in Los Angeles in 1918 at the age of 28 preceded by a growing reputation for exhilarating tent revivals. Within five years, Sister Aimee had established a new denomination—the International Church of the Foursquare Gospel—and built the 5,300-seat Angelus Temple, crowned by a pair of towering radio antennas that broadcast her sermons across the country on station KFSG. Of her many weekly sermons, the most anticipated was the Sunday evening spectacle of "sacred operas." These extravagant choreographed musicals featured costumed singers and actors, elaborate sets, and often animals. Sister Aimee, consistently mired in controversy for her suspected dalliances and ostentatious lifestyle, anticipated by several decades the televangelists whose theatrics and megachurches would dominate fundamentalist religion in America.

Sister Aimee stars in one of the elaborate "sacred operas" (left) staged by the wildly popular radio evangelist at her Angelus Temple in Echo Park (below).

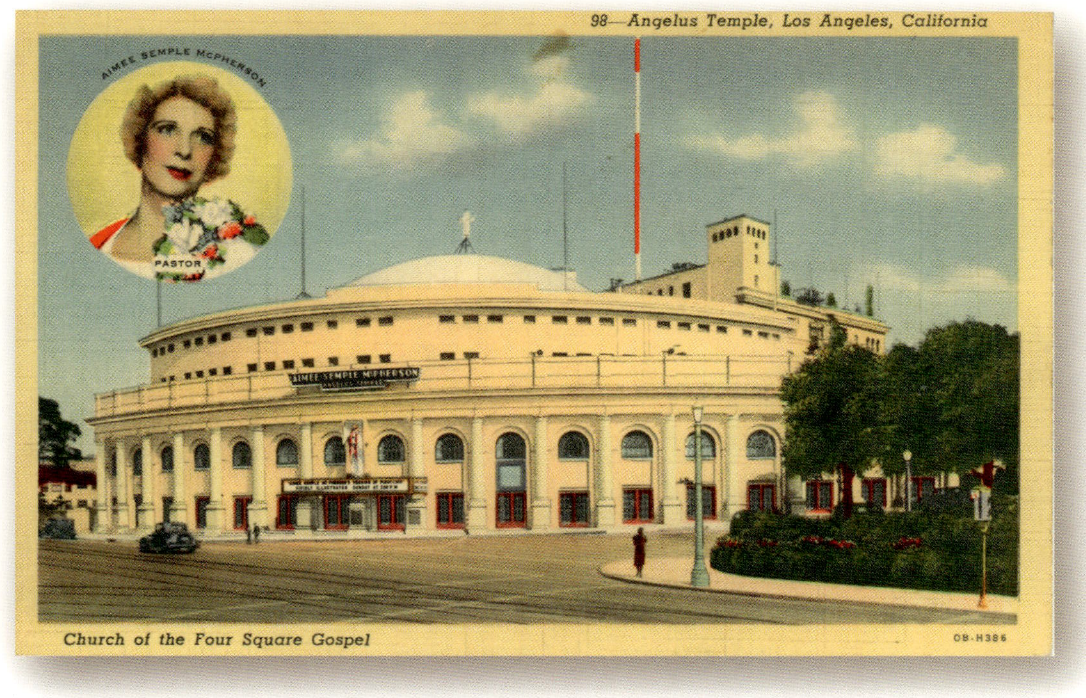

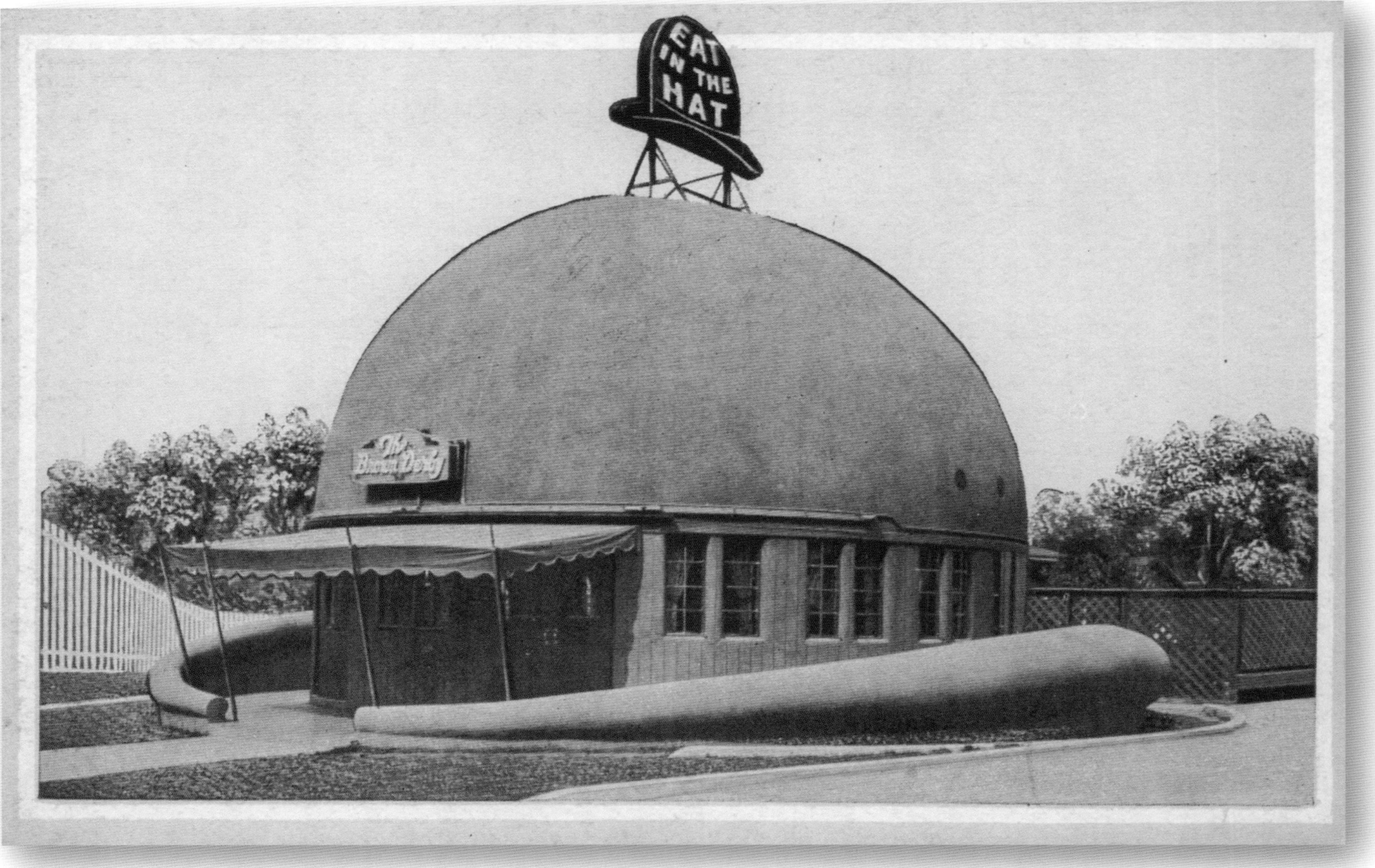


Downtown Los Angeles was the center of commerce, finance, mass transportation, and entertainment. It had evolved south from its eighteenth-century origins, with the Los Angeles River on the east acting as a buffer for a burgeoning manufacturing district. Certainly downtown's growth could have continued south. But instead, downtown headed west. It would be Wilshire Boulevard that became the major route from downtown to the Pacific Ocean. Named for land developer/publisher/socialist Henry Gaylord Wilshire, the boulevard that took his name began in 1895 as a wide four-block road west

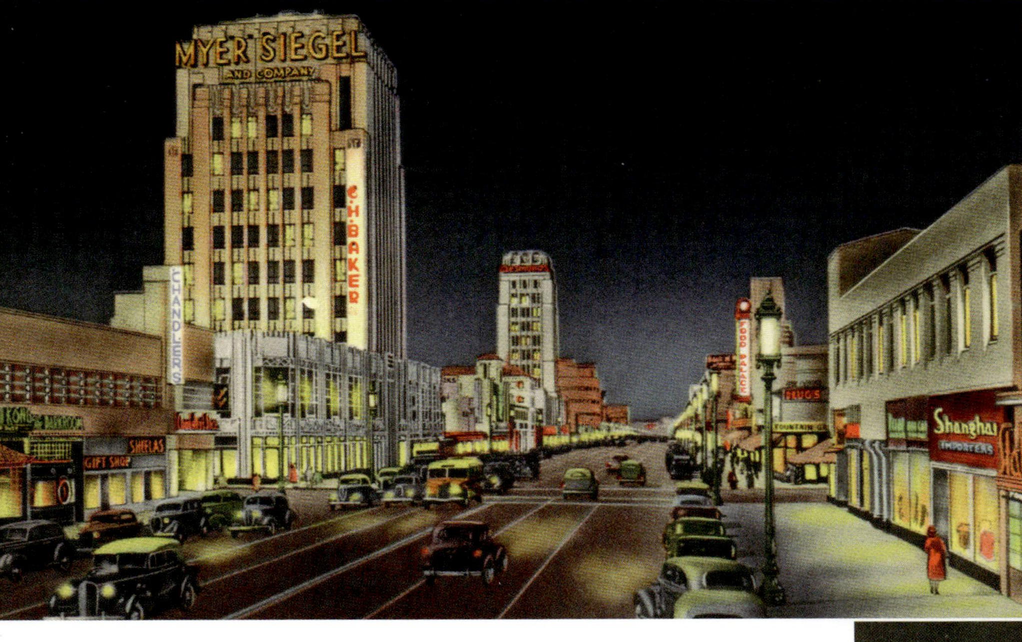


**FACING:** The original 1926 Brown Derby restaurant on Wilshire Boulevard near the Ambassador Hotel, before it was moved one block east in 1937. Its eye-catching design attracted speeding motorists, movie stars, and tourists.

**ABOVE:** The Miracle Mile on Wilshire Boulevard, the Main Street of Los Angeles.

**RIGHT:** Bullock's Wilshire, an Art Deco masterpiece that remains America's most beautiful department store building.

of Westlake Park (now MacArthur Park) through what Wilshire planned as an exclusive residential subdivision.

By the 1920s, Wilshire Boulevard was fulfilling its destiny as Los Angeles's Champs-Élysées, an elegant linear Main Street of class and sophistication. In 1921, the new Ambassador Hotel had a Wilshire Boulevard address. Eight years later, Bullock's became the first department store to establish a branch outside of downtown. Bullock's Wilshire—a masterpiece of high Art Deco design—had its main entrance facing the rear, where customers parked their cars, an innovation considered revolutionary at the time.

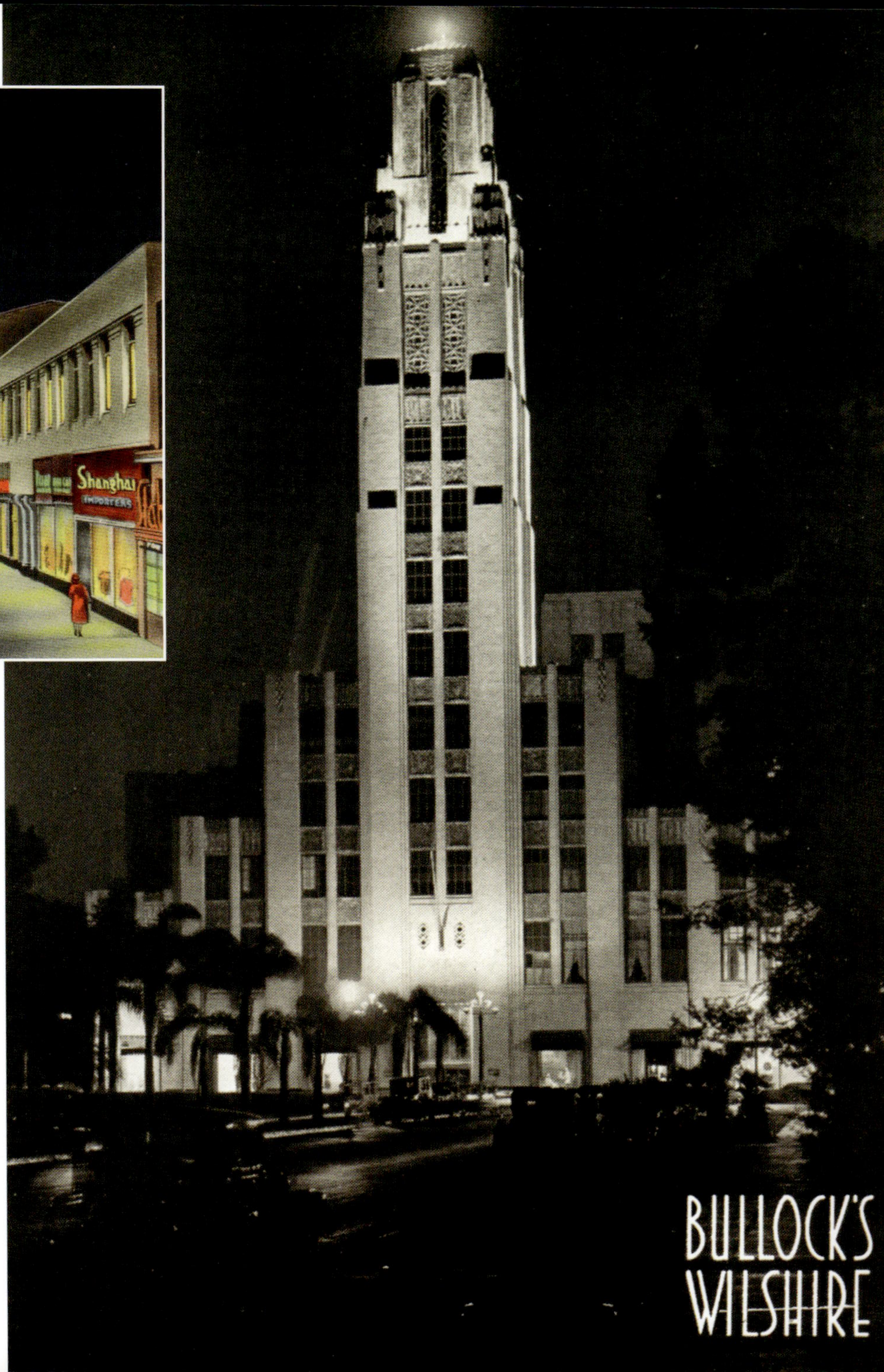

BULLOCK'S
WILSHIRE

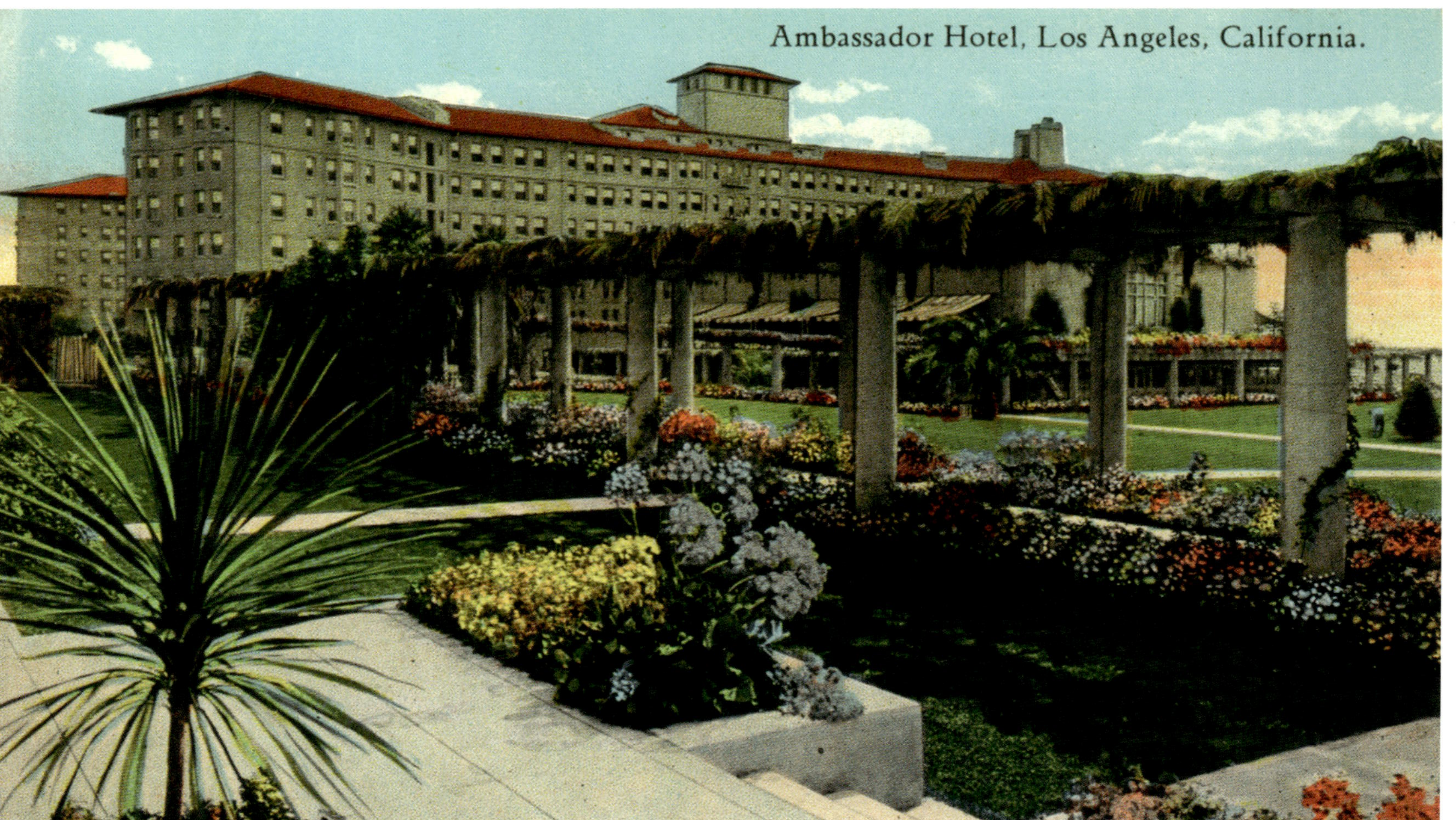


The opulent Ambassador Hotel on Wilshire Boulevard in 1921.

Over the years, Wilshire Boulevard spawned exclusive neighborhoods, the Miracle Mile shopping district, postwar corporate headquarters, and the Los Angeles County Museum of Art, while passing through the La Brea Tar Pits, Beverly Hills, Westwood, and Santa Monica.

One of these exclusive neighborhoods was the Mid-Wilshire District, where in the 1920s, chic multistory apartments and apartment hotels were built in the then-popular Italian Renaissance, French Chateau, Tudor, Colonial, and Spanish Colonial architectural styles. In fact, throughout Los Angeles the din of housing construction was never ending as Revival-style single-family dwellings, duplexes, fourplexes, bungalow courts, and apartment buildings were erected in a race to house an average of 1,300 new residents arriving every week.

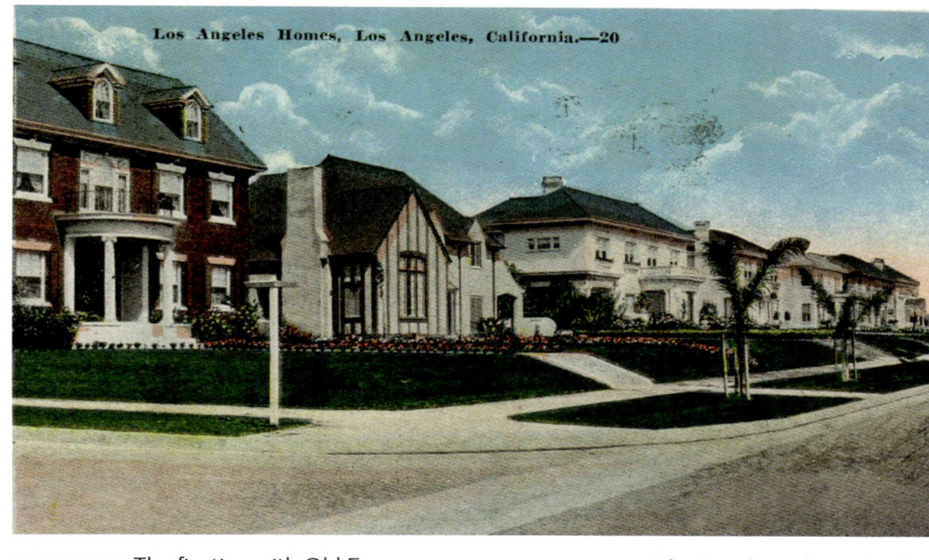


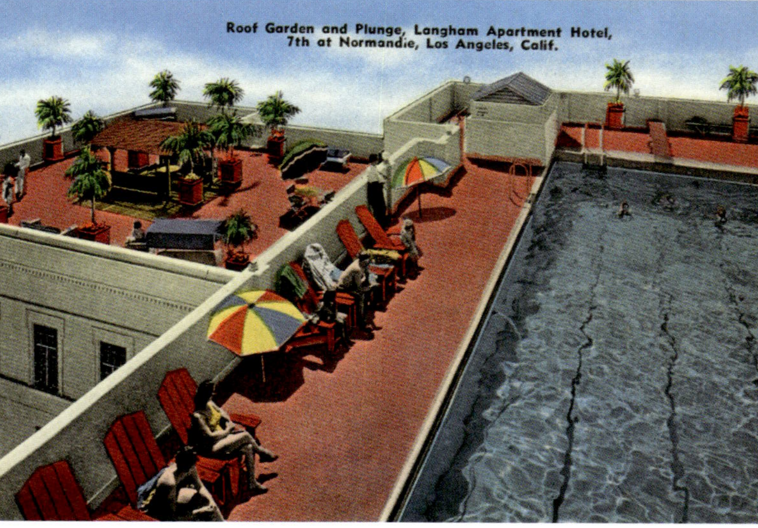


**ABOVE, LEFT:** The fixation with Old Europe reached its architectural peak in the 1920s, as these stately Colonial, Tudor, and Neoclassical Revival houses in Windsor Square demonstrate.

**ABOVE, RIGHT:** The Langham claimed to have "the only open air roof-top swimming pool in the world." It was one of many luxurious 1920s apartment hotels in the vicinity of the Ambassador Hotel.

**BELOW:** The ubiquitous bungalow court was a popular approach to housing the thousands migrating to Los Angeles in the 1920s.

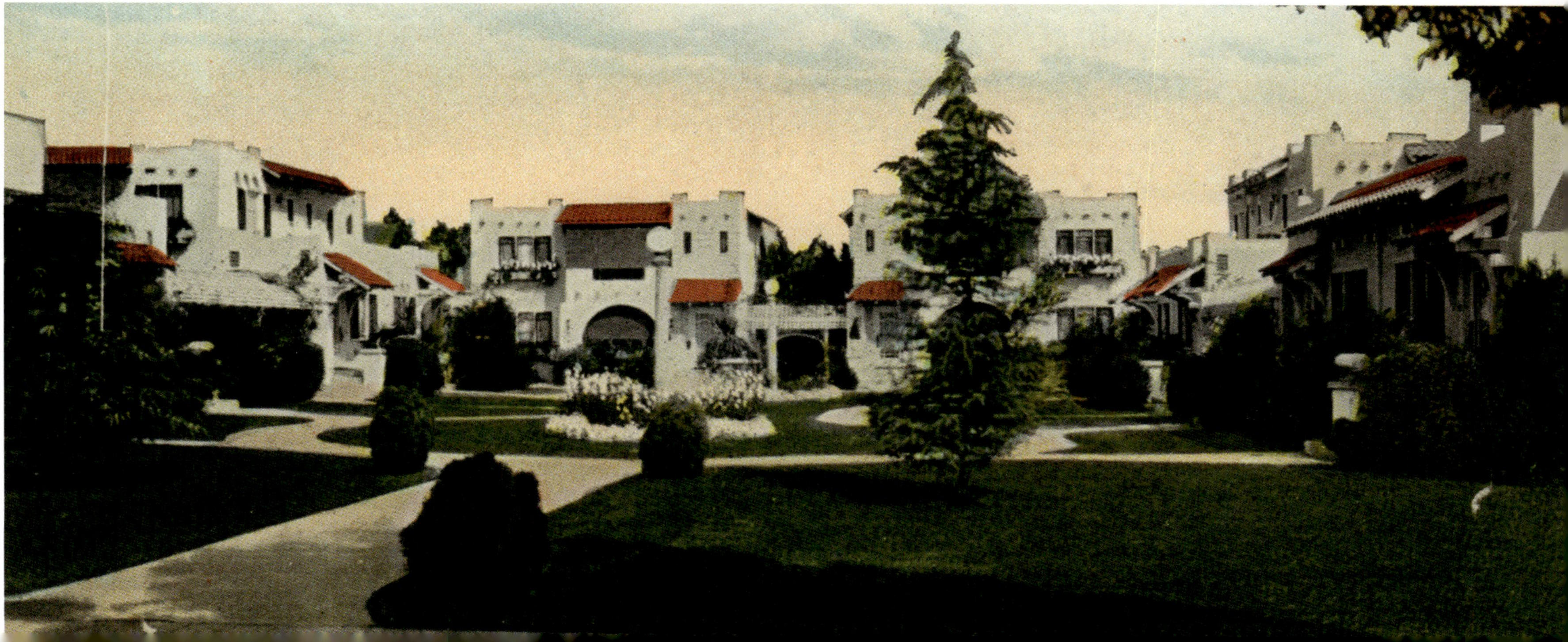

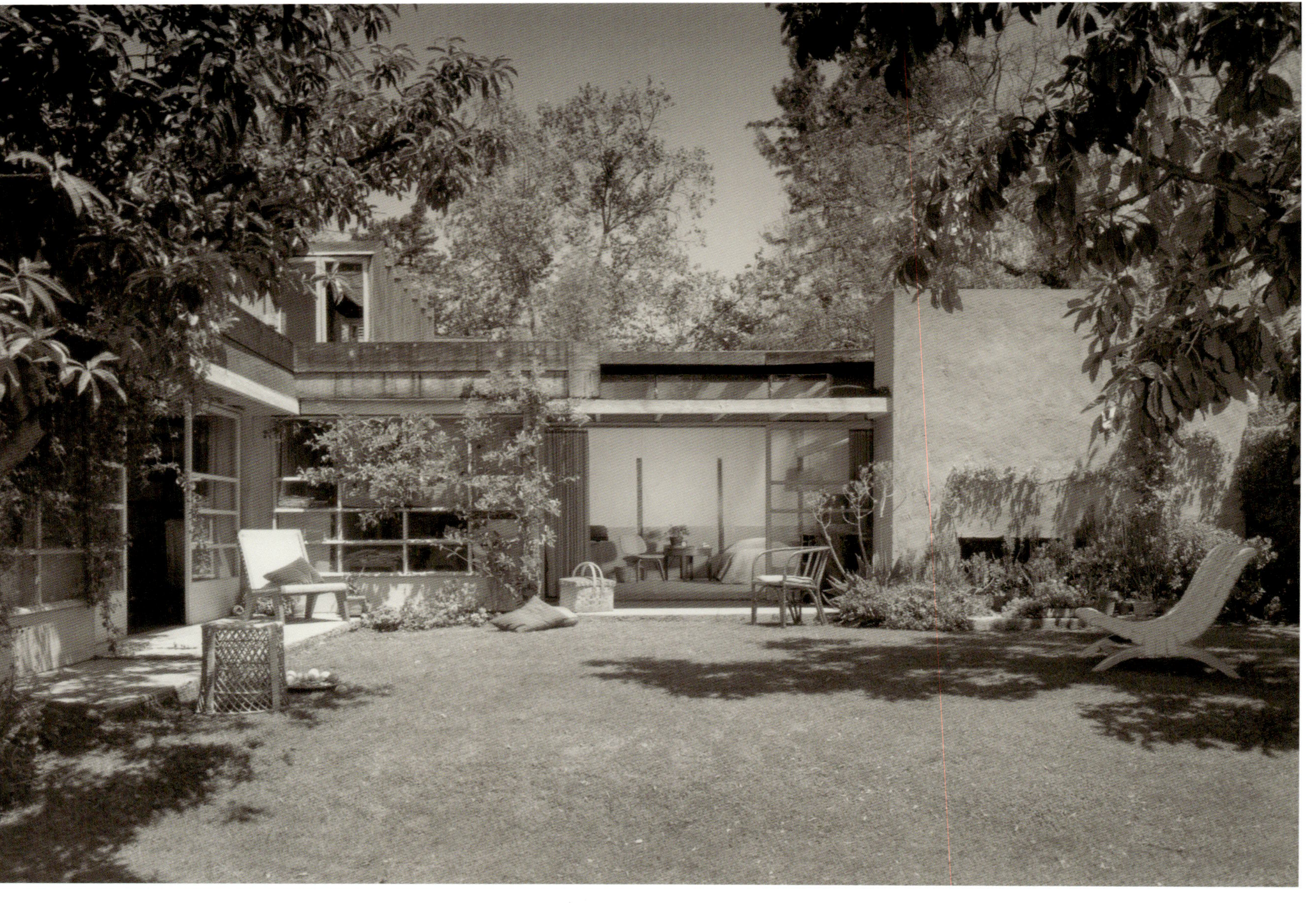

Bucking the Revival-style housing craze were two Austrian expatriate architects, Rudolph Schindler and Richard Neutra, whose handful of avant-garde houses that they designed in the 1920s would help usher in an entirely new approach to architecture in Los Angeles—Modernism.

**ABOVE:** Rudolph Schindler's Kings Road House, built in 1922, was a modern experiment in communal California living.

**FACING:** Richard Neutra's Lovell Health House (1927–1929) in Los Feliz defined International-style Modernism.

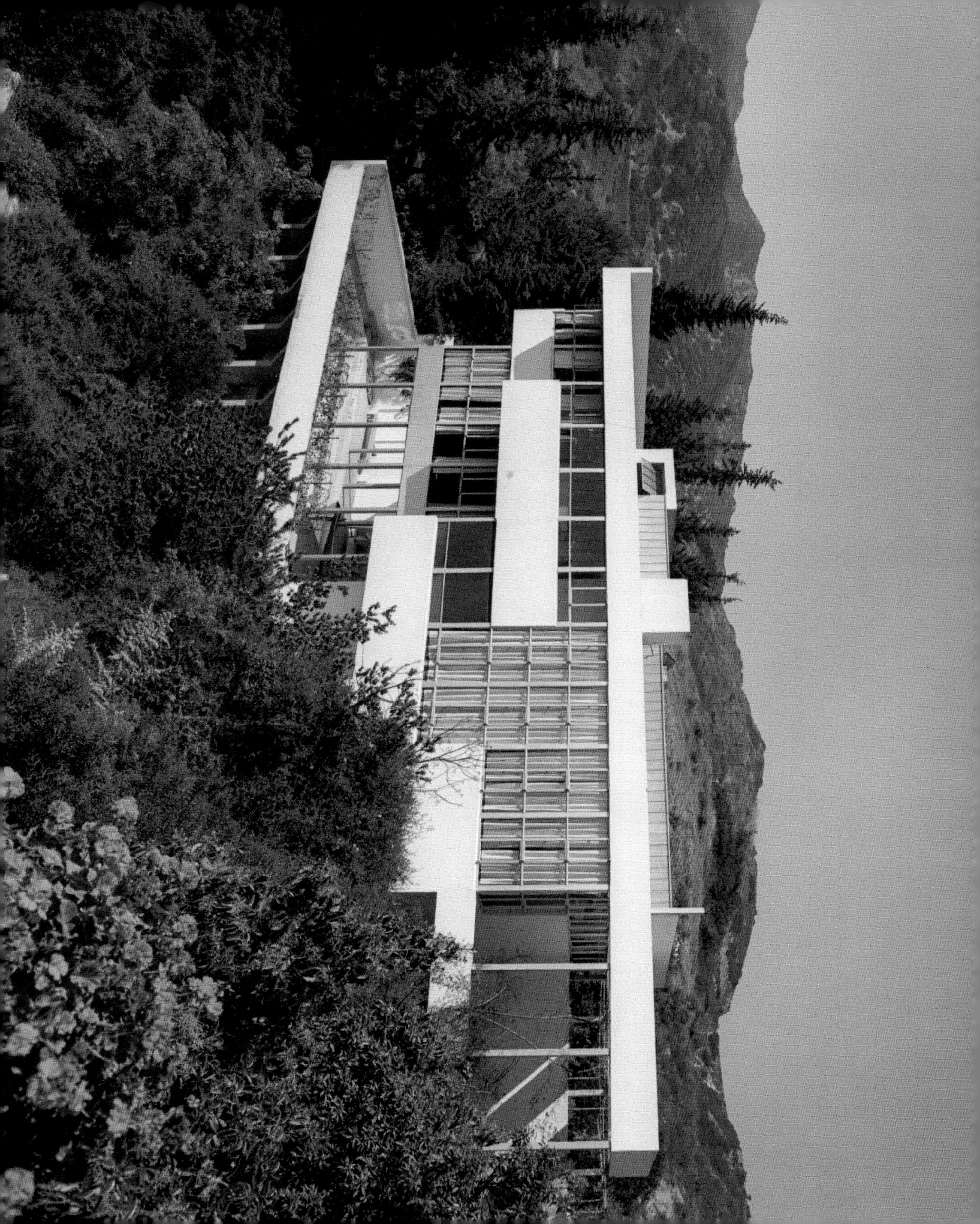

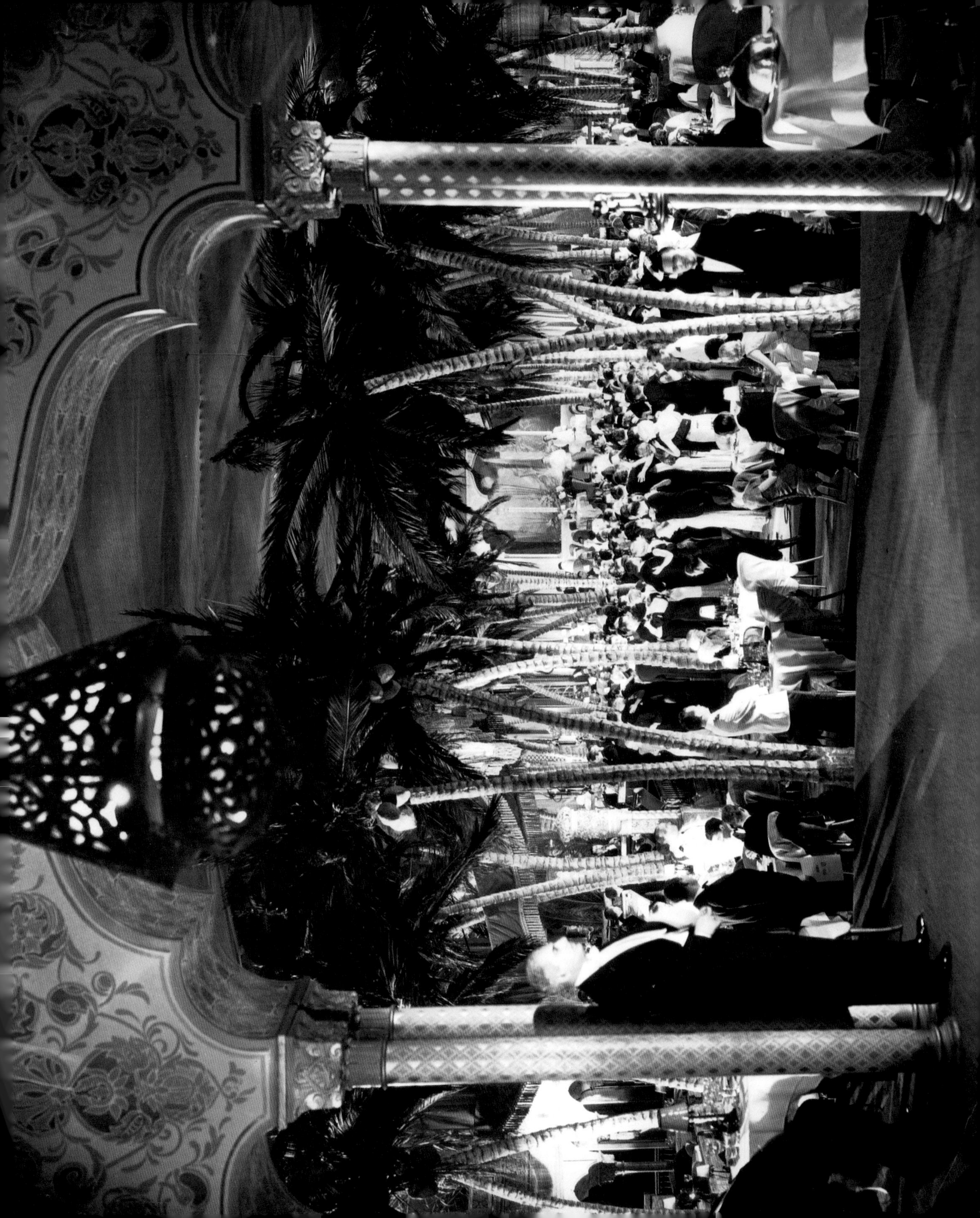

Prohibition created the speakeasy, as alcohol-fueled entertainment was forced underground. Much of the illegal activity, including backroom gambling, was centered along the Sunset Strip, one and a half miles of unincorporated land (today's West Hollywood) located just outside the jurisdiction of puritanical Los Angeles. From the 1930s through the 1950s, the Sunset Strip was where Hollywood people gathered at swank restaurants and nightclubs such as Ciro's, Mocambo, and the Clover Club (which also had gambling in a back room). In the late 1960s, the Sunset Strip was a center of countercultural music and fashion.

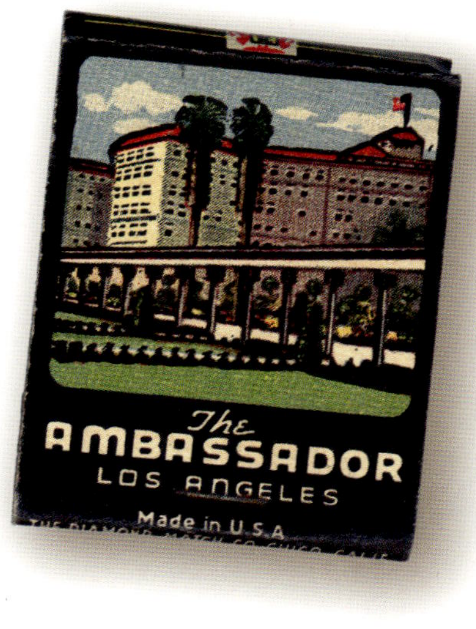


On Wilshire Boulevard, the Cocoanut Grove at the Ambassador Hotel attracted the black-tie set from Hancock Park, Pasadena, and San Marino in addition to the movie crowd. Opened in 1921, the Cocoanut Grove was the site of celebrity events such as the Academy Awards and splashy fundraisers during World War II.

Before the big Hollywood clubs appeared on the scene, the Palomar Ballroom on Vermont Avenue was billed as "the largest and most famous dance hall on the West Coast." Its dance floor accommodated over 4,000 couples, who were entertained by popular orchestras led by Glenn Miller, Tommy Dorsey, and Artie Shaw. It was destroyed by fire in 1939.

**FACING:** The smart set at the Ambassador's Cocoanut Grove. The Academy Awards were held there six times from 1930 to 1943.

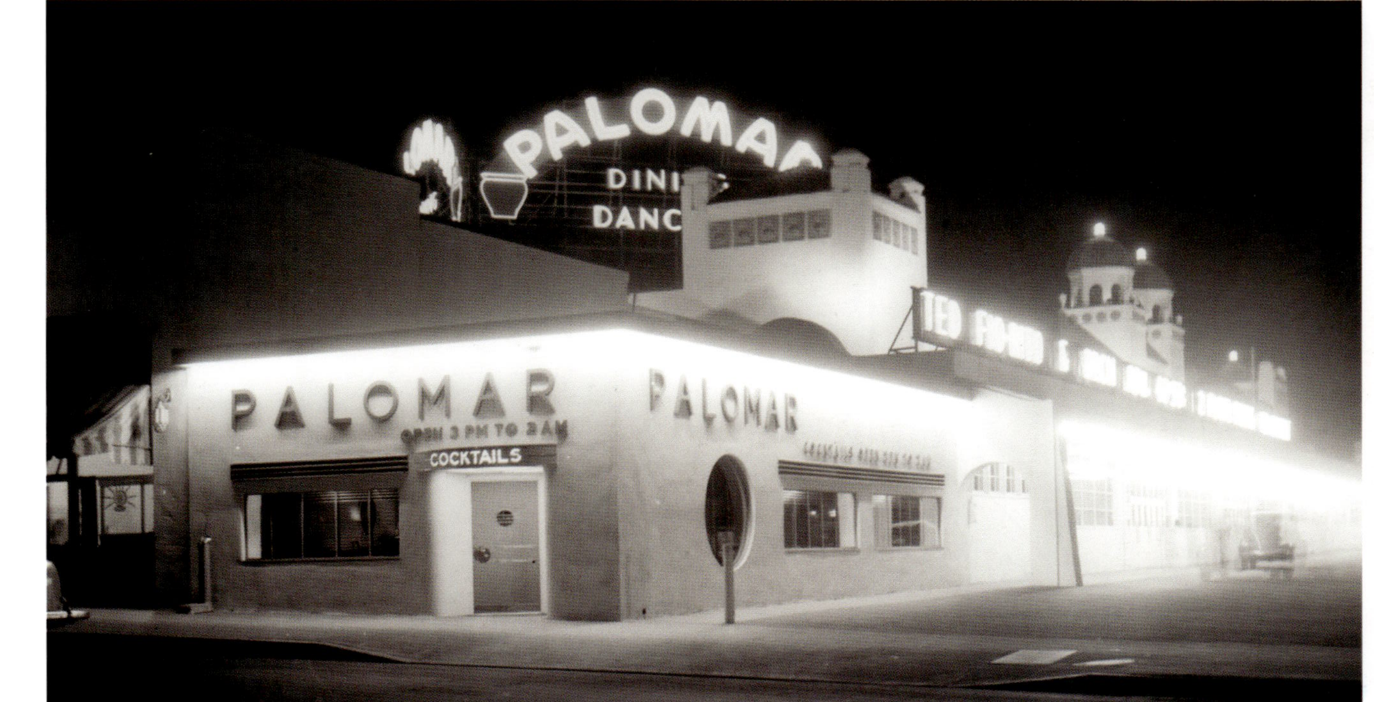


**RIGHT:** The mammoth Palomar Ballroom accommodated more than 4,000 couples.

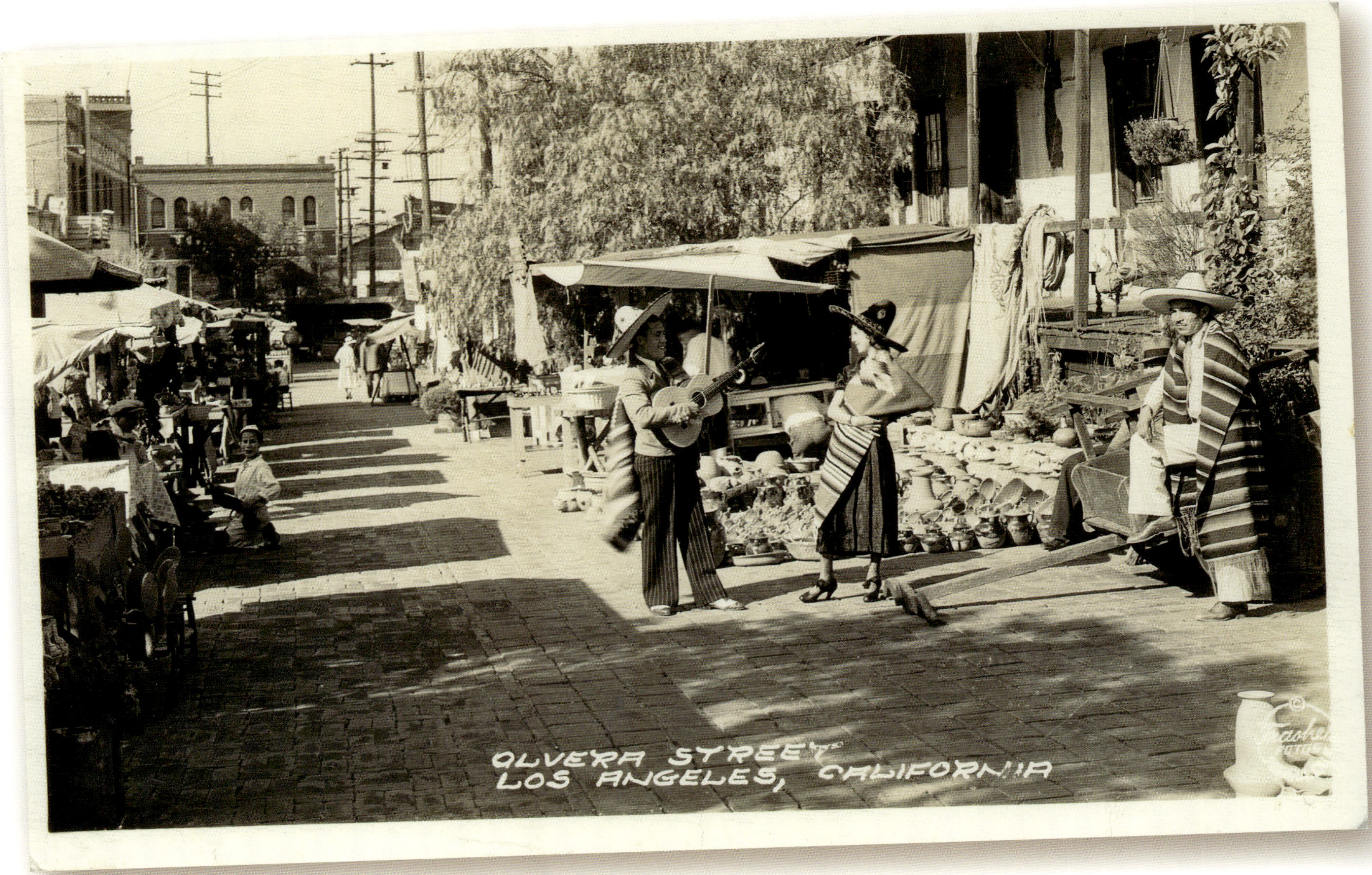

OLVERA STREET
LOS ANGELES, CALIFORNIA

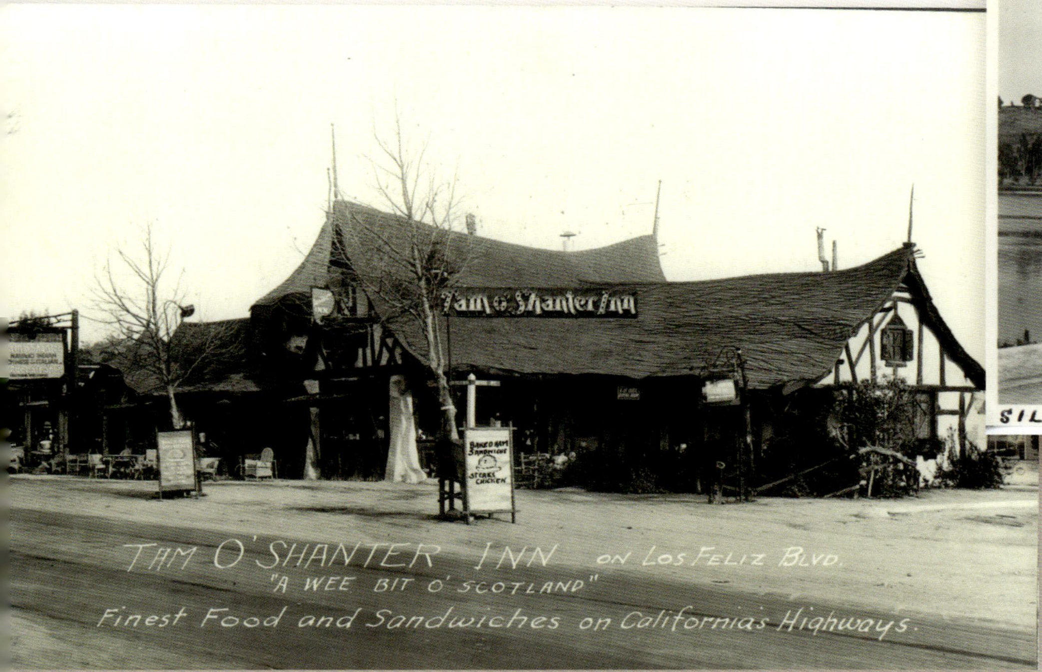

TAM O'SHANTER INN ON LOS FELIZ BLVD.
"A WEE BIT O' SCOTLAND"
Finest Food and Sandwiches on California's Highways.

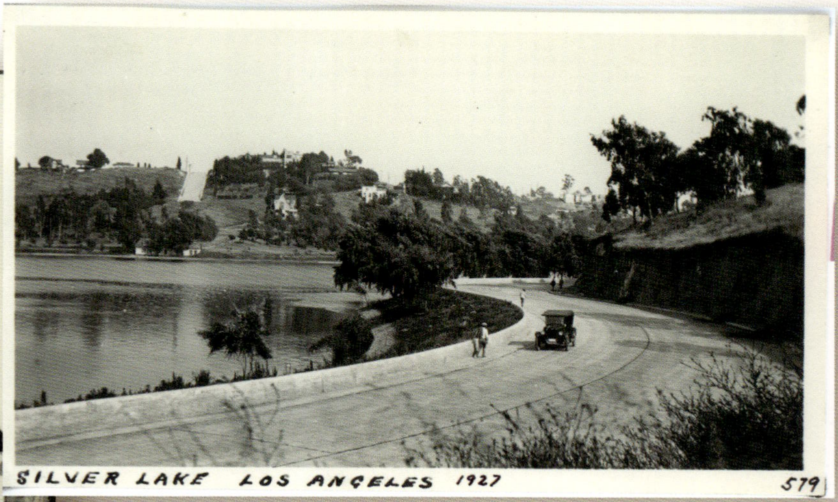

SILVER LAKE LOS ANGELES 1927 579

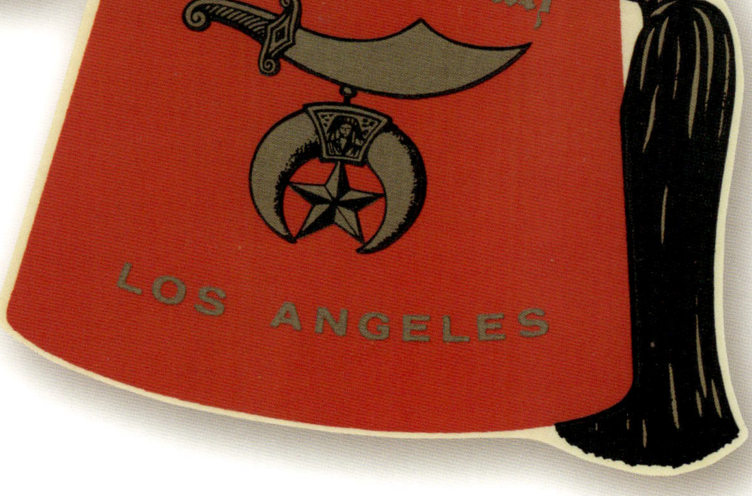


**ABOVE:** The Tam O'Shanter Inn opened in 1922 at its original Los Feliz Boulevard location between Hollywood and Pasadena. It is Los Angeles's longest-operating restaurant under continuous single-family ownership.

**ABOVE, RIGHT:** Silver Lake in 1927, when it was just being developed.

**FACING:** In 1929, civic booster Christine Sterling converted La Plaza's run-down Olvera Street into a romanticized version of a Mexican marketplace.

**RIGHT:** Al Malaikah ("The Angels") is the name of the Los Angeles chapter of the Ancient Arabic Order of the Nobles of the Mystic Shrine (the Shriners). The Shrine Auditorium is its Moorish-style temple, where Academy Awards and Grammy ceremonies have been held.

As the tallest building in Los Angeles—a position it would hold until 1964—the completion of the new City Hall in 1928 symbolized the city's triumph as the acknowledged capital of wealth and power in the American West.

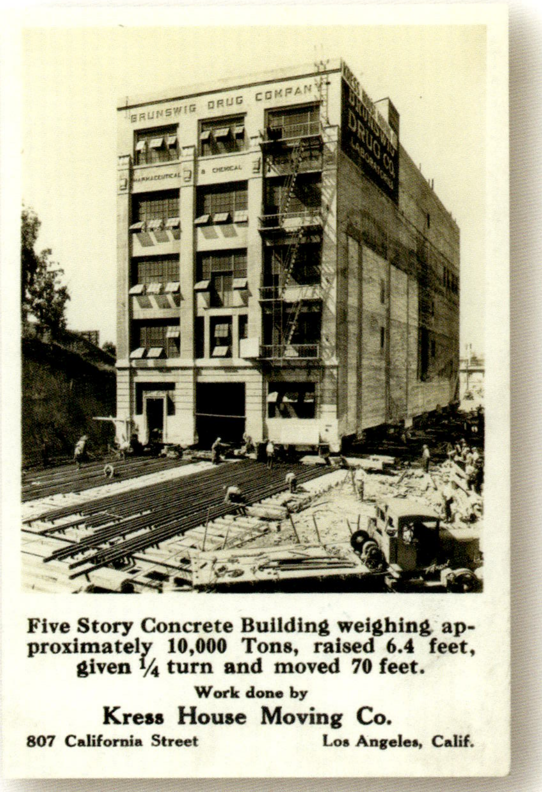


**ABOVE:** Street-widening projects made moving houses common in 1920s Los Angeles. However, moving—and turning—a five-story industrial building 70 feet was an amazing accomplishment in any decade.

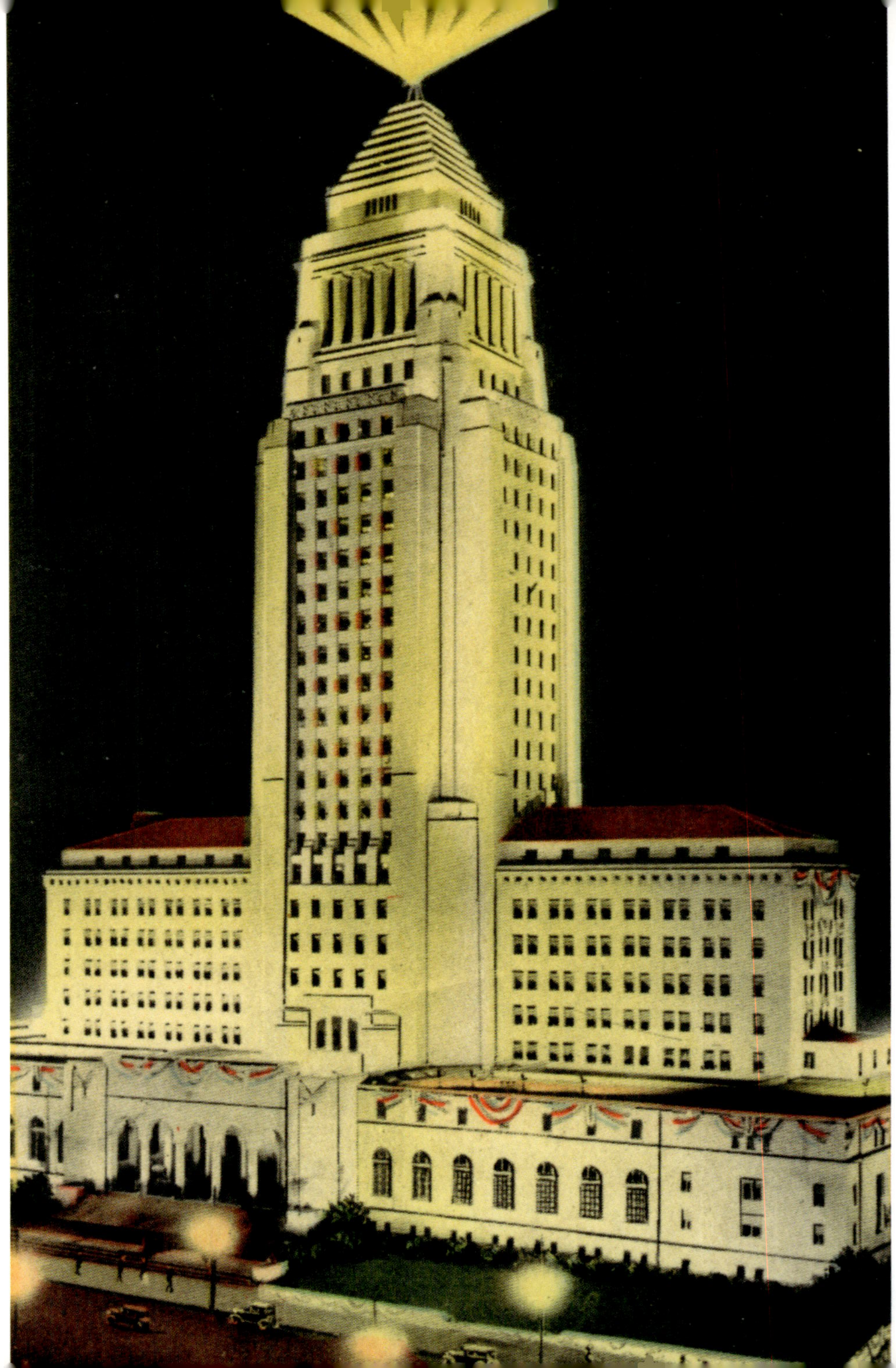

**RIGHT:** The new City Hall was Los Angeles's Parthenon, with its beacon proclaiming the city's status as the capital of the American West.

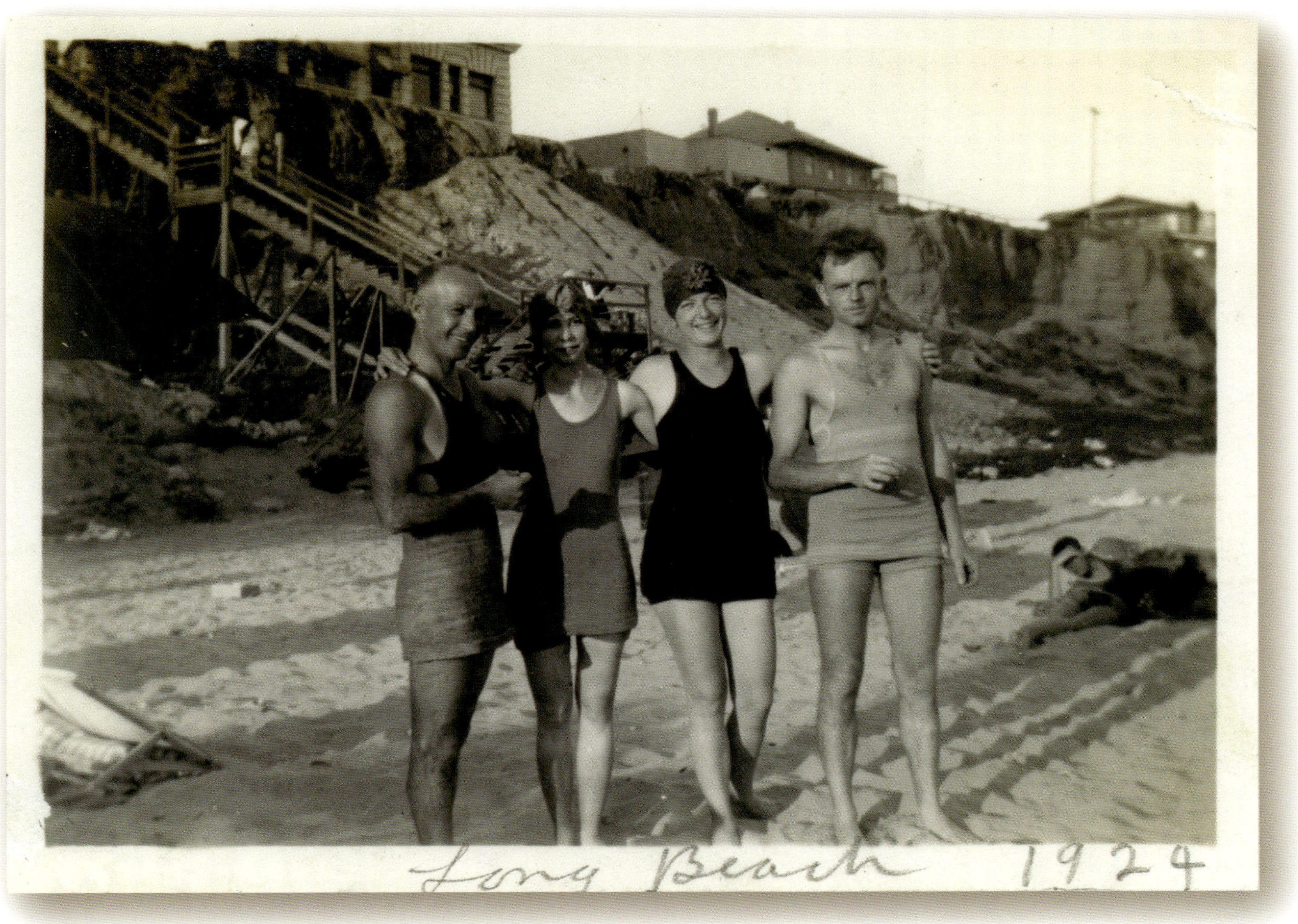


Celebrating the promised land at the western edge of America.

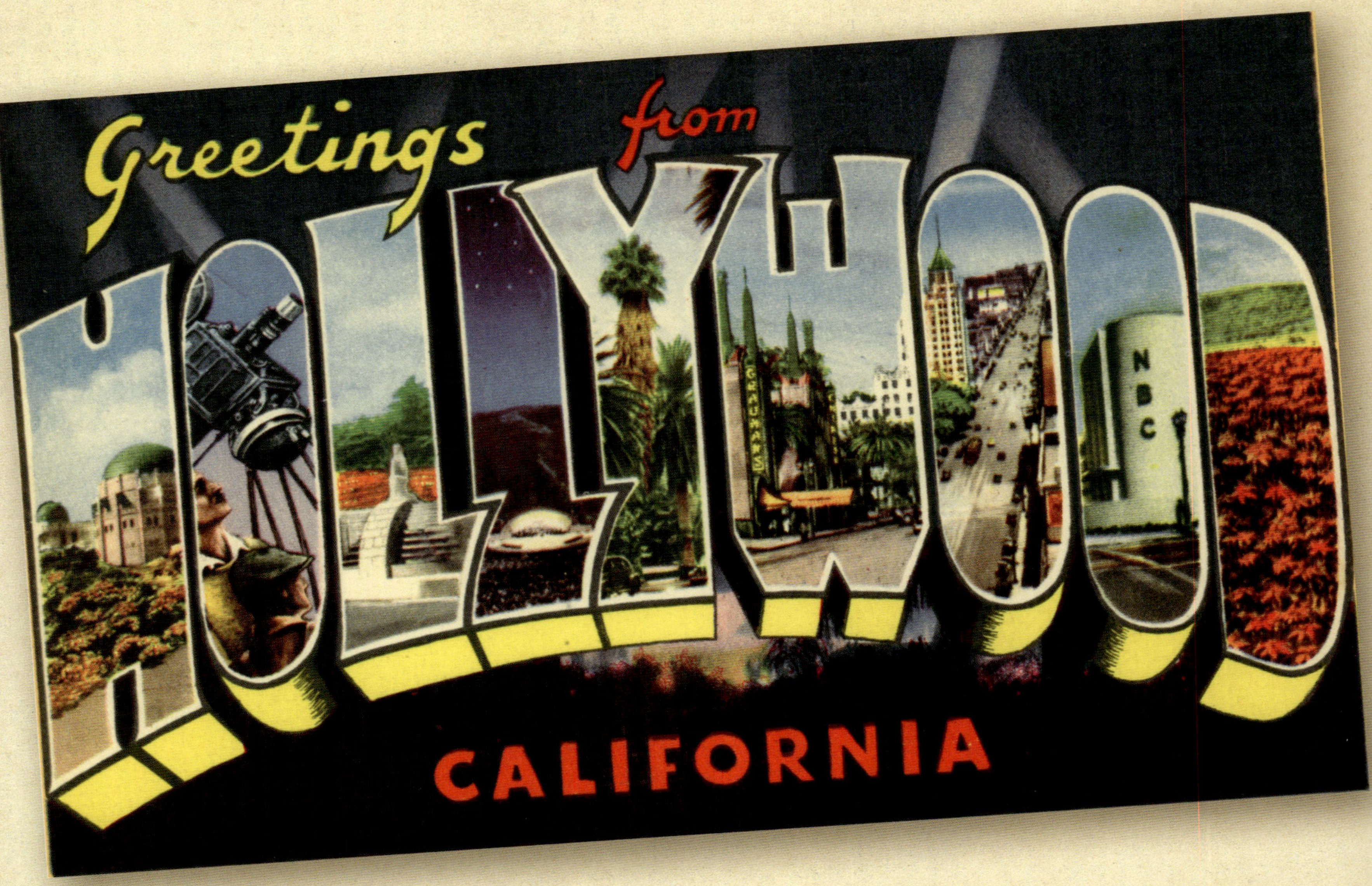
Greetings from
HOLLYWOOD
CALIFORNIA
NBC

# Depression, Corruption, War

## 1930–1945

As with the rest of the country, the Great Depression of the 1930s was painful for Southern Californians. Manufacturing declined, the real estate boom collapsed, oil production slowed. Even the movie industry suffered, as attendance initially fell in the early years of the economic crisis. Hollywood responded with lower ticket prices, double bills, promotional gimmicks, and most importantly movies that addressed people's doubts and fears. Initially gangster films dominated, along with over-the-top Busby Berkeley musicals and antic Marx Brothers comedies. Mae West became famous for the sexual innuendos and double entendres woven throughout her films. But as New Deal optimism grew in the second half of the Depression, movies became more hopeful, with outlaws vanquished and, due to self-imposed censorship, screwball comedies replacing sexually charged farces. During a time of extreme dislocation and hardship, Hollywood provided America with a narrative beyond mere escapism—one that celebrated individuality and up-from-the-bootstraps success, and a governmental and social order that was ultimately beneficial for the average man.

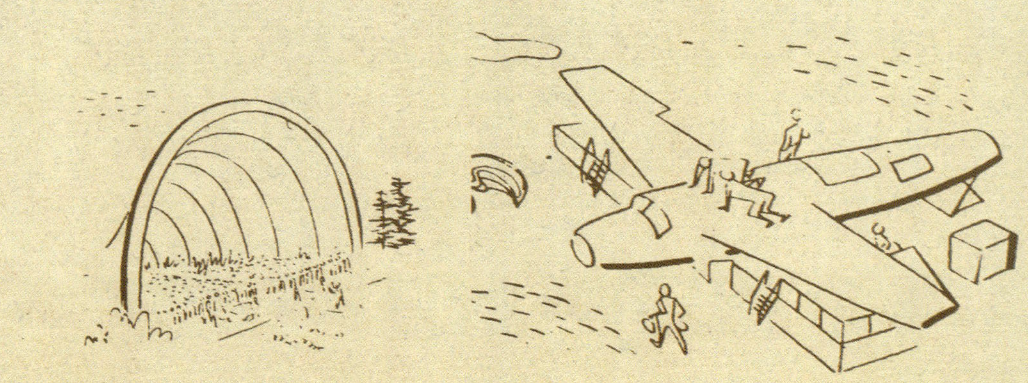

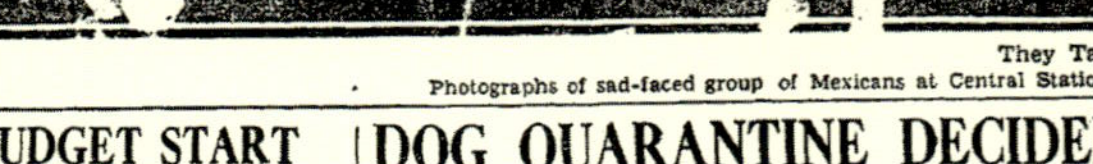

The Weather

FORECAST FOR LOS ANGELES AND SOUTHERN CALIFORNIA: Cloudy and local showers today and tomorrow; somewhat warmer. Maximum and minimum temperatures for yesterday: 60—55.

# Los Angeles Times

In Two Parts — 36 Pages

PART II — LOCAL SHEET — 18 PAGES

Vol. L. FRIDAY MORNING, APRIL 24, 1931. CITY NEWS—EDITORIAL—SOCIETY—THE DRAMA

## Mexicans and Families About to Embark on Trek Back to Native Land

They Take Few Belongings

Photographs of sad-faced group of Mexicans at Central Station yesterday preparing to leave the United States for their native land.

### HORDE DEPARTS FOR NATIVE SOIL

*Mexican Repatriates Leave on Homeward Trip*

*Eleven Hundred and Fifty Entrained Here*

*Tearful Scenes Enacted as They Bid City Adios*

One of the largest single groups of Mexican repatriates ever to leave in the vast migration back to Mexico—1150 men, women and children—departed yesterday on two sections of the Southern Pacific's Sunset Limited, bound for Nogales and El Paso, from which points they will be distributed inland in the southern republic.

Arrangements are being made through Consul-General De la Colina and Dr. Alejandro Wallace, head of the Mexican relief organization, to send away another 1000 early next week. Other shipments are planned weekly thereafter.

Negotiations also are under way between official Mexican and American authorities to charter a passenger boat in the near future to send an entire boatload of the returning Mexicans to Acapulco, from where they may make their respective ways inland to their former homes.

RAIL ACCOMMODATIONS

Of the group that left yesterday two-thirds will go to El Paso and the remainder to Nogales, according to the Southern Pacific bookings. Those for El Paso will be aided in their southward trek by the National Railway of Mexico, and those for Nogales will travel over the lines of the Southern Pacific de Mexico toward Guadalajara.

The rail accommodations for the repatriates consisted of two sections of the Sunset Limited, with eleven and nine coaches each. Loading began at 6:30 a.m., and continued until 10 o'clock. Southern Pacific officials ordered extra equip-

### BUDGET START SET BY MAYOR

*Work on Fiscal Year Task to Begin Next Monday*

*Estimates of Departments*

### DOG QUARANTINE DECIDED

*State Order Will Be Effective Within Ten Days; Health Officers Fear Rabies Spread*

Within ten days the State Department of Public Health will declare a quarantine on dogs in Los Angeles and Orange counties as part of a campaign to prevent the spread of rabies. Dr Giles S. Porter, director

### AIR BEACON TO AIM AT CITY FIELD

*Department of Commerce Also Allows Request to Flash Letters "L.A."*

### WOOD CLOSELY QUIZZED ON HOSPITAL CONDITIONS

*Head of General Institution Will Resume Stand Today in Hearing*

### The Lancer

by Harry Carr

POOR old Father Ricard isn't here to enjoy the triumph, but the scientists who spent most of their time ridiculing his rain predictions have coughed and hemmed and hawed and taken it all back.

Dr. Charles G. Abbott of the Smithsonian has come forth with an announcement that it is possible to predict rain for years in advance by the sun's radiation. Father Ricard told me that it would be possible to predict exactly what the weather would be like on the morning of July 2, 1999, or the year 3999—if any scientist would take the time to make the calculations.

The United States Weather Bureau has gone blissfully along on the theory that rainy days just kinda happen. As far as I can see the way the government predicts weather conditions is for the savant to stick his fist out of the window. If it comes back wet, he issues a bulletin saying that it might rain—but of course, again, it might not.

What I loved about Father Ricard was that he never perched on the fence.

HE HEWS TO THE LINE

Jackson A. Graves has been elected chairman of the board of directors of the Farmers' and Merchants' Bank. I haven't the slightest idea what that means, but I am prepared to cheer on

Documenting the forced repatriation of Mexicans and Mexican Americans in Los Angeles during the Depression. From 1929 to 1936, hundreds of thousands were expelled from across the country, over half of whom were American citizens.

In contrast, at the Depression's nadir, Mexican immigrants in Los Angeles County—many of whom were American citizens—were accused of stealing American jobs, and tens of thousands were forcibly repatriated to Mexico following police raids in local Mexican and Mexican American communities. This continued through the decade of the 1930s.

In the early 1930s, residents of Los Angeles's original Chinatown were evicted and most of the area razed for the construction of Union Station, the last major urban railroad station to be built in the United States. Soon after, two new Chinatowns competed to replace the old one. Christine Sterling, who had been responsible for the revamped "Old Mexico" Olvera Street, came up with the concept of a nearby Chinese village of restaurants, shops, and rickshaw rides staffed by costumed workers. She called it China City. At the same time, just up the street, a more ambitious New Chinatown was being built by Chinese businessmen. It featured a large central plaza with a blend of American and Chinese architecture. China City never caught on and was destroyed by fire in 1949. New Chinatown thrived for decades before declining, as Chinese communities developed in Monterey Park and other San Gabriel Valley cities.

**RIGHT:** Christine Sterling's "Exotic" China City opened in 1938 and was destroyed by fire in 1949.

**BELOW:** The original Chinatown was demolished to make way for downtown's Union Station, the "Last of the Great Railway Stations" in the United States when completed in 1939.

**BELOW, RIGHT:** Gin Ling Way marked the New Chinatown that Chinese businessmen financed in 1938. It survives to this day.

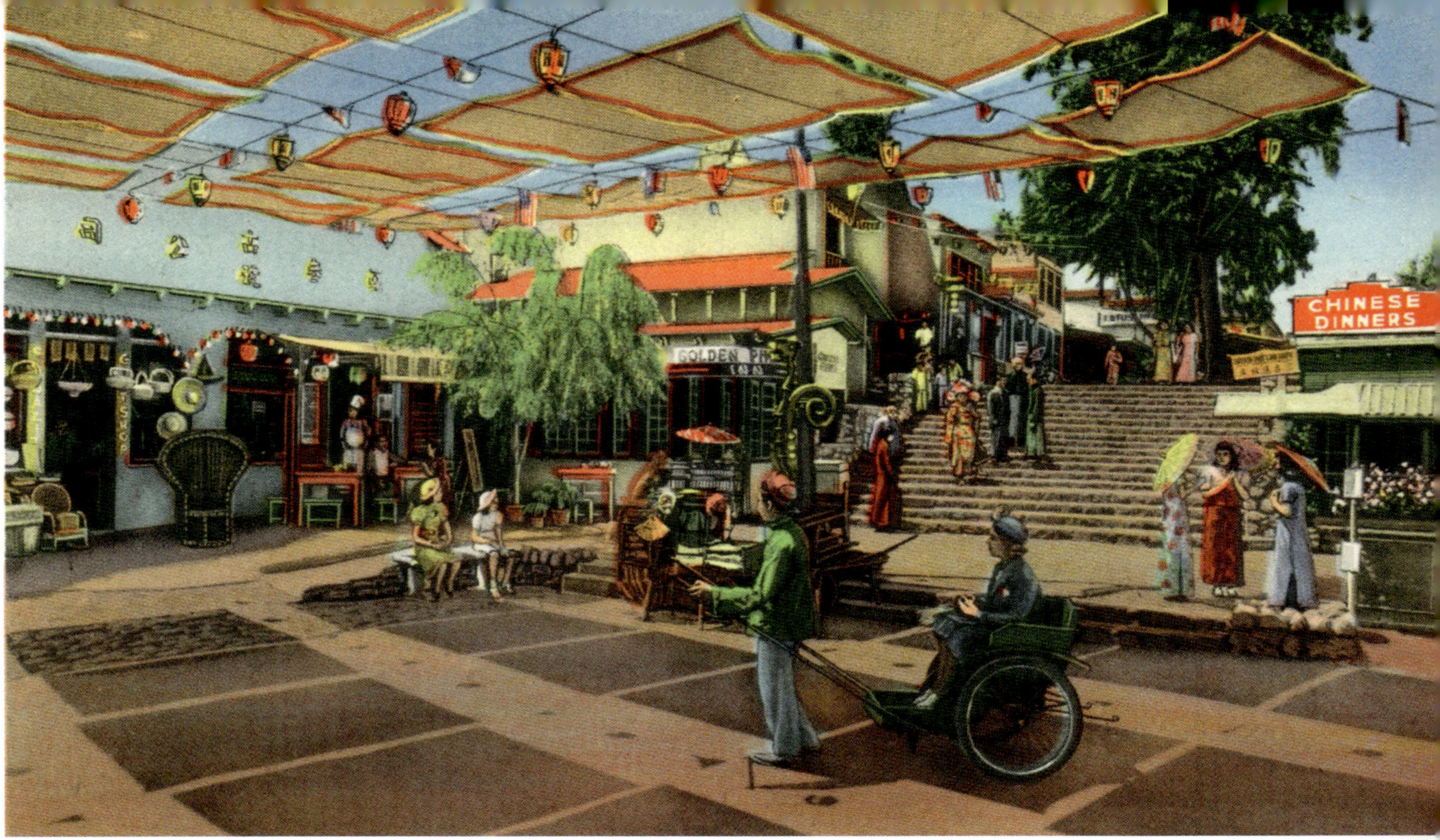

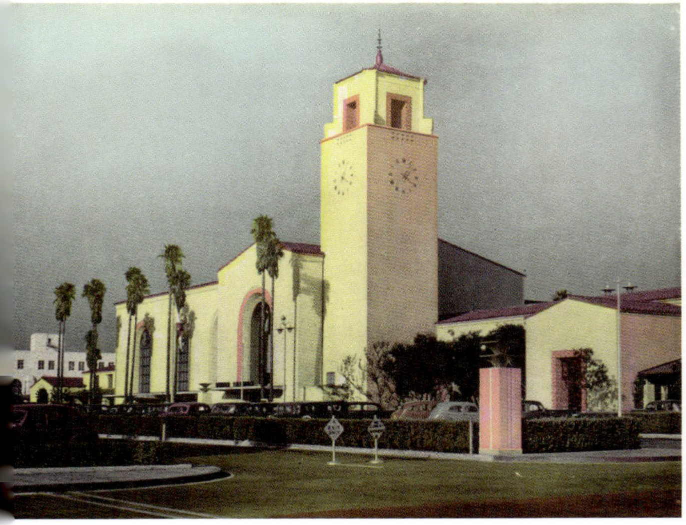

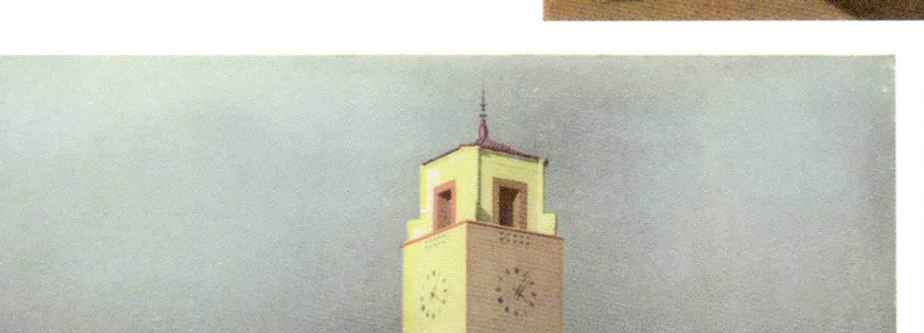

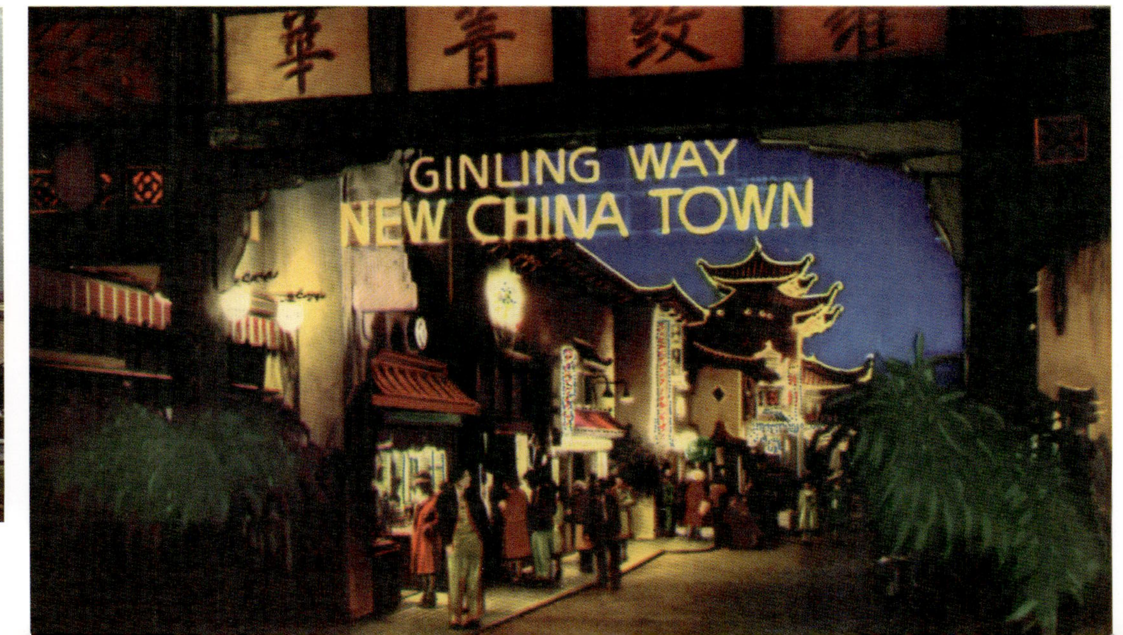

As if the region wasn't already suffering, 115 people were killed in 1933 when the Long Beach earthquake struck the area. Of the hundreds of brick buildings that collapsed in Long Beach and nearby Compton, schools were among the worst affected. Luckily, the temblor struck at 6 p.m., when most schools were empty.

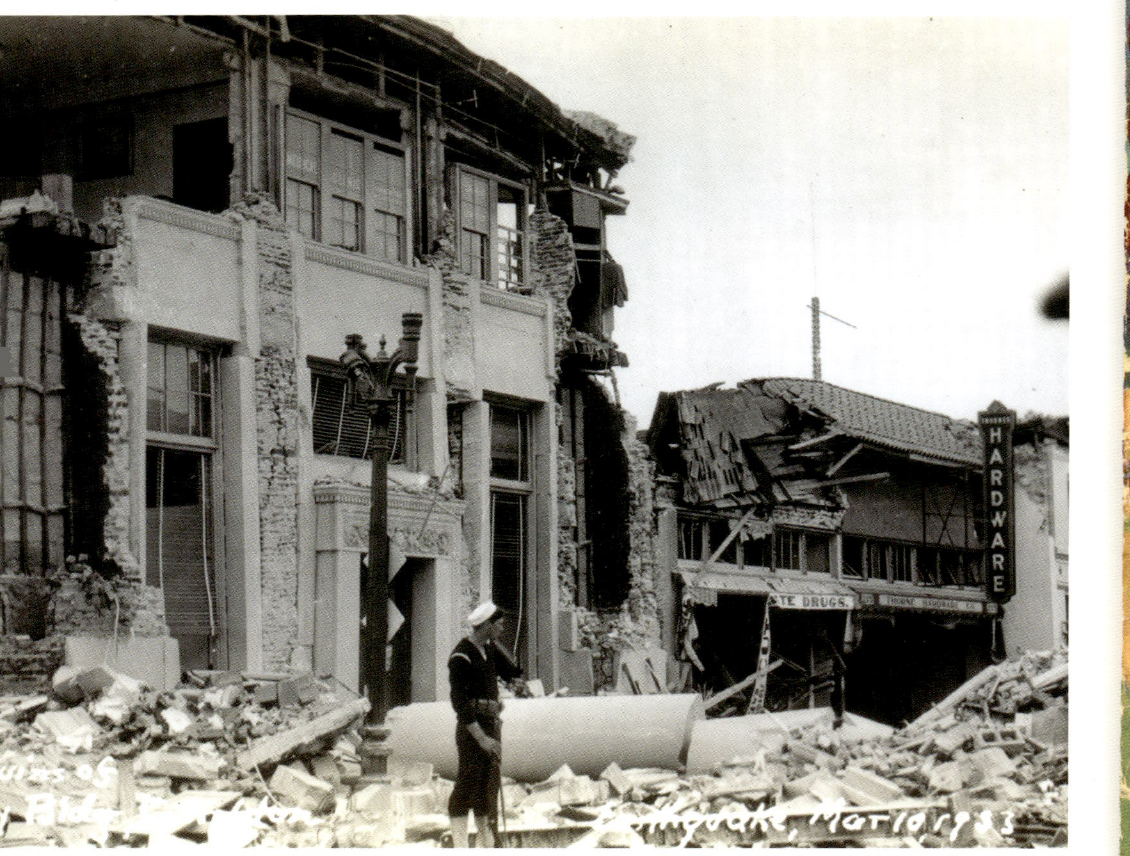


**ABOVE:** The 1933 Long Beach earthquake killed 115 people. Brick buildings were the first to collapse.

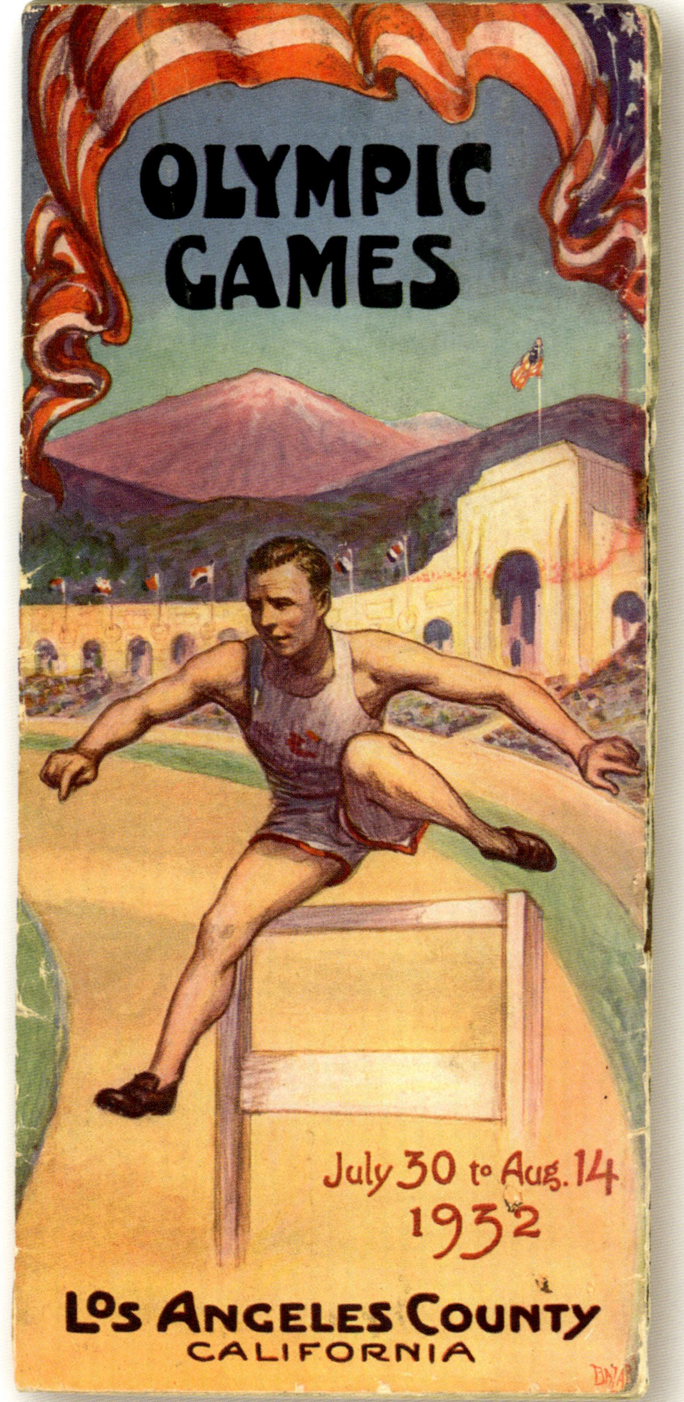


**RIGHT:** Despite the Depression, the 1932 Olympic Games in Los Angeles went ahead as scheduled, the city having built the Coliseum and other Olympic venues during the booming 1920s.

For a city so closely associated with the conservative midwesterners who had migrated there in the 1920s, it was shocking to what extent corruption would infiltrate the Los Angeles of the 1930s. Gambling, prostitution, extortion, and other vices were protected—and in some cases controlled—by crooked elements within the administration of Mayor Frank Shaw and Los Angeles Police Department Chief James Davis. Infuriated by the rampant corruption, Clifford Clinton, the owner of the popular Clifton's cafeterias, took the lead as a reformer who helped uncover the astonishing extent of civic and police involvement with the vice racket. For his efforts, Clinton survived the bombing of his house by a secret intelligence unit of the LAPD. Mayor Shaw, Chief Davis, and others were implicated in these and other crimes, with Shaw recalled by voters in 1938 and Davis fired a year later.

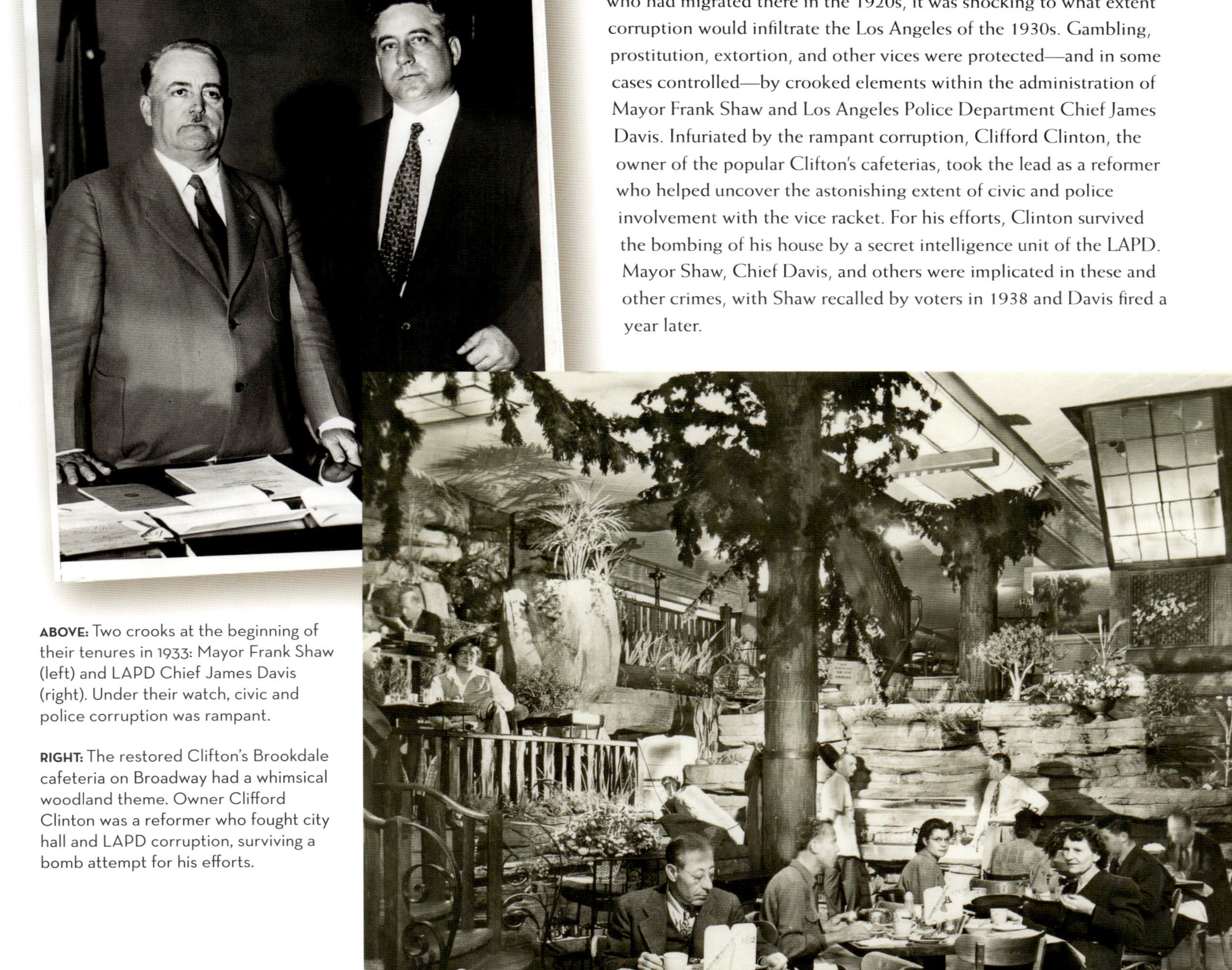

**ABOVE:** Two crooks at the beginning of their tenures in 1933: Mayor Frank Shaw (left) and LAPD Chief James Davis (right). Under their watch, civic and police corruption was rampant.

**RIGHT:** The restored Clifton's Brookdale cafeteria on Broadway had a whimsical woodland theme. Owner Clifford Clinton was a reformer who fought city hall and LAPD corruption, surviving a bomb attempt for his efforts.

# Mid-Wilshire

This amazing photo (right) depicts Wilshire Boulevard in the 1930s. On the lower right is Lafayette Park. Across the street, near the Eastside Beer and Ale billboard, is Simon's Sandwiches, a circular Streamline Moderne drive-in with a neon pylon designed by architect Wayne McAllister. Early houses with neat lawns still faced the boulevard. The Town House hotel is to the right, Bullock's Wilshire is in the center, the Gaylord apartment hotel in the middle distance, and the Ambassador Hotel at the upper left. Except for Simon's and the Ambassador, all still exist today.

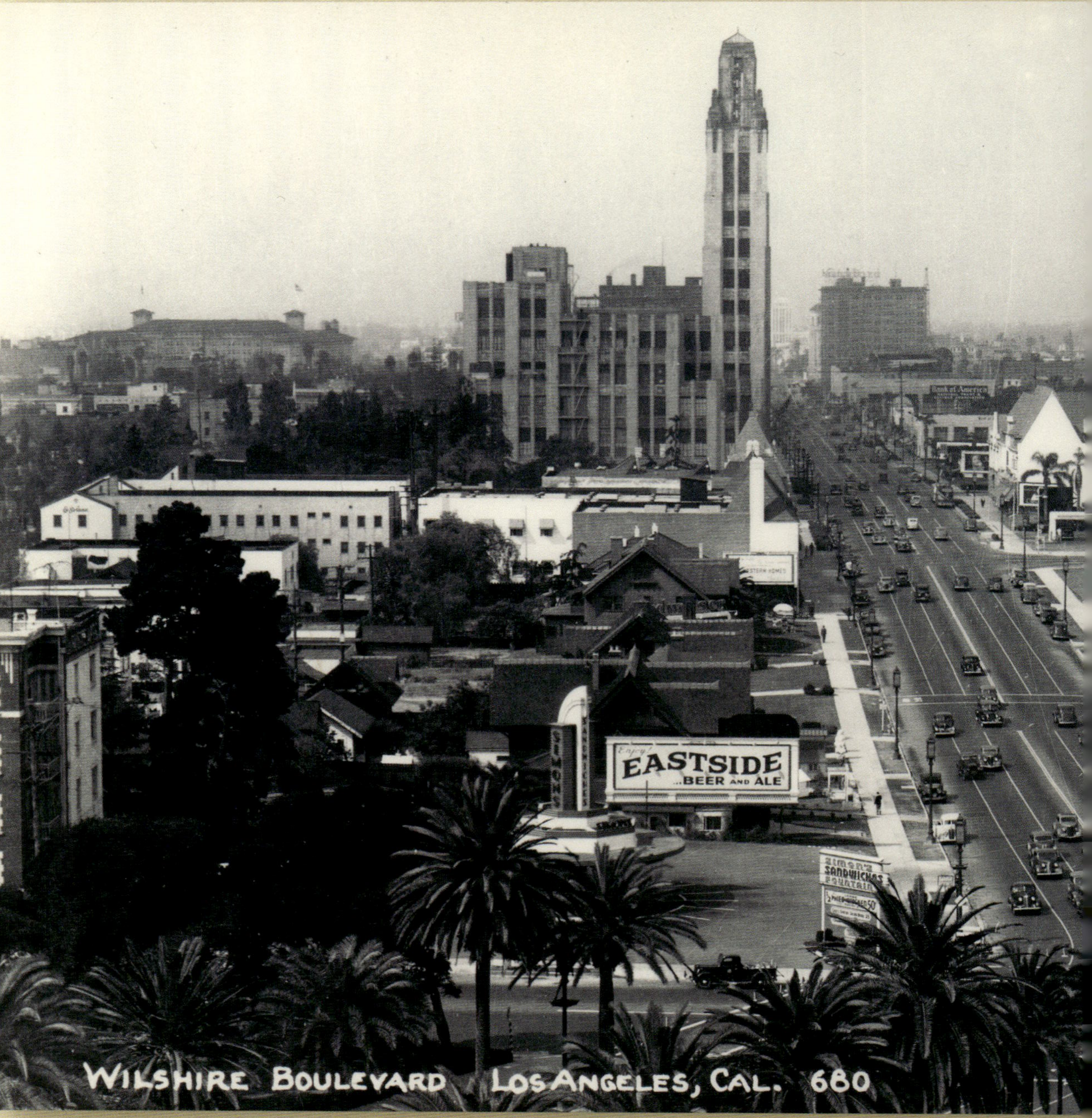

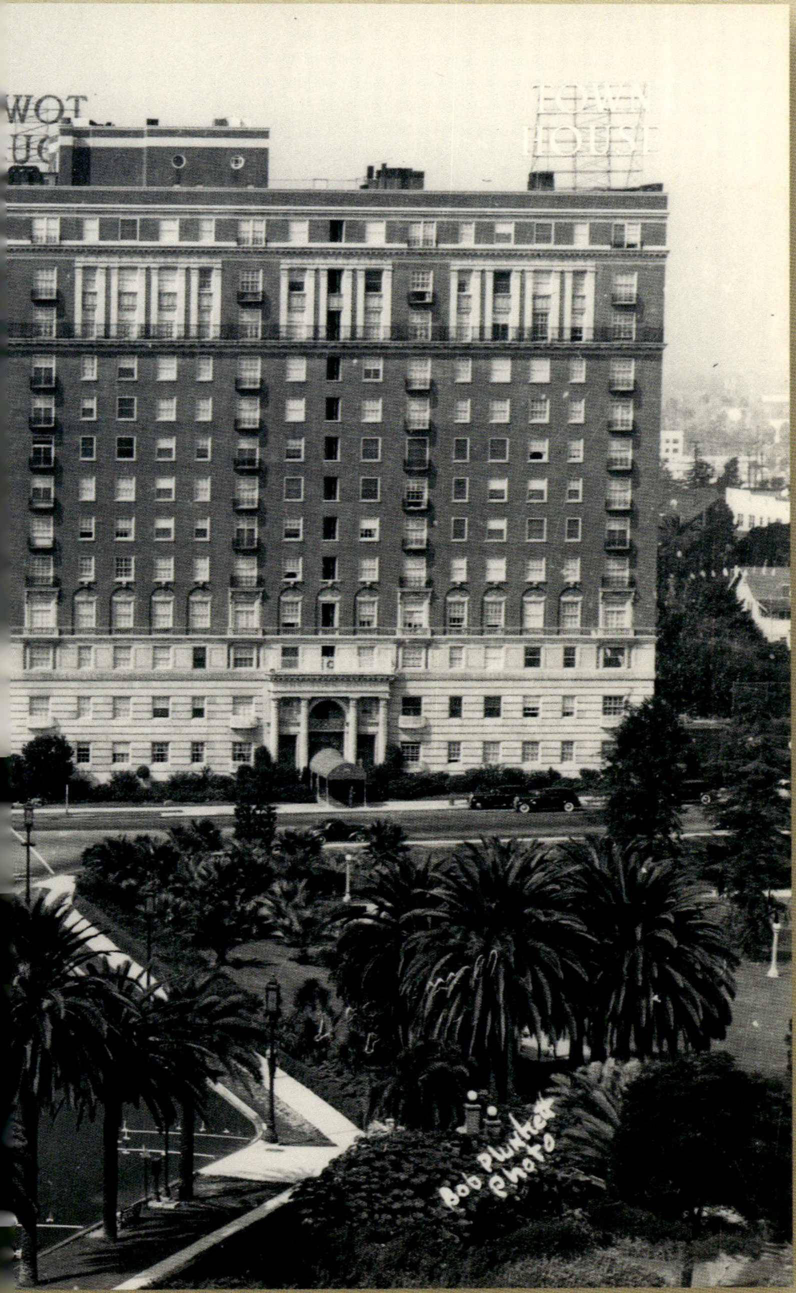

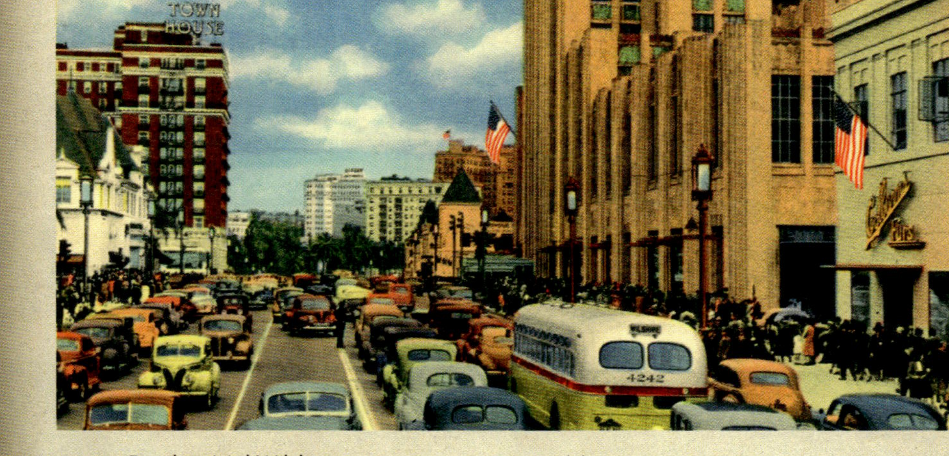


**ABOVE:** Bustling Mid-Wilshire in 1941. Bullock's Wilshire is at the middle right.

**BELOW:** Mystery creatures ponder the La Brea Tar Pits.

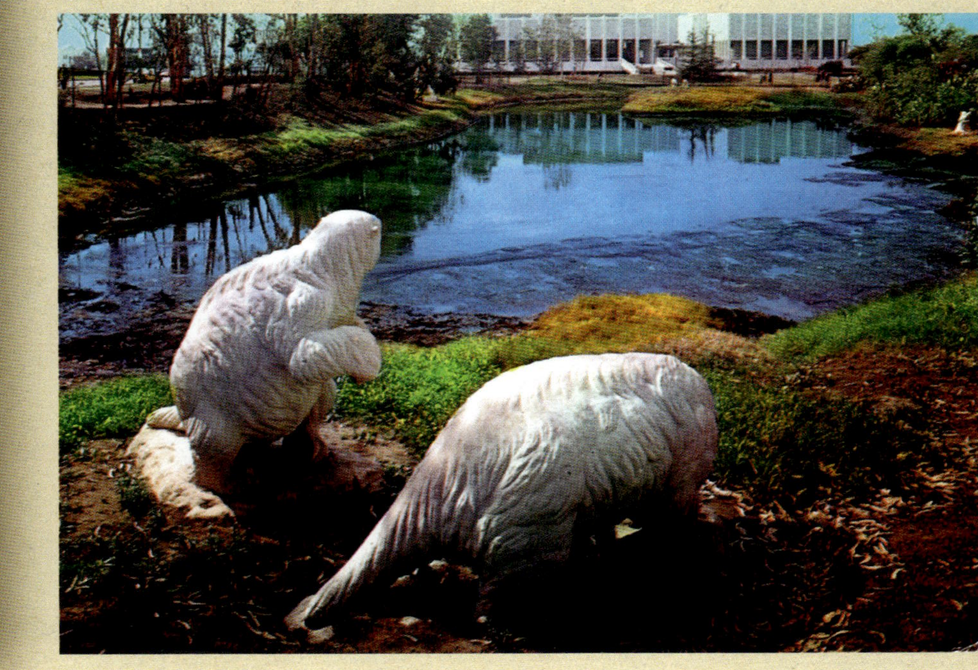

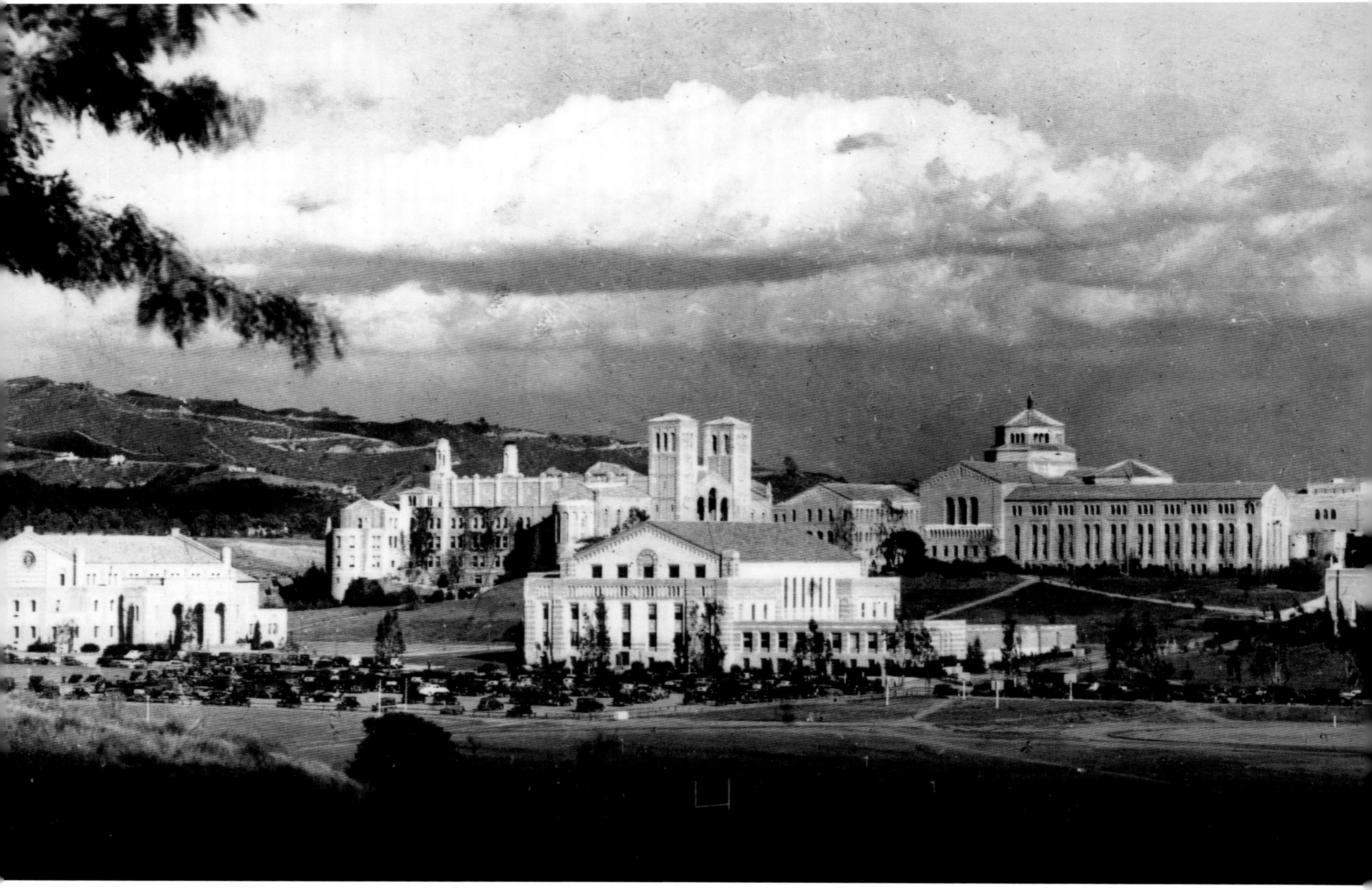

In the 1930s, before Westwood Village and Bel Air were developed, the UCLA campus was evocative of a Mediterranean hill town.

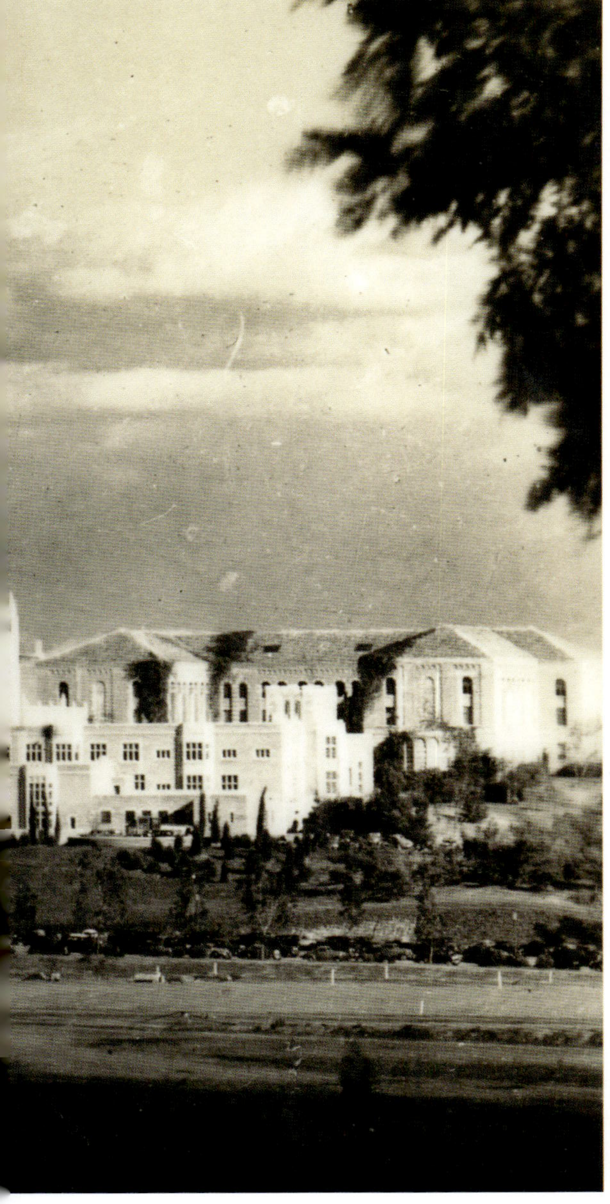

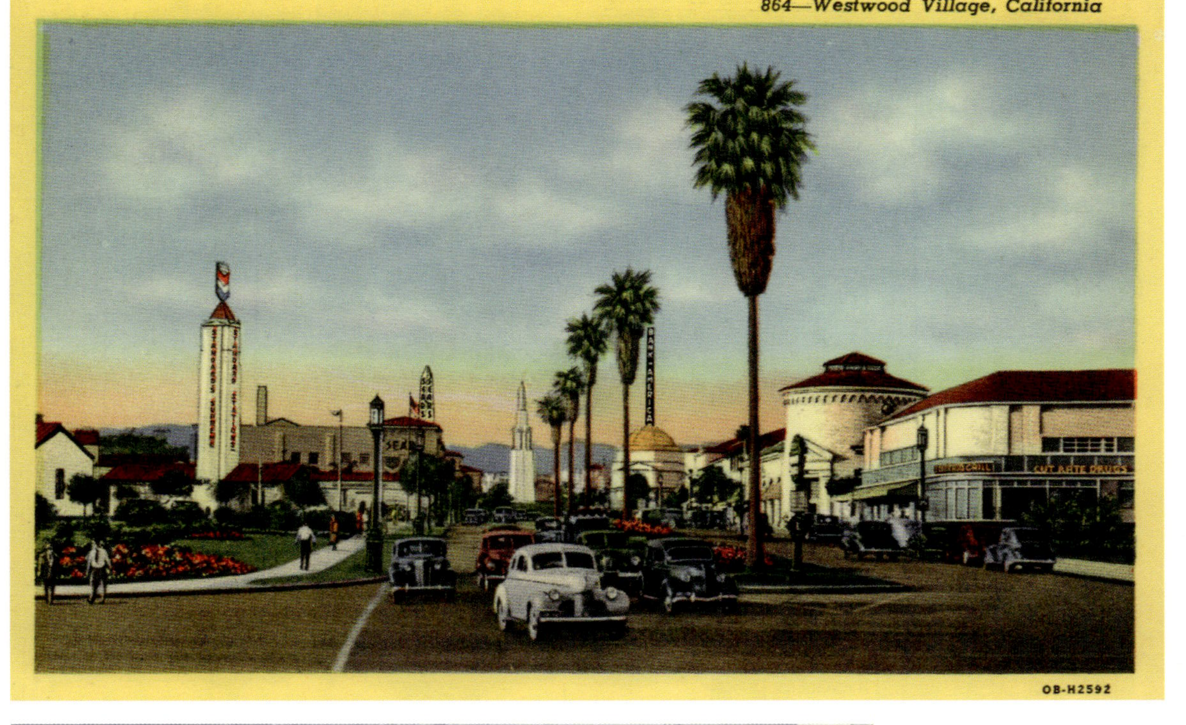


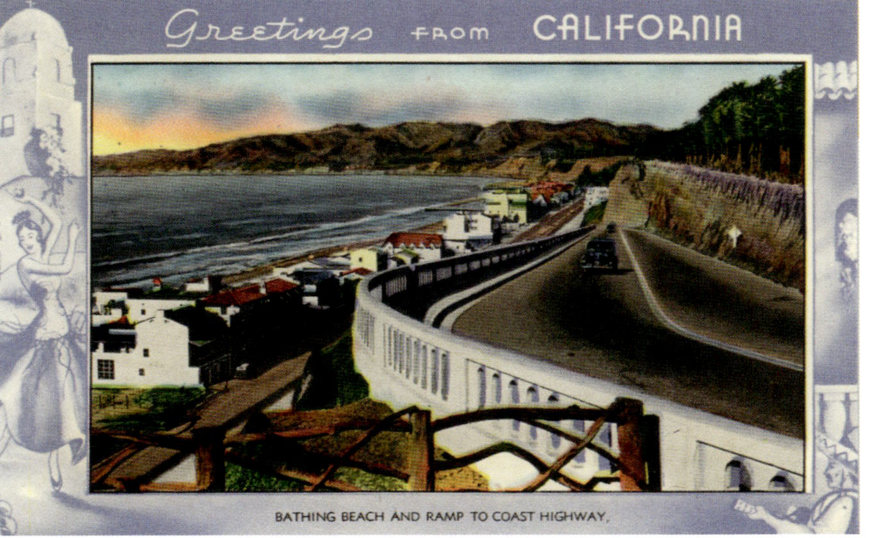


**ABOVE:** Westwood Village.

**LEFT:** The famous California Incline in Santa Monica.

Meanwhile offshore, pushing the boundaries of legality were gambling boats floating just outside California's three-mile jurisdictional limit. The most famous of these was former bootlegger Tony Cornero's SS *Rex*, "Anchored in calm waters off Santa Monica Pier," where water taxis sped patrons to and from the ship. With a capacity of 1,990, the *Rex* (a modified fishing barge) offered "Cuisine by Henri," bonded drinks, dancing to the rhythm of the Rex Mariners, and a round-the-clock casino. In 1939, authorities attempting to raid the *Rex* were repelled by the ship's defensive water cannons for nine days before Cornero finally surrendered. Just as the gambling ship era was ending, a dapper East Coast mobster arrived who would quickly become the new master of the Los Angeles underworld: Benjamin "Bugsy" Siegel." Mickey Cohen was his second in command.

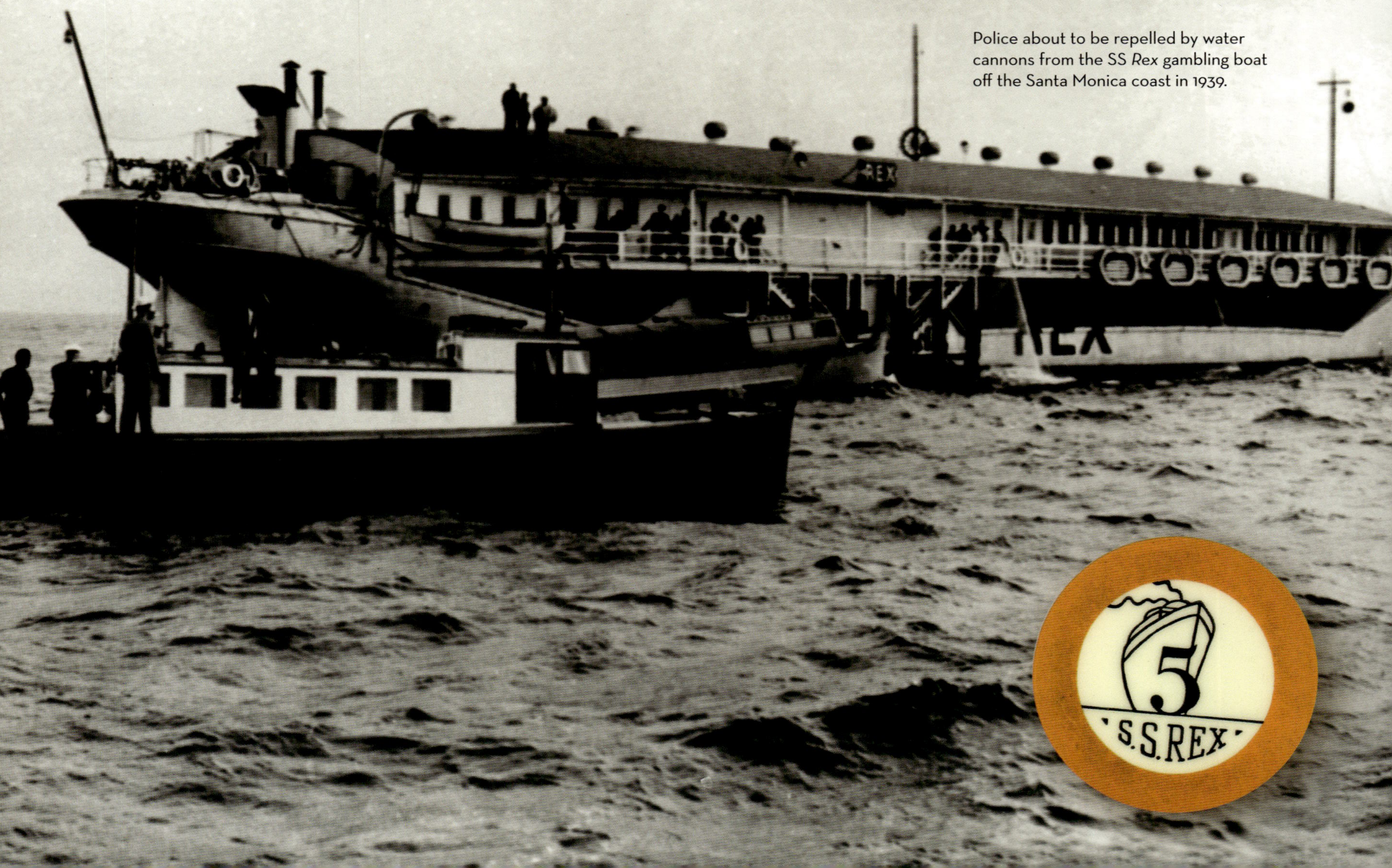


Police about to be repelled by water cannons from the SS *Rex* gambling boat off the Santa Monica coast in 1939.

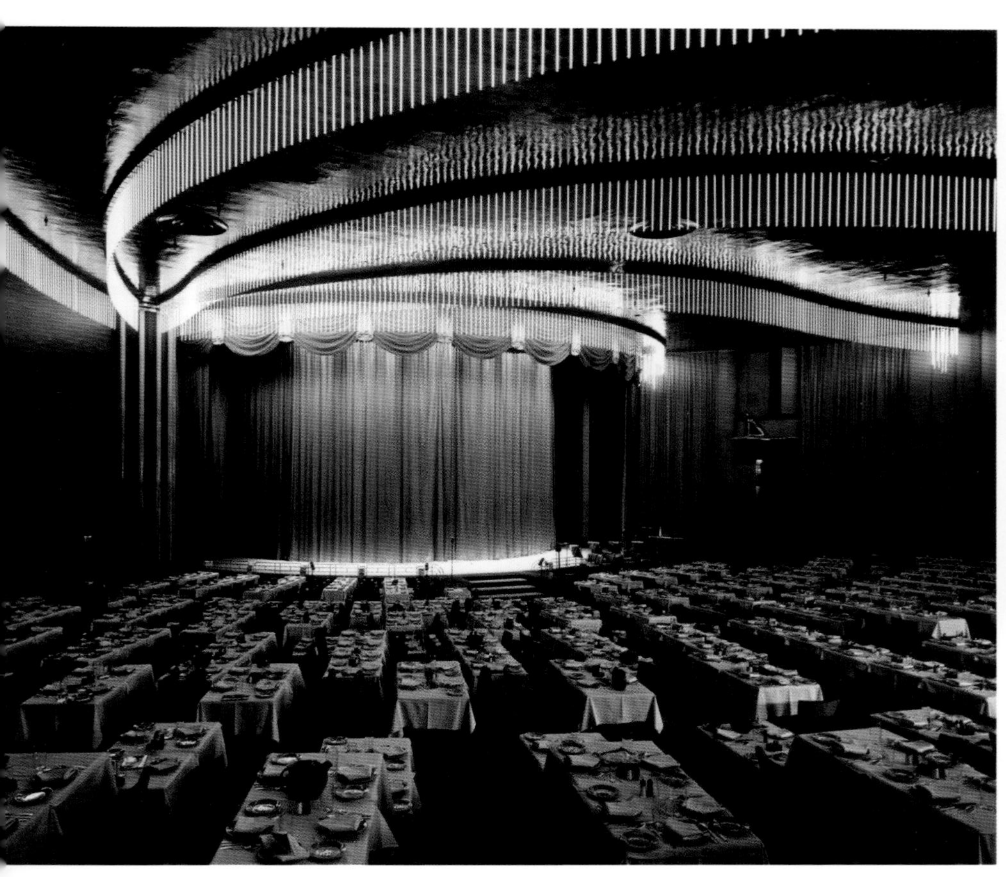

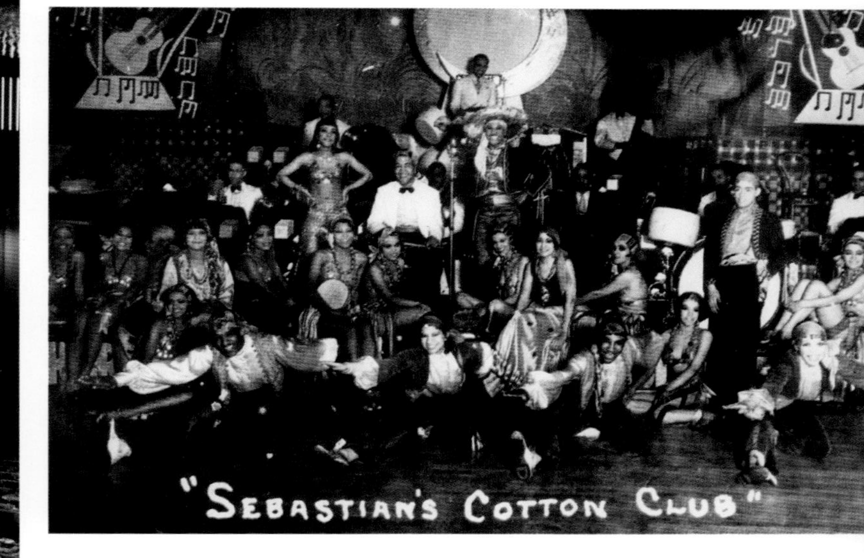


**LEFT:** "Through These Portals Pass the Most Beautiful Girls in the World" was the cheeky slogan for Earl Carroll's gargantuan Hollywood nightclub that he opened in 1938.

**ABOVE:** Frank Sebastian's Cotton Club—a swank Culver City dance hall featuring top black entertainers—doubled as a speakeasy and gambling joint for upscale whites from 1927 to 1939.

It's difficult to imagine today, but there was once a time—a bright and shining moment between the Great Depression and the 1960s—when adults frequented nightclubs to drink, dine, see a show, dance, and stay up late. It was a time when ordinary Angelenos in their fifties, sixties, and older would enjoy a midnight show and go to bed at 3 a.m. These days only twentysomethings have the stamina to be out past 10 p.m.

In contrast with recent decades, when celebrities generally avoid mixing with the public in social settings, the period of the 1930s and 1940s was a time when the studios demanded that their stars be regularly seen—and photographed—at nightclubs and restaurants, not just movie premieres and award ceremonies. At the very center of Hollywood nightlife was the Sunset Strip, an unincorporated area just outside the Los Angeles city limits in what is now the city of West Hollywood. Billy Wilkerson, publisher of the *Hollywood Reporter,* was a flamboyant entrepreneur who set the tone for Sunset Boulevard glamour with his Café Trocadero in 1934, and in 1940, Ciro's. The Trocadero was the intimate gathering spot for Hollywood's glitterati, and later became famous for the jitterbug and West Coast swing. It was a place where young dancers would gather to "cut loose, jump around, and go crazy." In the 1960s, rock clubs such as the Whisky a Go Go, Roxy, Pandora's Box, and London Fog ruled the Sunset Strip.

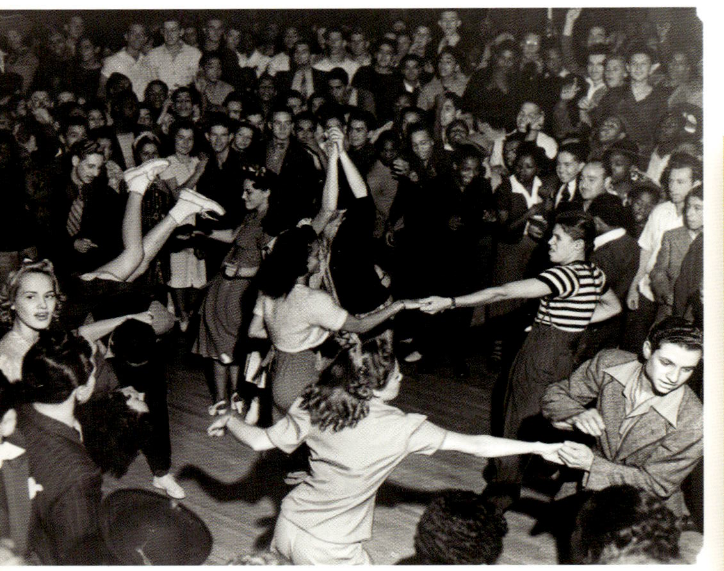

**ABOVE:** Twenty-five hundred kids of all races competing at the first annual jitterbug convention at the Palomar Ballroom in 1939.

**BELOW:** Simon's was one of Los Angeles's iconic 1930s streamlined drive-ins designed by architect Wayne McAllister.

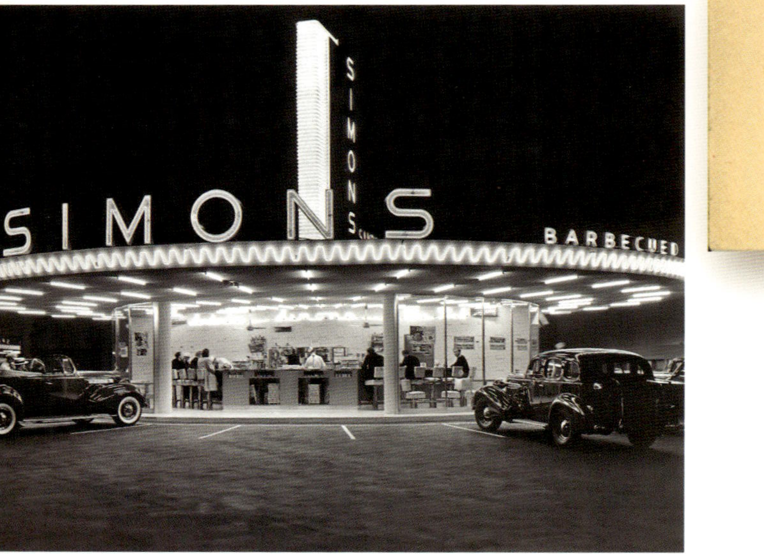


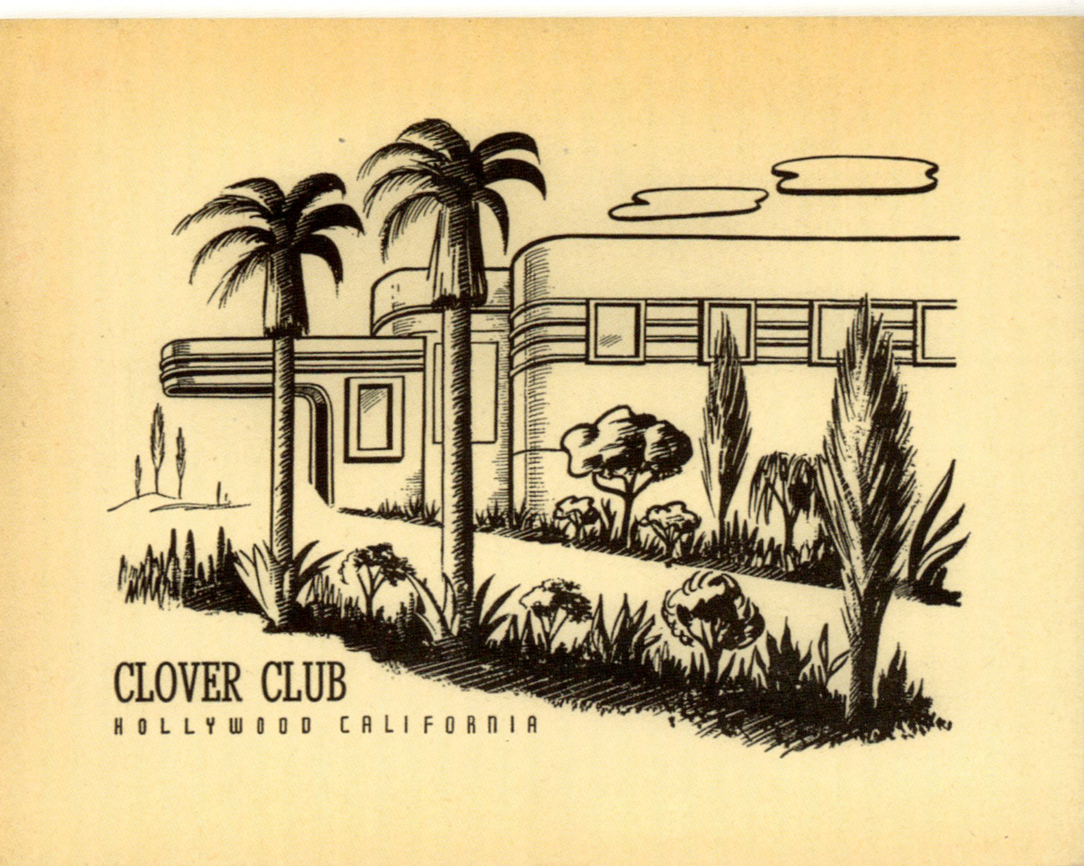


**ABOVE:** Among the most notorious of the backroom casinos was the Clover Club, situated just west of the legendary Chateau Marmont on the Sunset Strip.

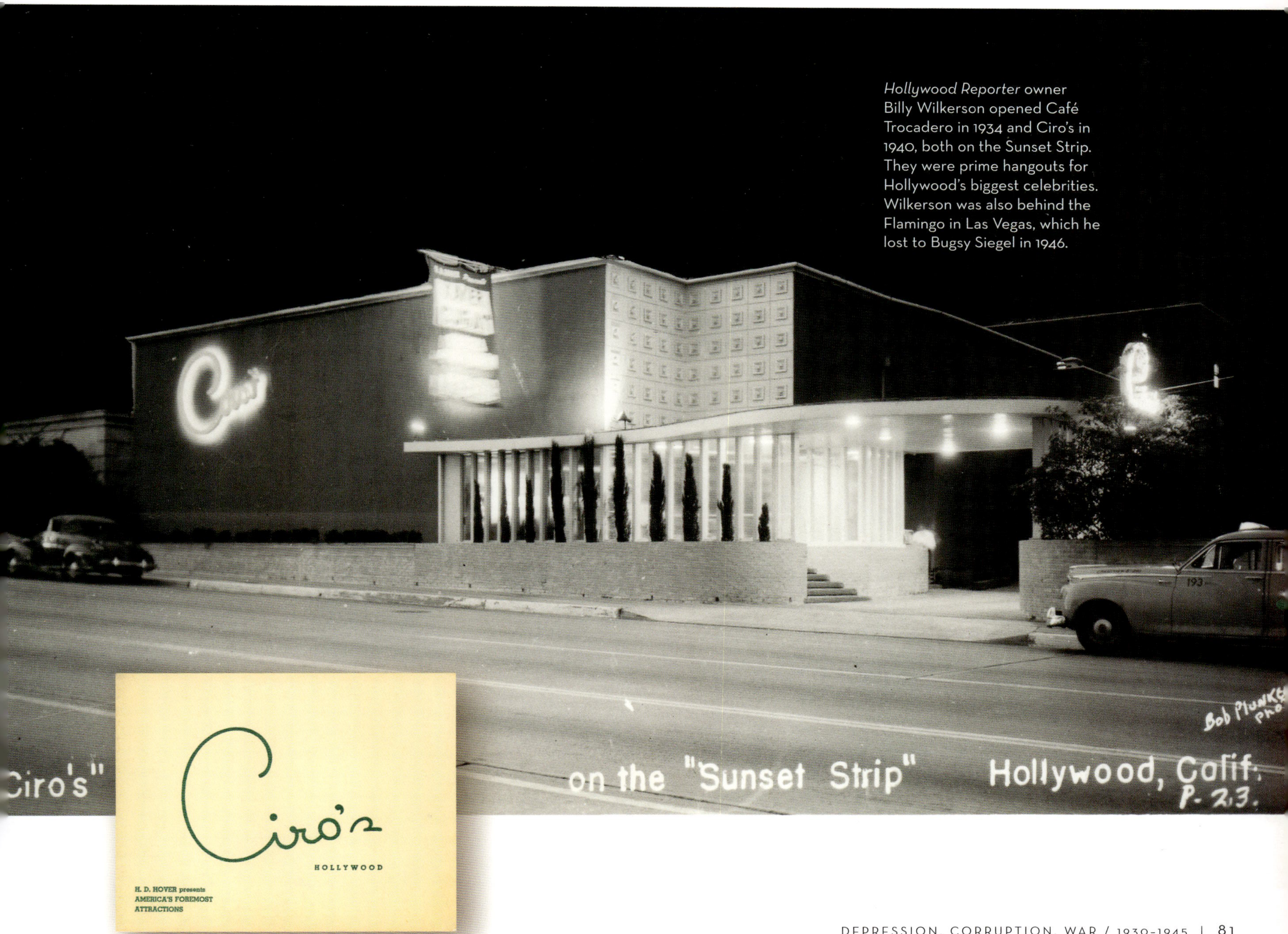

*Hollywood Reporter* owner Billy Wilkerson opened Café Trocadero in 1934 and Ciro's in 1940, both on the Sunset Strip. They were prime hangouts for Hollywood's biggest celebrities. Wilkerson was also behind the Flamingo in Las Vegas, which he lost to Bugsy Siegel in 1946.

Ciro's" on the "Sunset Strip" Hollywood, Calif. P-2.3.

Bob Plunkett Photo

Ciro's

HOLLYWOOD

H. D. HOVER presents
AMERICA'S FOREMOST
ATTRACTIONS

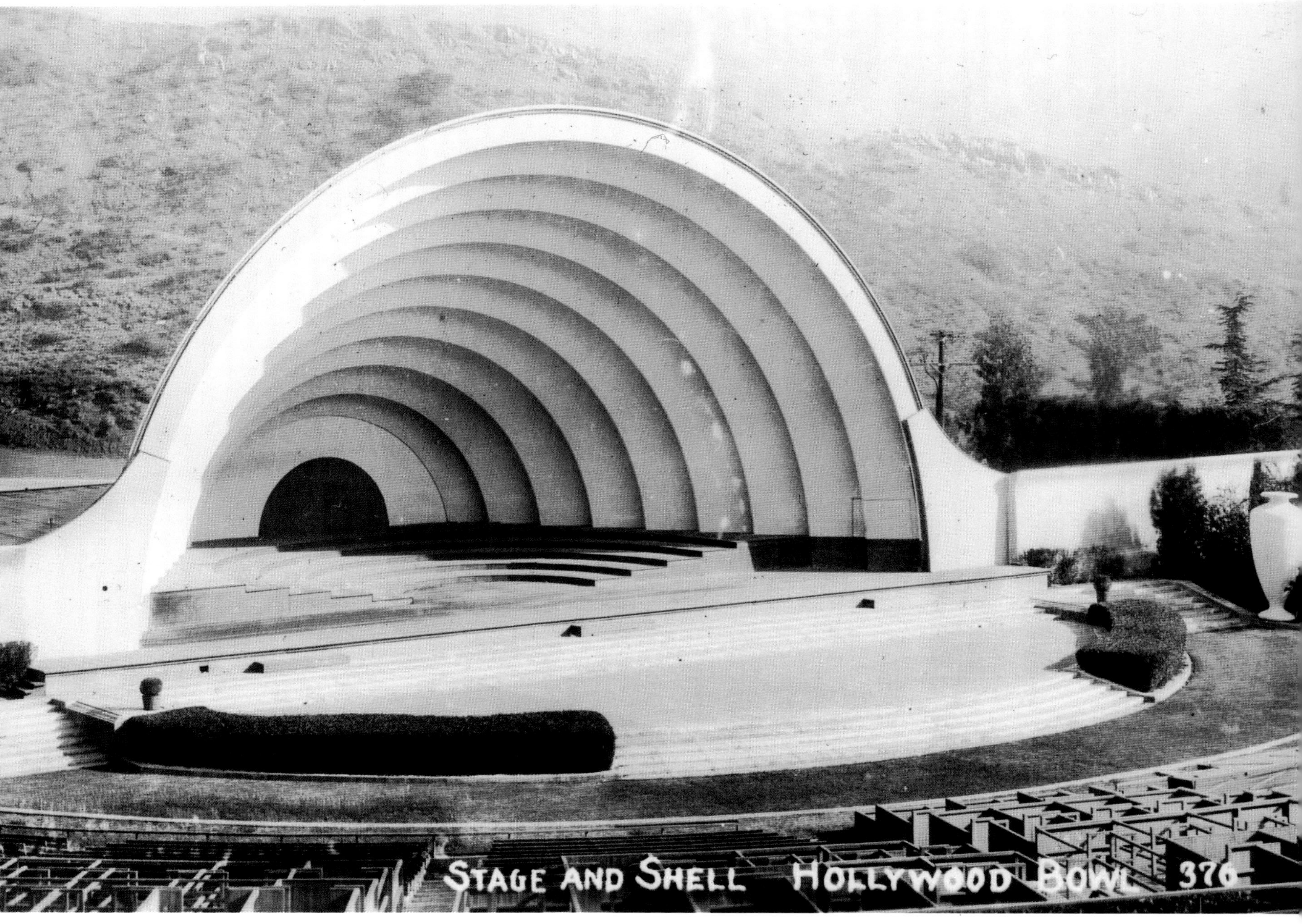
STAGE AND SHELL HOLLYWOOD BOWL 376

One of the most despairing books of the 1930s, which captured the sordid underbelly of Hollywood, was *The Day of the Locust* by Nathanael West. The novel—later made into a film—chronicles a set designer's descent into the degenerate world of a wannabe starlet and her parasitic hustler friends, who latch onto a lonely retiree from Iowa. The story ends at a movie premiere, when America's obsession with celebrity is taken to its logical extreme by a fanatical mob.

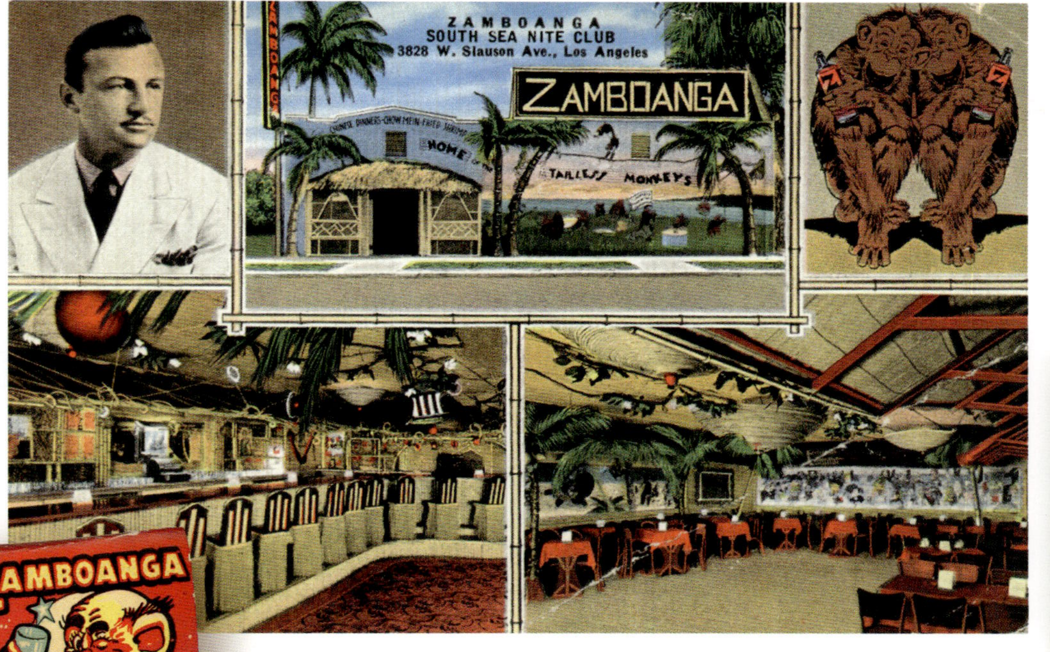


**ABOVE:** The pre-Tiki Zamboanga South Sea Nite Club in South Los Angeles was "The Home of the Tailless Monkeys," which was actually the club's signature cocktail.

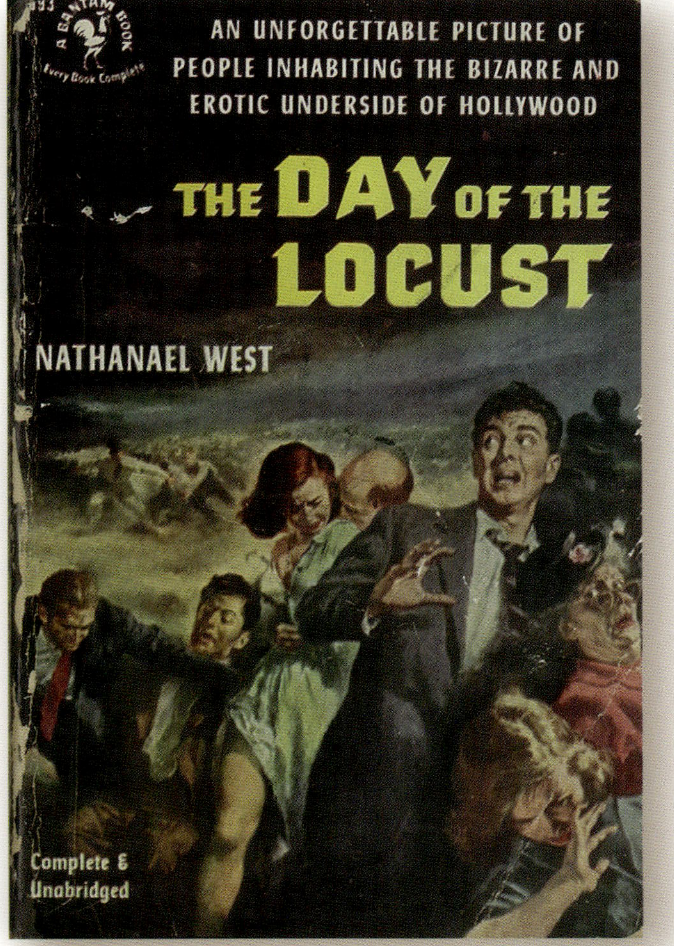


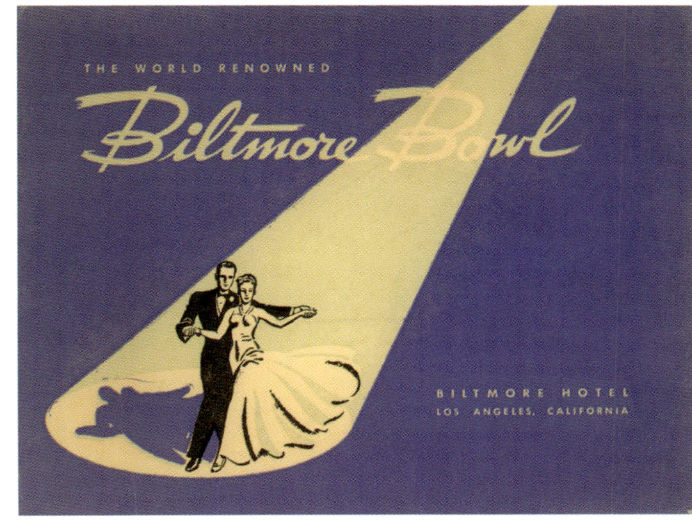


**FACING:** An early photo of the Hollywood Bowl.

**RIGHT:** The posh Biltmore Bowl, a large ballroom located in the deluxe Biltmore Hotel in downtown Los Angeles, opened in 1928.

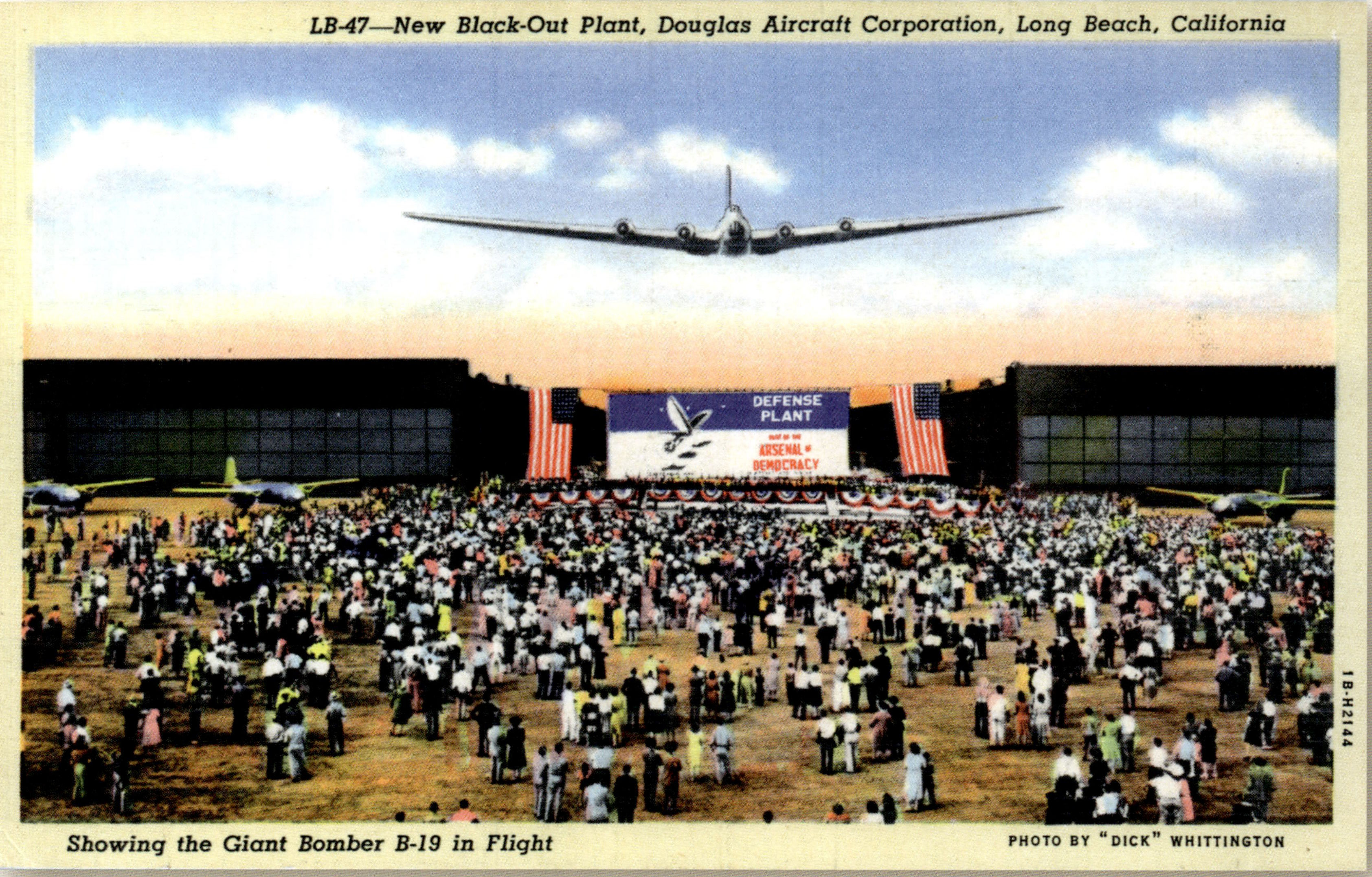


In anticipation of war, the federal government began placing huge orders for military aircraft as early as 1939. As a result, Southern California's burgeoning aircraft industry expanded enormously in capacity, hiring thousands of new workers. When war came in December 1941, the local shipbuilding industry likewise swelled with government orders and round-the-clock employment.

With men being sent to fight, factory workers were in short supply, so women were called to do "male jobs" that had traditionally been denied them. Locally, these "Rosie the Riveters" were machinists, technicians, and assembly-line workers in hundreds of plants throughout Southern California during World War II.

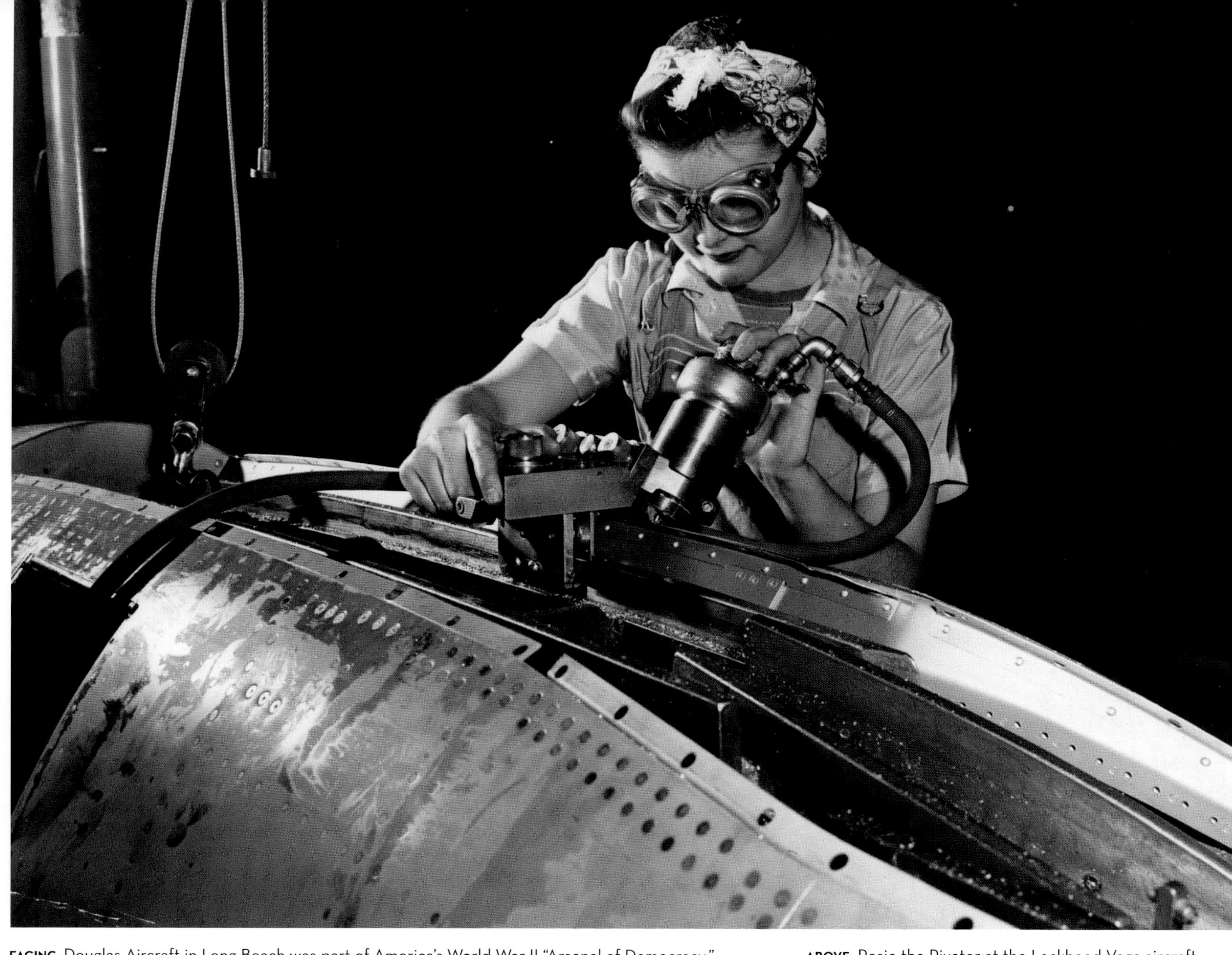

**FACING:** Douglas Aircraft in Long Beach was part of America's World War II "Arsenal of Democracy." This "blackout plant" emitted no light that could be seen by enemy bombers. It employed 47,000 in 1943, over half of whom were women.

**ABOVE:** Rosie the Riveter at the Lockheed Vega aircraft factory during World War II.

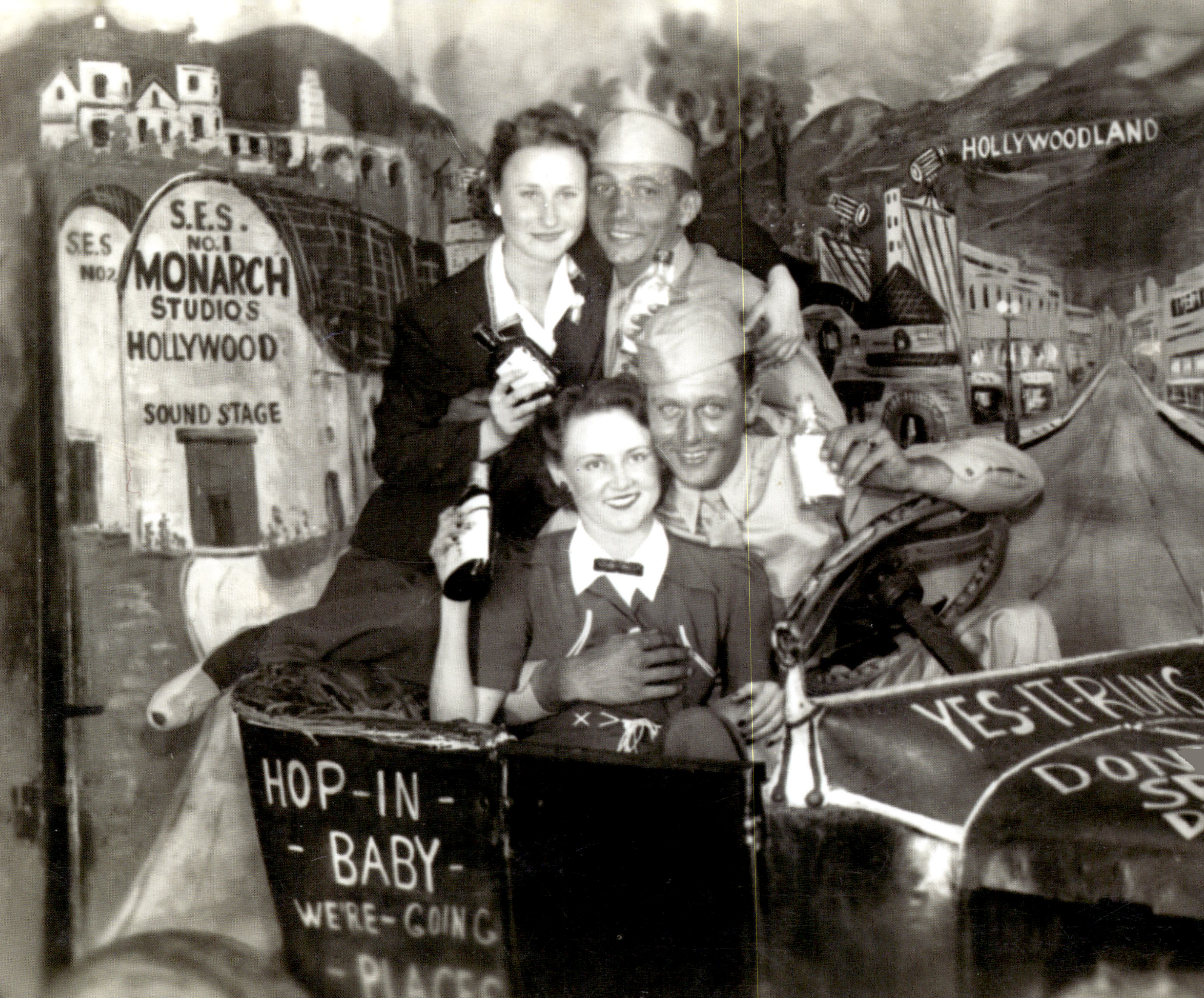
S.E.S.
NO. 1
MONARCH
STUDIOS
HOLLYWOOD
SOUND STAGE
S.E.S
NO2
HOLLYWOODLAND
HOP-IN-
-BABY-
WE'RE-GOING
YES-IT-RUNS

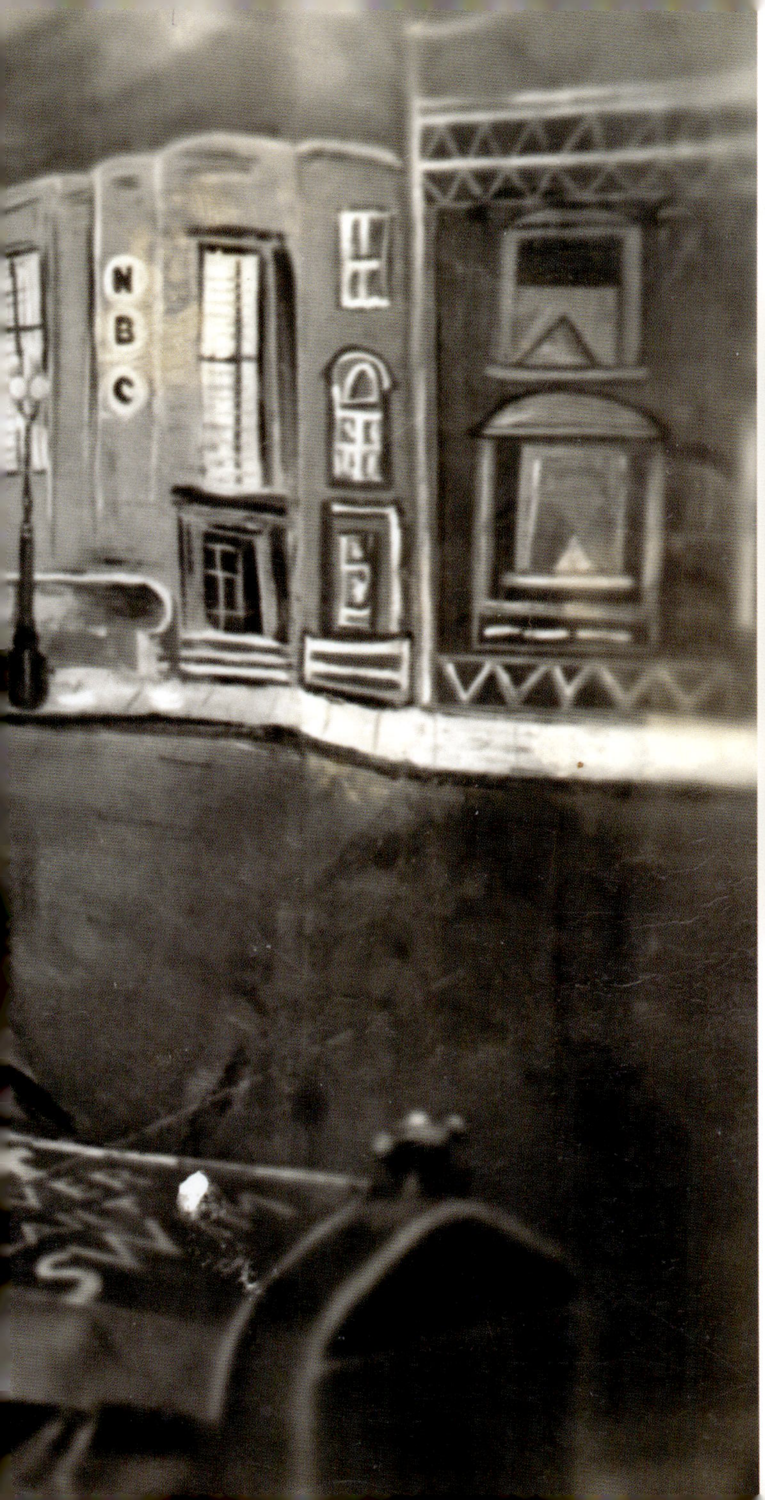

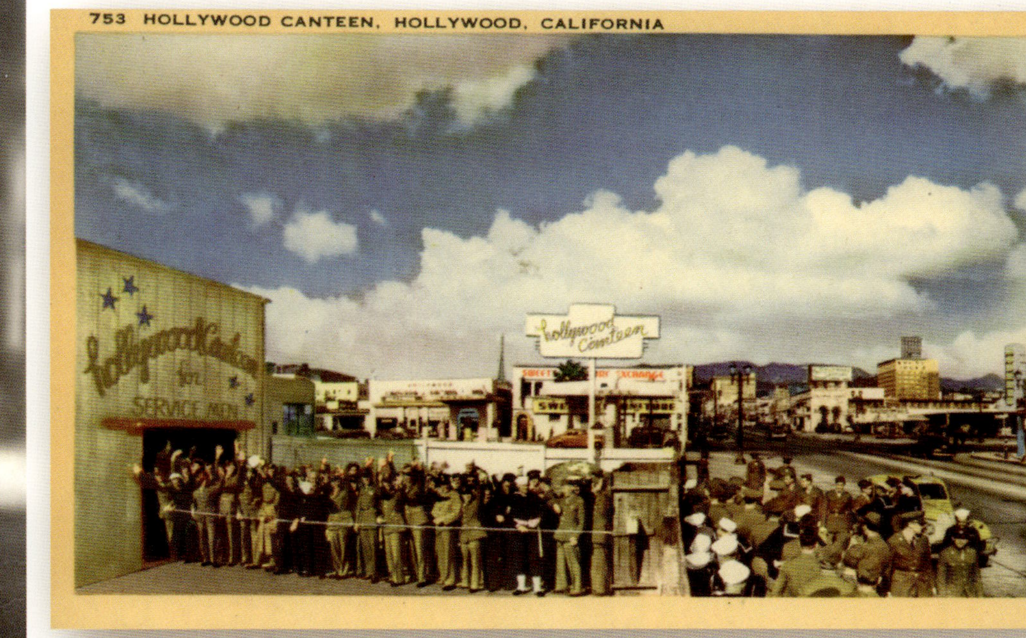


**ABOVE:** Movie studios and their stars created the Hollywood Canteen for servicemen and servicewomen passing through Los Angeles. Free meals, top entertainment, and the chance to dance with a celebrity made the venue enormously popular.

**LEFT:** Servicemen on leave yuk it up with their gals in a boozy novelty photo.

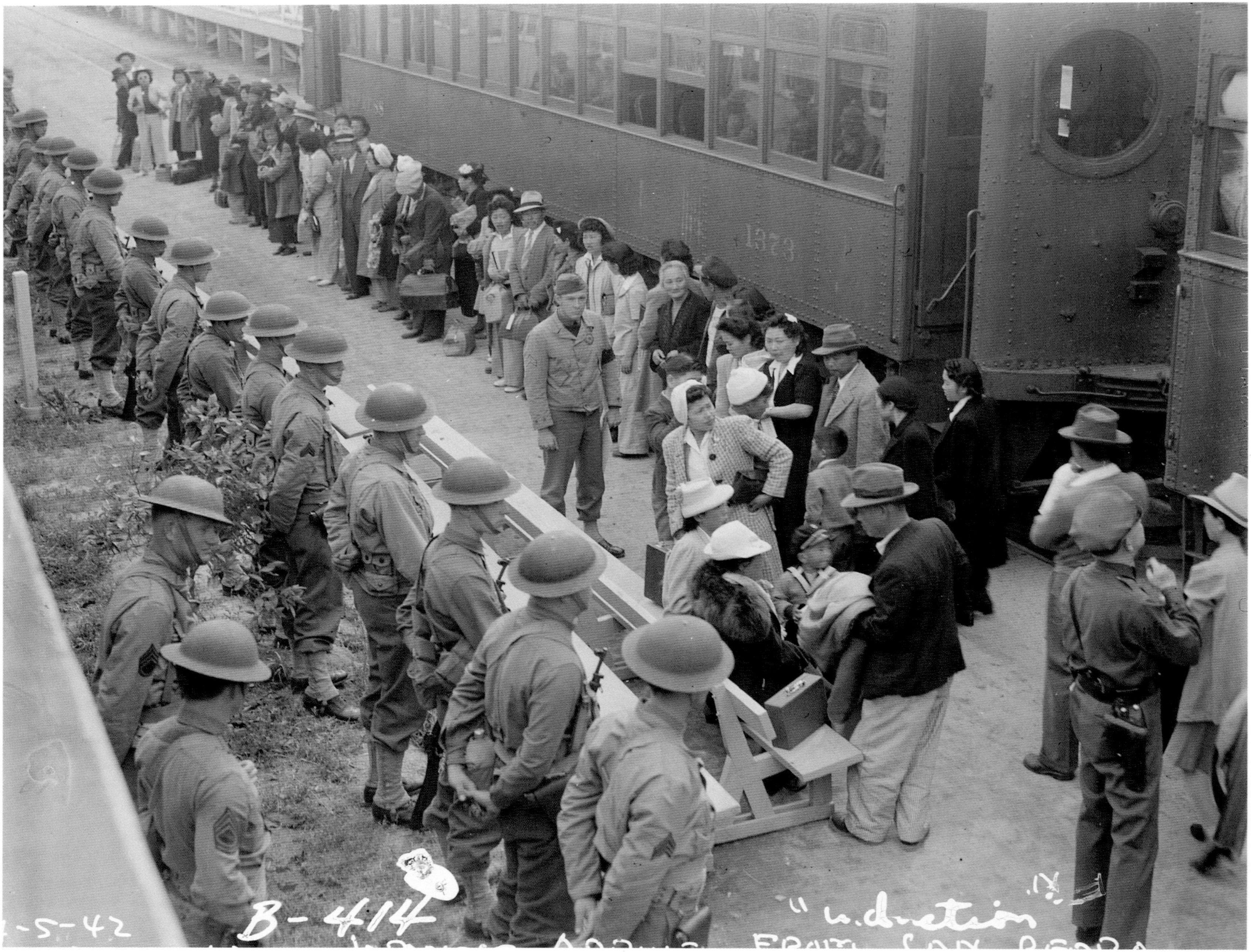

At the same time, tens of thousands of African Americans moved to California from the South for the many good-paying, highly skilled jobs available in the wartime defense industry. Part of the second great migration, these new residents settled primarily in the segregated areas of Los Angeles and Long Beach.

Following the attack on Pearl Harbor, unwarranted fear and racism, particularly in Los Angeles, led to one of the most shameful acts ever committed by the U.S. government on its own people. From 1942 to 1945, over 100,000 persons of Japanese descent living on the Pacific Coast—more than 60 percent of whom were United States citizens—were involuntarily forced into internment camps. Despite this outrage, thousands of Japanese American men joined the war effort, fighting in Europe in the army's 442nd Infantry Regiment that became the most highly decorated unit for its size in American history. At the war's end, many internees returned to Southern California to resume their lives, reestablish their businesses, and again pursue the American dream.

**FACING:** Japanese Americans in Los Angeles about to board the train for internment in distant camps.

**RIGHT:** Young Chicanos wearing zoot suits were attacked by servicemen in 1943, foreshadowing the ethnic and racial tensions that would haunt Los Angeles after World War II.

# Los Angeles Times

Wartime Weather

IN THREE PARTS—38 PAGES

Part II—LOCAL NEWS—20 Pages

TIMES OFFICE 202 West First Street Los Angeles 53, Calif.

VOL. LXII — CC — MONDAY MORNING, JUNE 7, 1943 — CITY NEWS—EDITORIAL—SOCIETY

## By The Way
with BILL HENRY

## Inquiry on Jap Activities Set
### Dies Group Here Will Investigate Loyalty of Those Released

How many Southern California Japanese were members of the sinister Black Dragon Society and what percentage of those recently released from war relocation centers are disloyal to the United States will be subjects of inquiry when the special Dies committee on un-American activities opens its hearing here tomorrow.

Representative John M. Costello of Los Angeles, who will act as chairman of the subcommittee, made this disclosure last night in announcing that the hearing, scheduled originally to open today, would be postponed until tomorrow because of the delayed arrival of two members of the committee.

*Members on Way*

The two Eastern members, Herman P. Eberharter (D.) Pa., and Karl E. Mundt (R.) S.D., are expected to arrive tonight. They are en route here by train.

"Our inquiry will be confined to un-American activities and to what extent subversive forces have been at work among the Japanese," Representative Costello explained.

The committee, it was said, also plans to inquire into the reasons for the release of approximately 1000 Japanese weekly from war relocation camps and as to what steps have been taken by War Relocation Authority representatives to determine whether or not those released are loyal to the United States.

*To Inform Public*

Although most of the sessions of the committee, which will be held in the Federal Building, will be closed to the public, Costello said that arrangements were being made to keep the public advised as to conditions existing in the war relocation centers.

## Zoot Suiters Learn Lesson in Fights With Servicemen

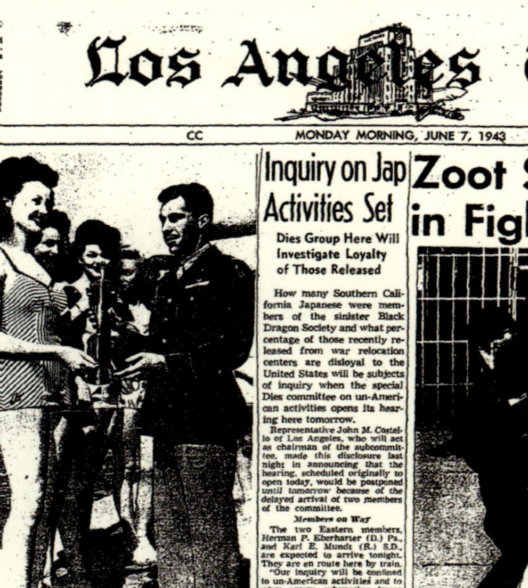

LINE UP FOR BOOKING—"Zoot suiters" are stripped of clothing by servicemen, mostly sailors, in East Los Angeles roundup of youths. They appear at County Jail.

## Gangs Stay Off Streets After Dark

Those gamin dandies, the zoot suiters, having learned a great moral lesson from servicemen, mostly sailors, who took over their instruction three days ago, are staying home nights.

With the exception of 61 youths booked in County Jail on misdemeanor charges, wearers of the garish costume that has become a hallmark of juvenile delinquency are apparently "unfrocked."

These were the conclusions reached last night by Capt. David Croushorn, commanding Sheriff's men at the Hall of Justice during night patrols, and Capt. Harry Seager, night Chief of Police.

*Street Fights Rage*

The officers have directed some 200 extra police and 100 deputies who for the last 72 hours maintained vigils at widely scattered points in the eastern sections of the city during a long series of more or less bloody encounters between gangs of zooters and servicemen.

Strife between the two factions arose as a result of beatings of individual sailors by juvenile street bands and, in two cases, assaults on women relatives of servicemen.

These attacks by zooters occurred over a period of several days. The counterattack did not last as long.

*None in Sight*

Main St. from First to Sixth, California and Temple Sts., Carmelita at Brooklyn and other focuses of habitual zoot-suit congregation all were empty of male zooters last evening, the authorities reported.

PRESENTATION—Maj. F. F. Pope presents cup to June Harris, who won Earl Carroll girls' beauty contest at benefit aquatic contest at Beverly-Wilshire Hotel.

## Baccalaureate Service Heard by 750 at U.C.L.A.

## Girls Compete in Benefit to Aid Officers

## Two Launched in 25 Hours

## William H. Allen Jr., 89, of Title Company, Dies

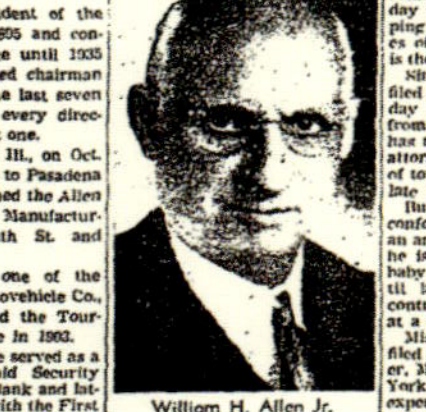

William H. Allen Jr.

## Chaplin Plans Legal Reply to Paternity Suit

## Salesman Dies of Beating Injuries

## Couple Will Reach 50th Milestone Today

## Californians on African Wounded List

## Alley Grading Set

## Lifeguards Can't Tell 'Zoot Suit' Bathers

## Home Picnic Attracts 3000

## Daily Dimout Reminder

COLLEGE DAYS NEARLY OVER FOR THEM—Members of U.C.L.A. summer graduating class march in procession to baccalaureate services in Royce Hall.

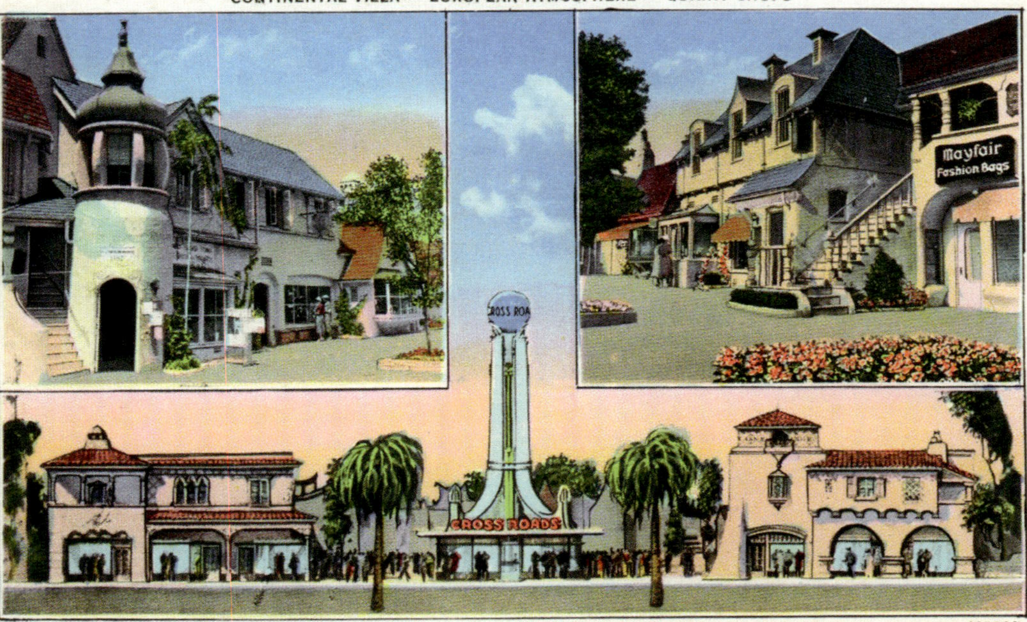


**LEFT:** Crossroads of the World on Sunset Boulevard (1936) was one of the earliest outdoor shopping malls. Its blue neon globe rotates to this day.

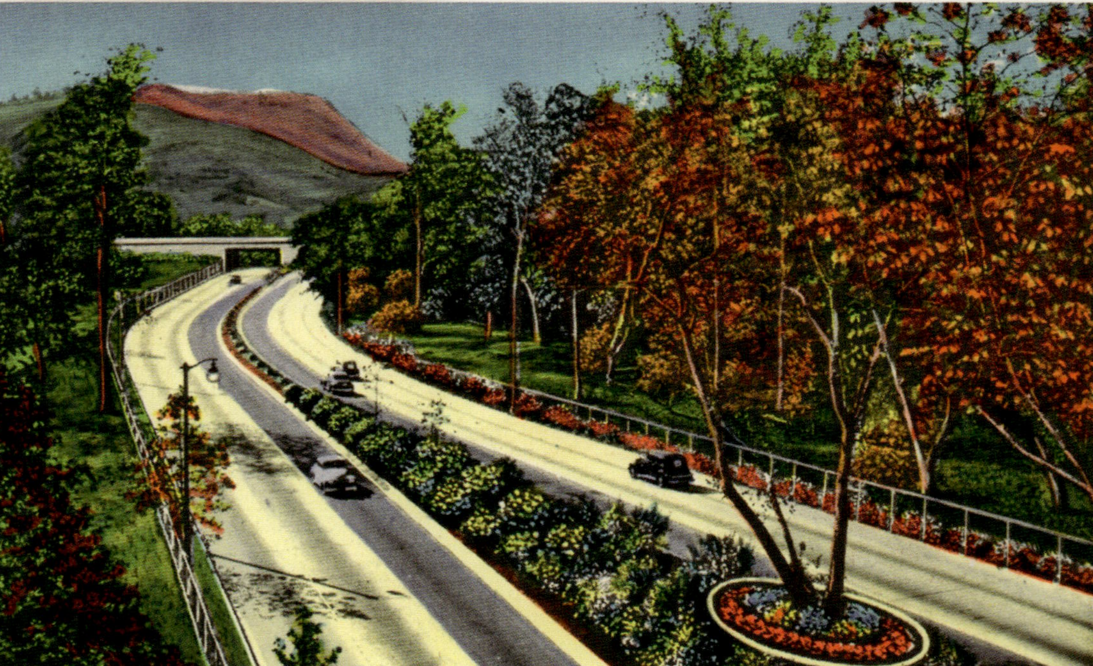

**RIGHT:** The Arroyo Seco Parkway (later known as the Pasadena Freeway until 2010, when the original name was restored) was one of the first "restricted access highways" in America. Note the charming landscaped center strip that made it a parkway.

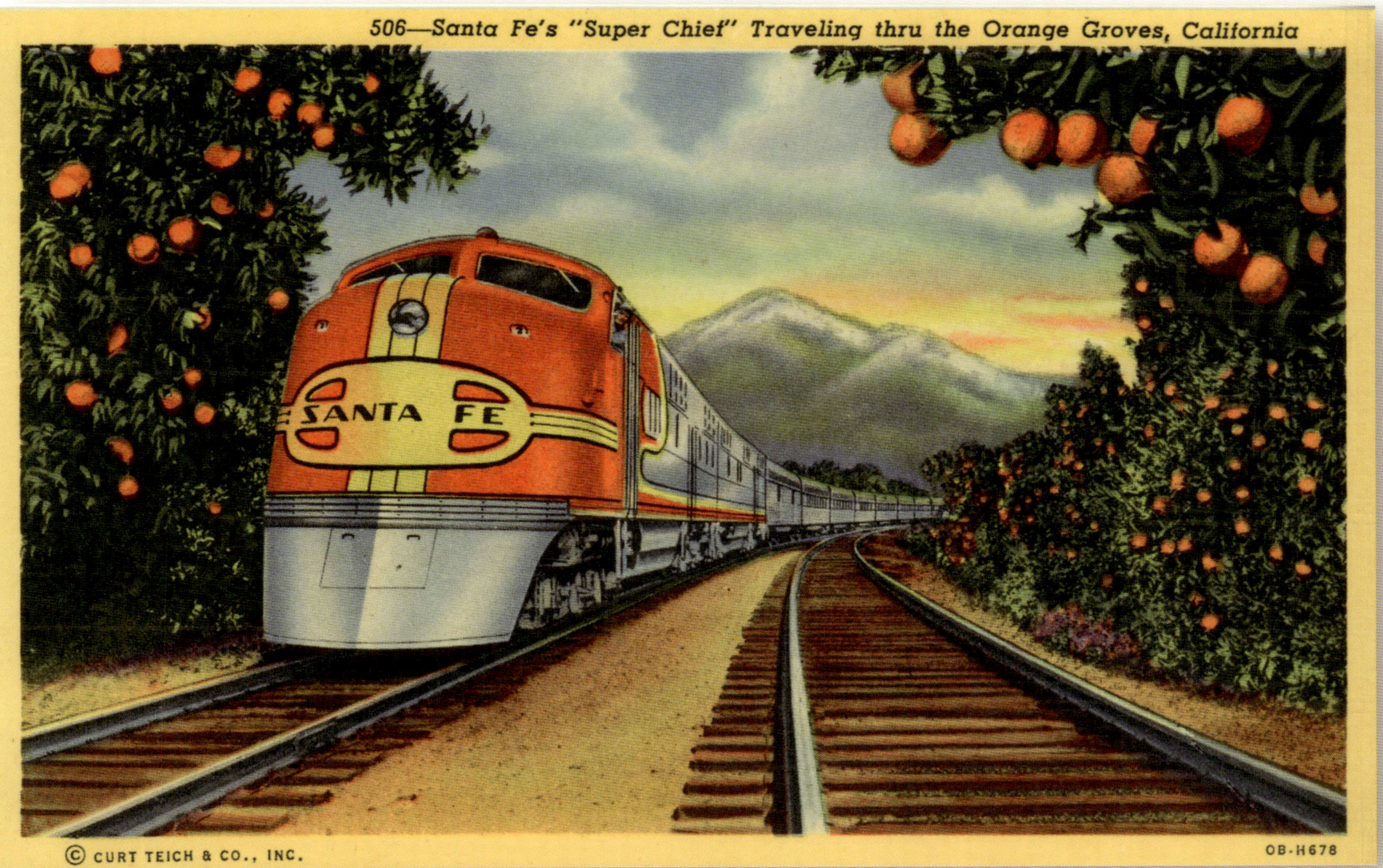


The Santa Fe *Super Chief* as it glides through the lovely orange groves that would be replaced by tract housing after the war.

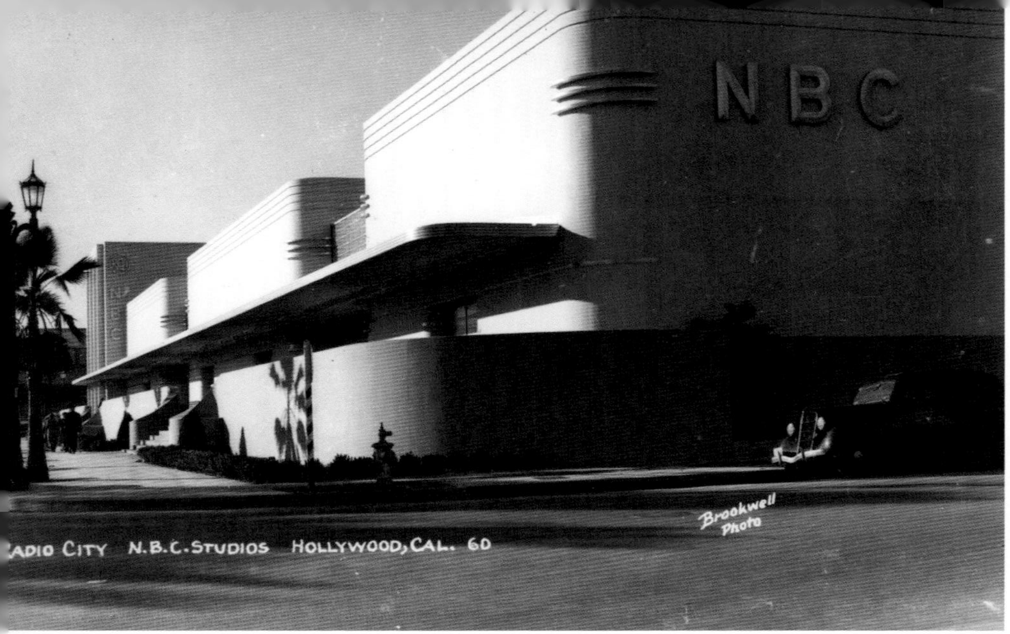

ADIO CITY N.B.C. STUDIOS HOLLYWOOD, CAL. 60

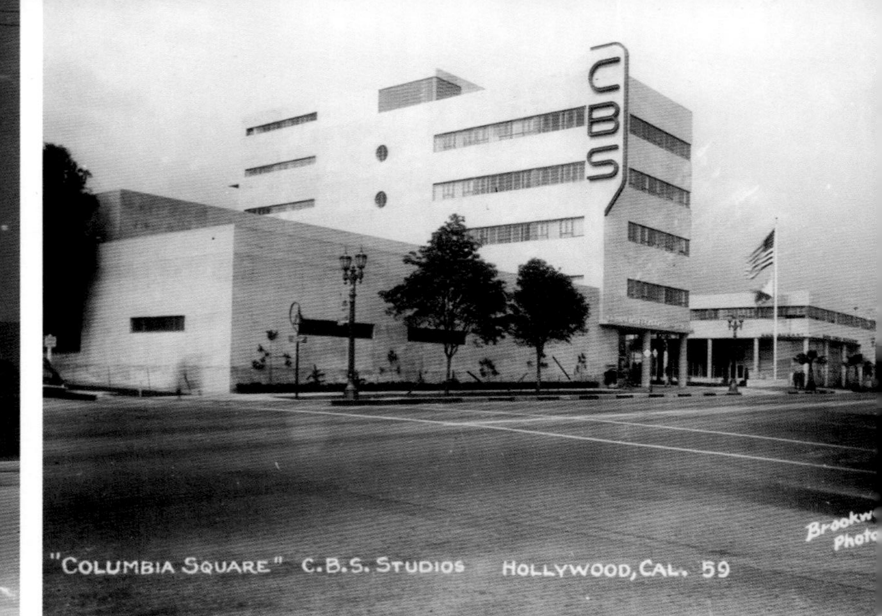

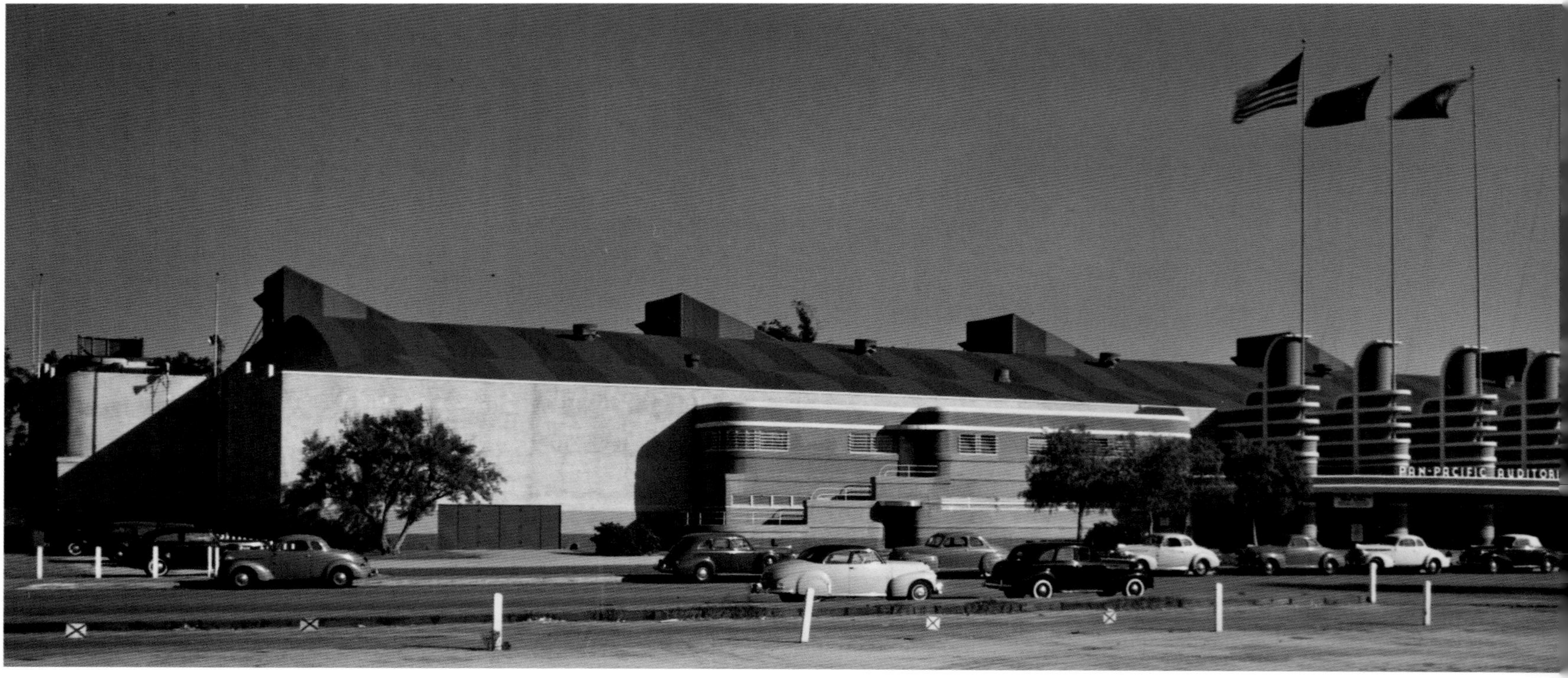

**FACING, LEFT:** The 1938 NBC Radio City at Sunset and Vine was a Streamline Moderne masterpiece.

**FACING, RIGHT:** CBS's Columbia Square radio studio in Hollywood (1938) was an International-style modern marvel designed by architect William Lescaze.

**RIGHT:** Architect S. Charles Lee's streamlined Academy Theater in Inglewood was completed in 1939. It is now a church.

**BELOW:** The peak of Streamline Moderne styling was the 1935 Pan-Pacific Auditorium by architects Wurdeman and Becket. Fire claimed the landmark in 1989.

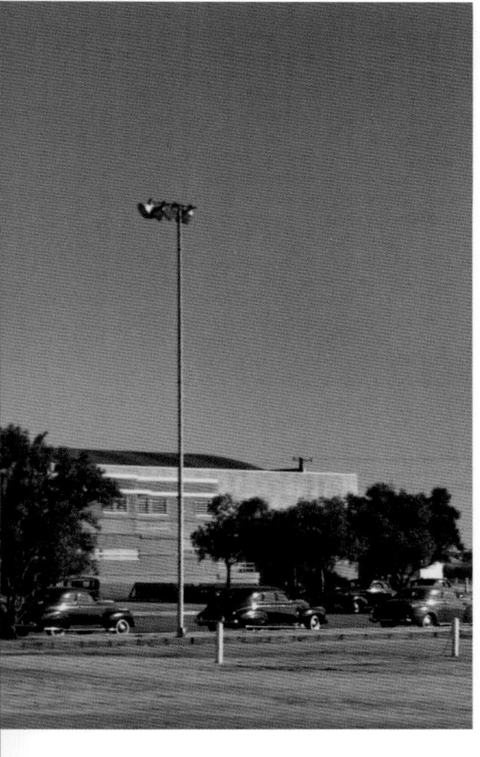

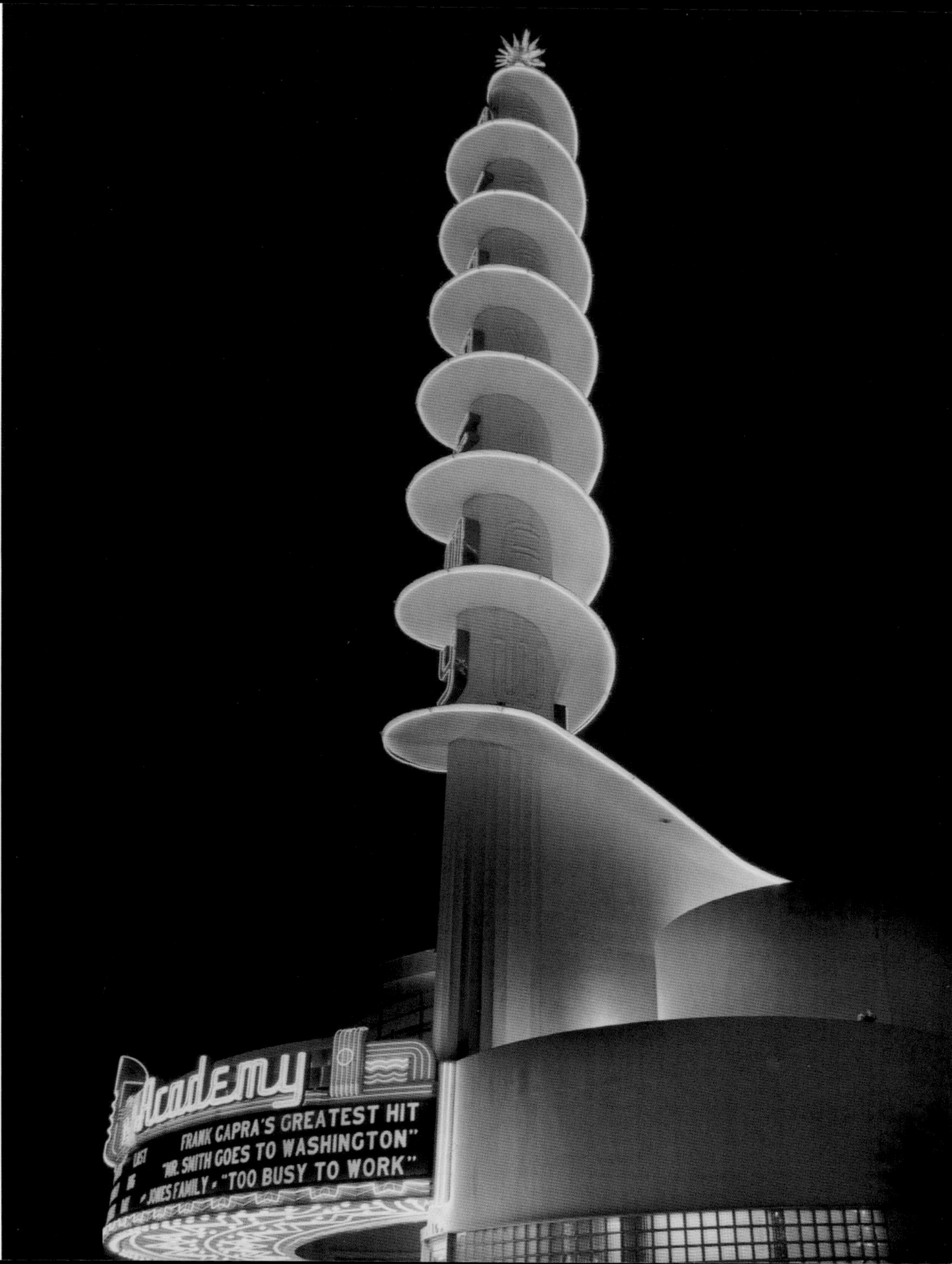

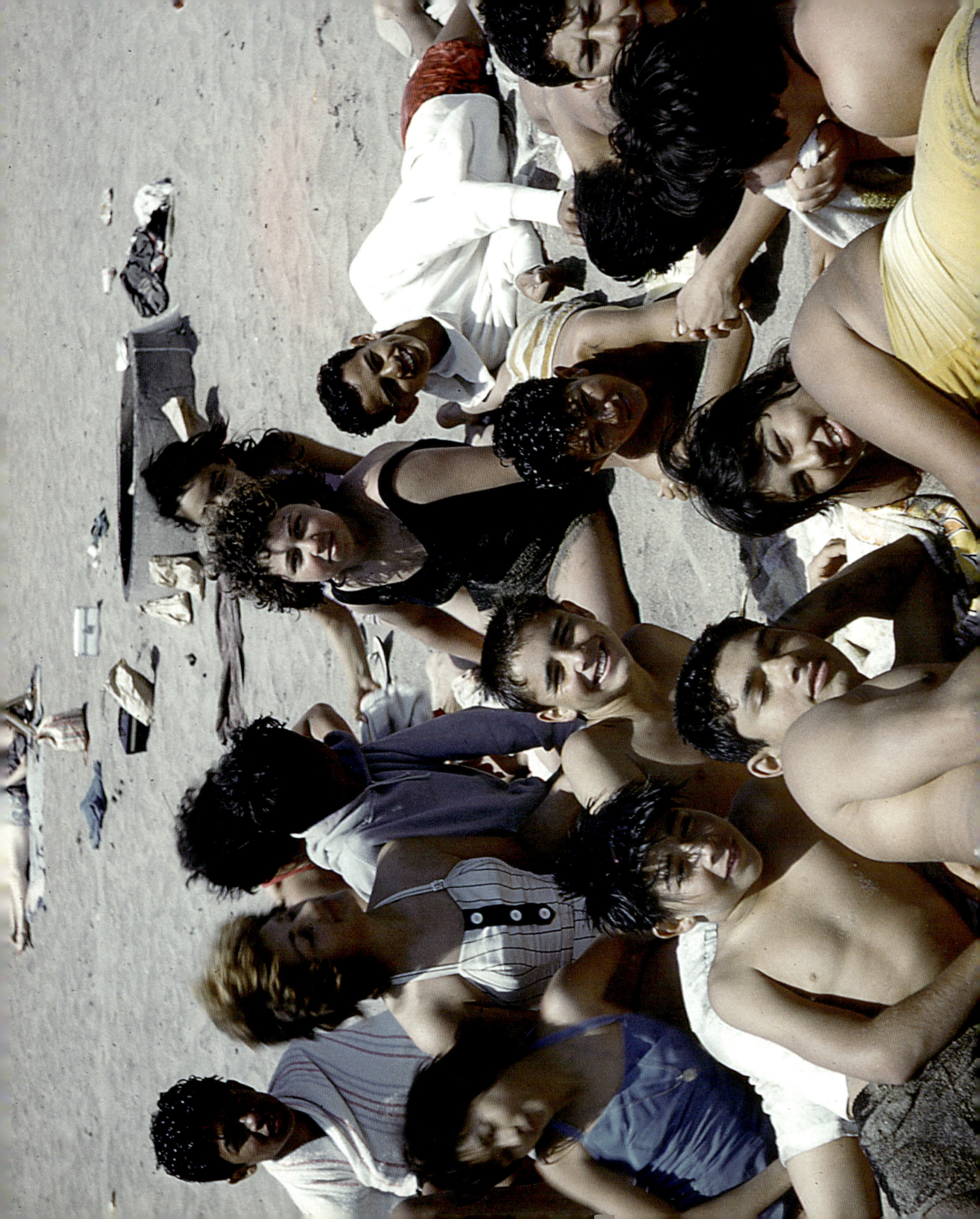

# Paradise

## 1945–1965

The two decades after World War II were the fulfillment of decades of hype and boosterism promoting Los Angeles as America's "City of the Future." Between 1940 and 1960, the population of Los Angeles County went from 2,785,643 to 6,039,834, an increase of 117 percent. As agriculture and oil production tapered off, the aerospace, electronics, and entertainment industries boomed; auto, tire, steel, appliance, furniture, and textile manufacturing flourished; and tract home development proliferated across the Southland.

Citrus groves made way for expanding San Gabriel Valley cities such as Covina, West Covina, Arcadia, Duarte, Azusa, Diamond Bar, Glendora, Rosemead, and San Dimas. The postwar housing boom in the San Fernando Valley (aka "the Valley") encompassed the districts of Encino, Sherman Oaks, Woodland Hills, Canoga Park, North Hollywood, Van Nuys, and many others. Returning veterans and working families qualified for low-interest loans, making home ownership for the average American possible for the first time since the start of the Great Depression.

**FACING:** On the beach with students from the predominantly Latino Lincoln High in 1961.

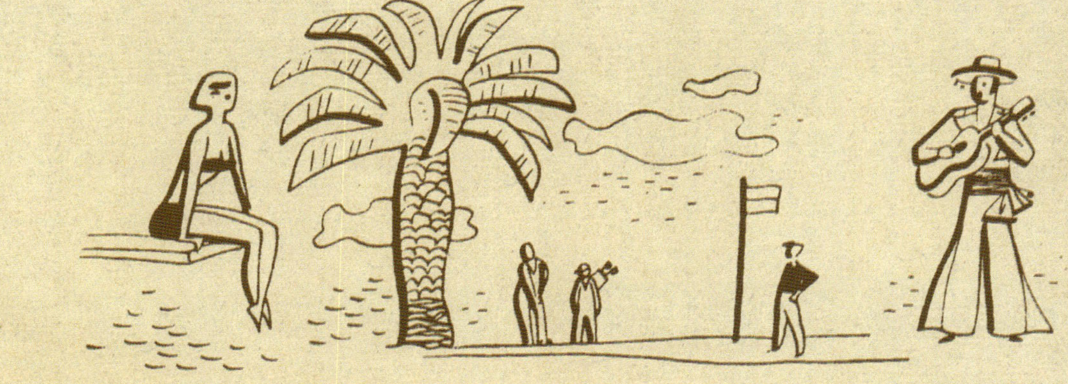

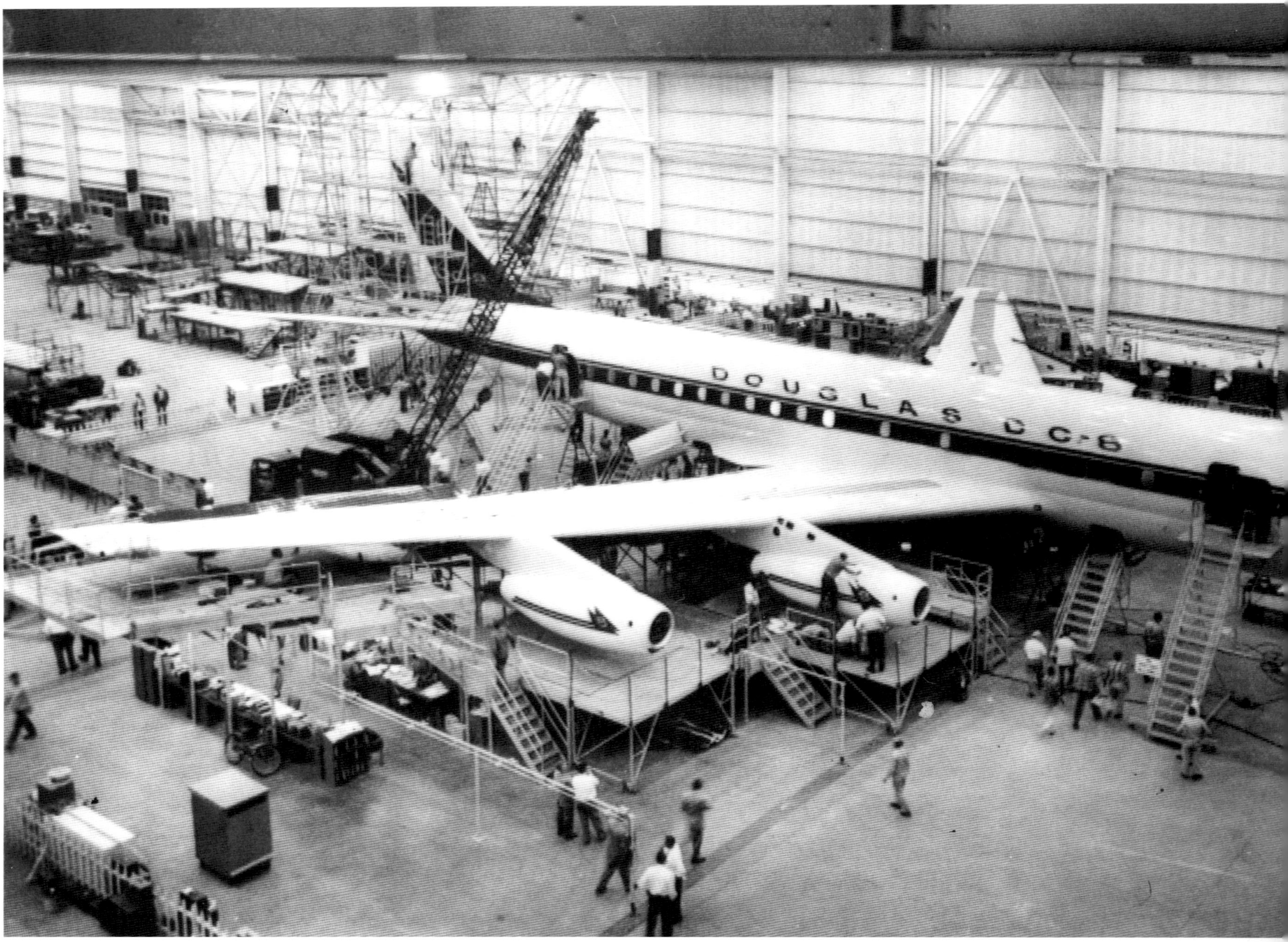

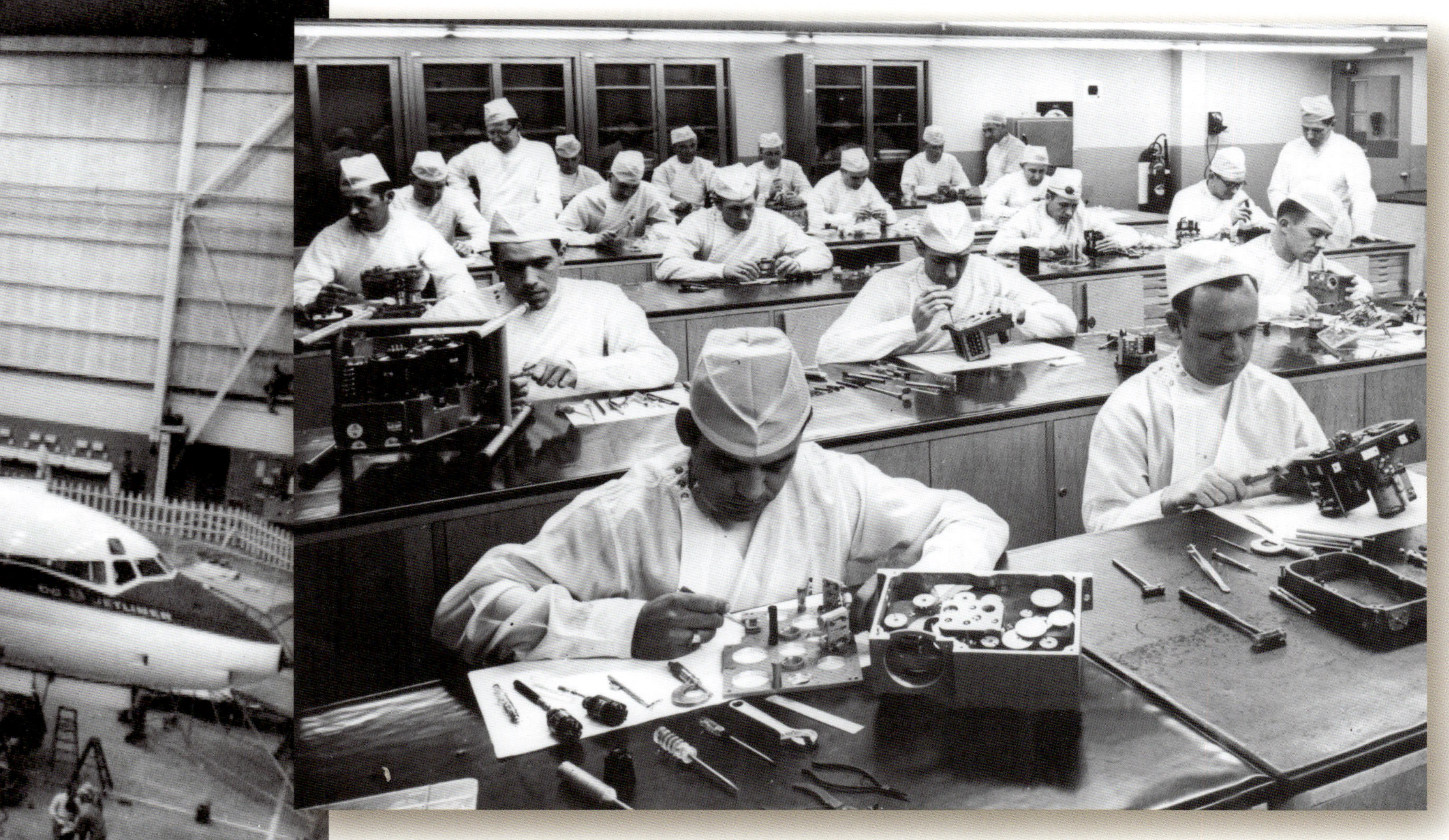

**LEFT:** Building the sleek new DC-8 jetliner at the Douglas Aircraft factory in Long Beach in 1958. Jets made air travel affordable for millions of Americans.

**ABOVE:** At North American Aviation's Autonetics Division in Downey, caps and gowns keep the assembly area dust free.

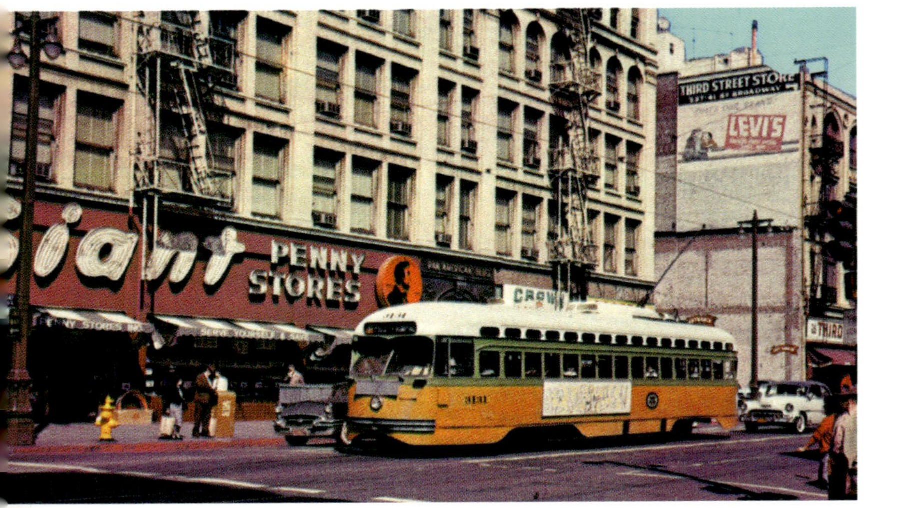

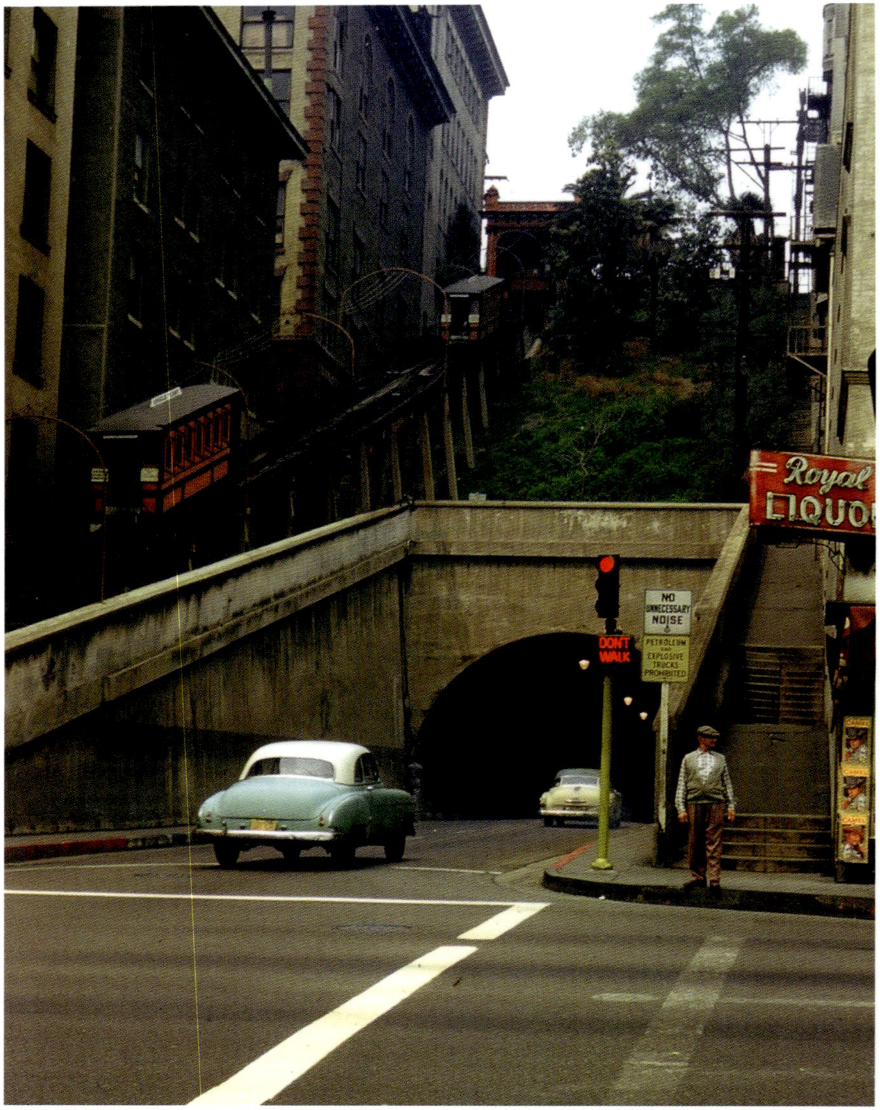

**ABOVE:** A Yellow Car on Broadway, just before the system was dismantled in 1963.

**RIGHT:** Angels Flight trolley before 1960s urban renewal razed every building in the photo.

**FACING, TOP LEFT:** Like many other San Gabriel Valley cities, tract housing replaced citrus groves in West Covina after World War II.

**FACING, BOTTOM LEFT:** A new suburban Food Giant, "where every penny counts."

**FACING, RIGHT:** Nese Realty's dynamic sales team in Highland Park.

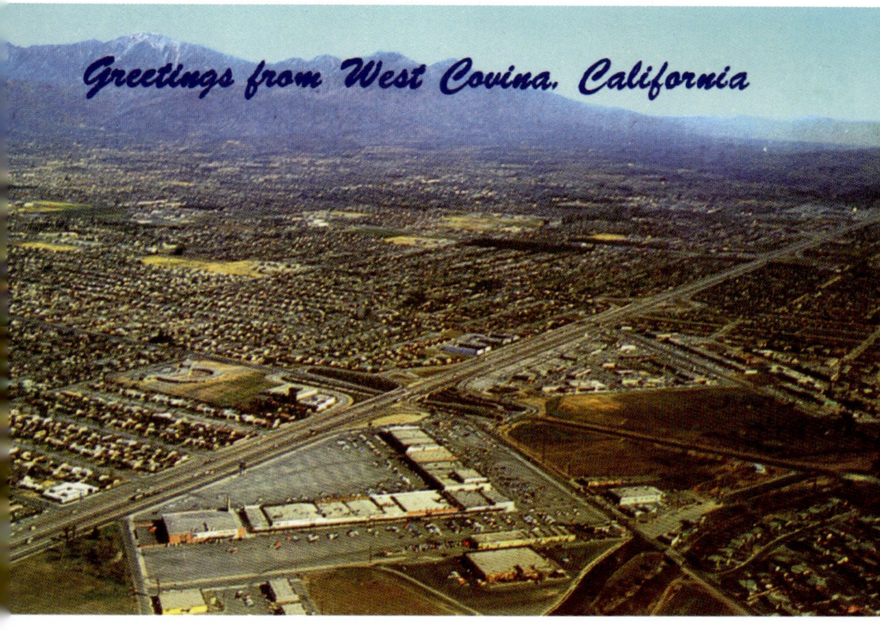
Greetings from West Covina, California

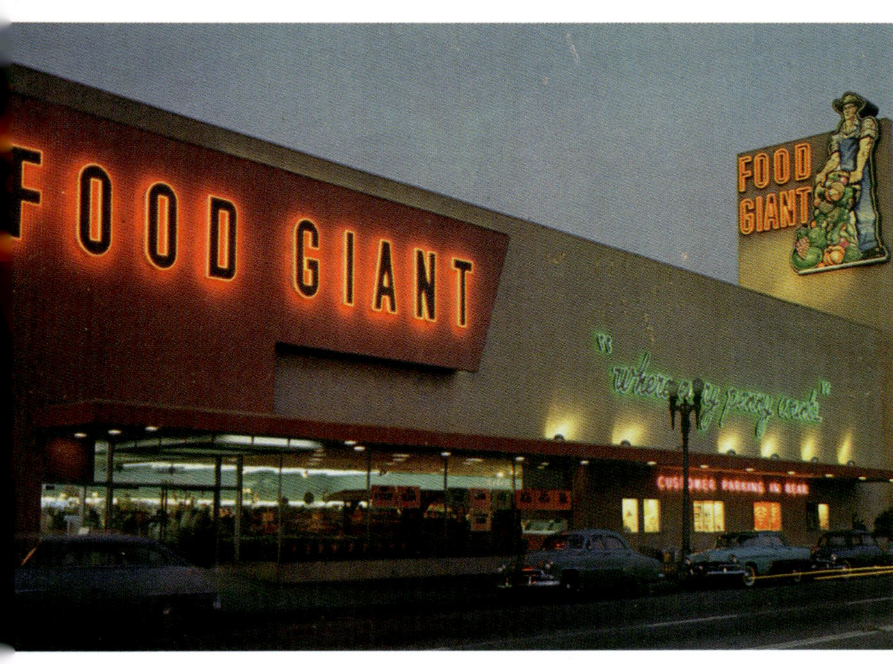
FOOD GIANT
FOOD
GIANT
"where every penny counts"
CUSTOMER PARKING IN REAR

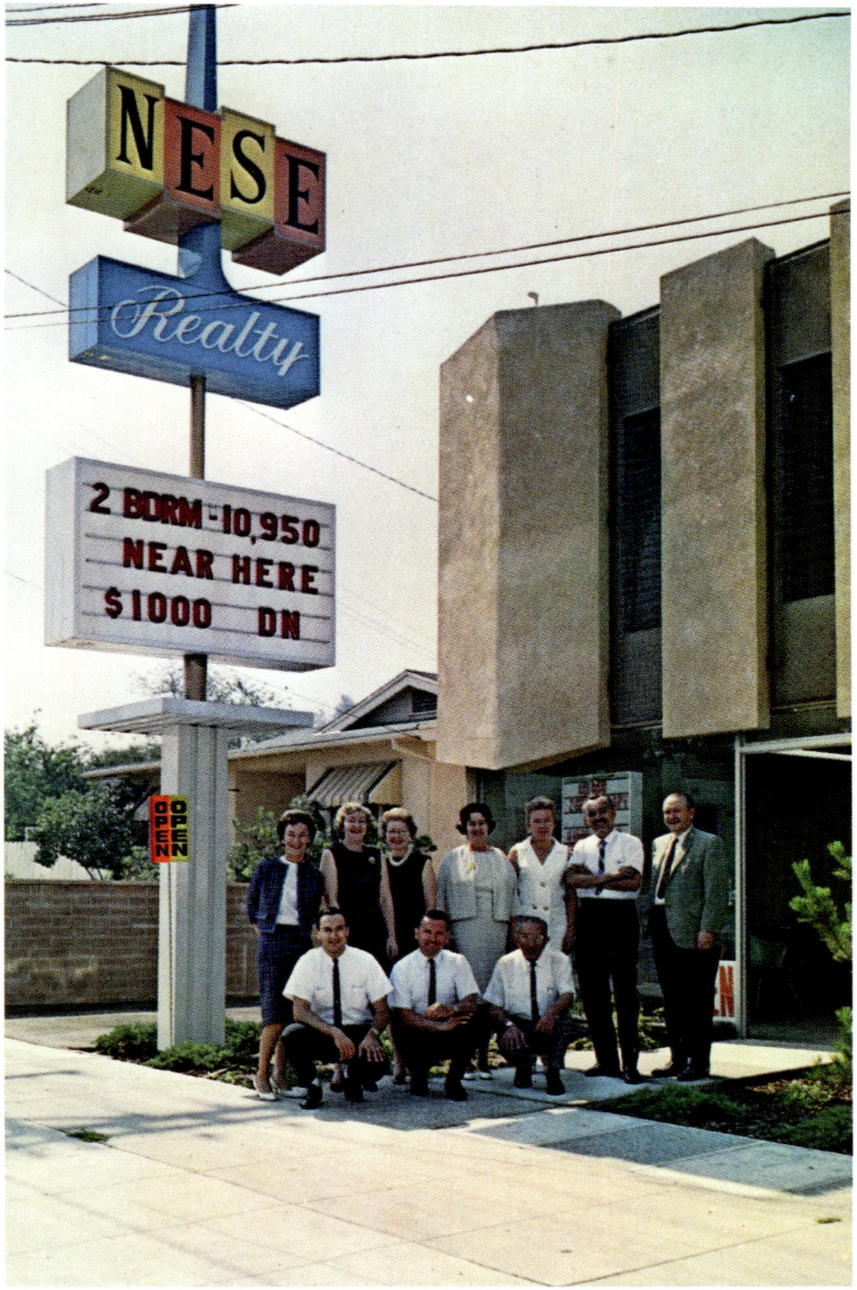

NESE
Realty
2 BDRM-10,950
NEAR HERE
$1000 DN
OPEN
OPEN

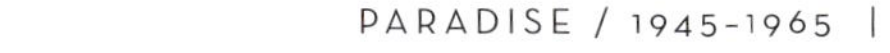

Of the postwar suburban boomtowns, perhaps Lakewood was the most iconic. Located just north of Long Beach on what had been lima bean fields, 17,500 houses were built between 1949, when the tract broke ground, and 1953, when the project was completed. In the center of this planned community was a massive new shopping center, one of America's largest. With a population of 70,000, its residents voted to incorporate as the City of Lakewood in 1954.

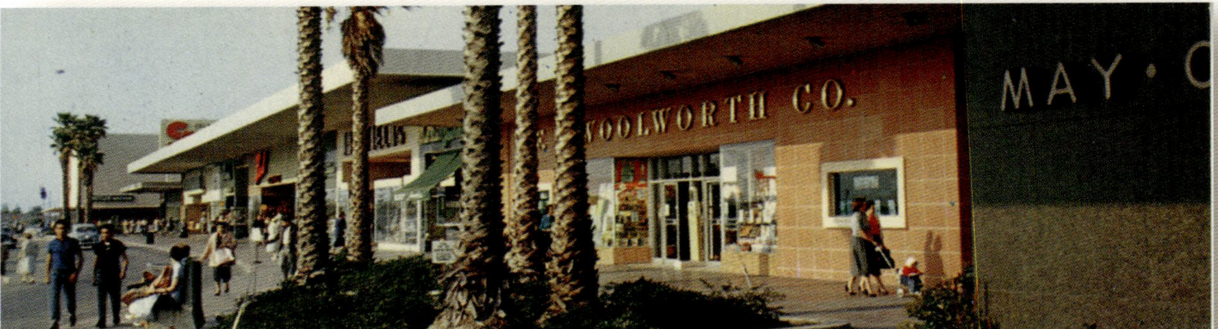


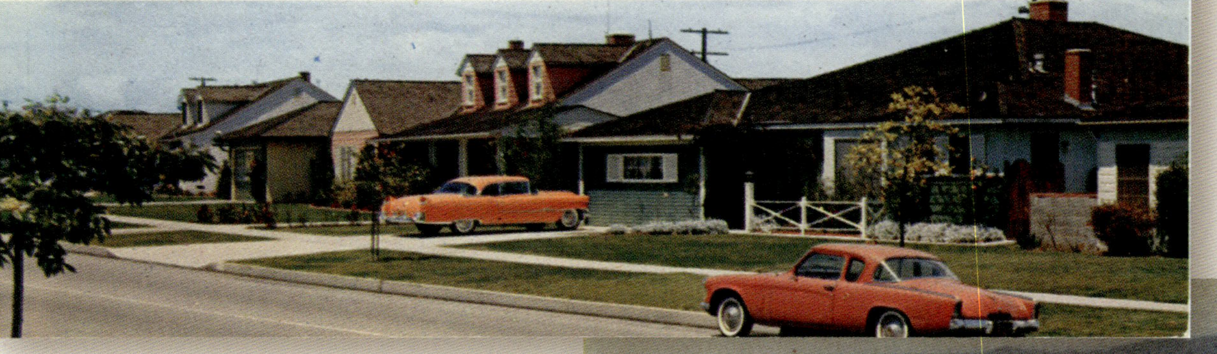


**ABOVE:** In five years, lima bean fields were transformed into the city of Lakewood, with 17,500 houses.

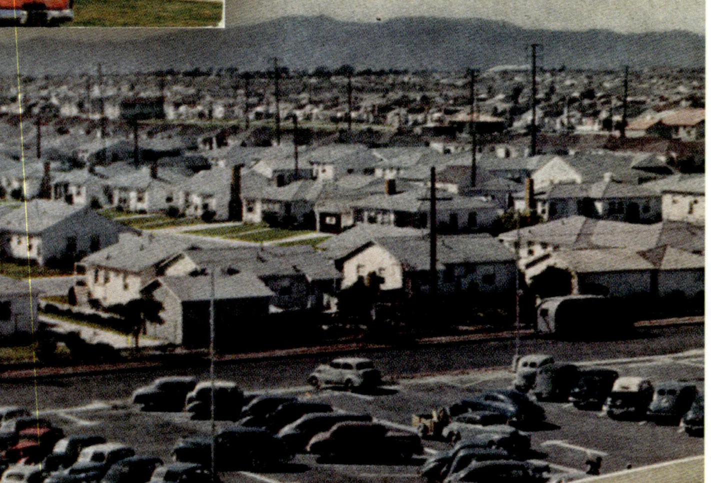

**RIGHT:** Westchester was another postwar boomtown.

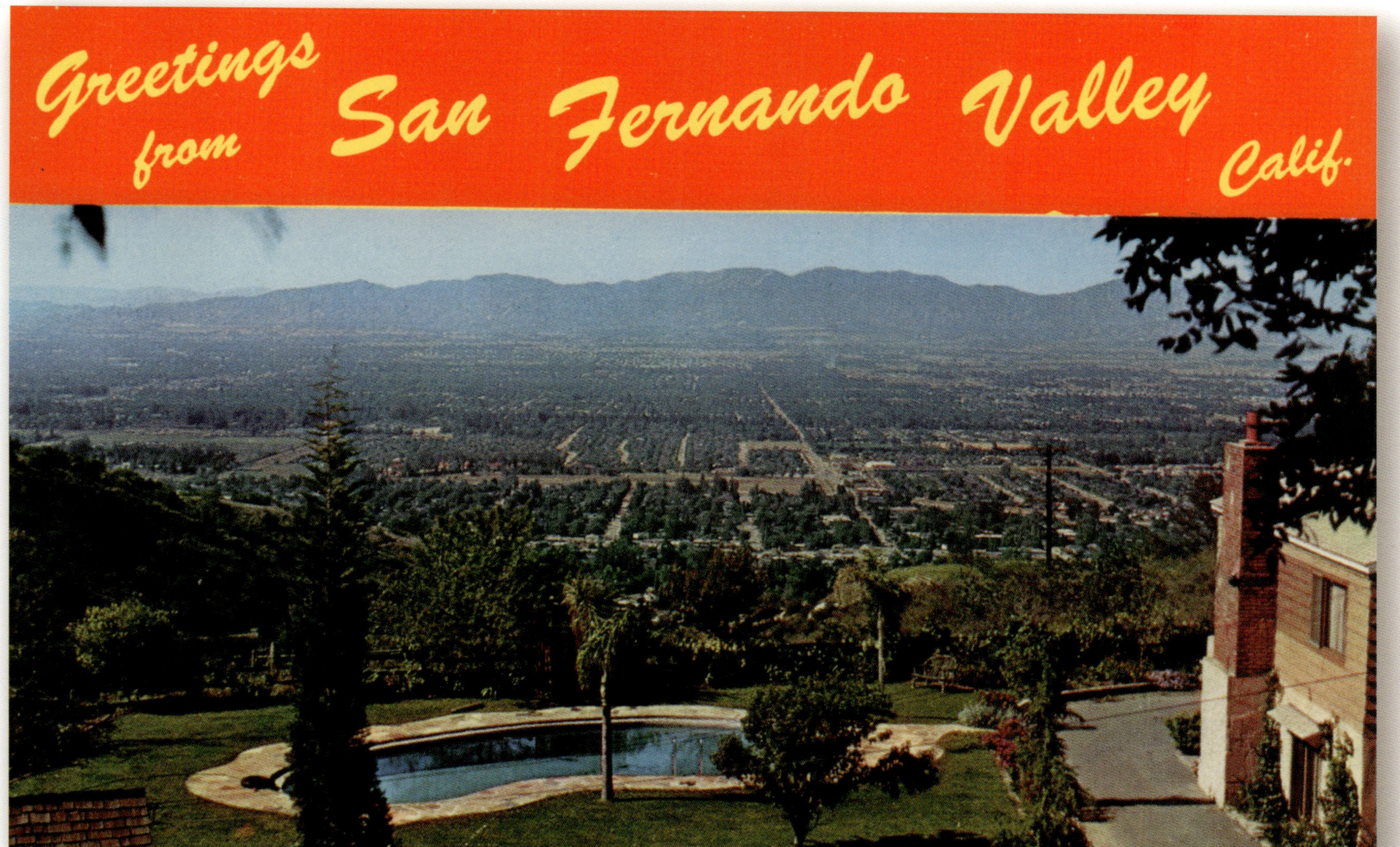


The postwar housing boom in the San Fernando Valley encompassed the districts of Encino, Sherman Oaks, Woodland Hills, Canoga Park, North Hollywood, Van Nuys, and many others.

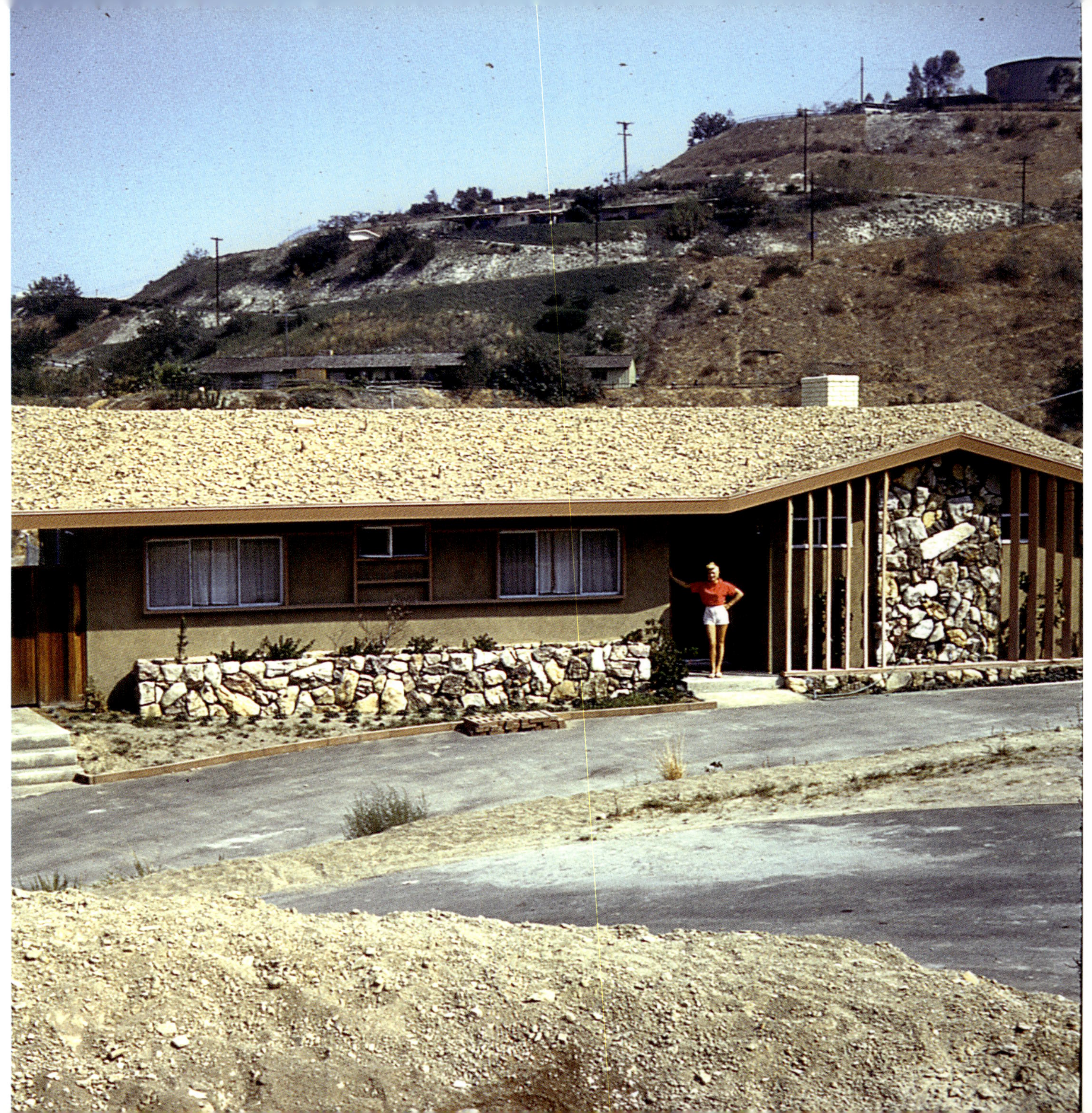

Doris shows off her new digs.

Postwar Los Angeles wasn't yet ready for high-style Modern housing. Instead, mass-produced, low-cost residential tracts consisted of minimal stucco boxes with traditional elements such as hipped roofs and wood-framed windows. Ranch was another popular style, which harkened back to the Old West. Low and sprawling, Ranch houses were usually one story with shingle cladding, wood windows with shutters, deep overhanging eaves, and exposed rafters.

**BELOW:** A typical 1950s Southern California suburban Ranch house.

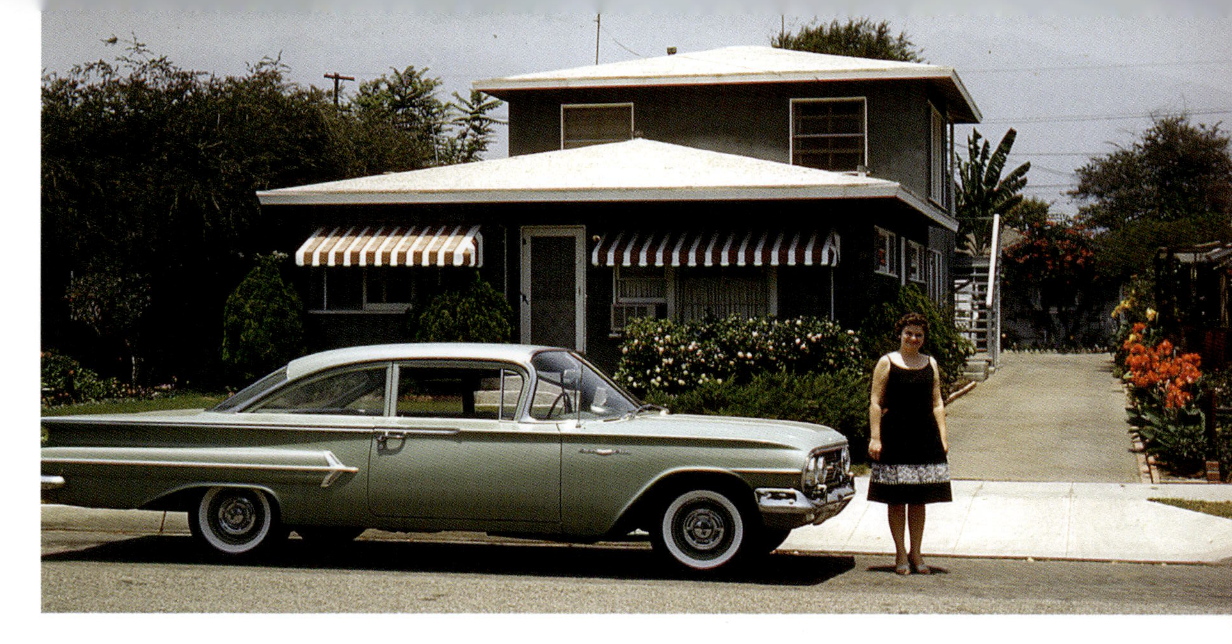

**RIGHT:** Donette with her beloved 1960 Chevy Bel Air at her Arcadia duplex.

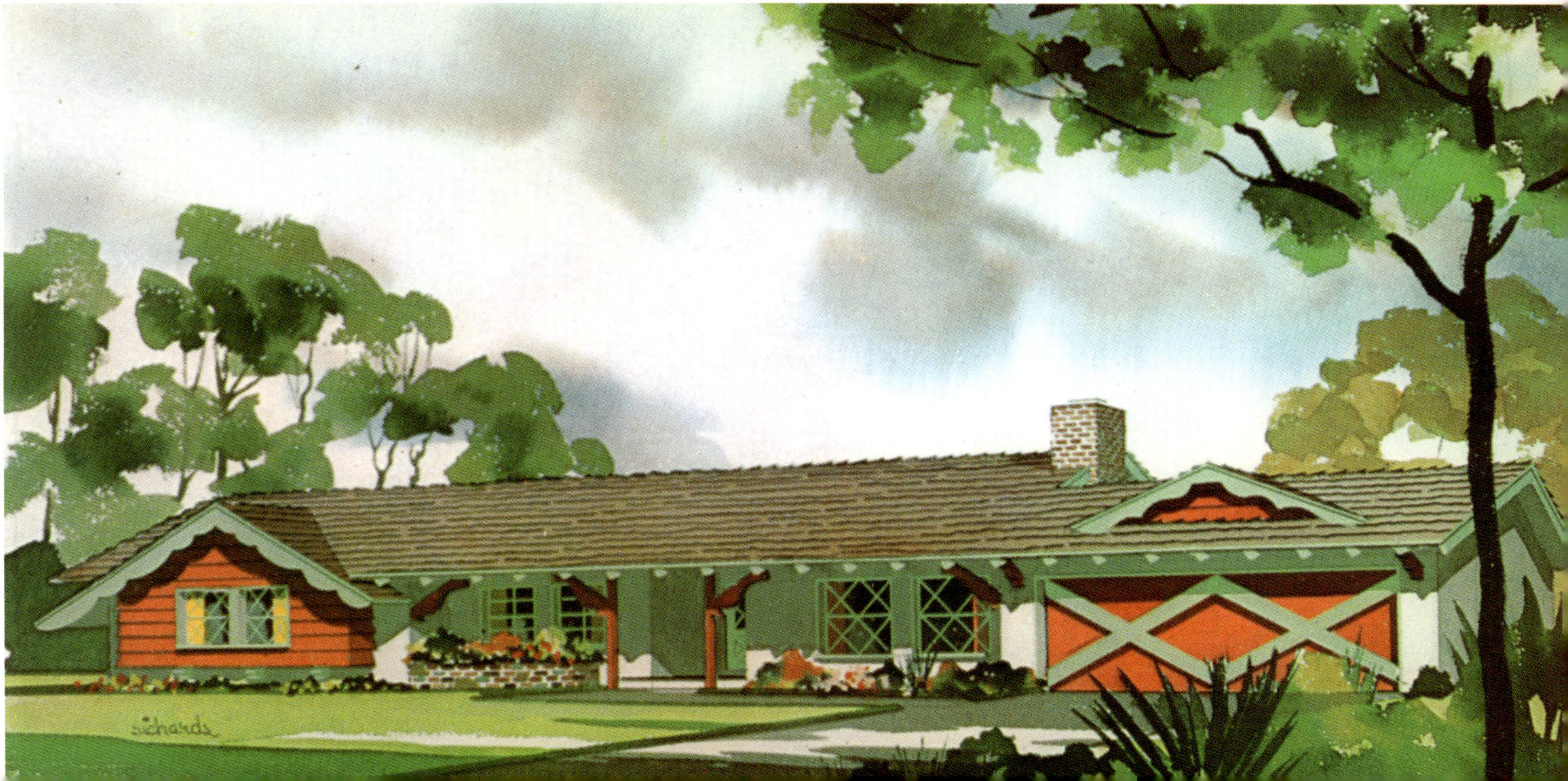

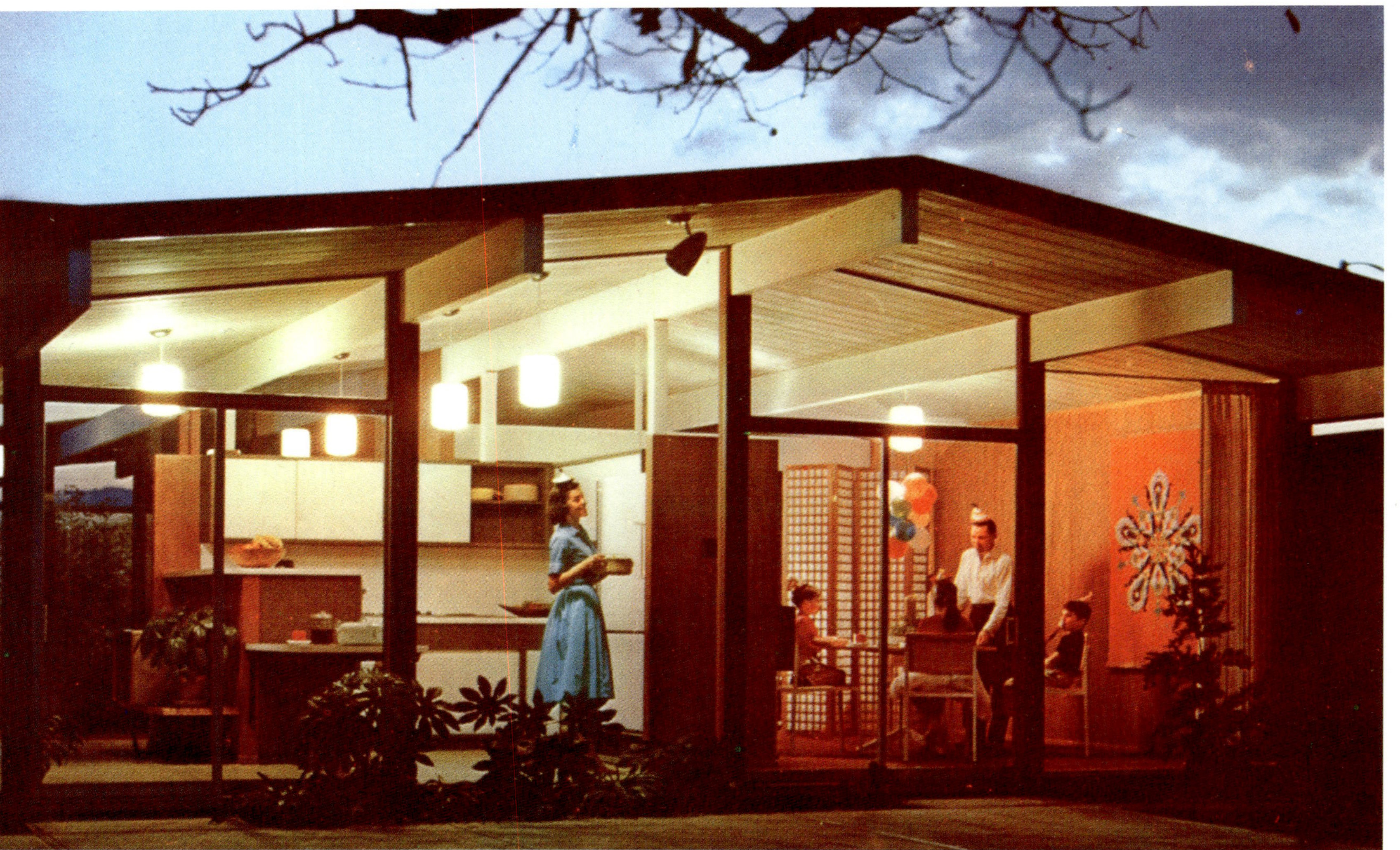

**ABOVE:** Avant-garde buyers opted for the architect-designed Midcentury Modern tract homes of developer Joseph Eichler, which defined indoor-outdoor living for the middle class.

For more daring buyers, the region's talented Modern architects designed custom homes with clean lines, flat or low-pitched roofs, open floor plans, and sliding glass doors for indoor-outdoor living. Similarly, commercial buildings of the era were often architecturally bold. The Modern designs of office buildings, shopping centers, car dealerships, banks, and restaurants expressed the bright, optimistic future that defined postwar Los Angeles.

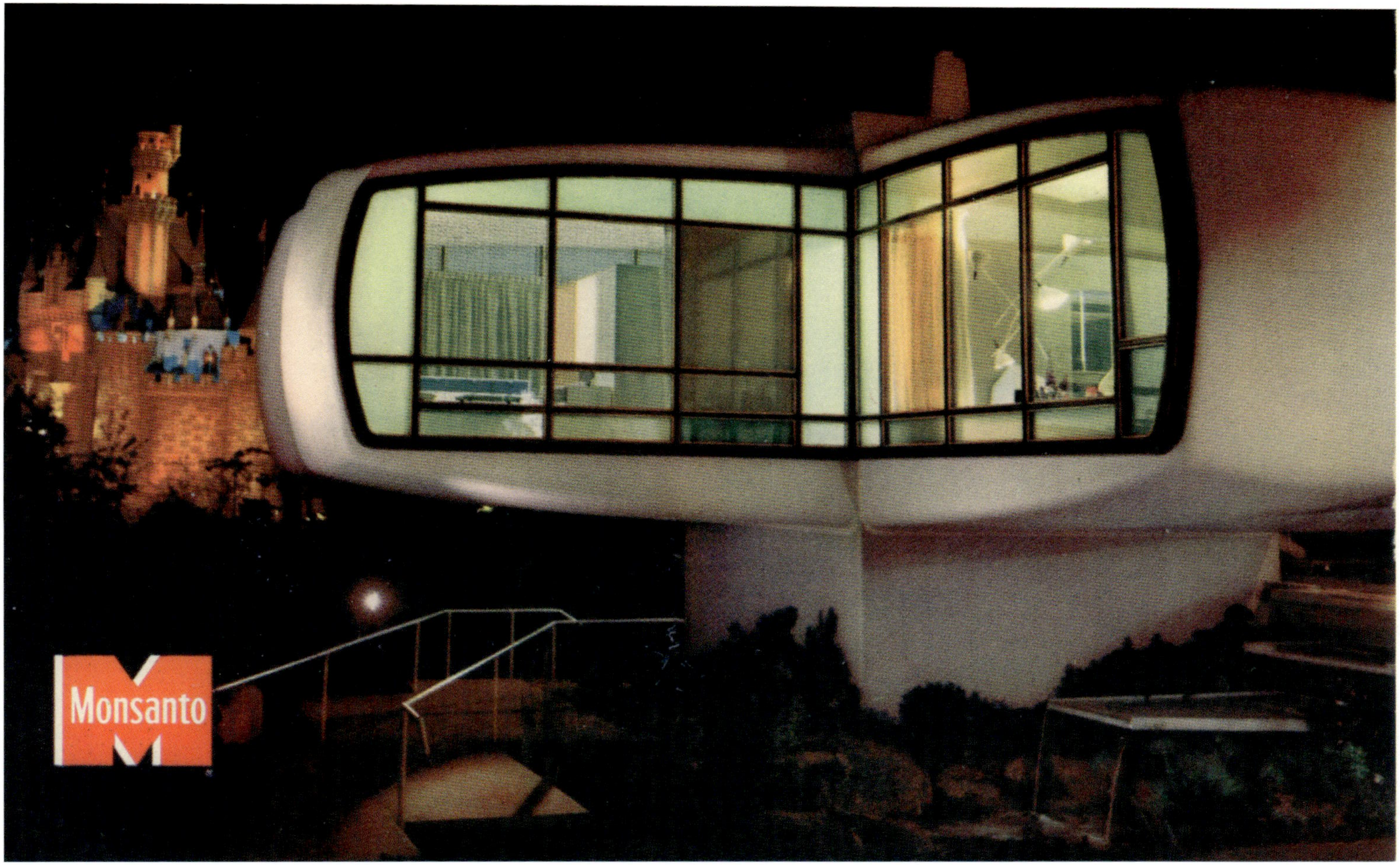

**ABOVE:** Monsanto Company promoted the all-plastic "House of the Future" at Disneyland's Tomorrowland. The future didn't turn out quite that way.

**RIGHT:** An outdoor classroom in the California sun.

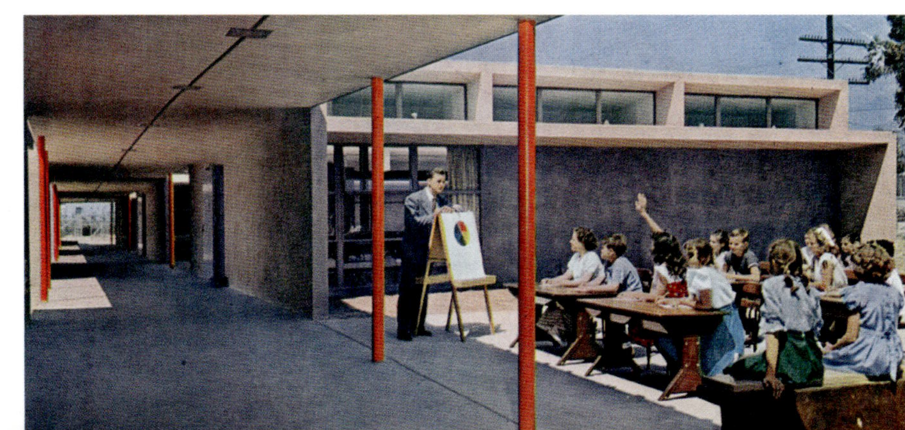

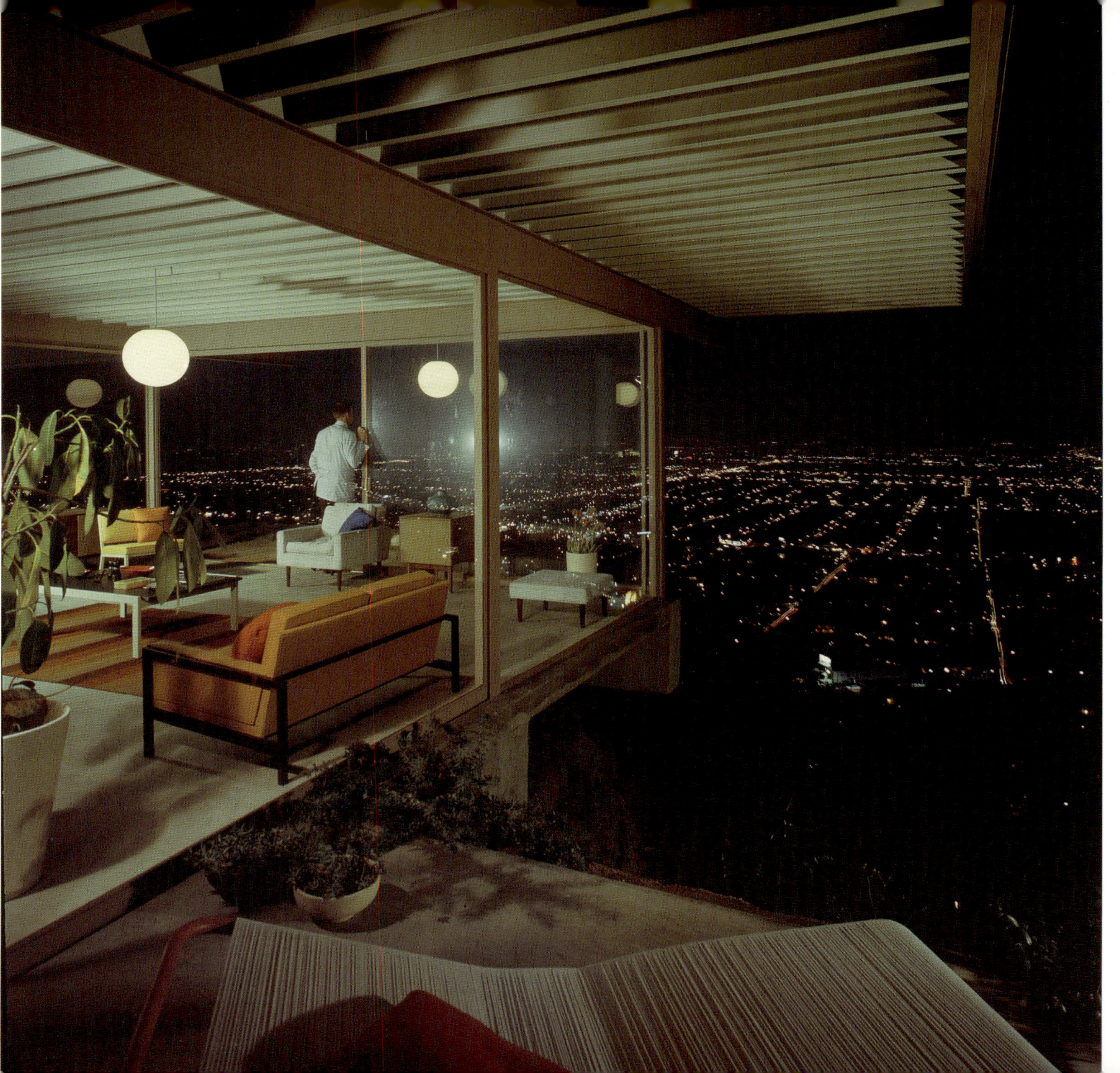

Famed photographer Julius Shulman documented these Midcentury Modern homes by talented young architects who experimented with new materials, floor plans, and concepts for contemporary living: the 1960 Case Study House #22 by Pierre Koenig (facing), and the 1960 Chemosphere House by John Lautner (above).

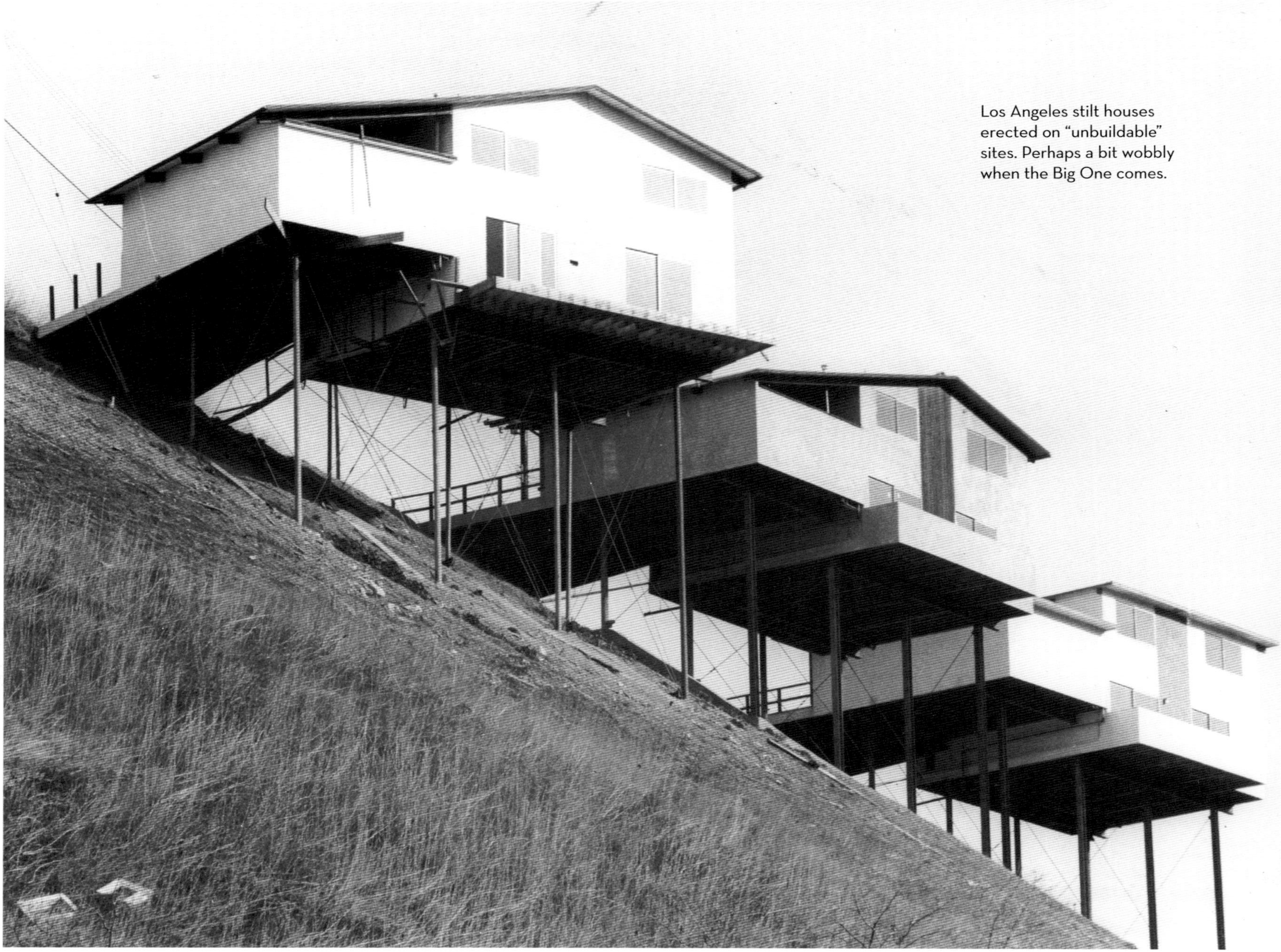

Los Angeles stilt houses erected on “unbuildable” sites. Perhaps a bit wobbly when the Big One comes.

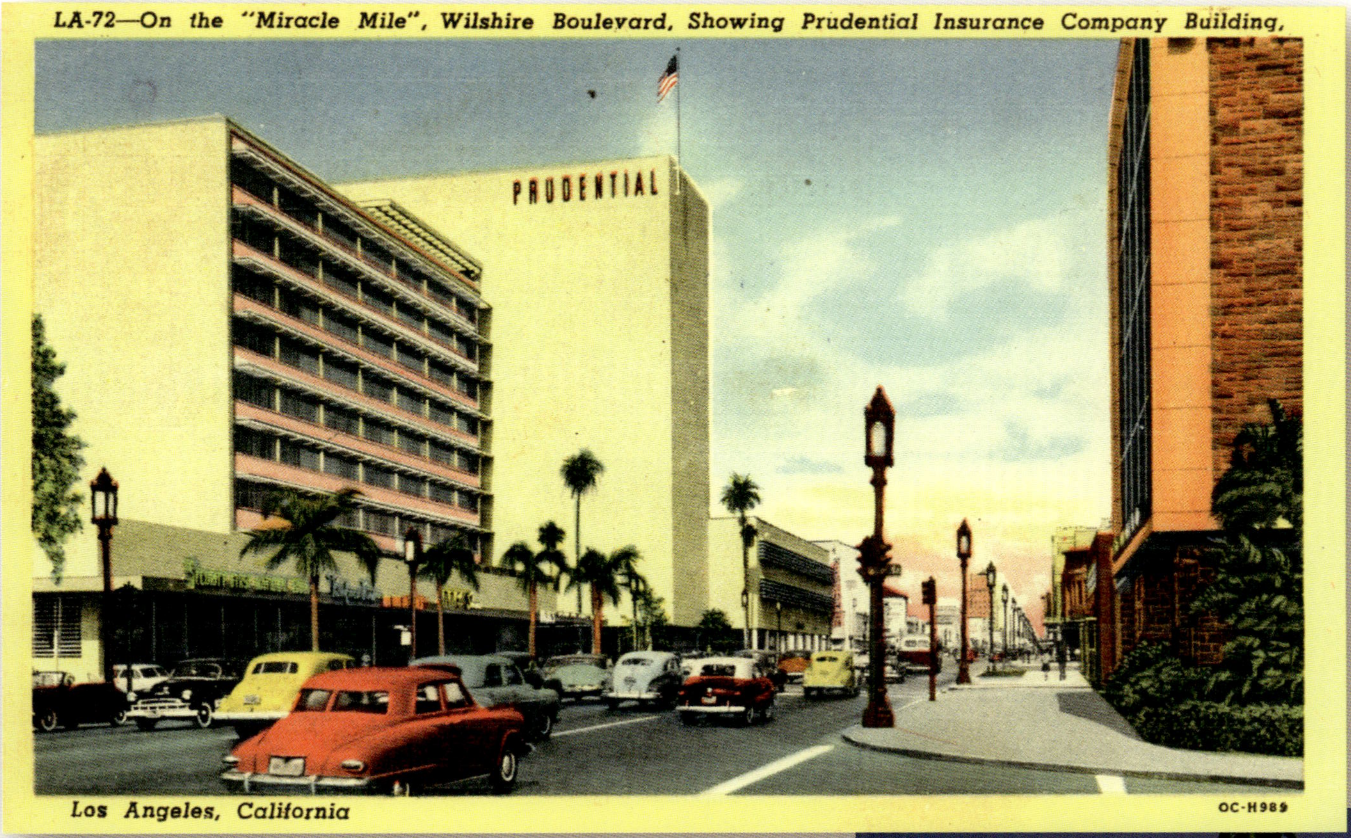

LA-72—On the "Miracle Mile", Wilshire Boulevard, Showing Prudential Insurance Company Building,

PRUDENTIAL

Los Angeles, California

OC-H989

**ABOVE:** Wurdeman and Becket's 1948 Prudential Building on Wilshire Boulevard's Miracle Mile was one of the earliest Modern office buildings in Los Angeles.

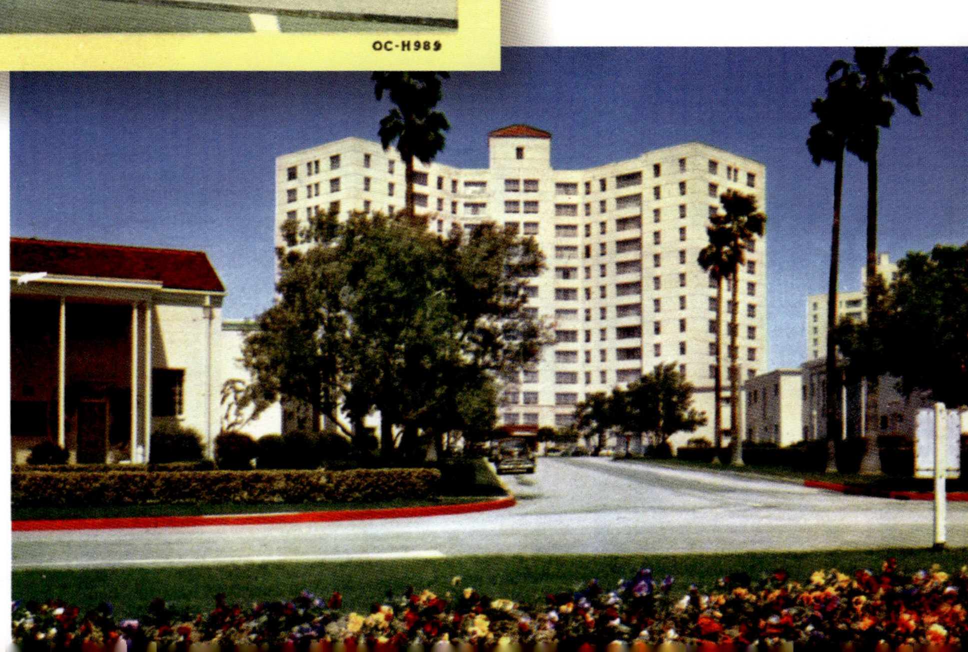

**RIGHT:** Park La Brea, a sprawling apartment complex in Los Angeles's Fairfax District. The 31 Colonial Modern townhouses were built in 1941. The 18 X-shaped high-rises appeared in 1948.

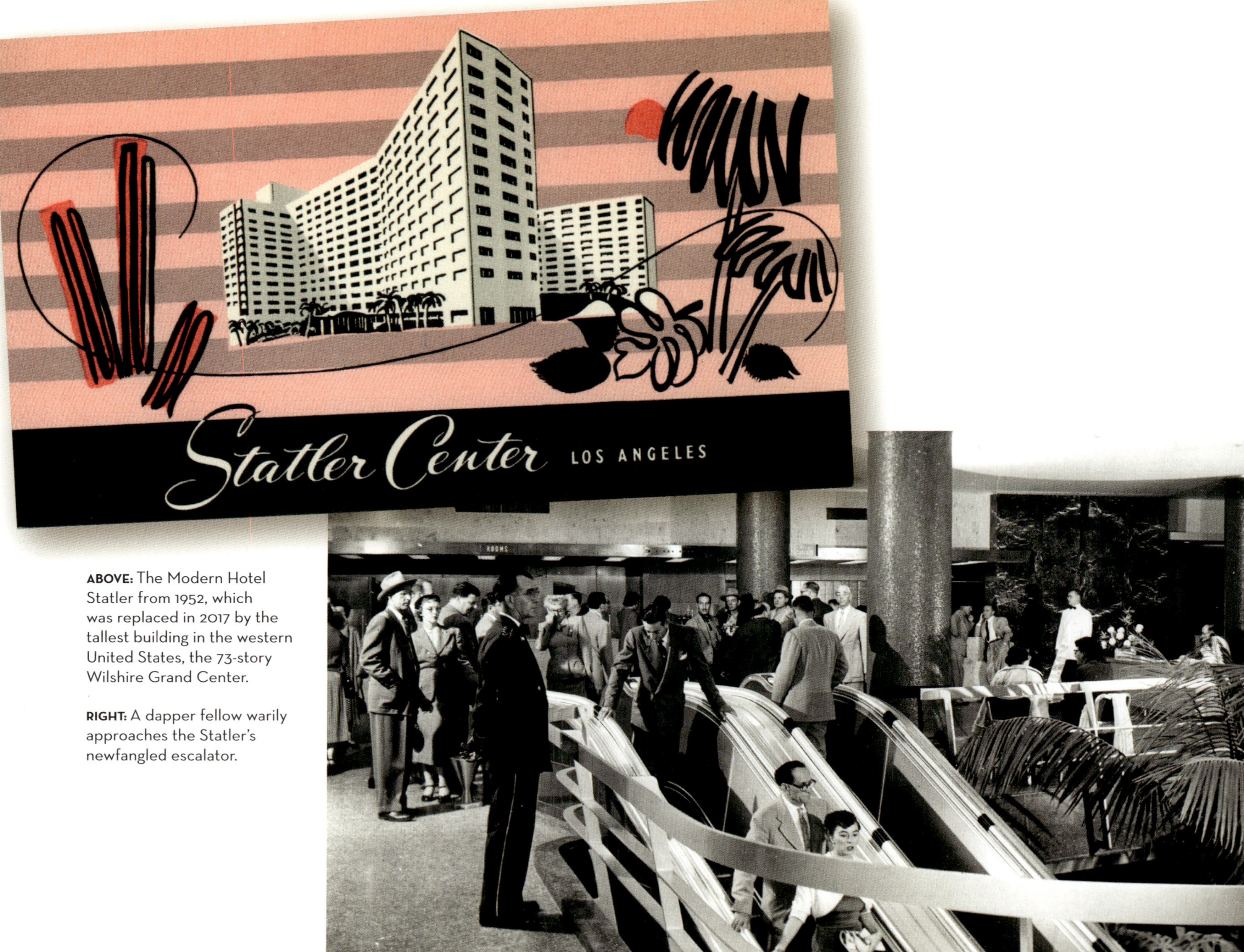


**ABOVE:** The Modern Hotel Statler from 1952, which was replaced in 2017 by the tallest building in the western United States, the 73-story Wilshire Grand Center.

**RIGHT:** A dapper fellow warily approaches the Statler's newfangled escalator.

“From Television City in Hollywood” was the voice-over introducing many TV shows taped there. Architect William Pereira’s ultramodern design was completed in 1952.

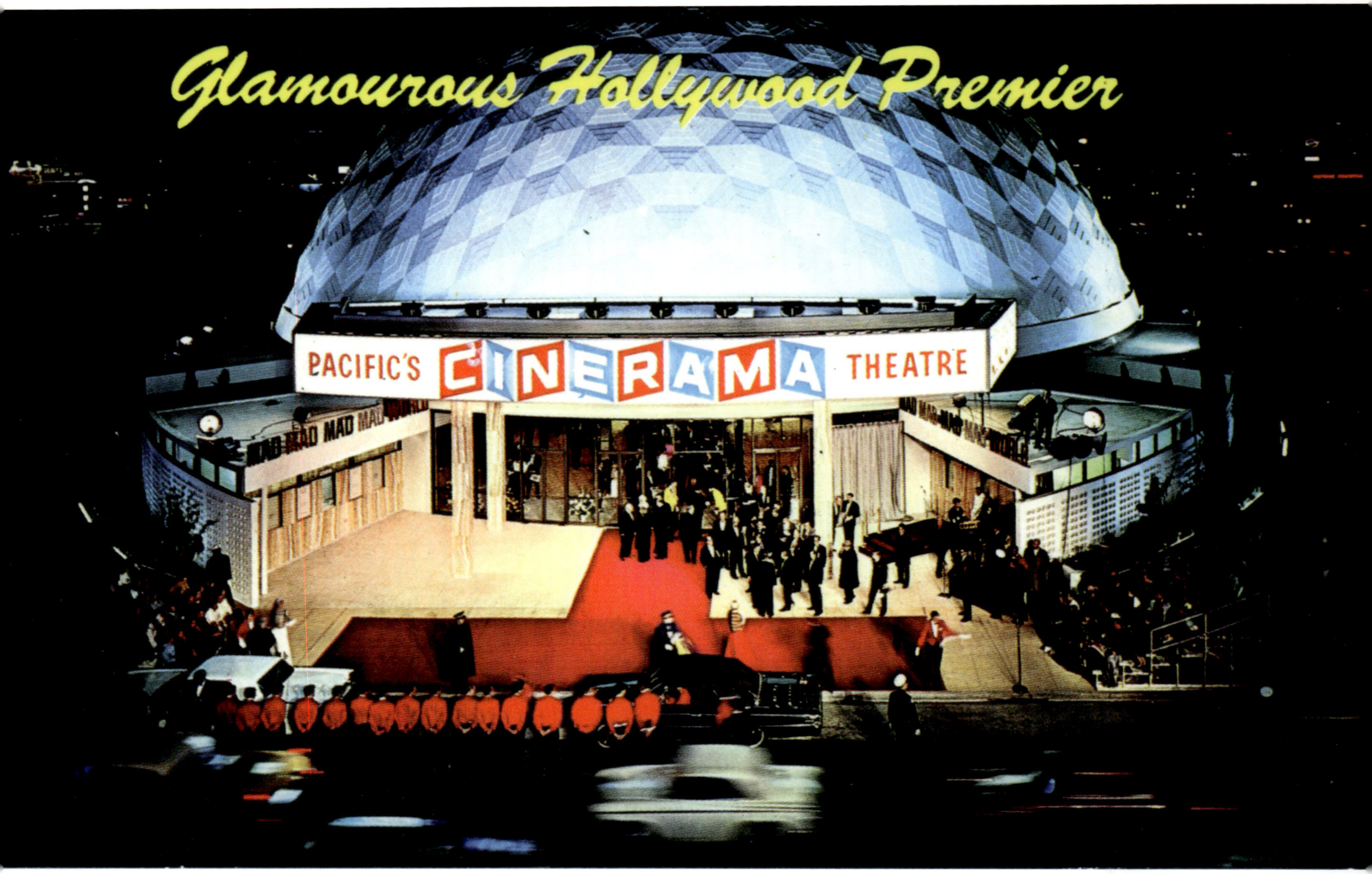

Hollywood's Cinerama Dome at its opening in 1963.

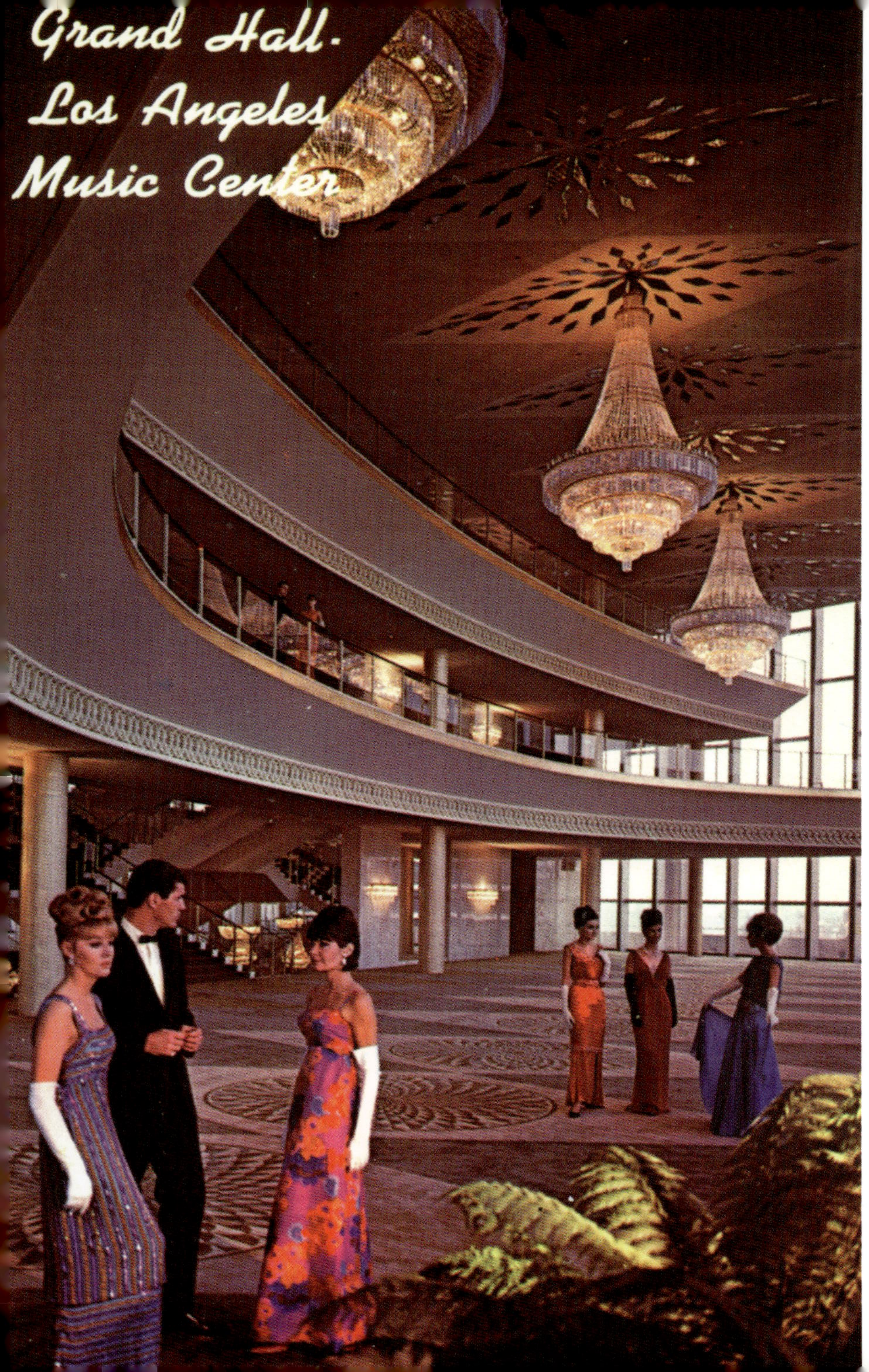

Grand Hall.
Los Angeles
Music Center

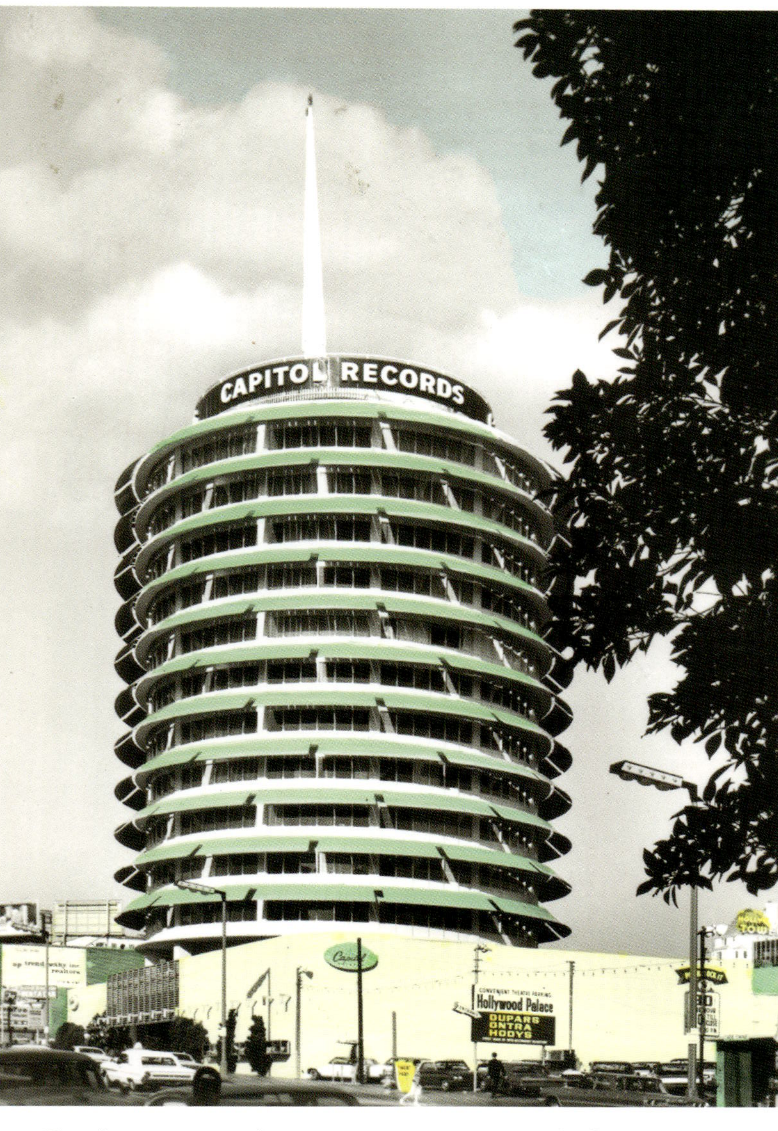


**LEFT:** The elegant Los Angeles Music Center affirmed the city's status as an important cultural center when completed in 1964. It was designed by Welton Becket & Associates, the architects of Hollywood's Capitol Records Tower and Cinerama Dome.

**ABOVE:** The futuristic 1956 Capitol Records Tower was one of the world's first round office buildings. The light atop its spire spells "Hollywood" in Morse code.

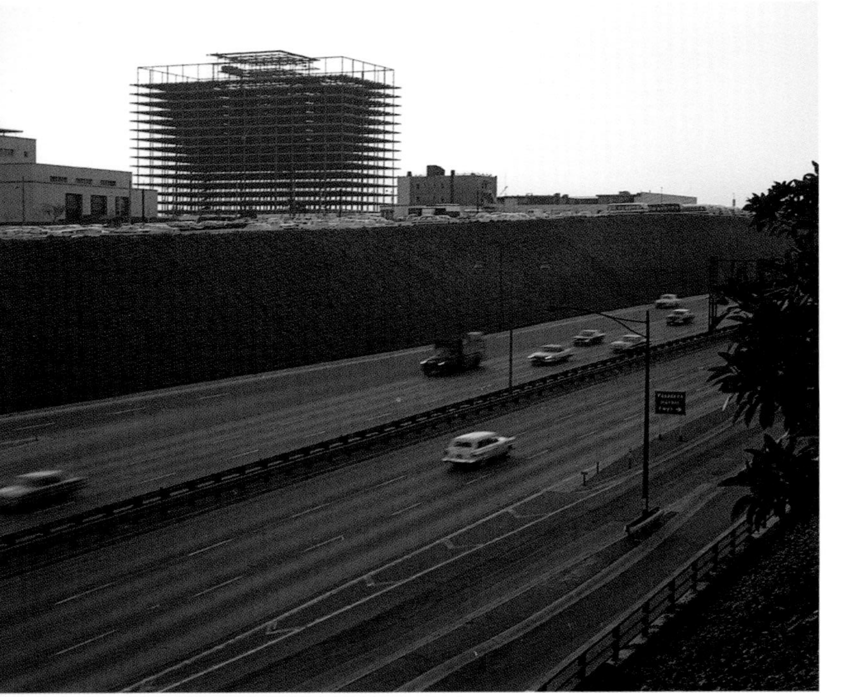

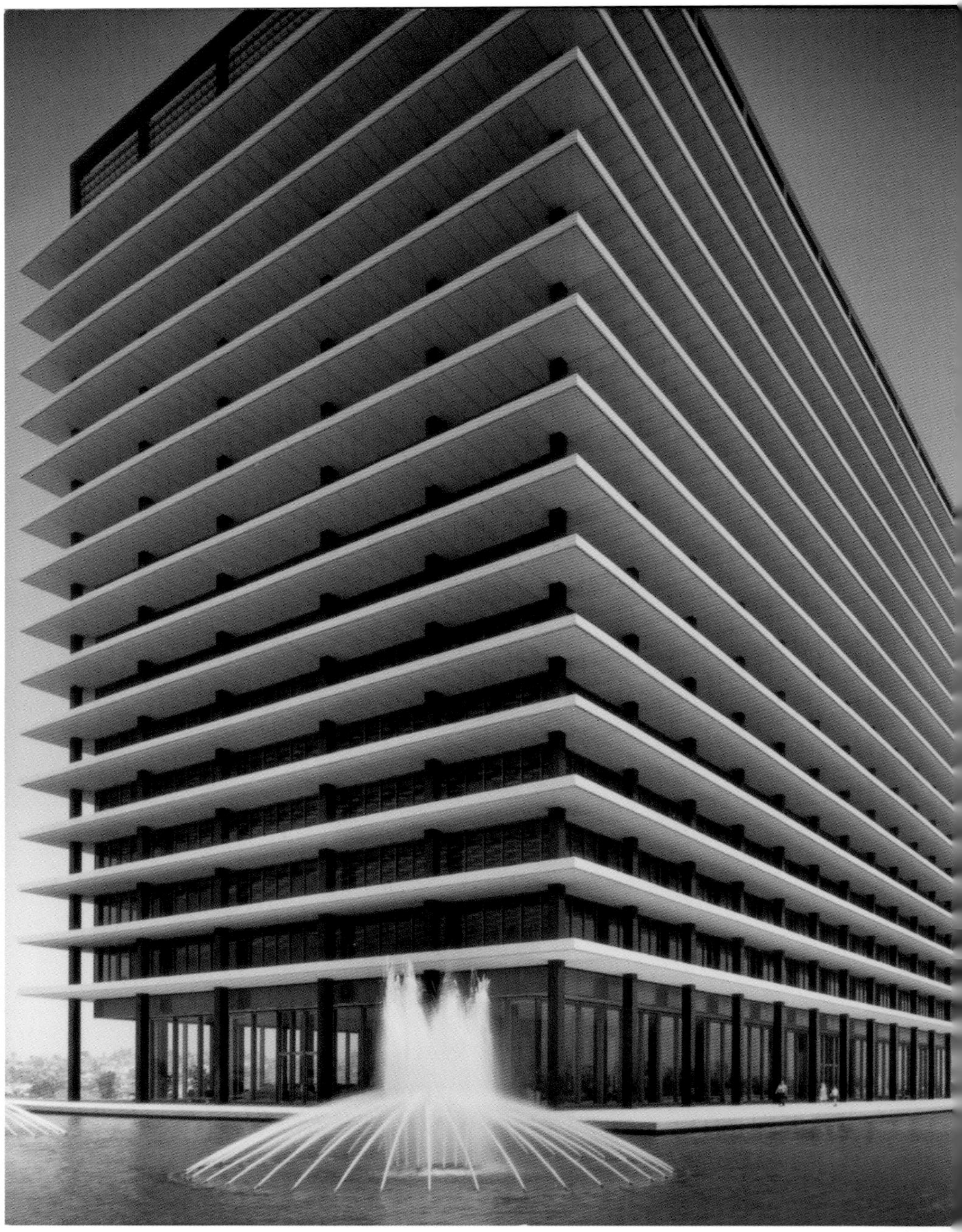

The monumental Department of Water and Power Building by Albert C. Martin under construction in 1964, with the Hollywood Freeway in the foreground (above). A modern temple dedicated to the worship of water (right).

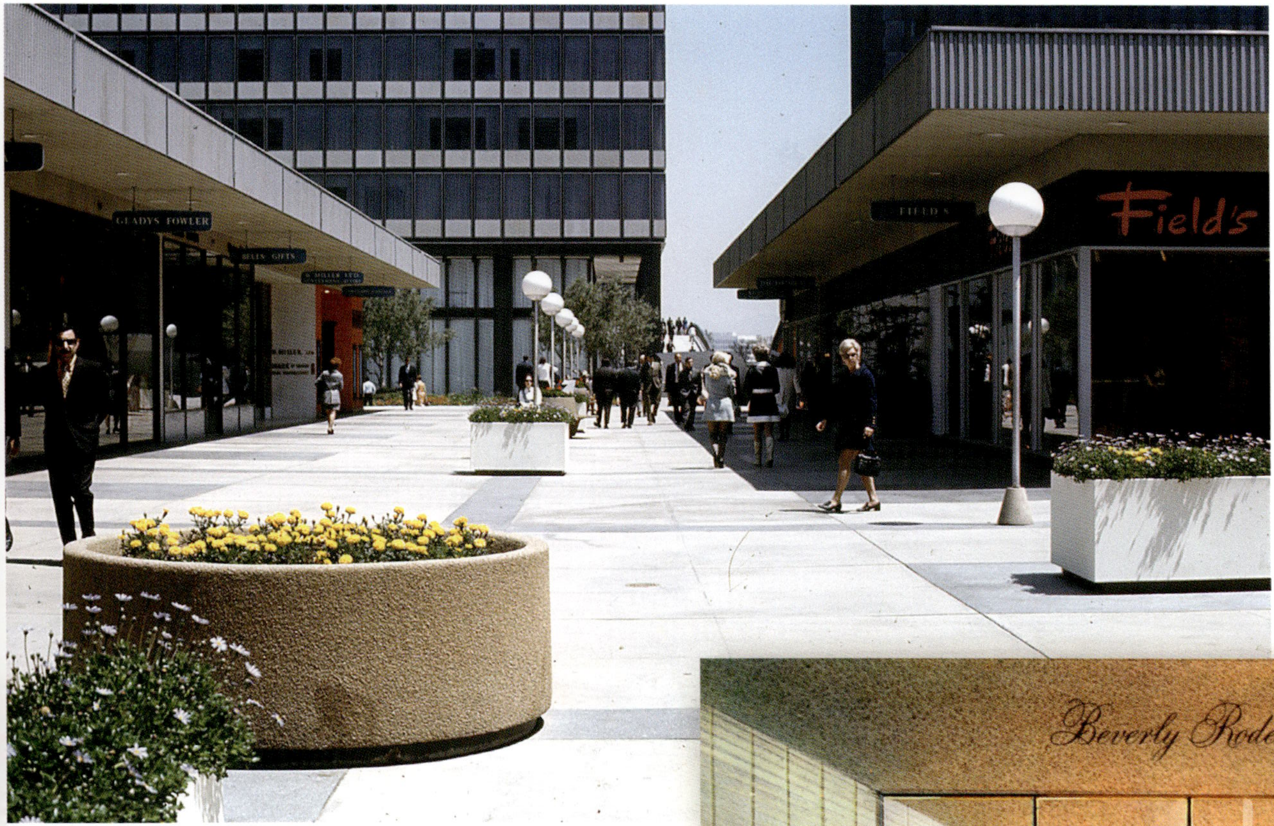

**LEFT:** Smart and sophisticated, Century City was a futuristic "city within a city." Located on the 176-acre former back lot of 20th Century Fox, its first buildings were completed in 1963. The Century Square Shopping Center, shown here, opened a year later.

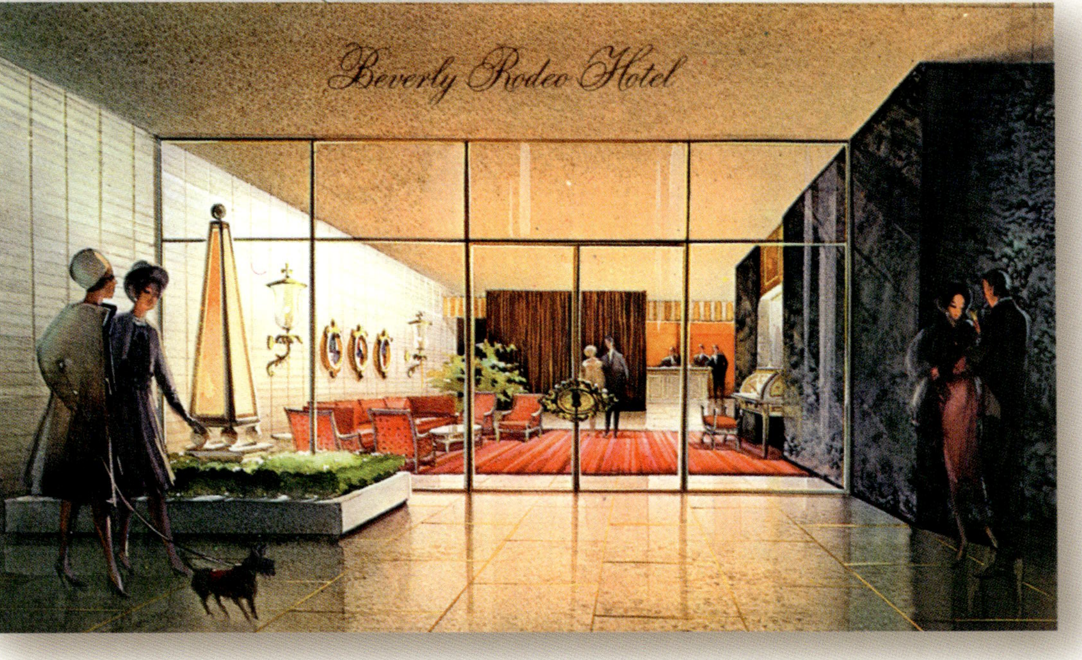


**RIGHT:** The Beverly Rodeo Hotel, classical elegance in an ultramodern setting—the definition of the Hollywood Regency style.

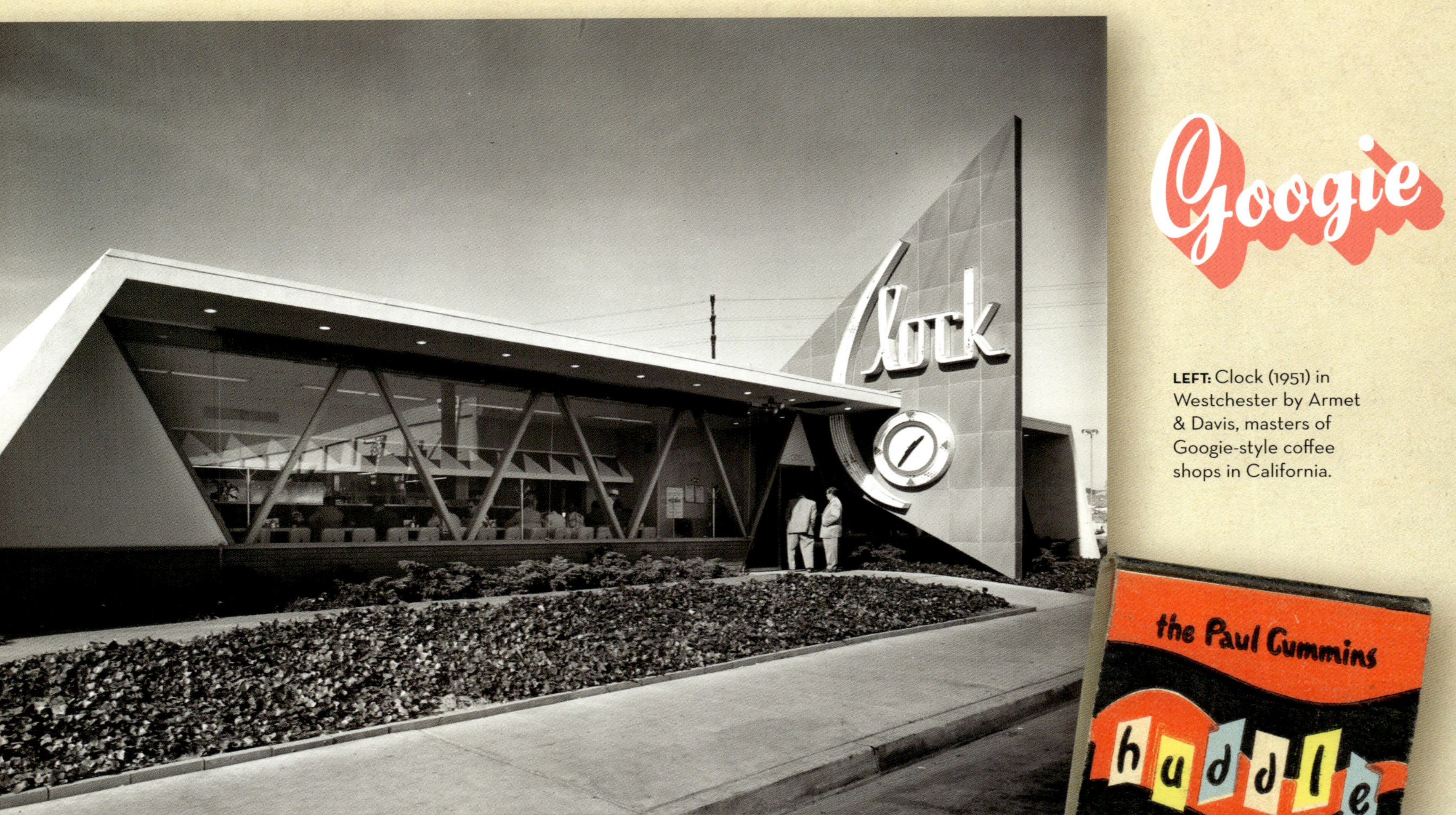


# Googie

**LEFT:** Clock (1951) in Westchester by Armet & Davis, masters of Googie-style coffee shops in California.

Popular Modernism found its greatest expression in the Googie style, applied to supermarkets, automobile showrooms, car washes, liquor stores, bowling alleys, and coffee shops. Googie, named after the Sunset Boulevard coffee shop Googie's, where the style first appeared, featured exaggerated and often colorful architectural elements combined with large neon-lit signage to draw the attention of speeding motorists. In addition, the ability to "bring the outdoors in" made possible through the technology of floor-to-ceiling plate glass windows was a typical Googie design feature. In the late '50s and early '60s, Jet Age elements such as uplifted or tilting rooflines were particularly emphasized. Los Angeles–based architects Louis Armet and Eldon Davis, John Lautner, Douglas Honnold, and Martin Stern Jr. were all masters of the Googie style.

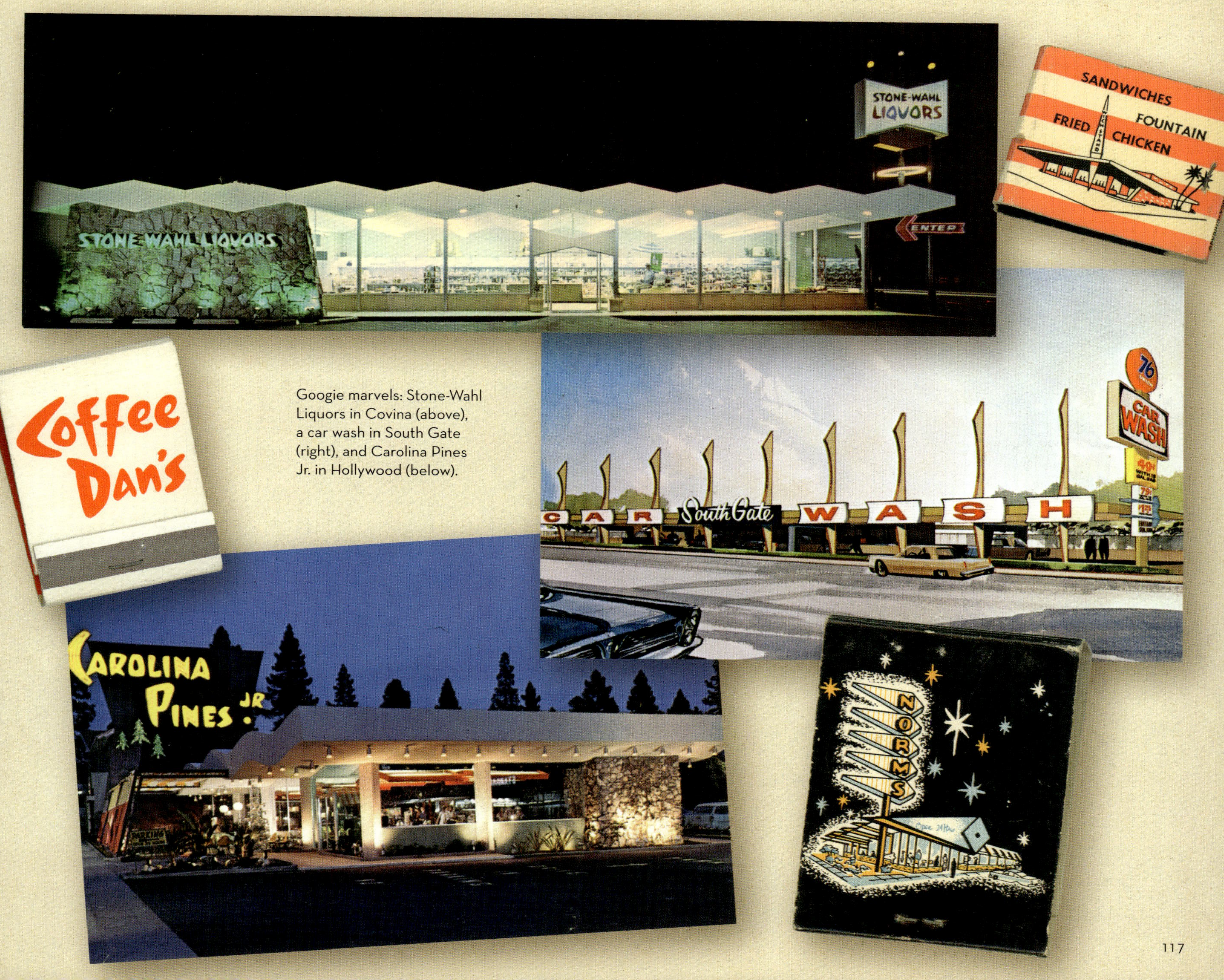


Googie marvels: Stone-Wahl Liquors in Covina (above), a car wash in South Gate (right), and Carolina Pines Jr. in Hollywood (below).

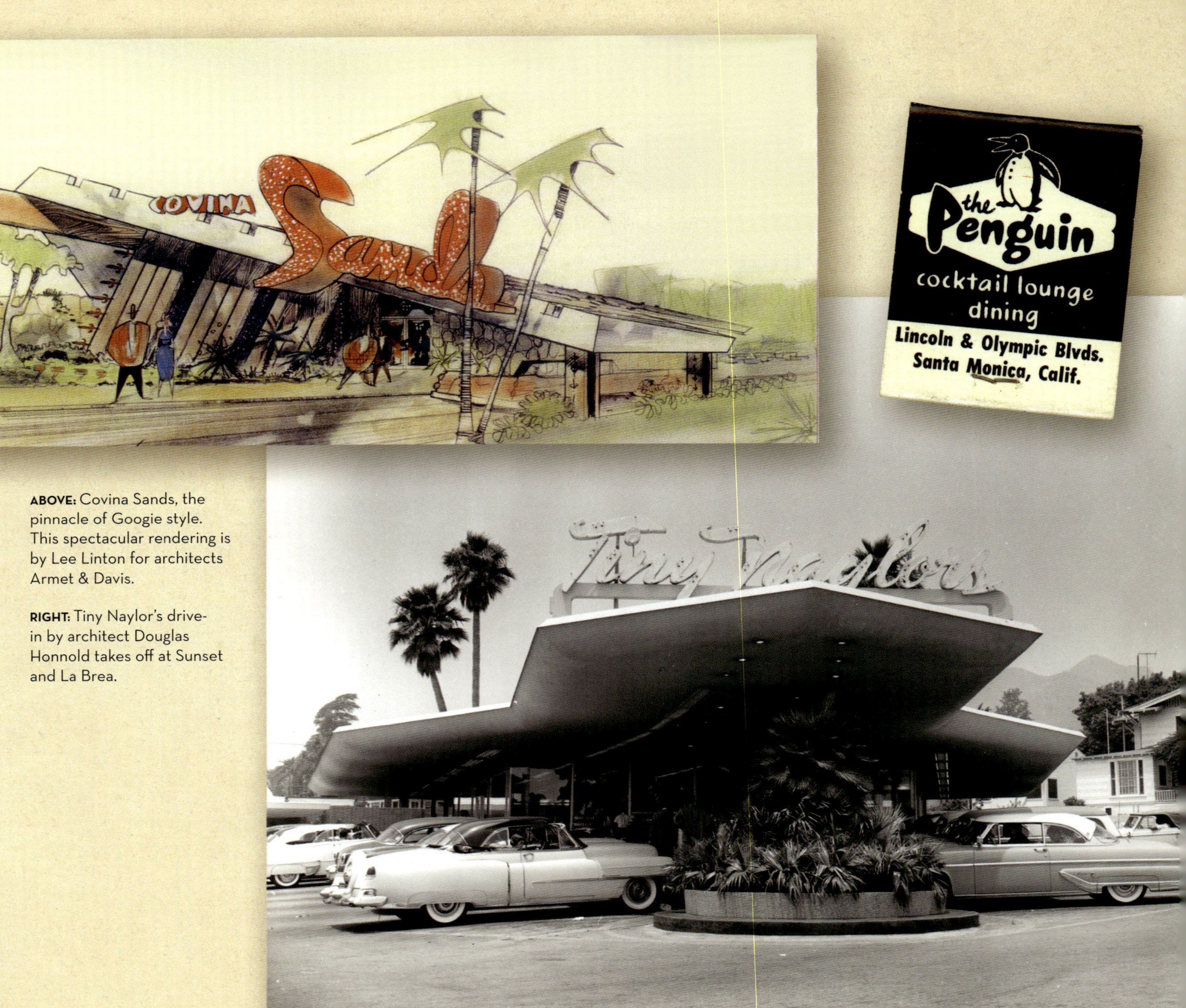


**ABOVE:** Covina Sands, the pinnacle of Googie style. This spectacular rendering is by Lee Linton for architects Armet & Davis.

**RIGHT:** Tiny Naylor's drive-in by architect Douglas Honnold takes off at Sunset and La Brea.

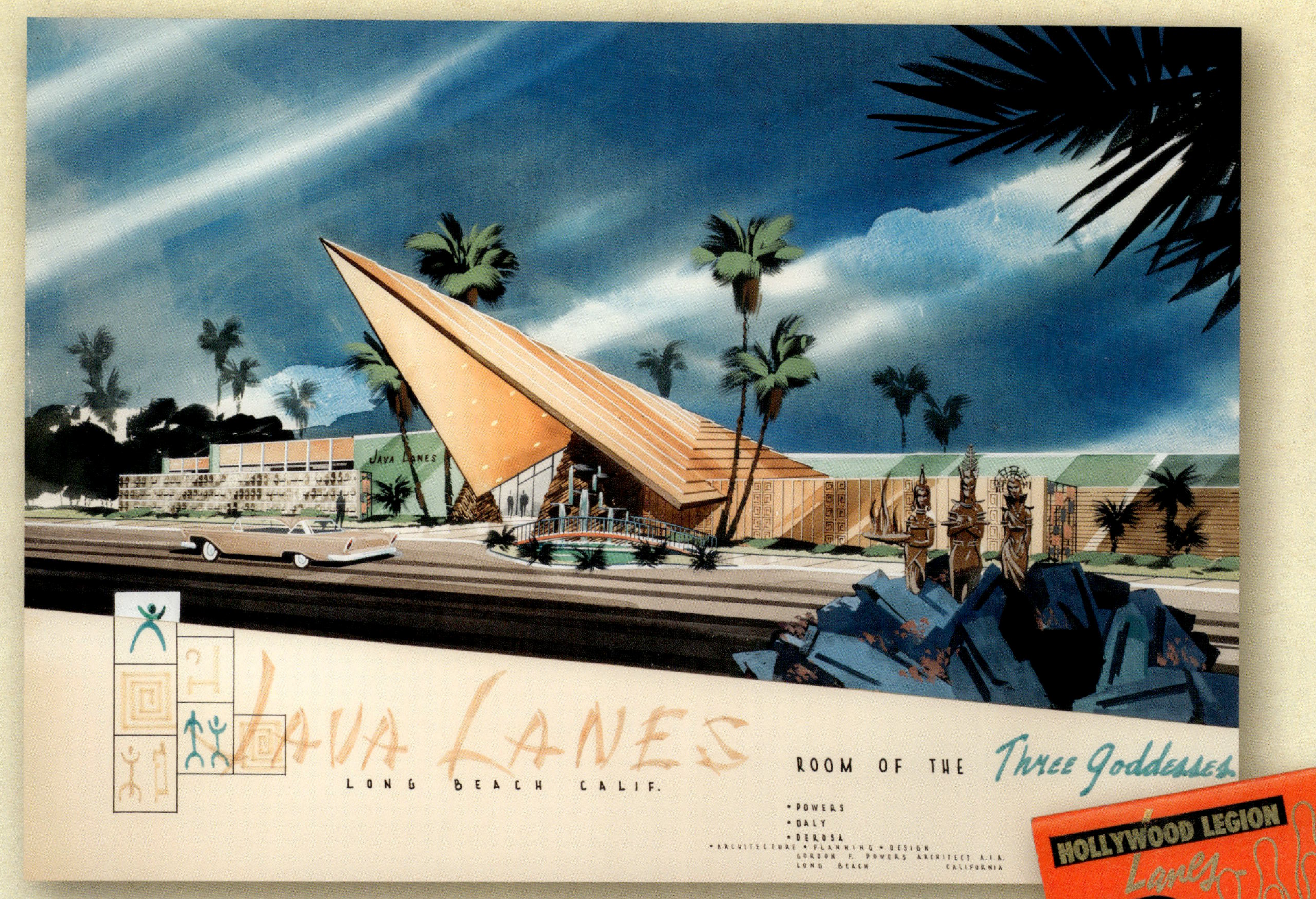


ABOVE: Java Lanes in Long Beach typified the elaborate, exotically themed entertainment/bowling centers built between 1955 and the early 1960s.

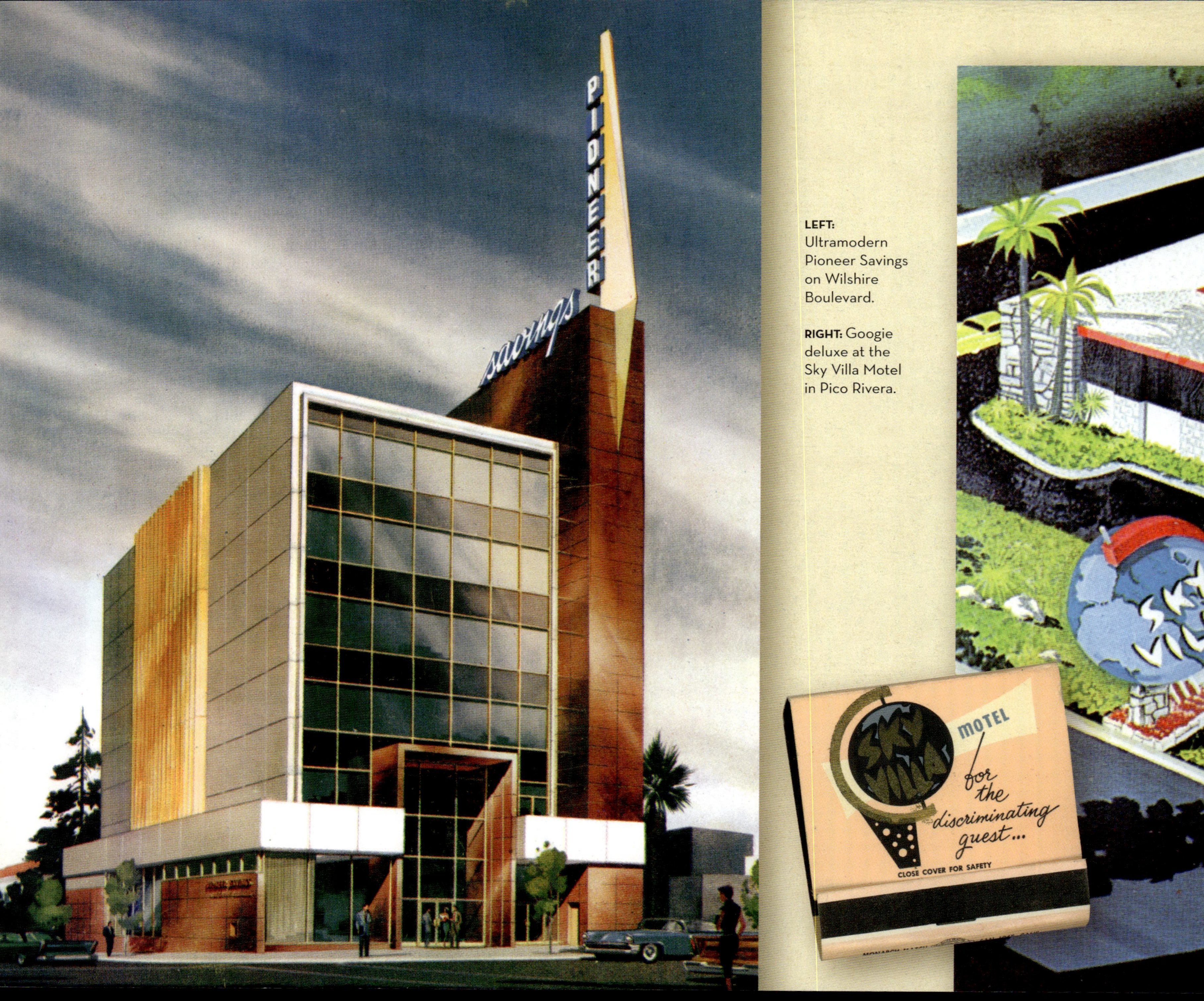


**LEFT:** Ultramodern Pioneer Savings on Wilshire Boulevard.

**RIGHT:** Googie deluxe at the Sky Villa Motel in Pico Rivera.

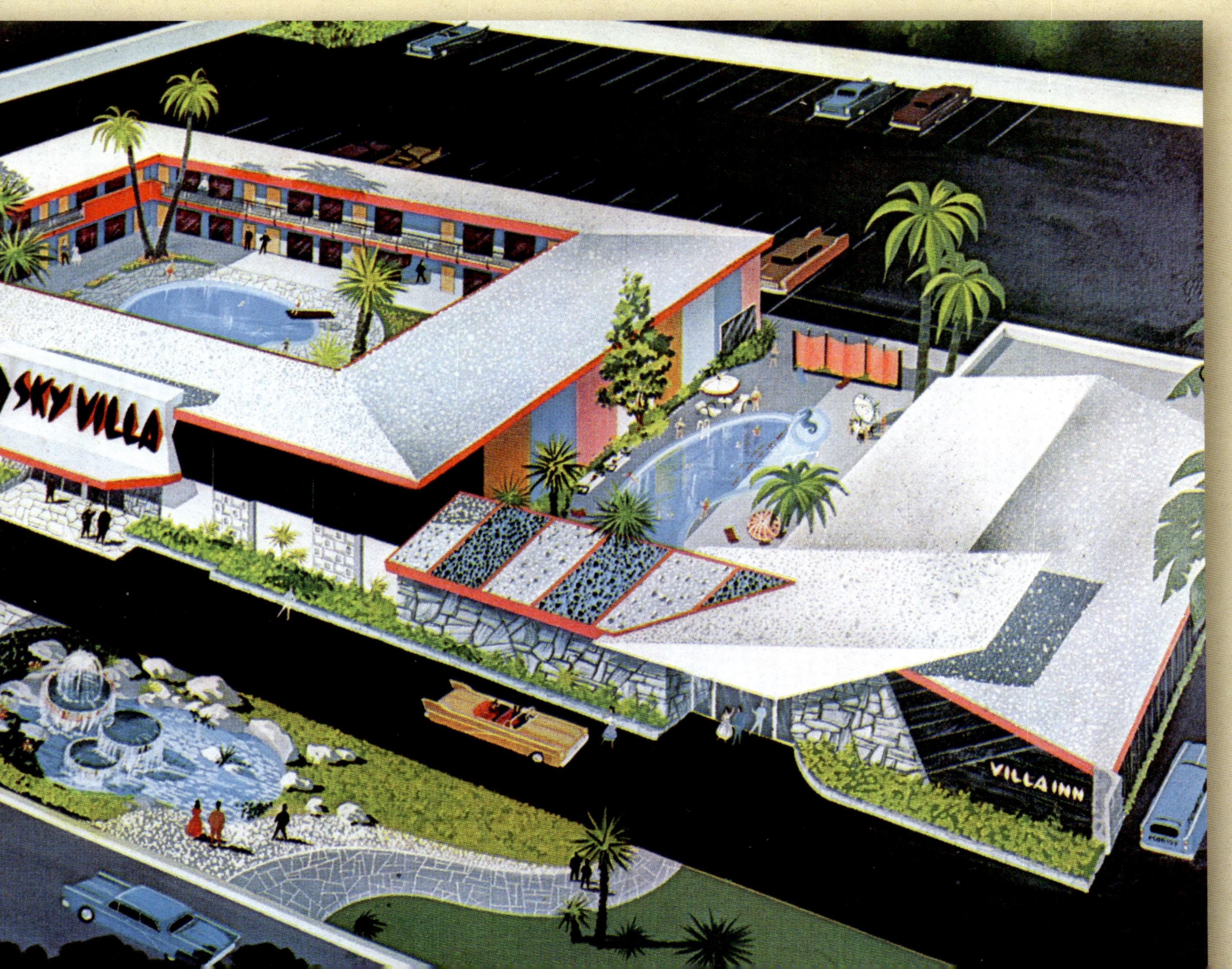
SKY VILLA
VILLA INN

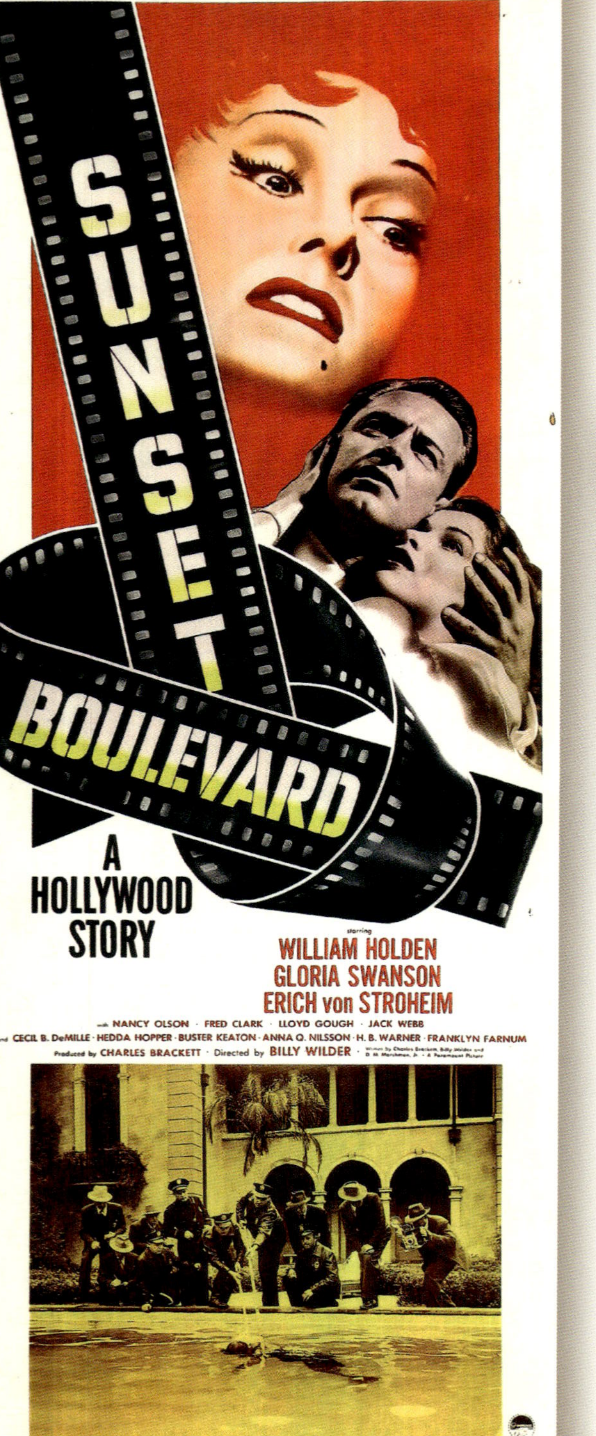


After Bugsy Siegel was shot dead in the living room of his girlfriend's Beverly Hills house in 1947, Mickey Cohen took over the Los Angeles rackets. Cohen's flamboyant lifestyle fed true crime tabloids that delved into the underbelly of booming postwar Los Angeles. Hollywood movies mirrored the era in the dark melodramas filmed on location in the streets and neighborhoods of the city. Known as "film noir" and shot mainly in shadowy black and white, these movies featured femmes fatales, flawed heroes or antiheroes, and cynical private eyes. The noir films most associated with Los Angeles are *Double Indemnity* (1944), *Sunset Boulevard* (1950), and *Kiss Me Deadly* (1955).

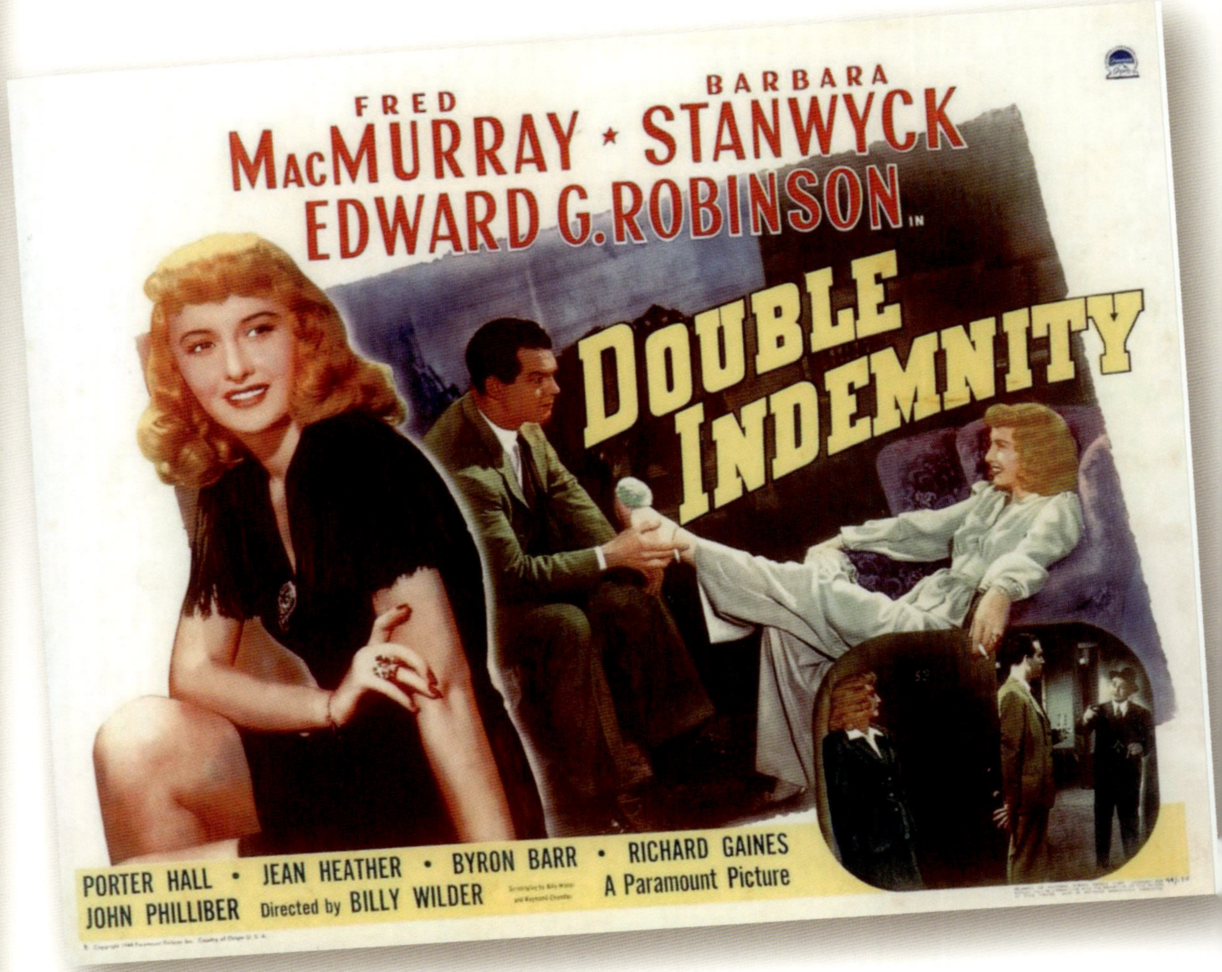

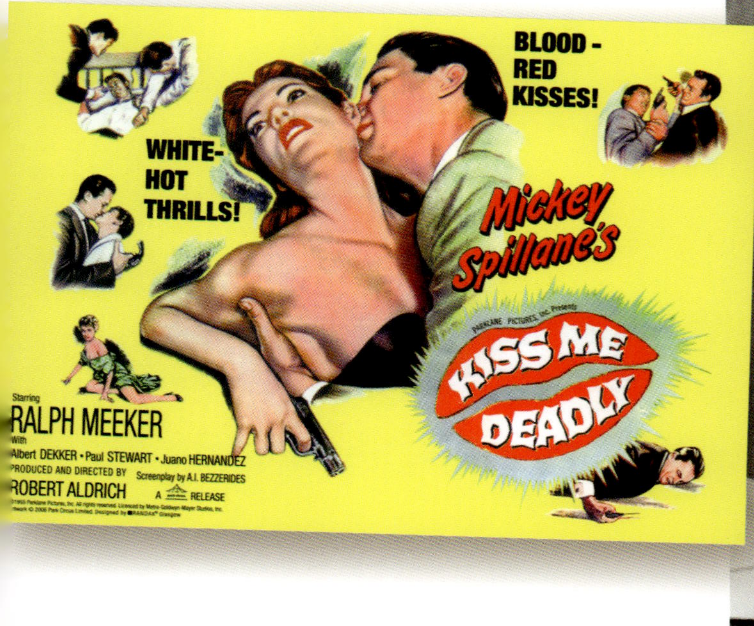

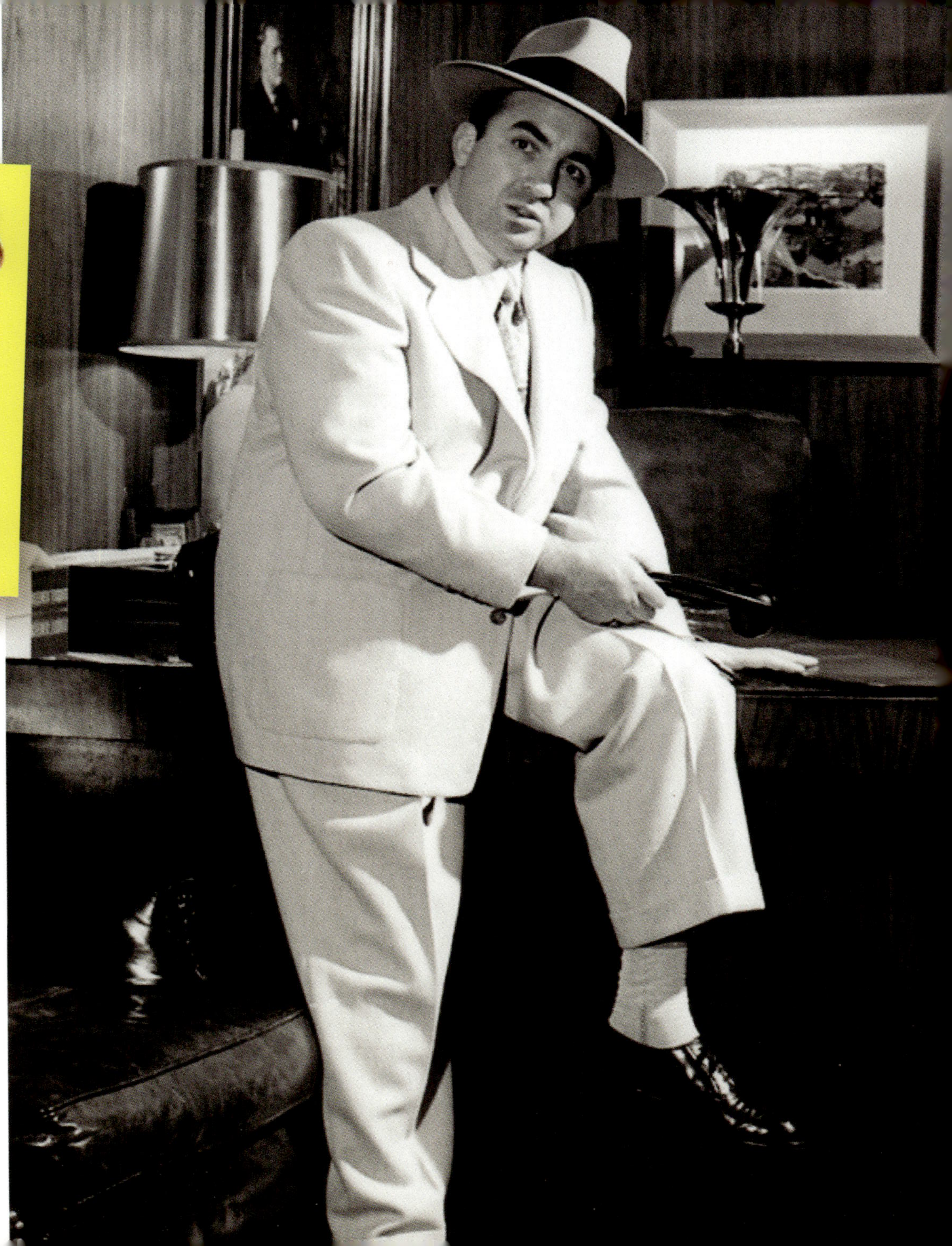

**RIGHT:** Mob boss and snappy dresser Mickey Cohen takes a call in his wood-paneled office.

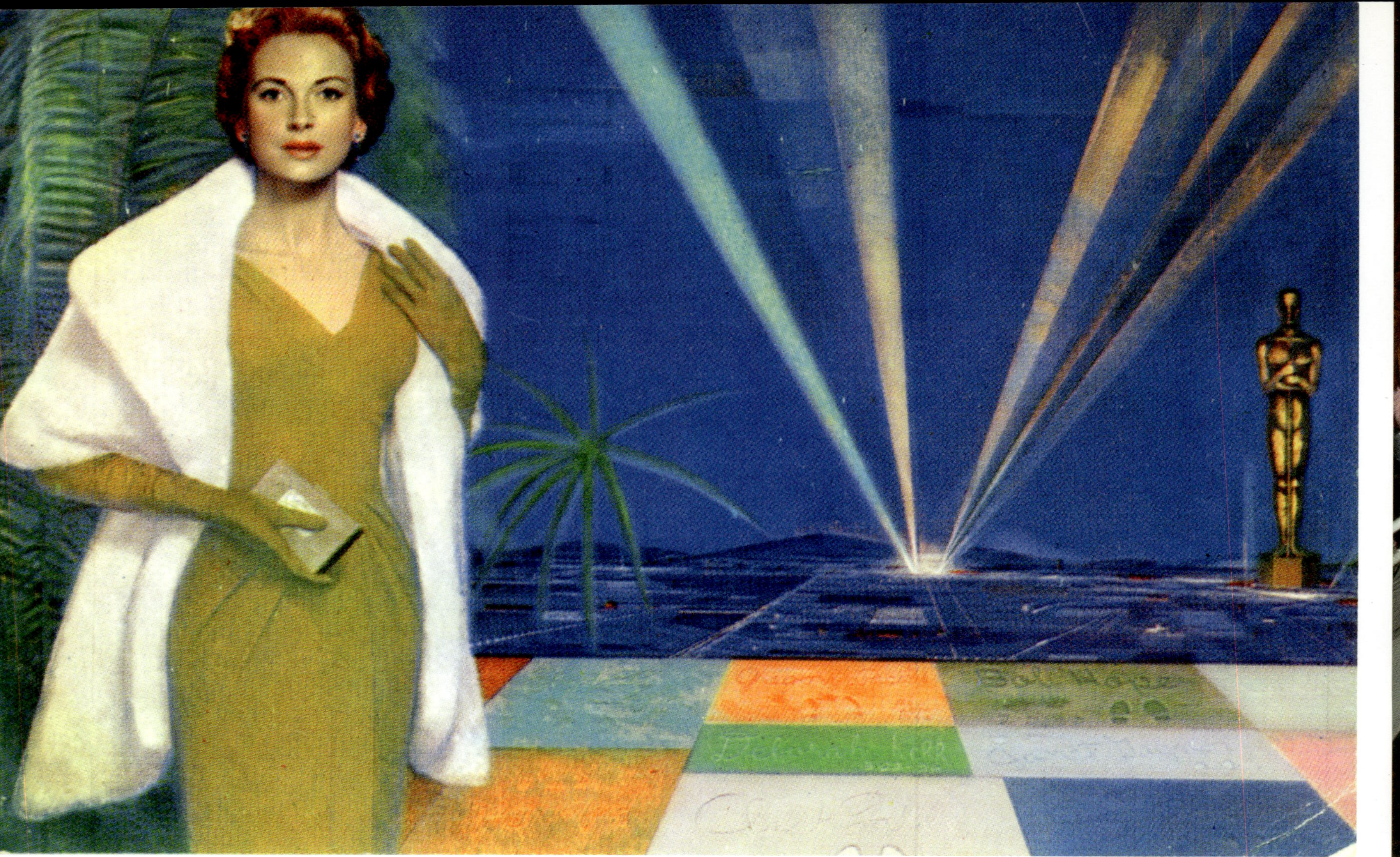

*Hollywood* by artist Maric Zamparelli.

By the mid-1950s, television challenged movies as the dominant form of mass entertainment. In response, motion picture studios produced extravagant epic films like *The Ten Commandments*, *Ben-Hur*, and *Cleopatra*, and gimmicks like 3-D films, Cinerama, CinemaScope, and VistaVision. Yet Hollywood continued to employ thousands as the home of both movie and television studios.

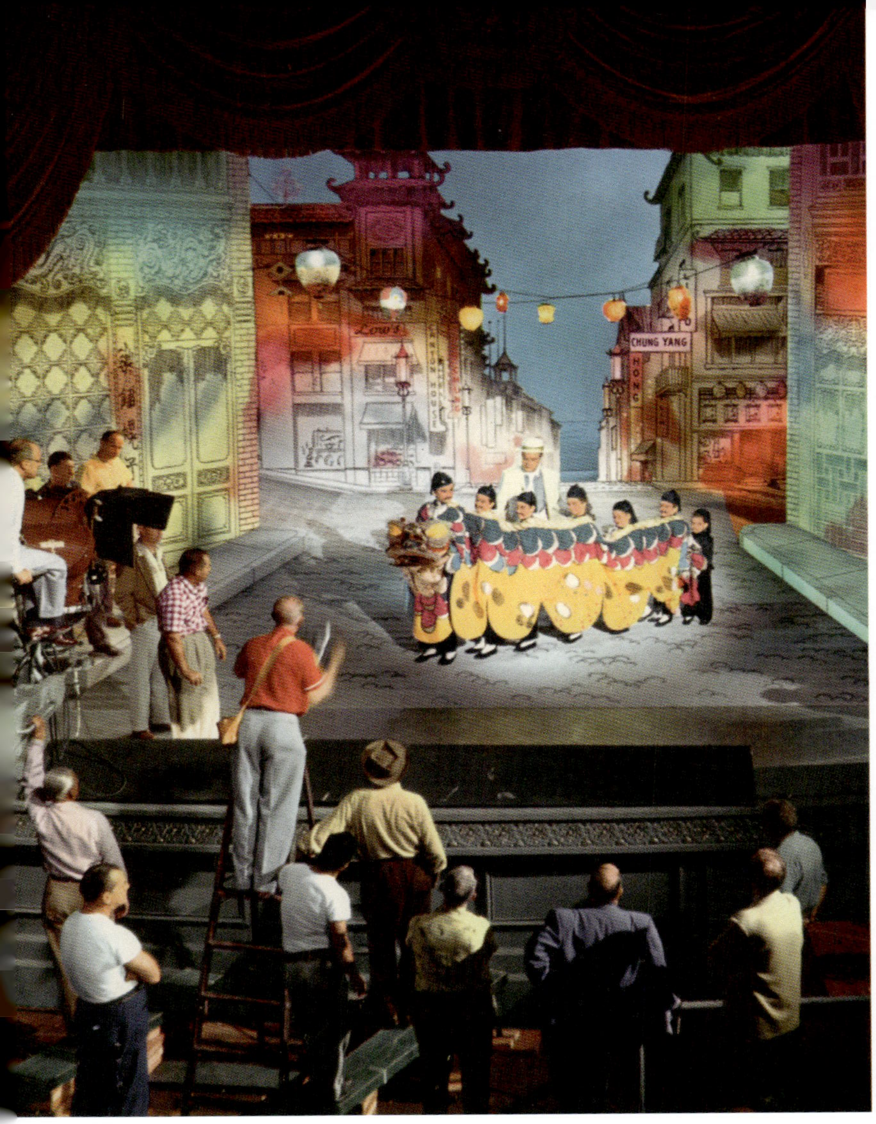

**ABOVE:** On set with Bob Hope and his Chinese friends.

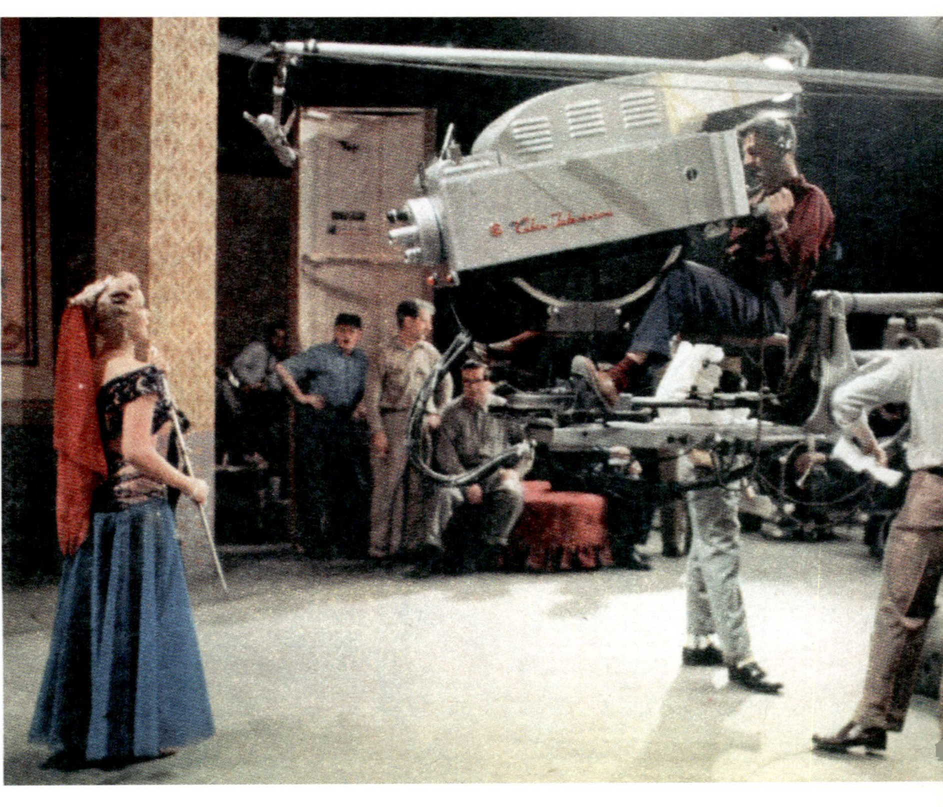

**ABOVE, RIGHT:** Introducing color television!

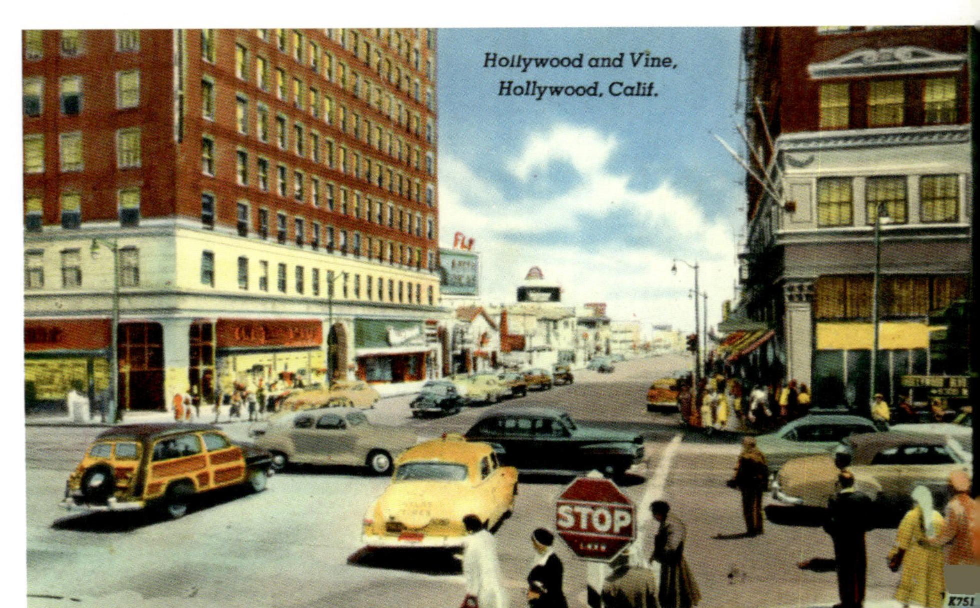


**BELOW, RIGHT:** Bustling Hollywood and Vine in the early 1950s.

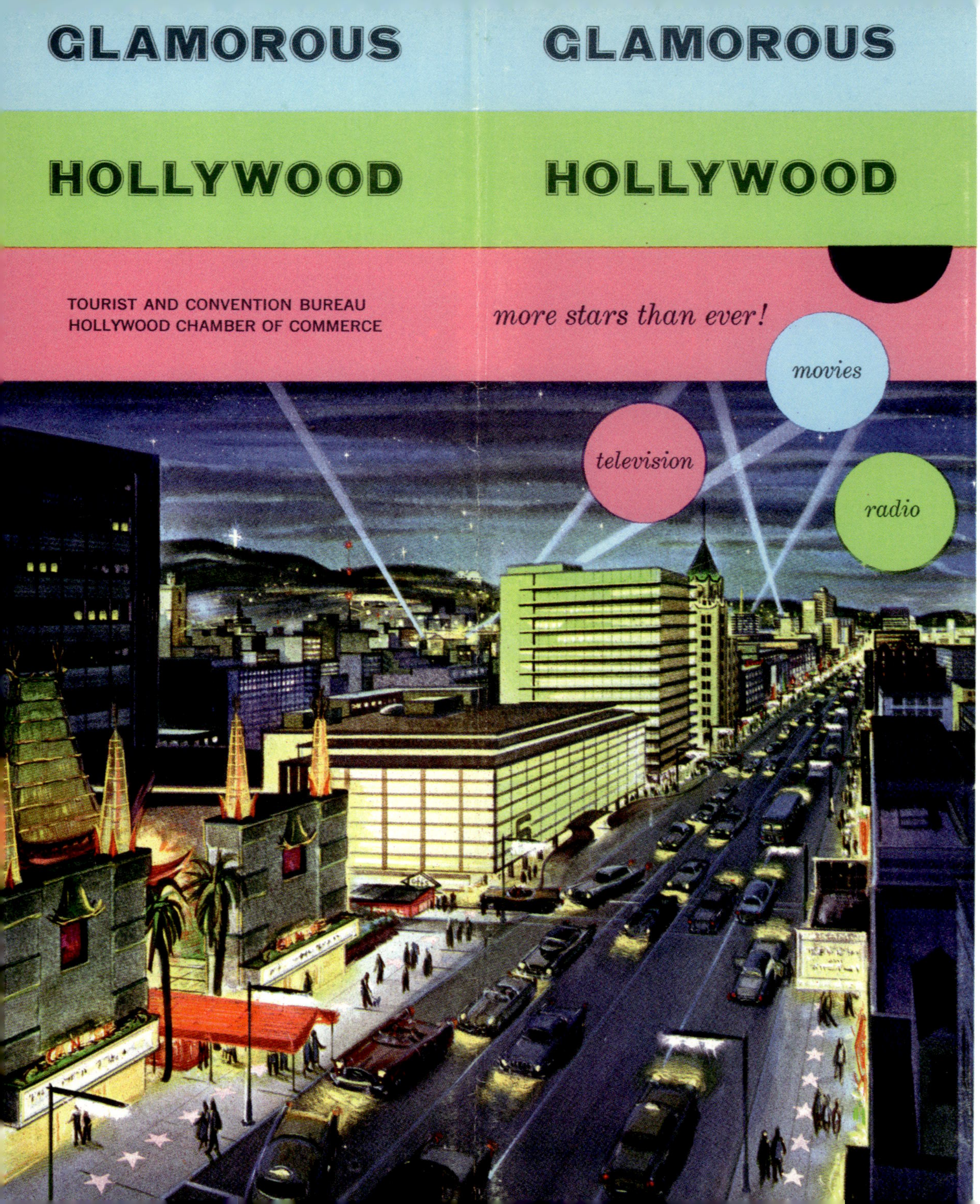

GLAMOROUS GLAMOROUS

HOLLYWOOD HOLLYWOOD

TOURIST AND CONVENTION BUREAU
HOLLYWOOD CHAMBER OF COMMERCE

*more stars than ever!*

*movies*

*television*

*radio*

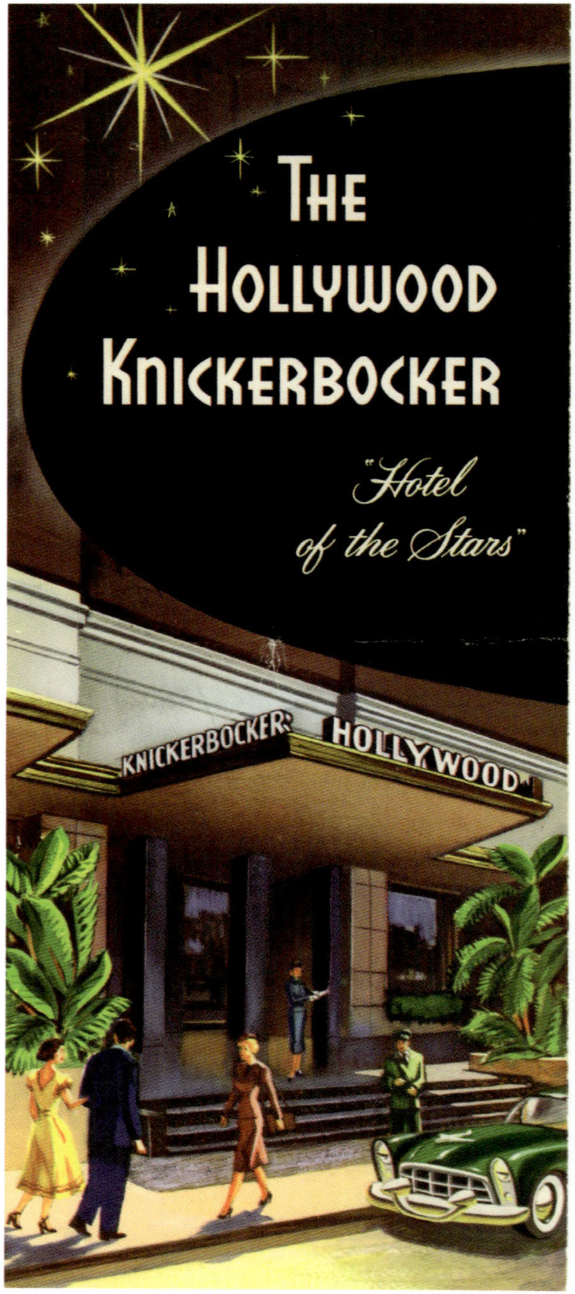

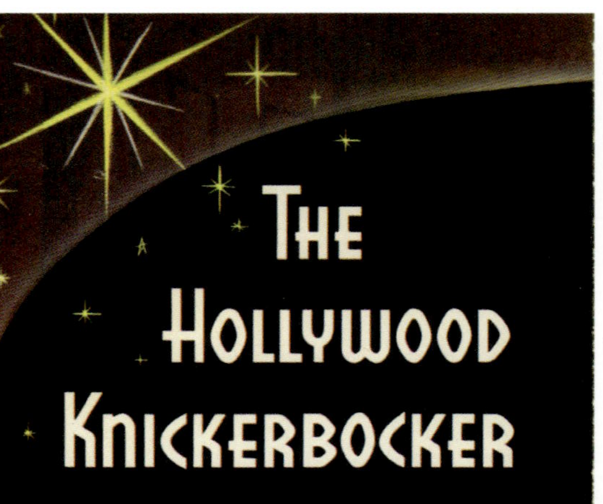

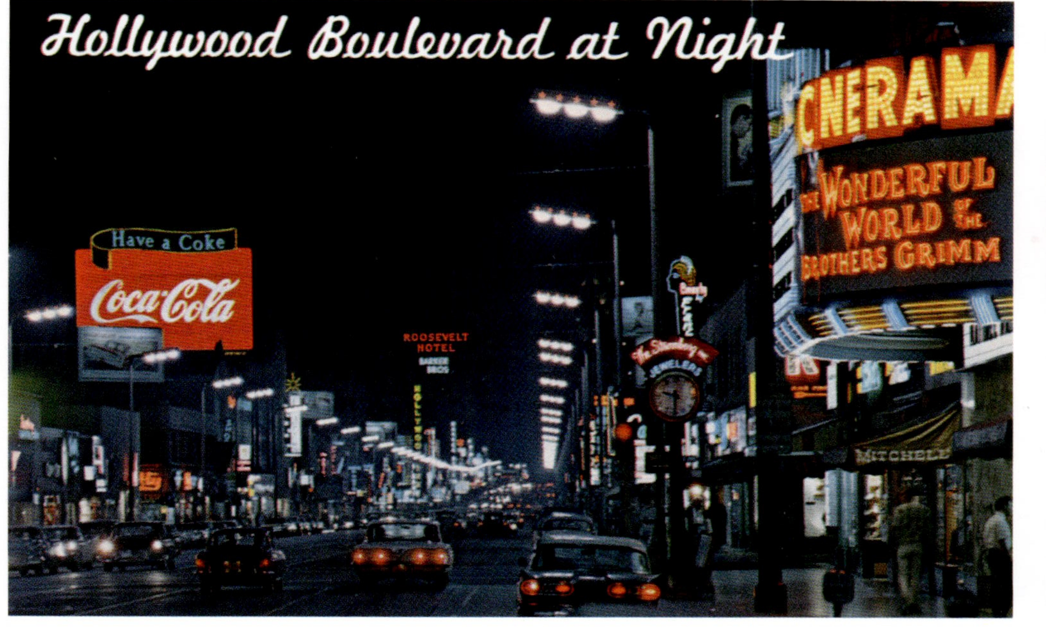


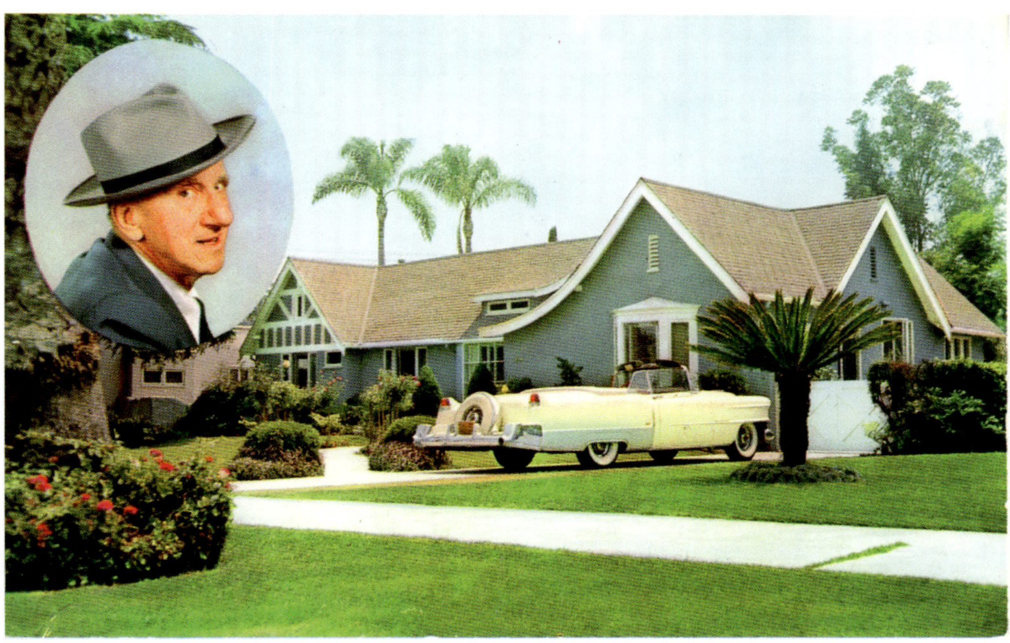

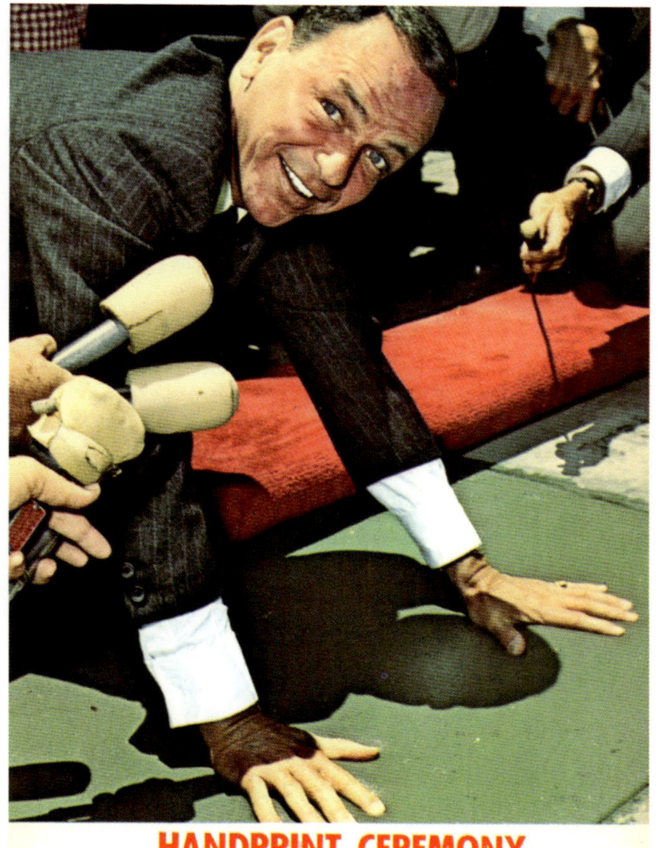


**ABOVE:** Frank Sinatra's handprints immortalized in concrete at Grauman's Chinese Theatre in 1965.

**LEFT:** Comedian Jimmy "The Schnoz" Durante's Cadillac convertible in the driveway of his Beverly Hills home in 1957.

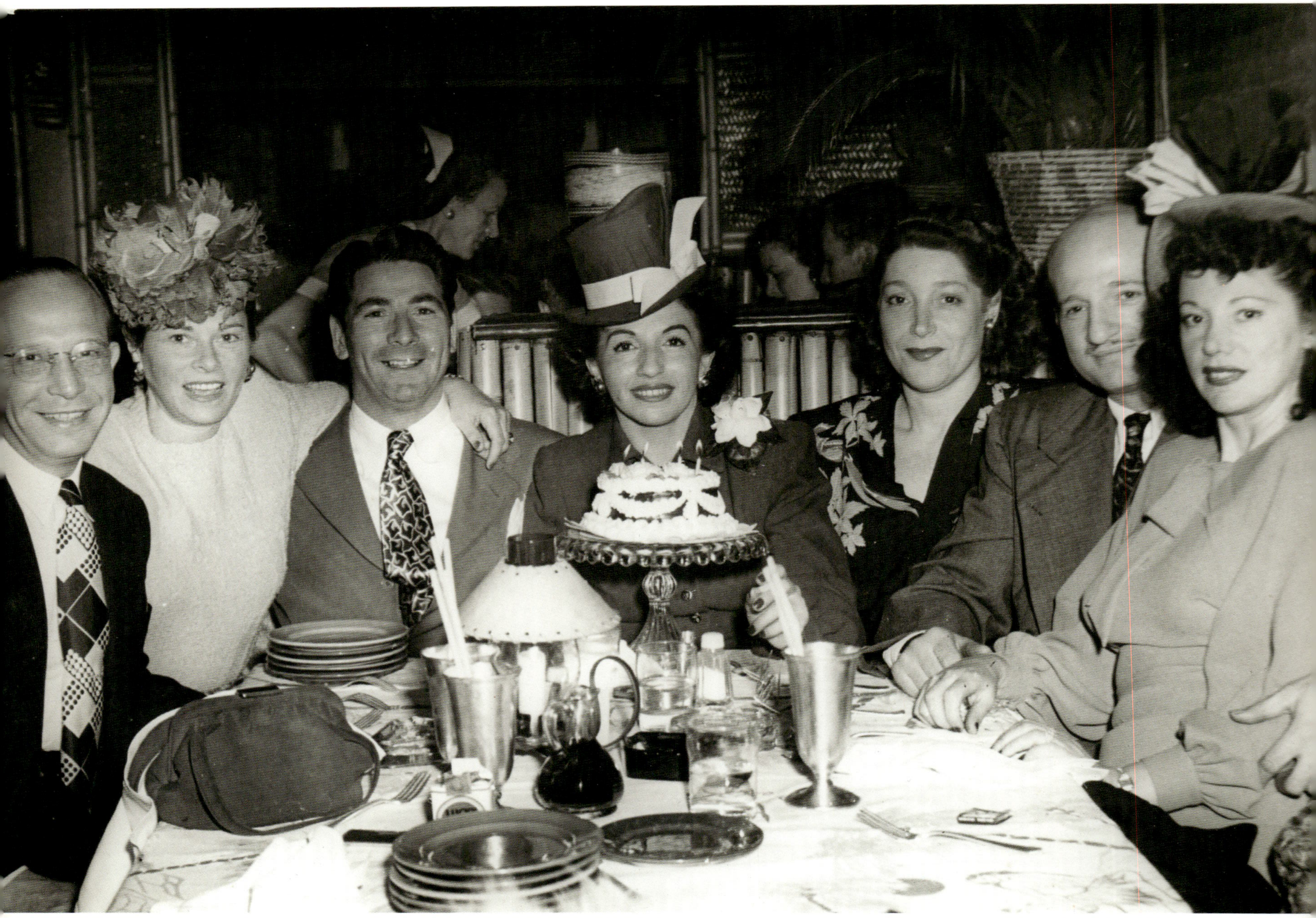

Los Angeles after dark meant nightclubs, fine restaurants, cafés, movie theaters, and burlesque houses. But it was the presence of Hollywood and the possibility of dining or dancing in the company of a radio, motion picture, or television star that made Los Angeles unique in American nightlife.

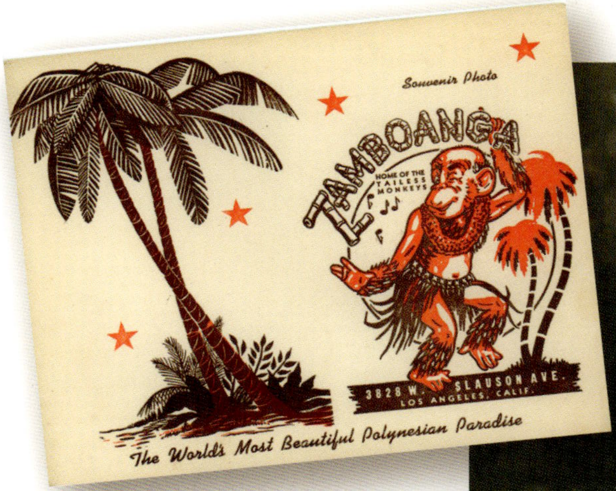

Nightclubs such as the Cocoanut Grove on Wilshire Boulevard, downtown's Biltmore Bowl, and those on the Sunset Strip were where the tony set gathered. The average Joe went to the bigger, livelier nightclubs in Hollywood and other parts of the city, such as the Palomar, Zenda Ballroom, and Palladium.

**FACING:** Celebrating Doris's birthday, March 16, 1947, at Sugie's Tropics.

**RIGHT:** True love at Zamboanga, Home of the Tailless Monkeys.

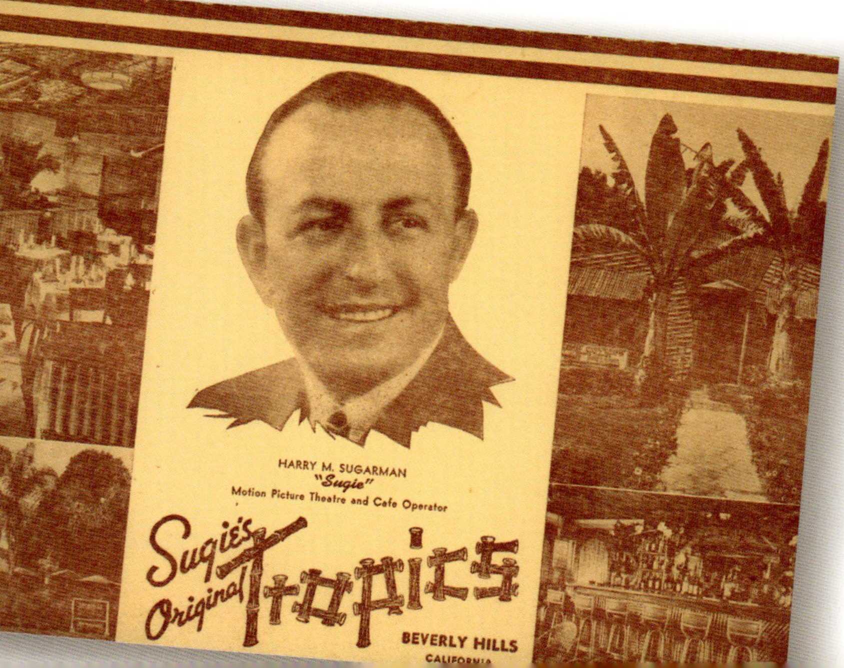

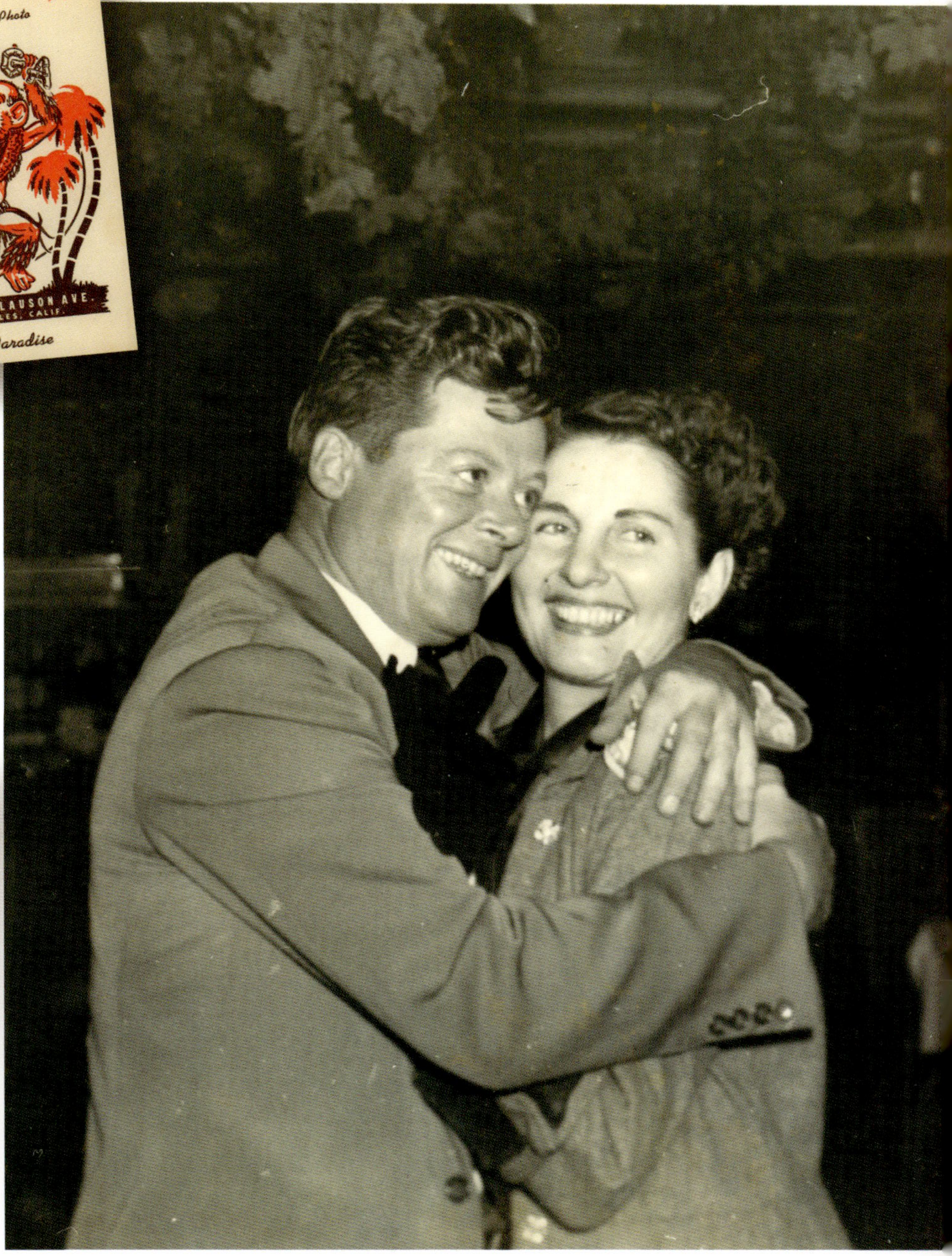

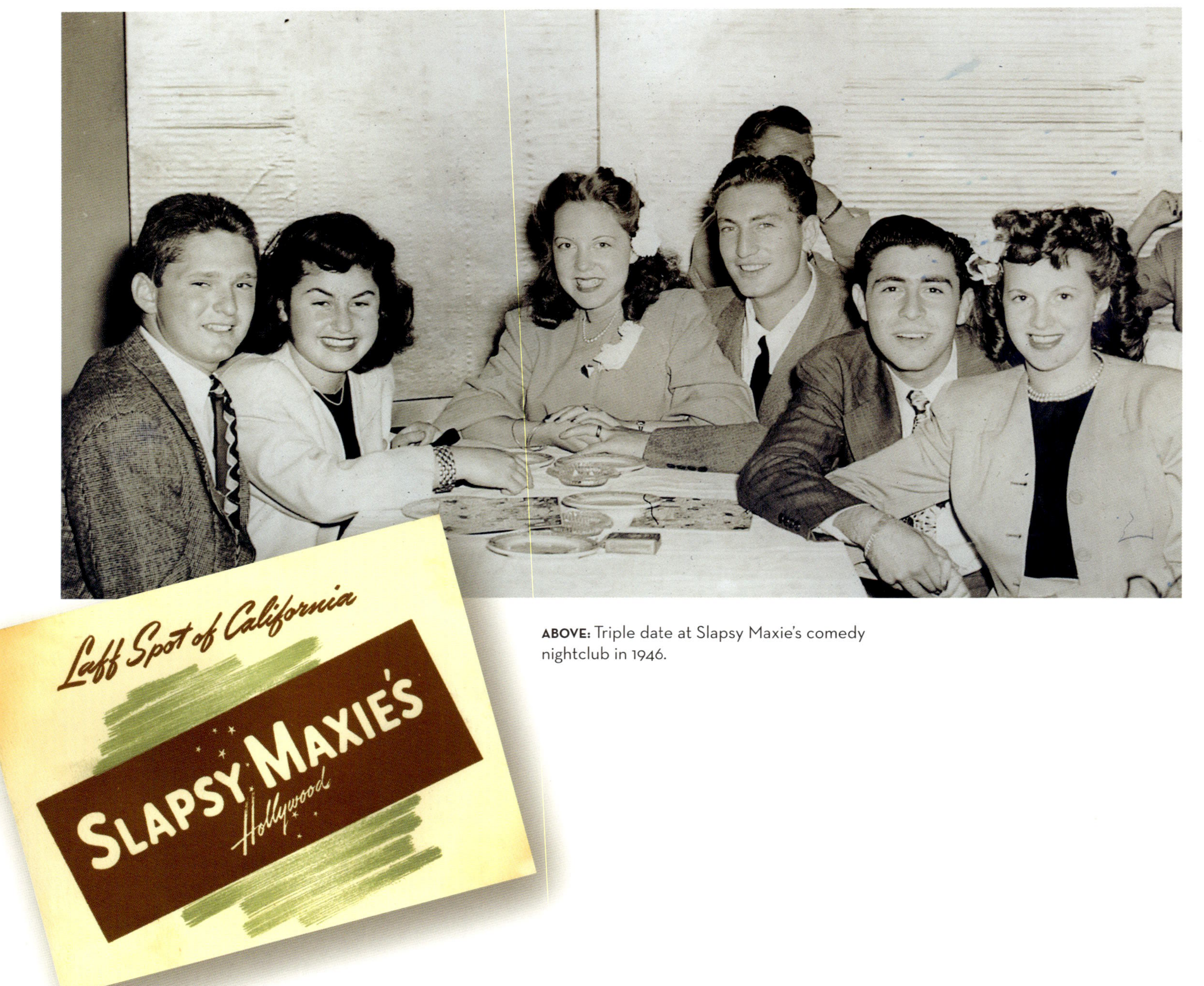


**ABOVE:** Triple date at Slapsy Maxie's comedy nightclub in 1946.

The ceiling above the bar had to be raised to accommodate the seriously big hair of these go-go girls at the Playgirl Club near Disneyland.

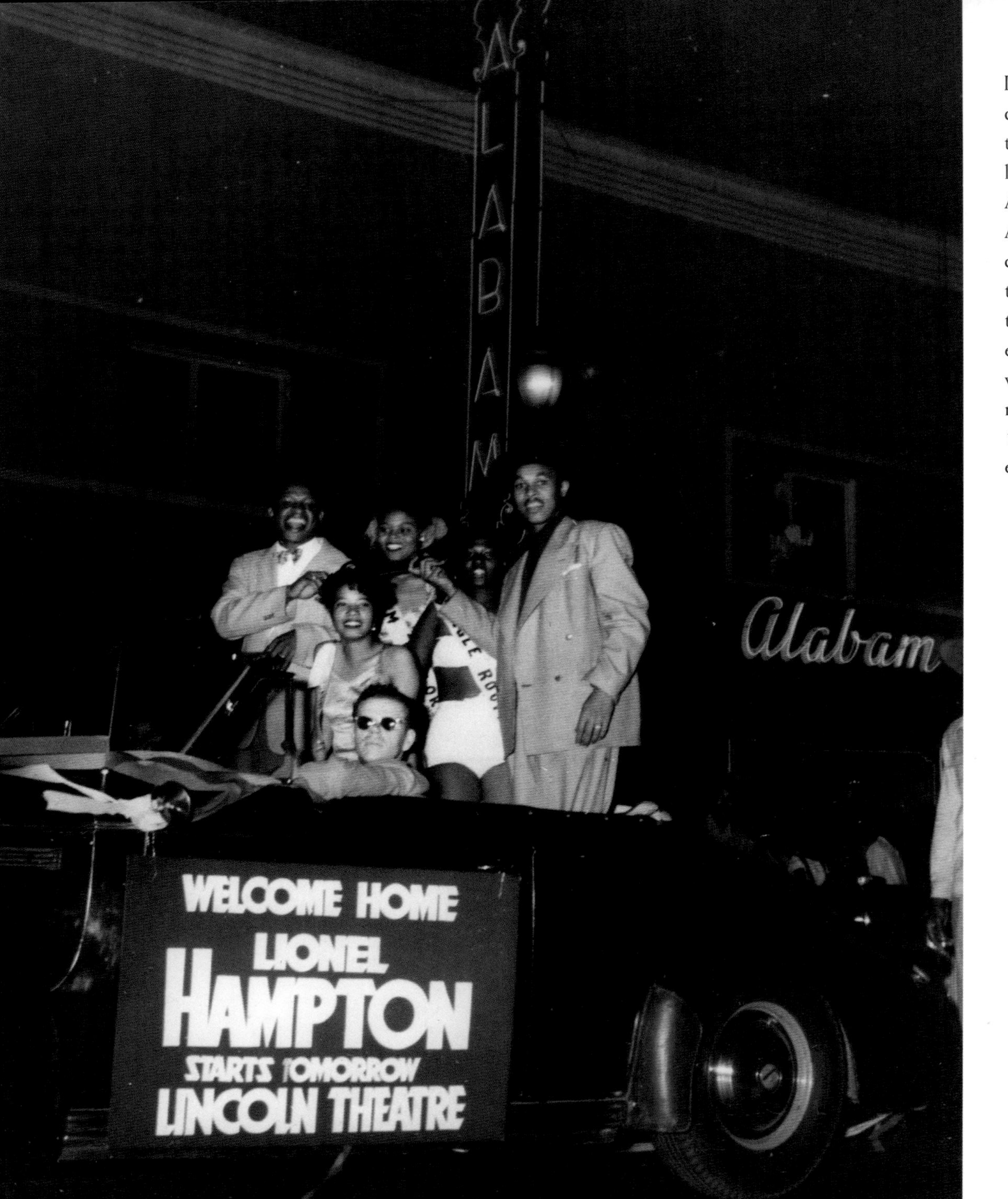


Despite the 1948 U.S. Supreme Court decision outlawing deed restrictions that prevented African Americans from living in white neighborhoods, Los Angeles remained highly segregated. As a result, African Americans were concentrated in areas south of downtown to approximately West 58th Street, in the Watts district, and small enclaves elsewhere in the city. Bisecting this area was Central Avenue, a commercial and residential corridor that from the late 1920s through the mid-1950s was the entertainment hub of black Los Angeles.

**LEFT:** Lionel Hampton (far left) promotes his show at the Lincoln Theatre. Club Alabam is in the background.

**RIGHT:** Dressed to the nines at Club Alabam on Central Avenue.

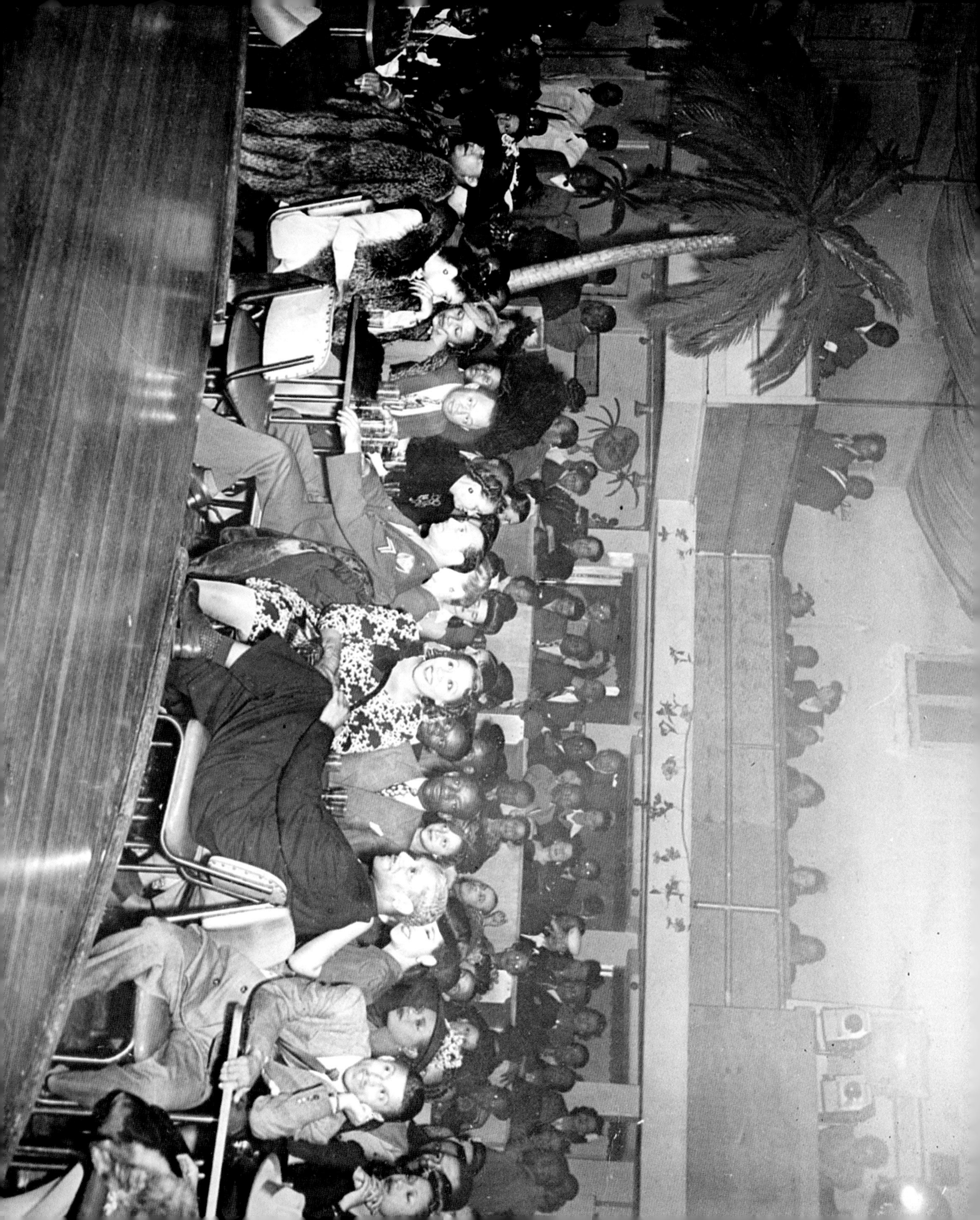

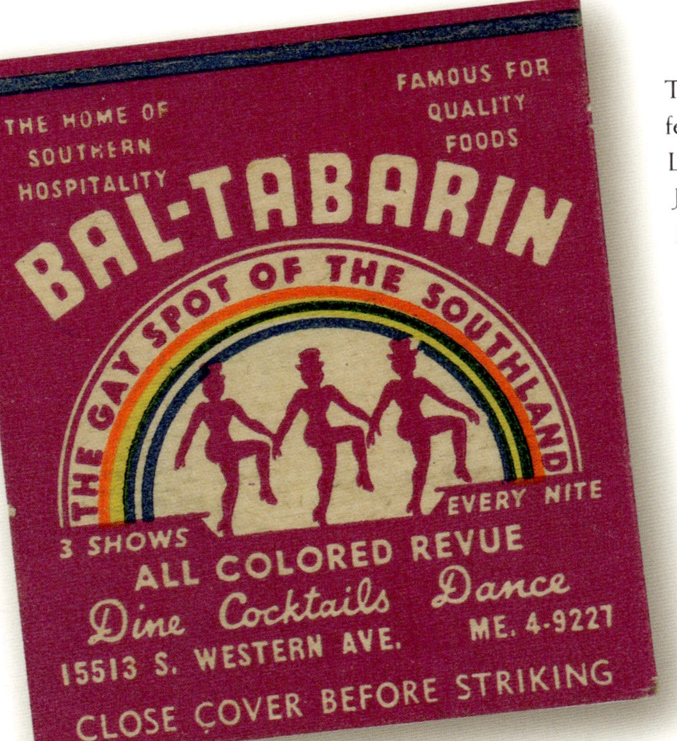


There were various terms used for the nightclubs that featured, and were patronized by, African Americans. The Last Word was the "East Side's Smartest Sepia Night Club." Joe Morris's Plantation Club, "California's Largest Harlem Night Club," was at 108th and Central. The Bal-Tabarin Cafe had its "All Colored Revue." At the Club Oasis at Western Avenue and 39th Street, black performers (including Sarah Vaughan) put on "spectacular bronze extravaganzas." Also on Central Avenue during this period were the Club Alabam, Downbeat, Jack's Basket Room, Club Congo, Savoy Ballroom, and the Lincoln Theatre. The Dunbar Hotel, the most prestigious African American hotel in the city, had a famous nightclub of its own. These were all integrated clubs, and adventurous whites would make the trek to Central Avenue to experience music far more dynamic than the typical fare found on the Sunset Strip and in Hollywood.

**FACING:** Raising a shot glass at the Cricket Club, where "it's fun to have fun."

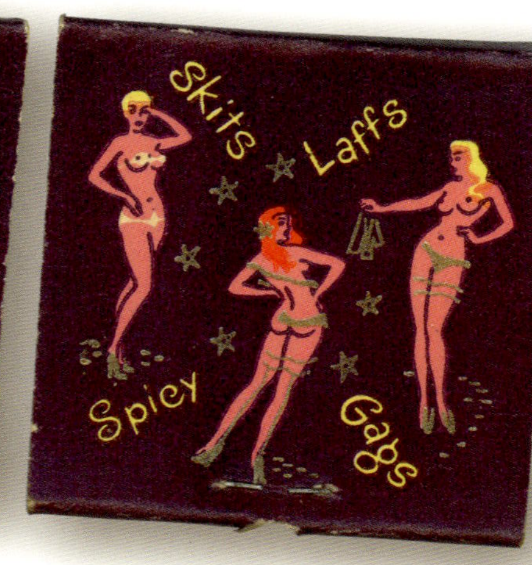


**RIGHT:** The Red Feather at 8618 South Figueroa in South Los Angeles advertised "Special Attraction Monday Nite Only All Colored Burlesque Revue."

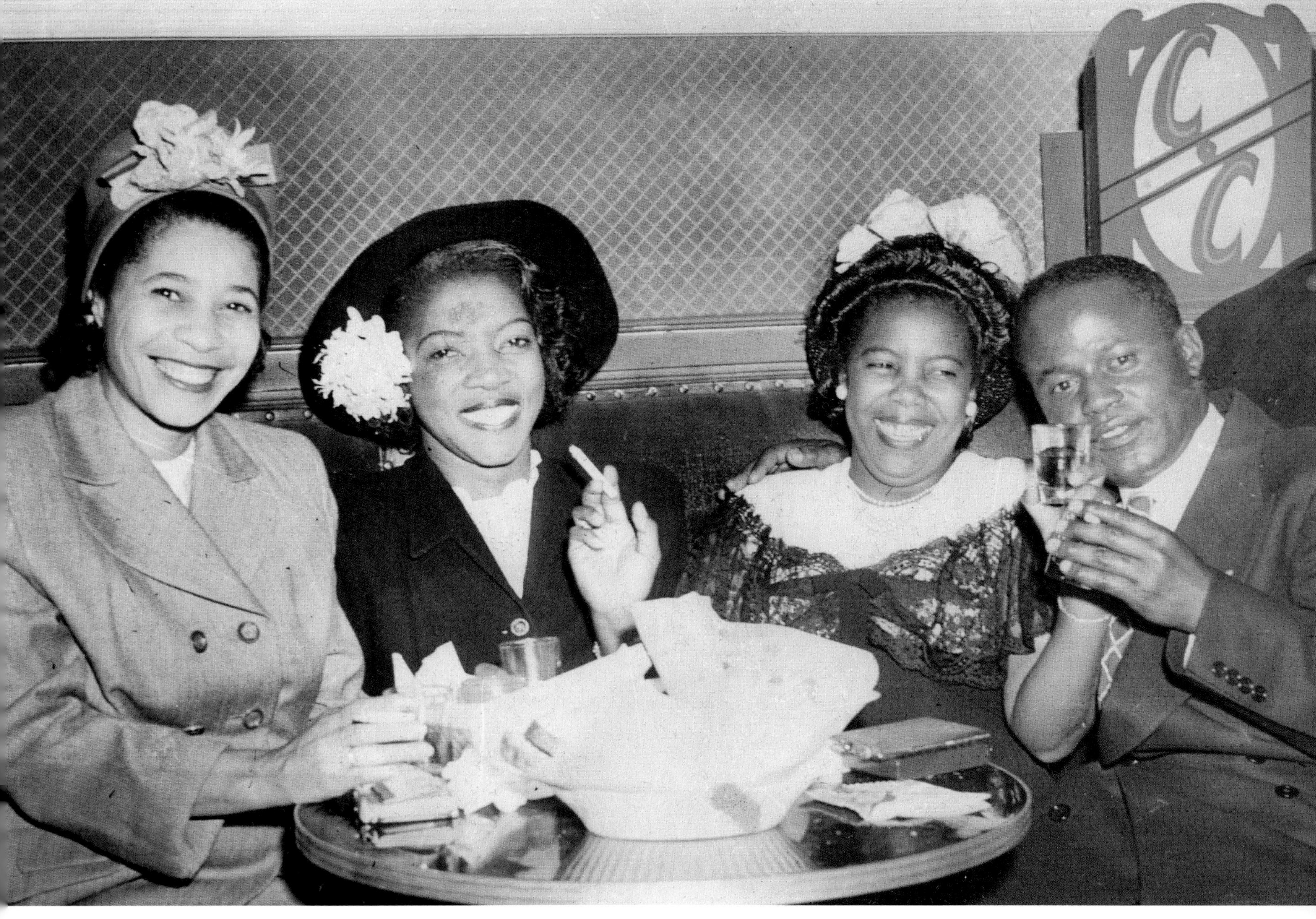

**LEFT:** Having their picture taken at the Zenda Ballroom. Inside the photo folder was written, "In remembrance of a brief friendship which I hope will not be like 'ships in the nite.' Anje Narajo. 5-17-52."

**FACING:** Les Brown conducts his orchestra at the Hollywood Palladium, New Year's Eve, 1951.

One of the few big dance halls to welcome Mexican Americans was the Zenda Ballroom in downtown Los Angeles. Once a whites-only venue, entrepreneur Joe Garcia took over the 2,500-person-capacity dance hall in the early 1950s and began booking performers such as Tito Puente and mambo king Pérez Prado, who were very popular with Latino audiences.

Zenda
BALLROOM - CAFE
936 W. 7th St. Los Angeles 17, Calif.
Dance to a Name Band
Every Saturday Night
8:00 p.m. to 2:00 a.m.
Rumba Matinee
every Sun. afternoon
4:00 to 8:00 p.m.
ZENDA BALLROOM is available for weddings, dances & parties
Phone Vandyke 8384 or Madison 9-9384

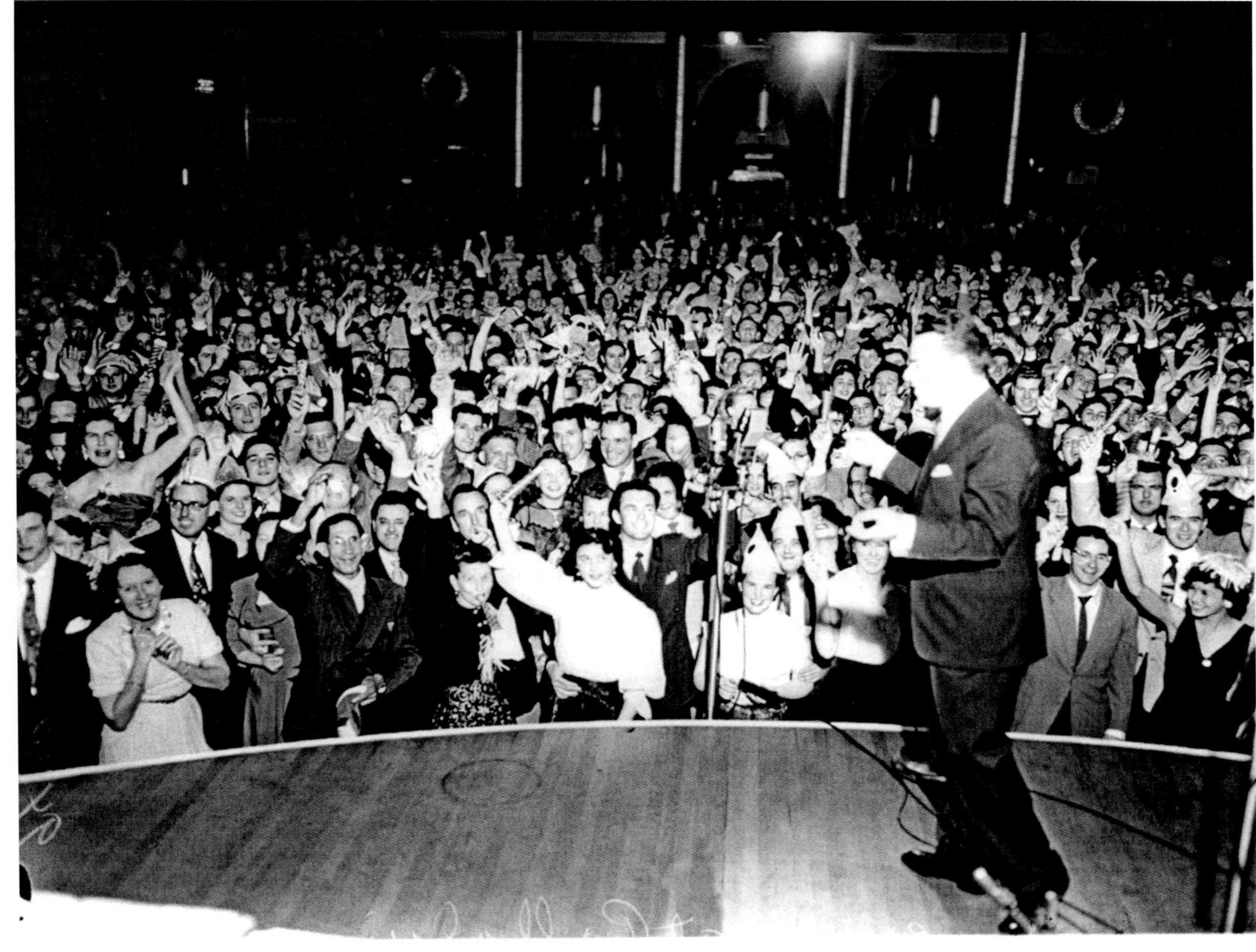

Los Angeles also had a vibrant burlesque scene in the 1950s. The Colony Club on Western Avenue in Gardena was a popular mixed-race venue with three shows nightly until 2 a.m. On Tuesday nights its "Famous Battle of the Burlesque Queens" brought in the crowds.

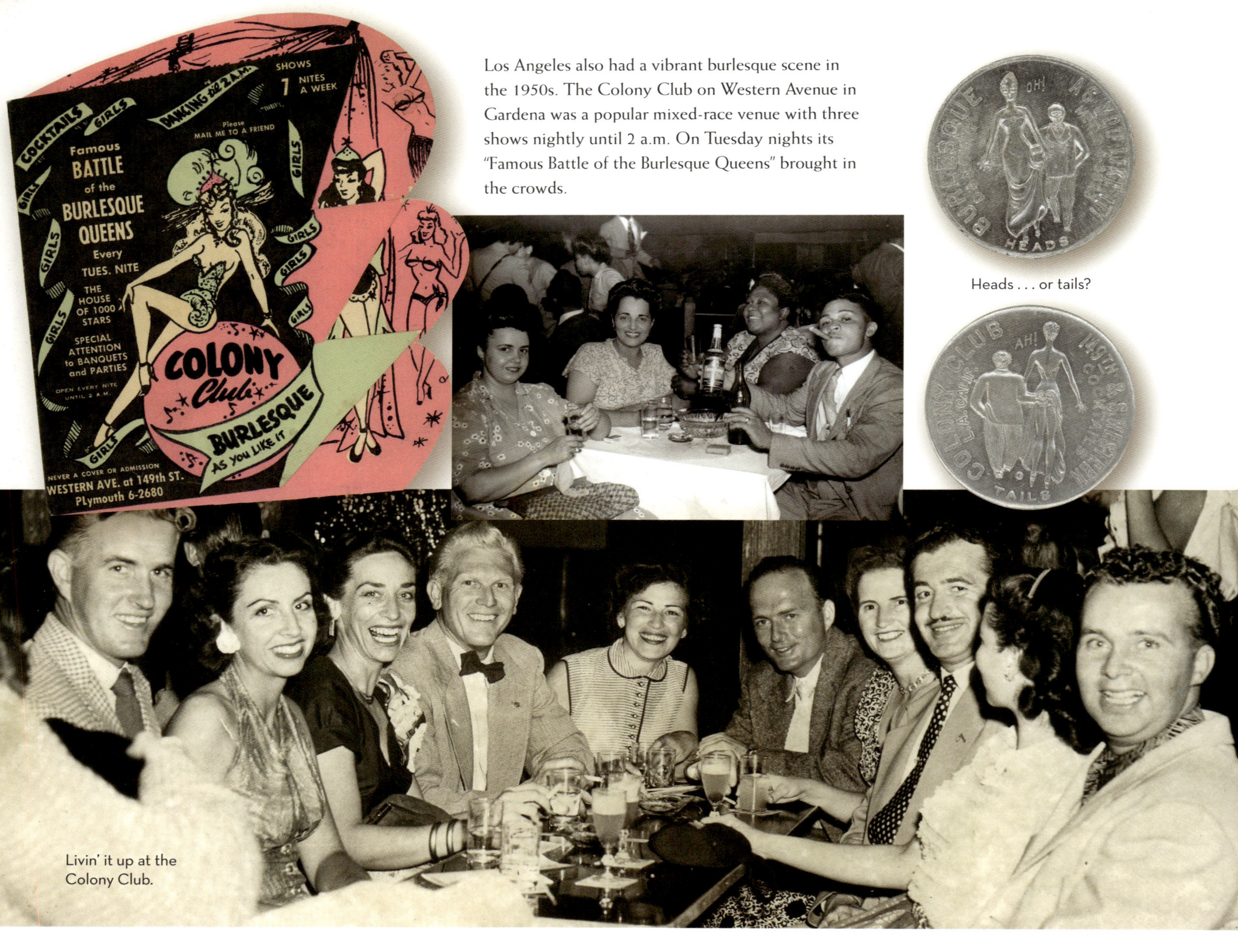


Heads . . . or tails?

Livin' it up at the Colony Club.

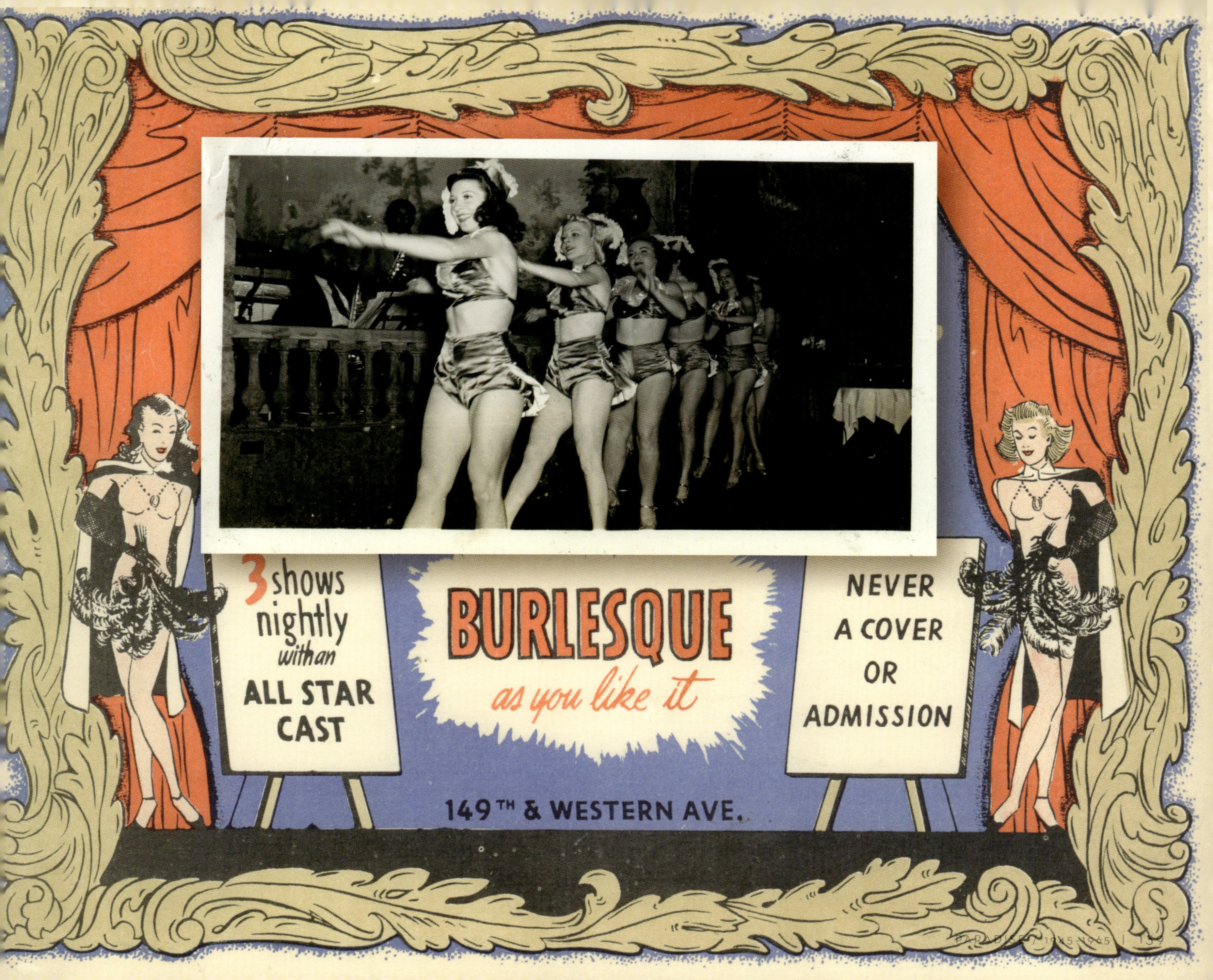
3 shows nightly with an ALL STAR CAST
BURLESQUE
as you like it
NEVER A COVER OR ADMISSION
149TH & WESTERN AVE.

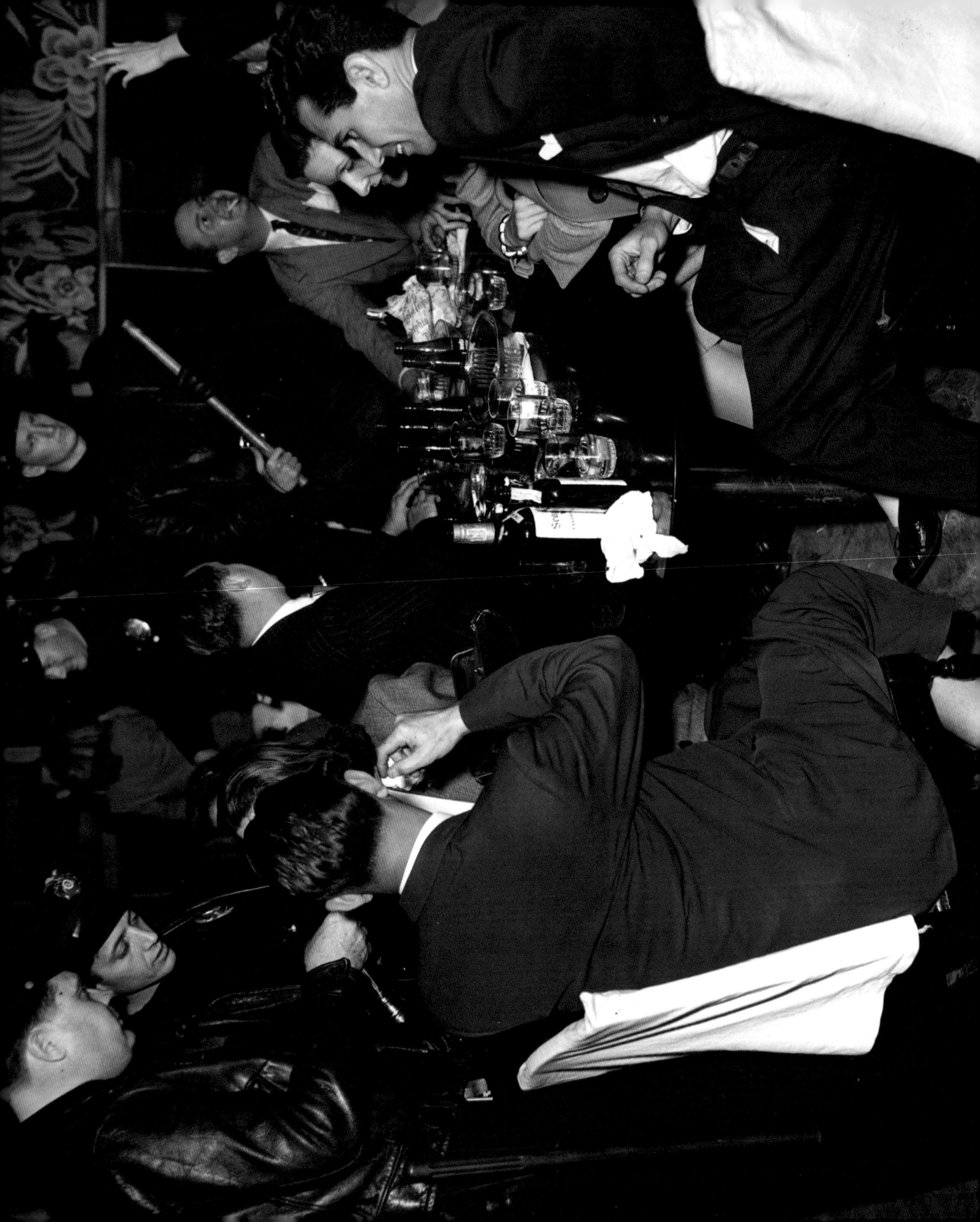

**FACING:** A police raid at the Casa Blanca nightclub in San Pedro, 1947. The *Los Angeles Times* called it "a breeding place of crime."

**RIGHT:** Disc jockey Bob Eubanks—later the host of *The Newlywed Game*—opened a chain of Cinnamon Cinder clubs, including this one in Studio City, so that underage teens could have a nightclub of their own. Lookin' cool in '63.

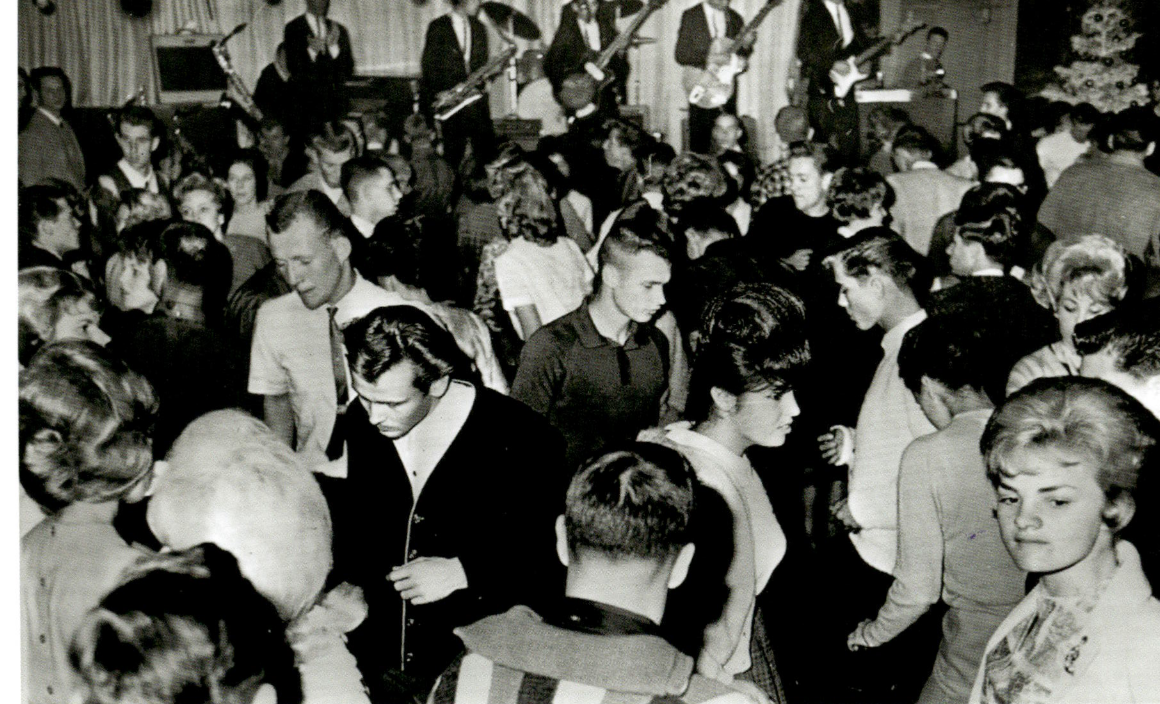

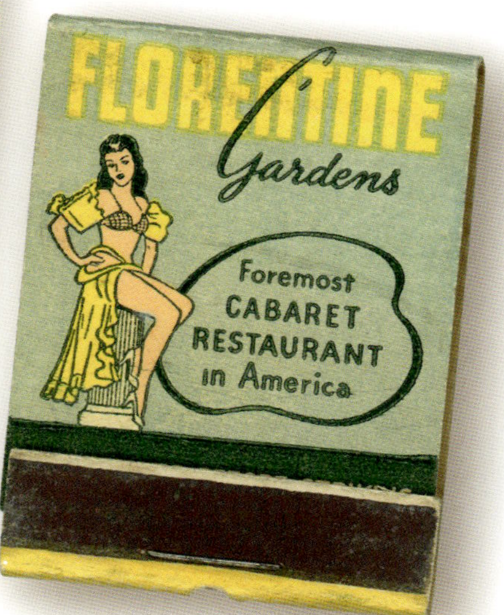


**LEFT AND BELOW:** Another Hollywood dinner theater was Florentine Gardens, with acts that ranged from Sophie Tucker to partially clad chorus girls strutting onstage while the crowd dined on mediocre Italian food.

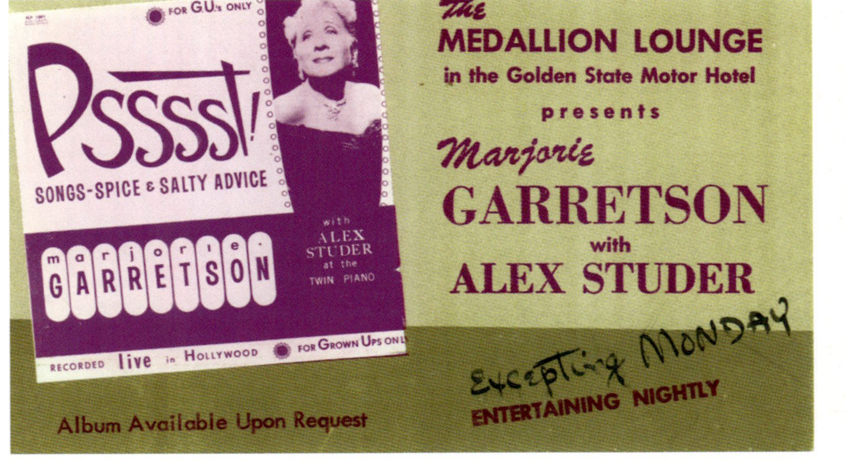


**BELOW, RIGHT:** Pssssst! The Medallion Lounge presents Marjorie Garretson's songs, spice, and salty advice—for grown-ups only.

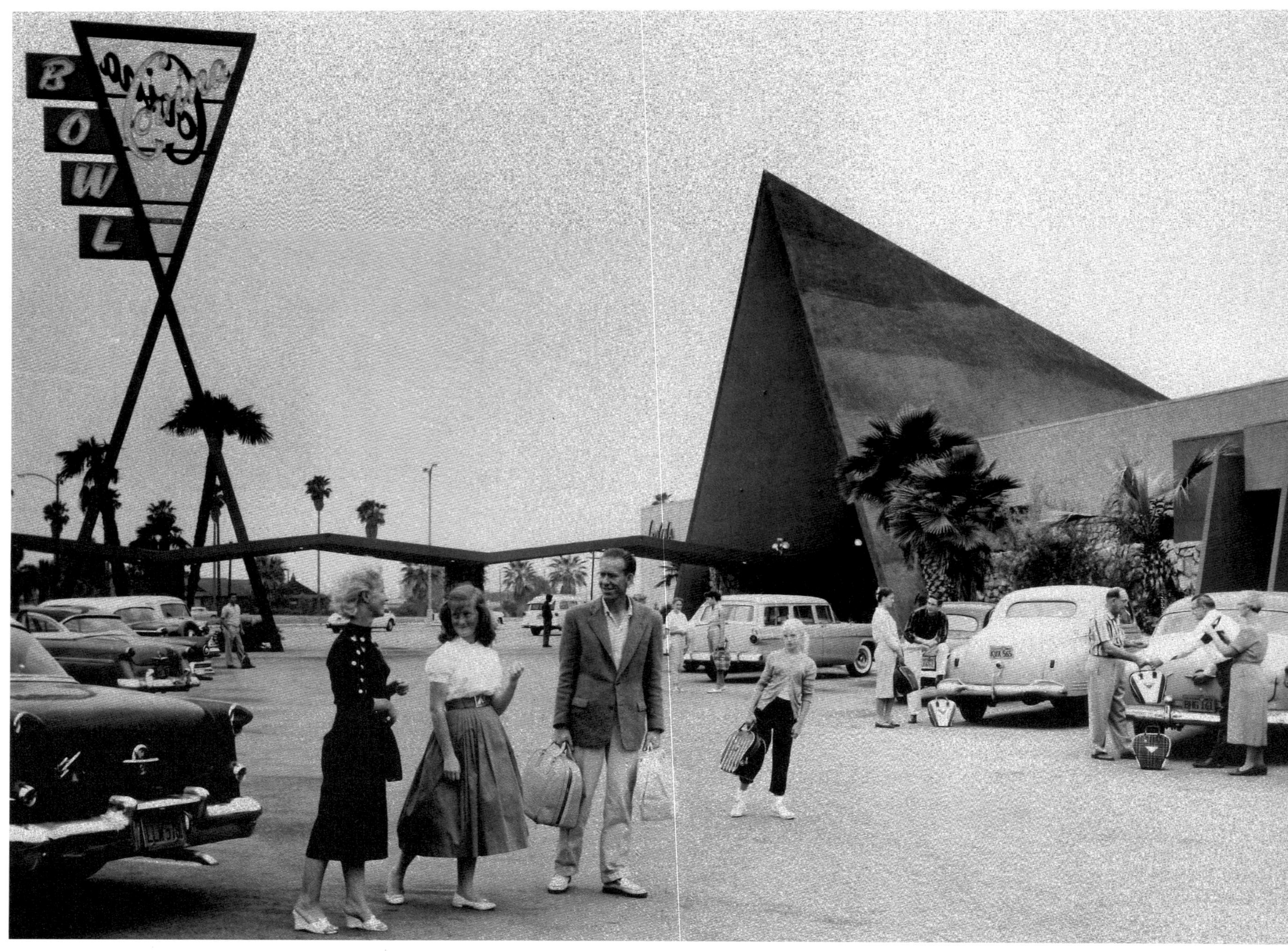
BOWL

Not surprisingly, entertainment in the region's new suburbs—unlike urban Los Angeles—was more sedate. Family bowling centers and drive-in theaters were the norm. Teenagers hung out at carhop restaurants and cruised the boulevards in hot rods. Churches were everywhere. For the adults, there were piano bars and cocktail lounges, most with nightly dancing.

**FACING:** Family fun in 1955 at Covina Bowl, America's first full-service bowling center with coffee shop, children's day care, banquet and meeting rooms, beauty parlor, and retail stores. There was even a cocktail lounge with live entertainment.

**BELOW:** Checking their iPhones in 1952.

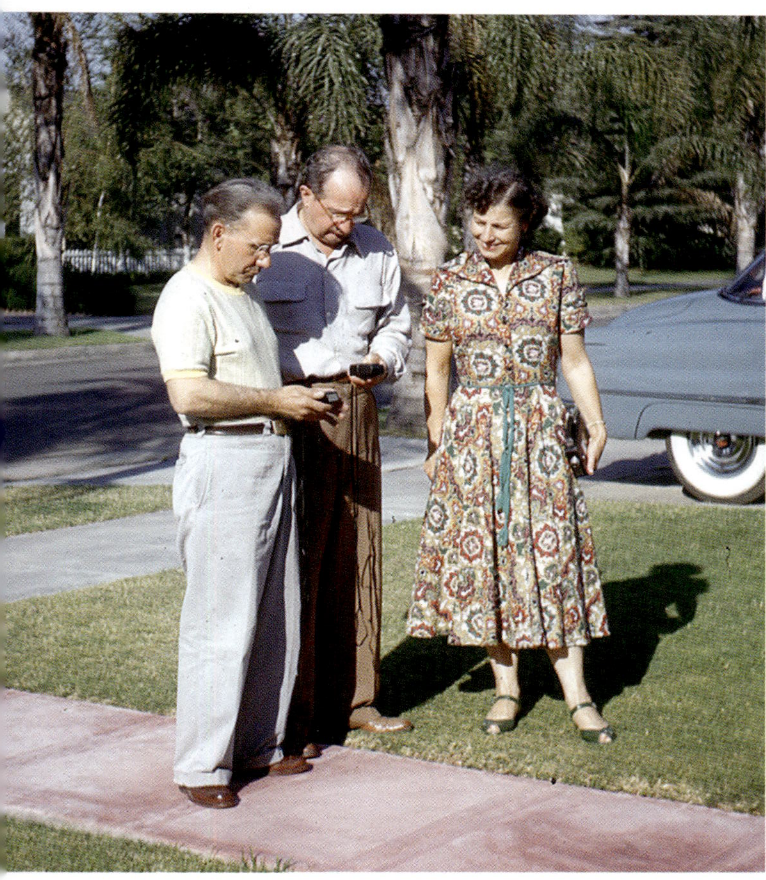

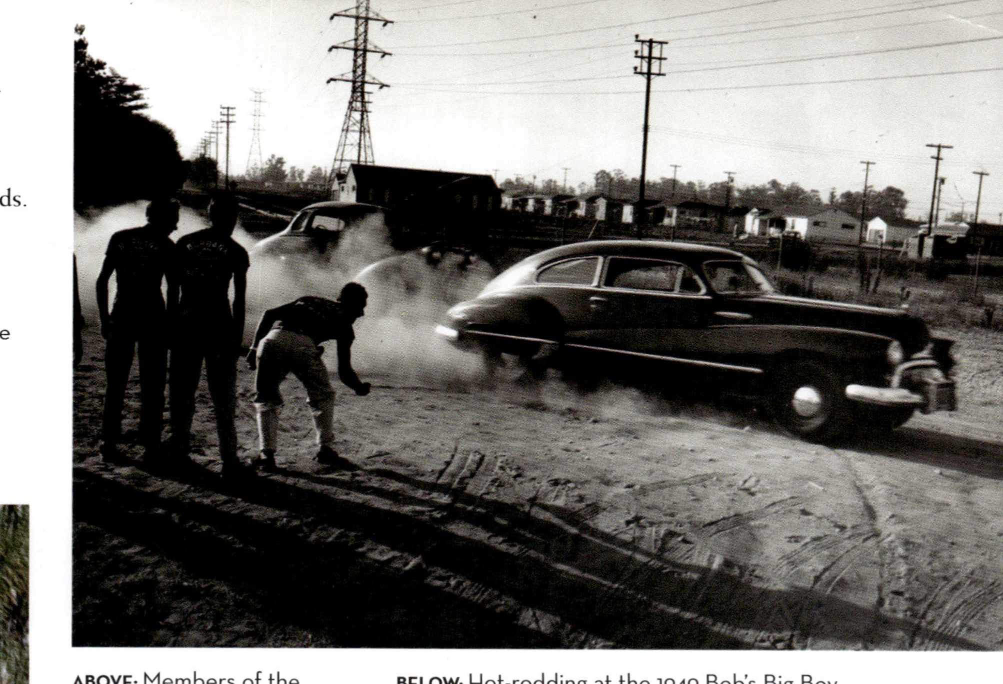

**ABOVE:** Members of the Burbank Prowlers with their souped-up hot rod.

**BELOW:** Hot-rodding at the 1949 Bob's Big Boy in Toluca Lake. This designated California landmark welcomes car clubs to this day.

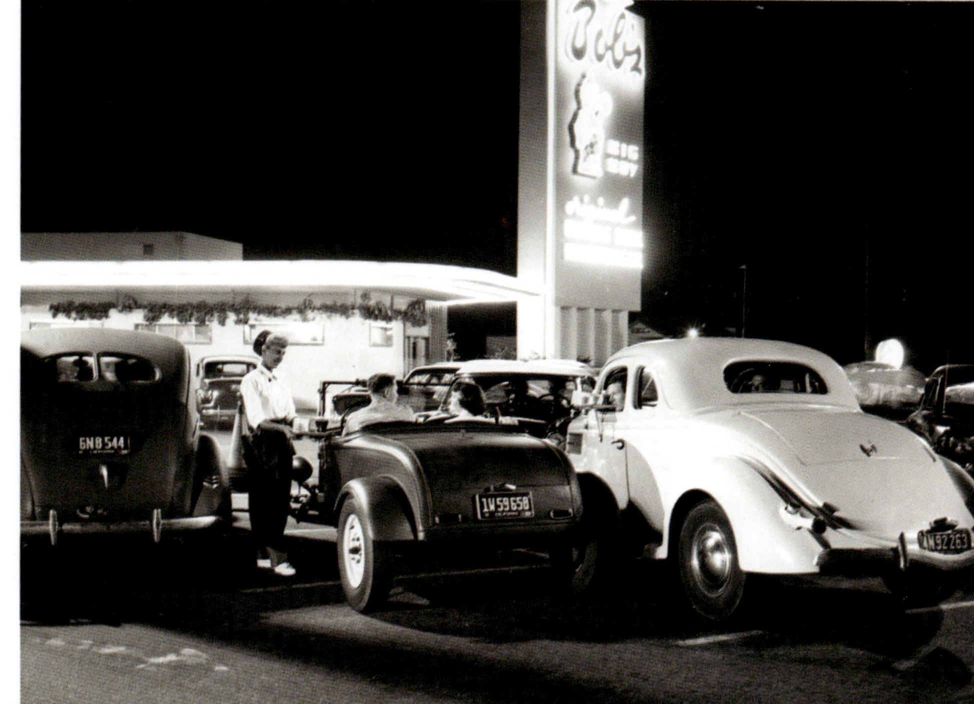

Surfing at Malibu

# Surf's Up!

Malibu, Santa Monica, Redondo, Hermosa, Huntington, Laguna, Venice. The Beach Boys, Dick Dale and the Del-Tones, Muscle Beach, Gidget. In the early 1960s, Southern California was fused in the popular imagination with surfing, beach parties, youth, and freedom.

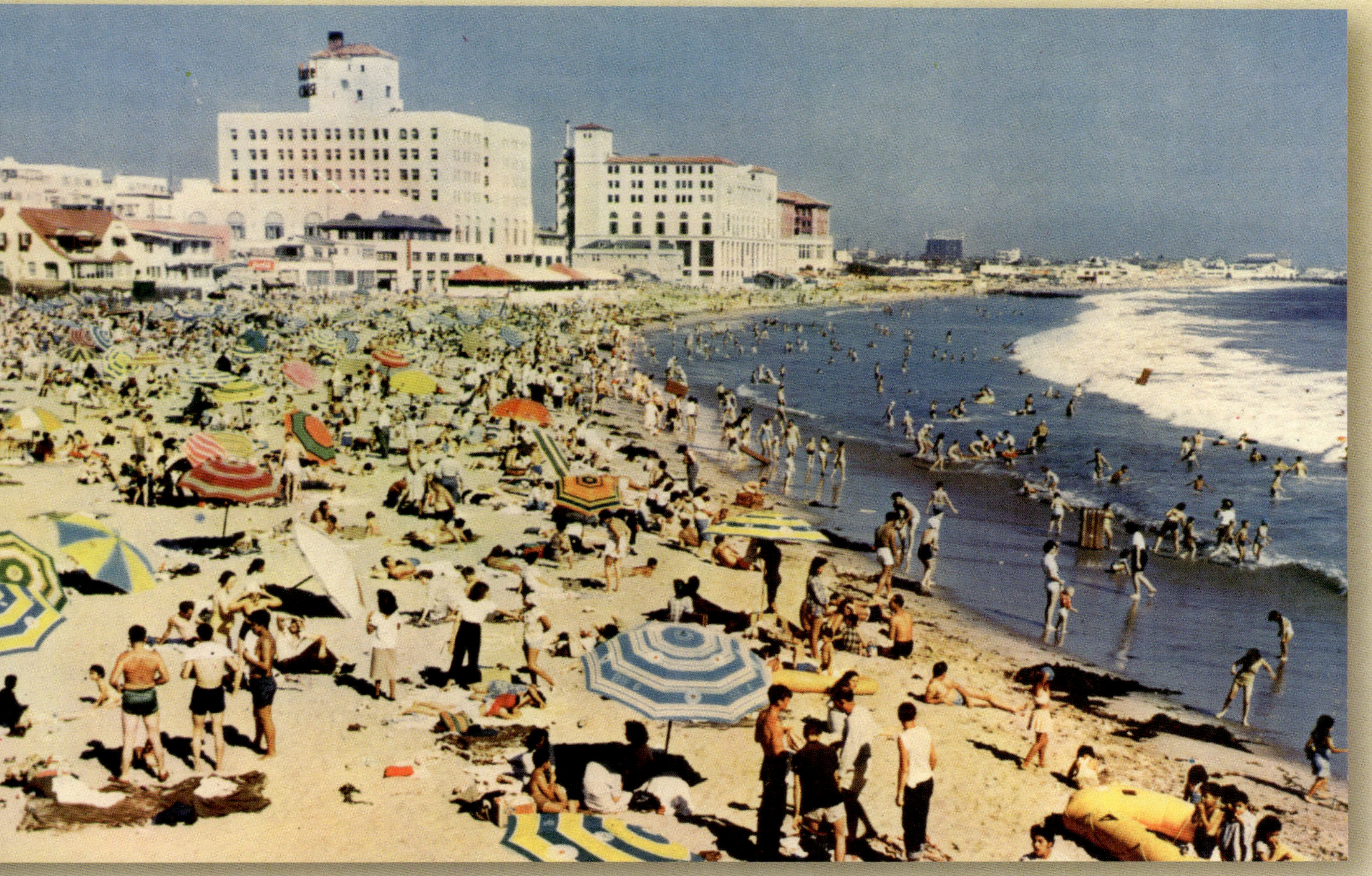

Santa Monica was a bit more crowded than Malibu.

# Smog

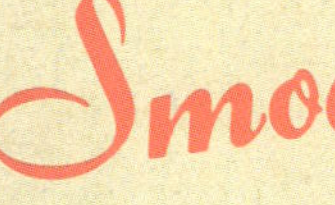

The Los Angeles region is a basin with mountains to the north and east, and the Pacific Ocean to the west and south. Often air is trapped in a "temperature inversion," which is a blanket of warm air that holds smoke and coastal fog—smog—close to the ground. Smog alerts were common when the brownish haze made visibility poor and breathing difficult. It took decades, starting in the 1960s, to apply technologies necessary to reduce air pollution from the region's millions of cars.

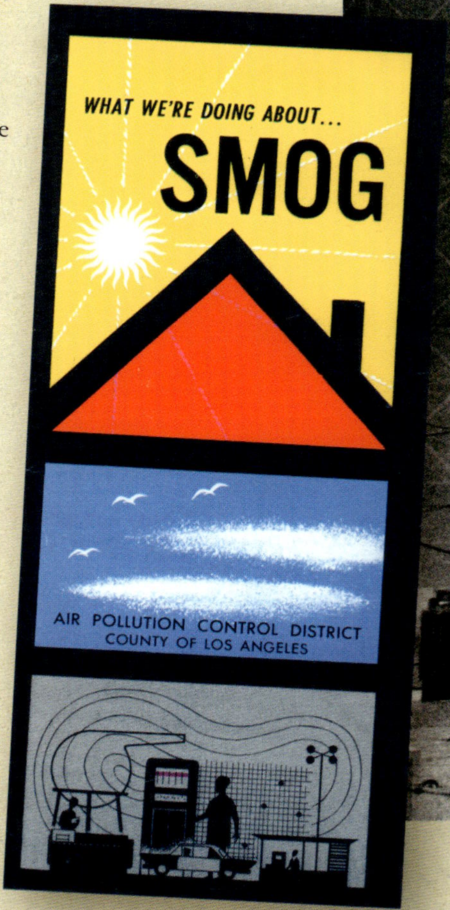

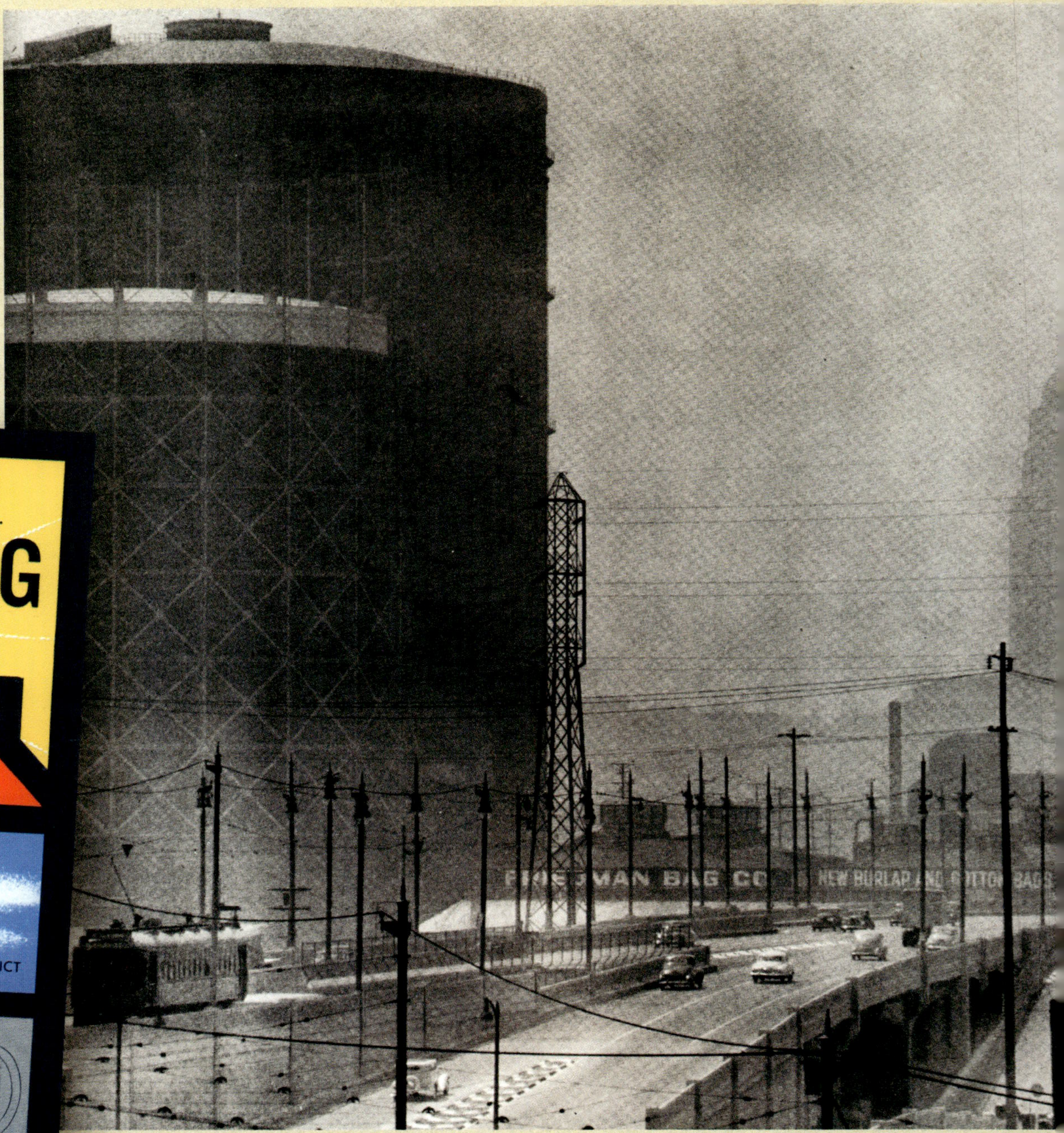

**FAR RIGHT:** Smog envelops downtown Los Angeles.

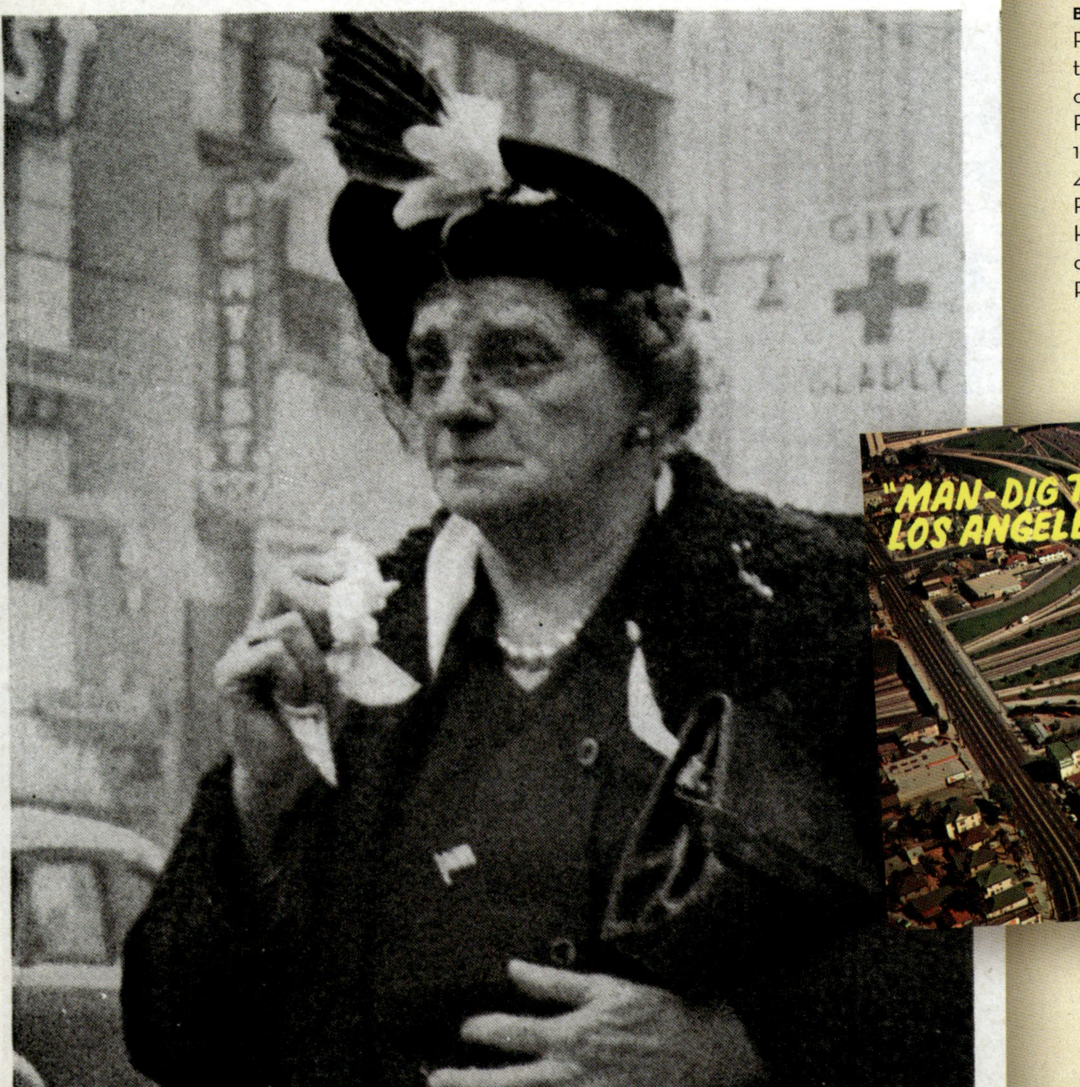

**IRRITANT** smog irritates citizens. A factory by-product, it tries tempers and starts tears.



**BELOW:** The Golden State Freeway (I-5), from Los Angeles to Orange County, was completed in 1956, the Ventura Freeway (101, 134) opened in 1960, the San Diego Freeway (I-405) in 1961, the Santa Monica Freeway (I-10) in 1963, and the Harbor Freeway (110), from downtown south towards San Pedro, in the late 1950s.

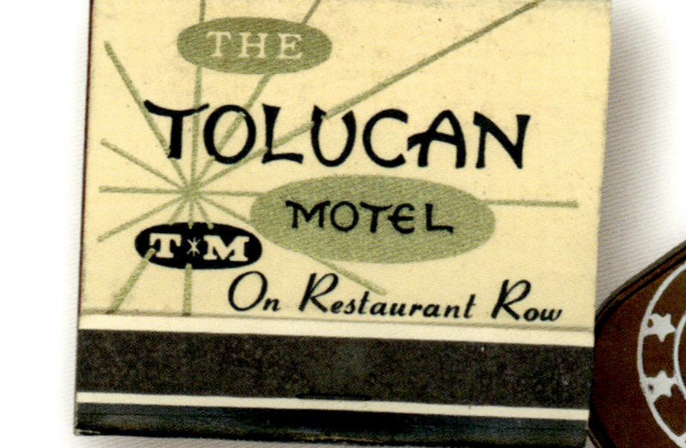


**ABOVE:** The Fabulous Flamingo Motel in North Hollywood in the flamboyant Dingbat style.

As tourism exploded after World War II, independent mom-and-pop motels blossomed along Southland highways to accommodate travelers. To capture the eye and wallet of motorists, owners outdid each other with fanciful and often exotic themes, swimming pools, and televisions in every room. Yet by the 1970s, freeways had bypassed and corporate chains decimated the independents, purging the roadside of a fun, quirky, and uniquely American phenomenon.

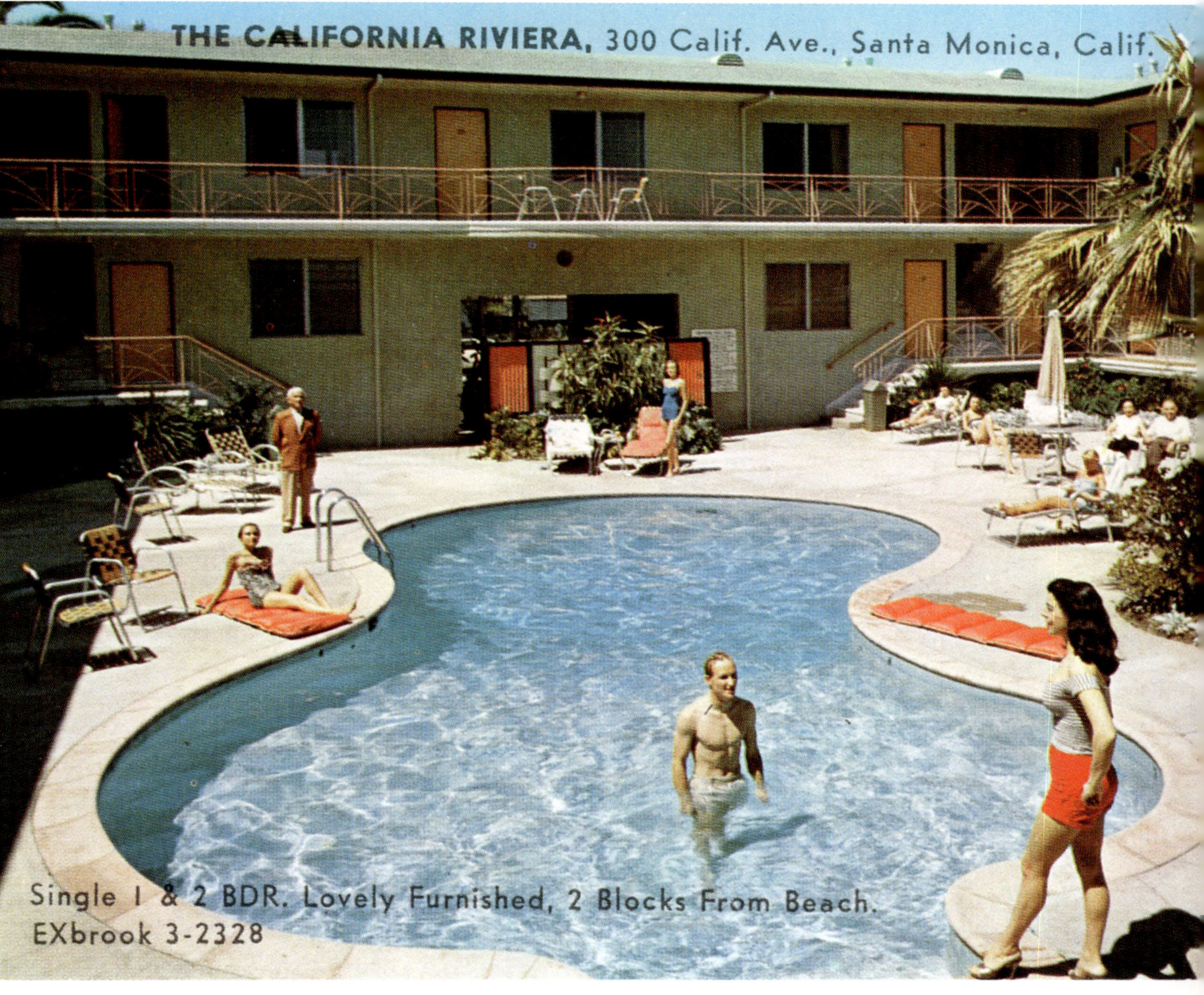


Awkward posing at The California Riviera apartments in Santa Monica. No suntans allowed.

**RIGHT:** The African American-owned Palm Vue Motel in South Central Los Angeles advertised "People of all races welcome" because most motels were still segregated in 1961.

**BELOW, RIGHT:** The Tiki-Chinese Kona Kai Motel near Disneyland.

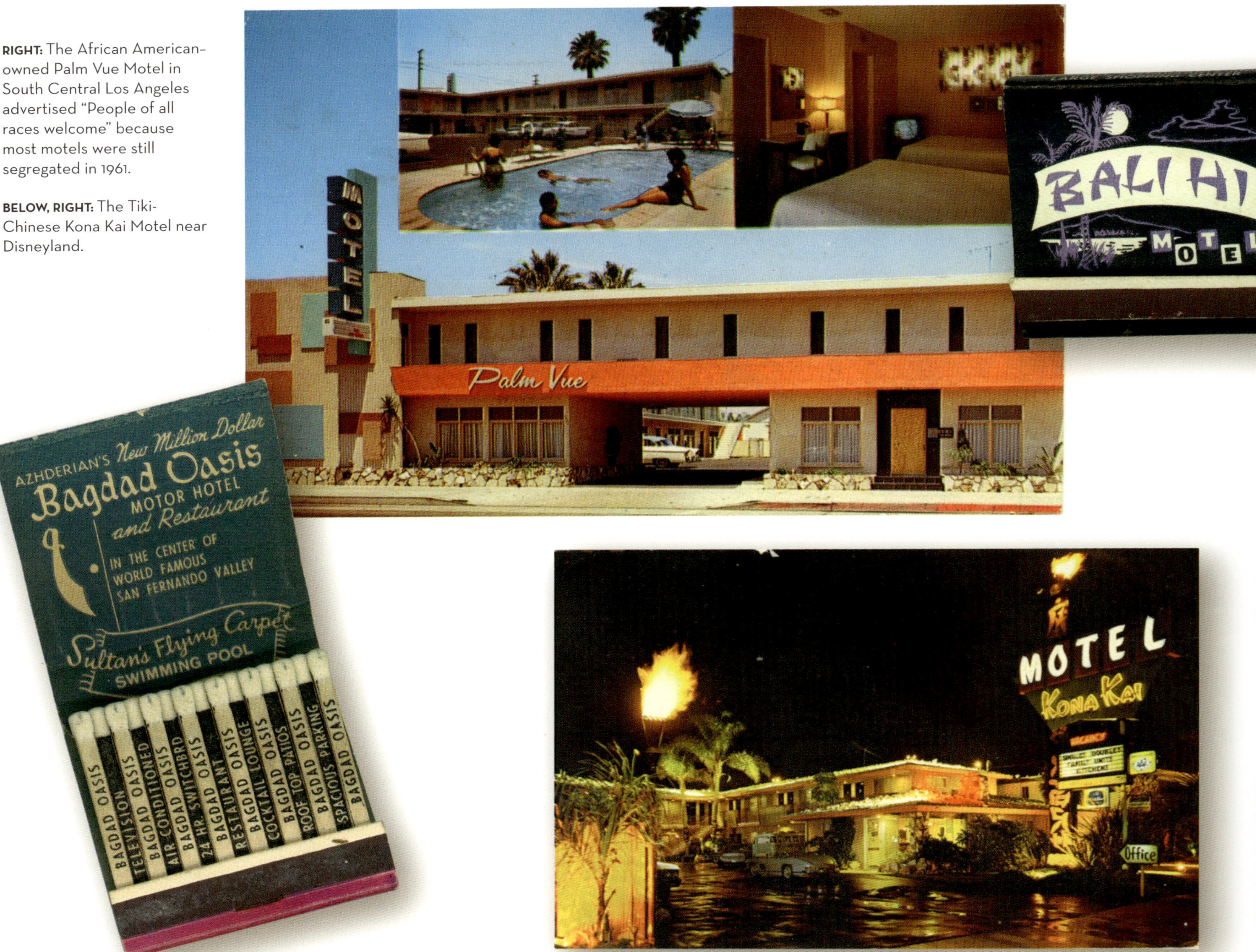

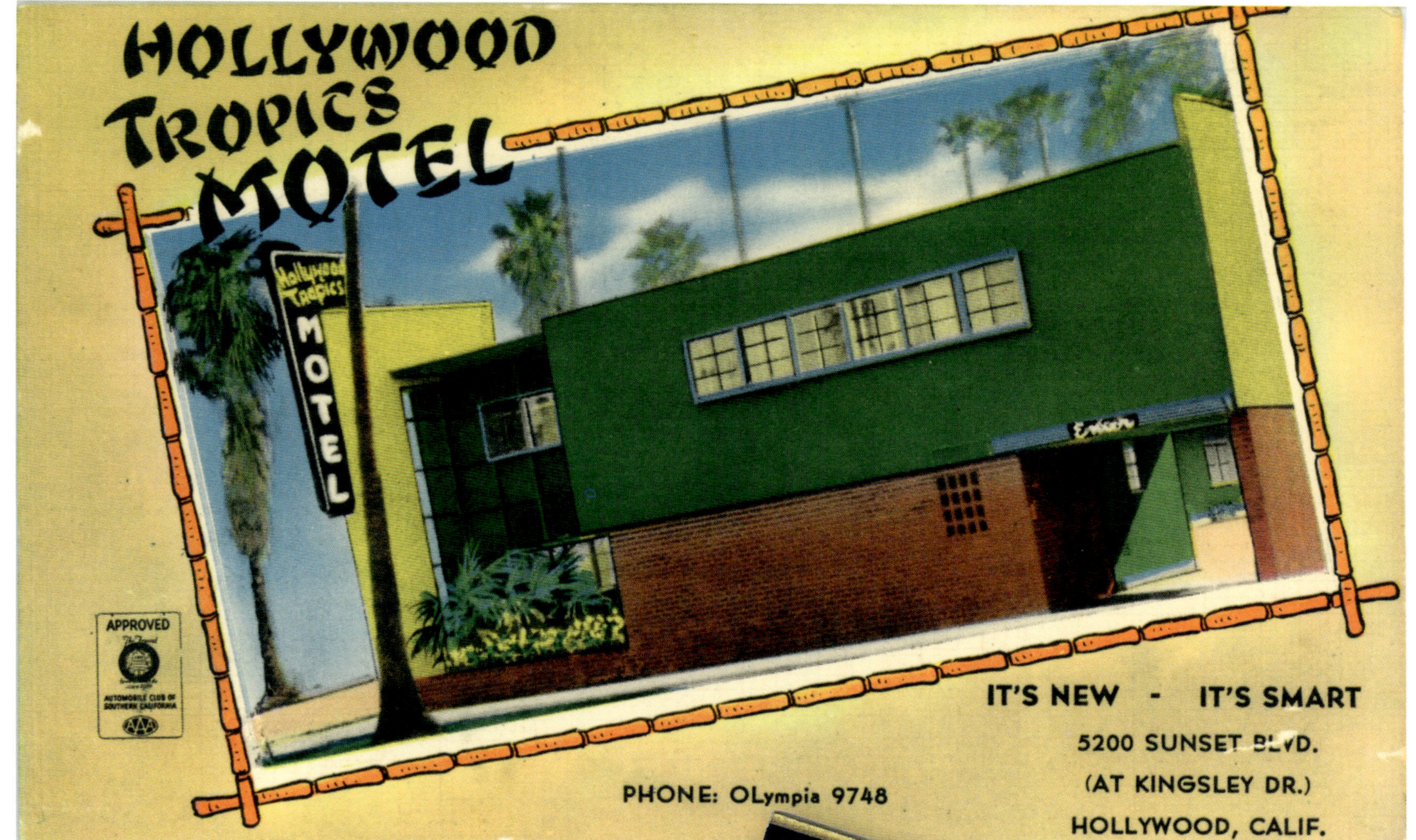


**ABOVE:** "It's New—It's Smart" at the Hollywood Tropics Motel on Sunset Blvd. The back of the postcard proclaimed, "In the '✶' Light, near NBC, CBS, RKO and Paramount Studios; The Blackouts; The Drunkard; Turn-About; Earl Carrolls; Brown Derby."

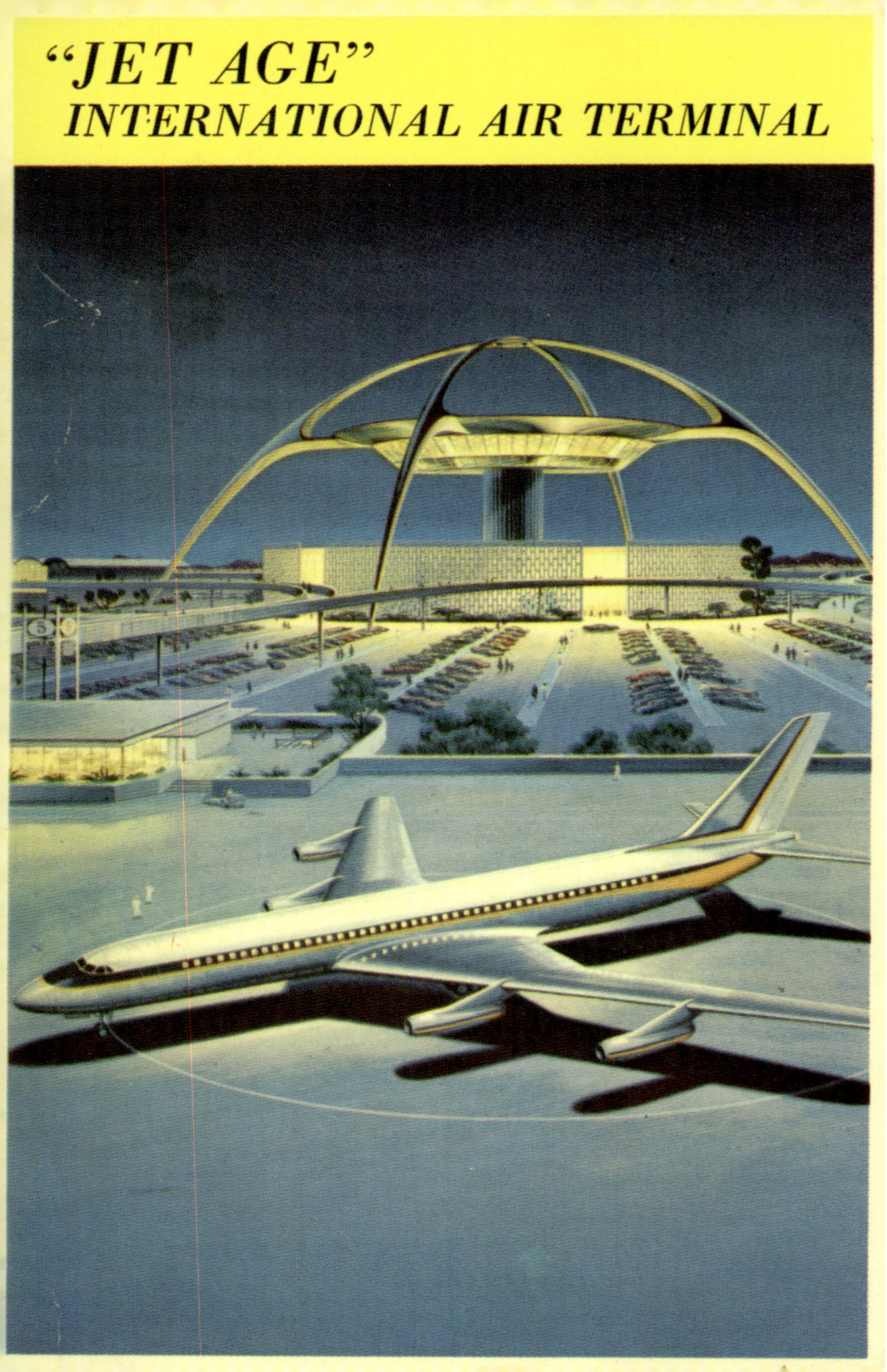

"JET AGE"
INTERNATIONAL AIR TERMINAL

Jet travel necessitated vast airport expansions across the country. In response, a consortium of local architects designed an entirely new LAX with passenger service beginning in 1962. Its focal point was the futuristic Theme Building, a restaurant and observation deck with the theme being—of course—the Jet Age!

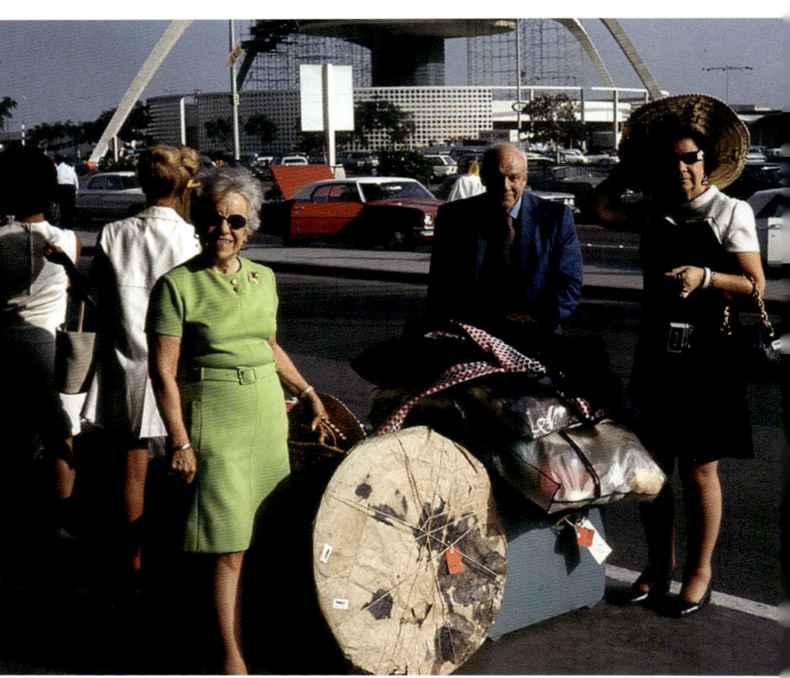

**ABOVE:** Traveling light.

**LEFT:** The theme of the 1961 Theme Building at LAX was the Jet Age. It housed the Skyhigh Restaurant & Cocktail Lounge, never the control tower or the Jetson family.

**FACING:** Off to Germany to visit Oma Freida in 1962.

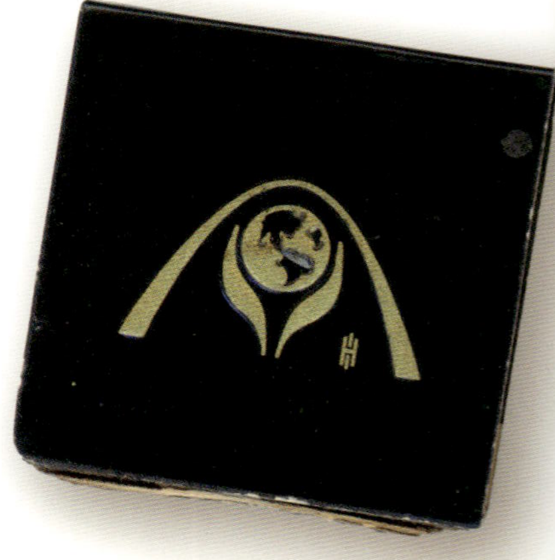

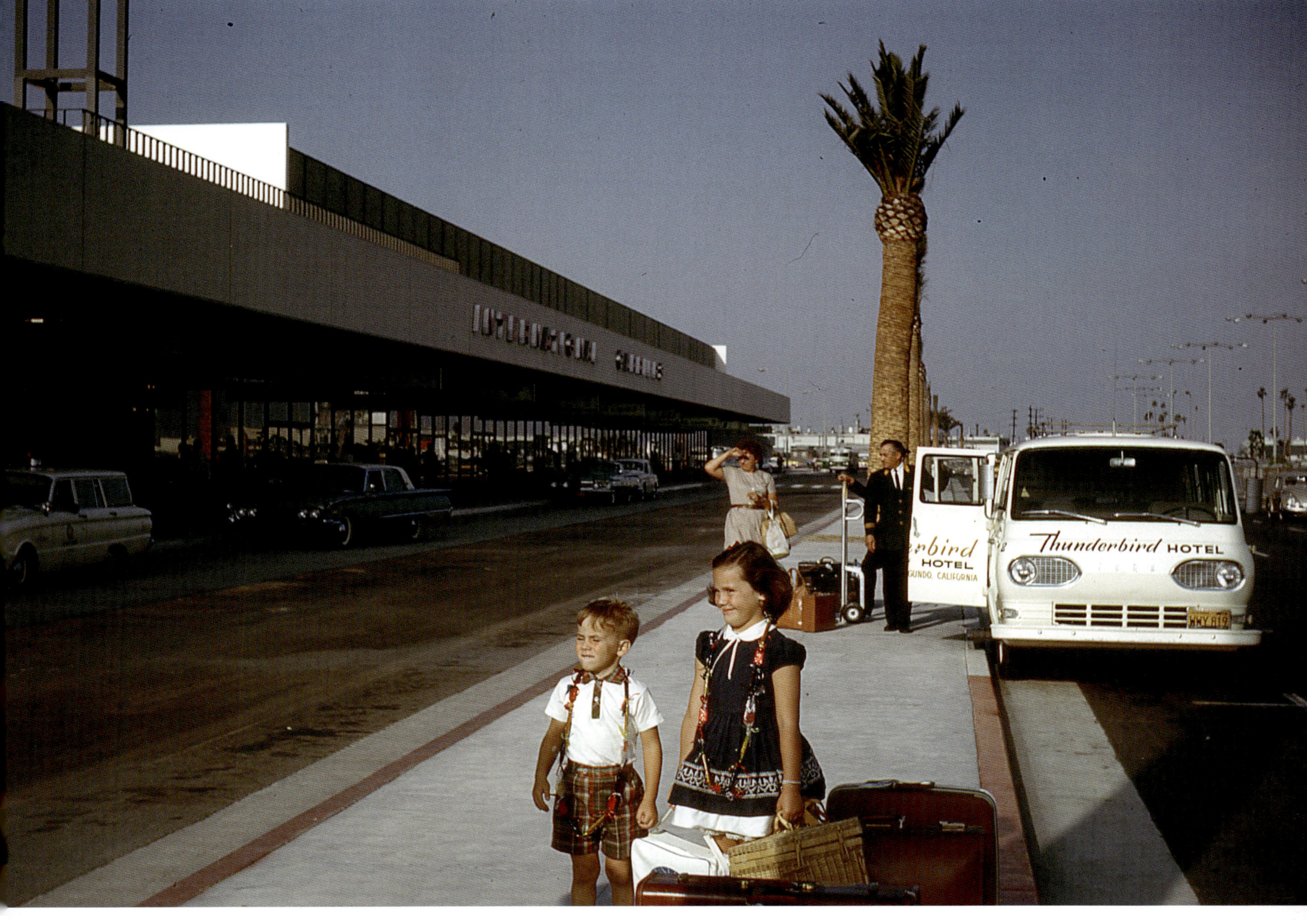
Thunderbird HOTEL
HOTEL

# Dining Out

Dining out in postwar Los Angeles meant choosing from a panoply of options. Polynesian palaces, working-class cafeterias, coffee shops, drive-ins, chop suey joints, steakhouses, continental-style fine dining restaurants, hamburger stands, and the birth of fast food, among many others.

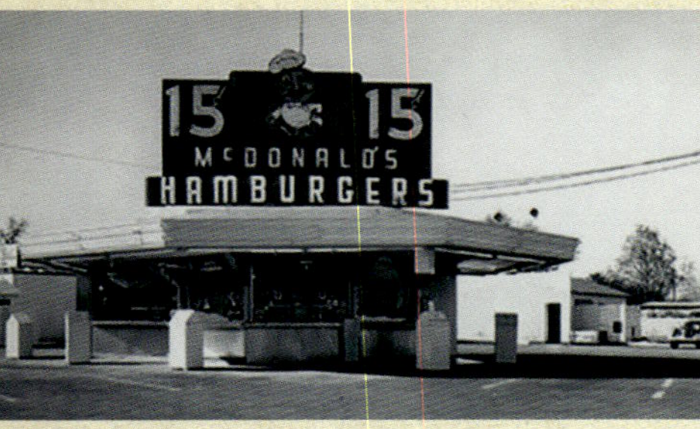


**ABOVE:** McDonald's began as a small self-service hamburger stand in nearby San Bernardino in 1948. By the time Ray Kroc franchised his first location in Des Plaines, Illinois, in 1955, there were already around a dozen McDonald's restaurants in the Southwest.

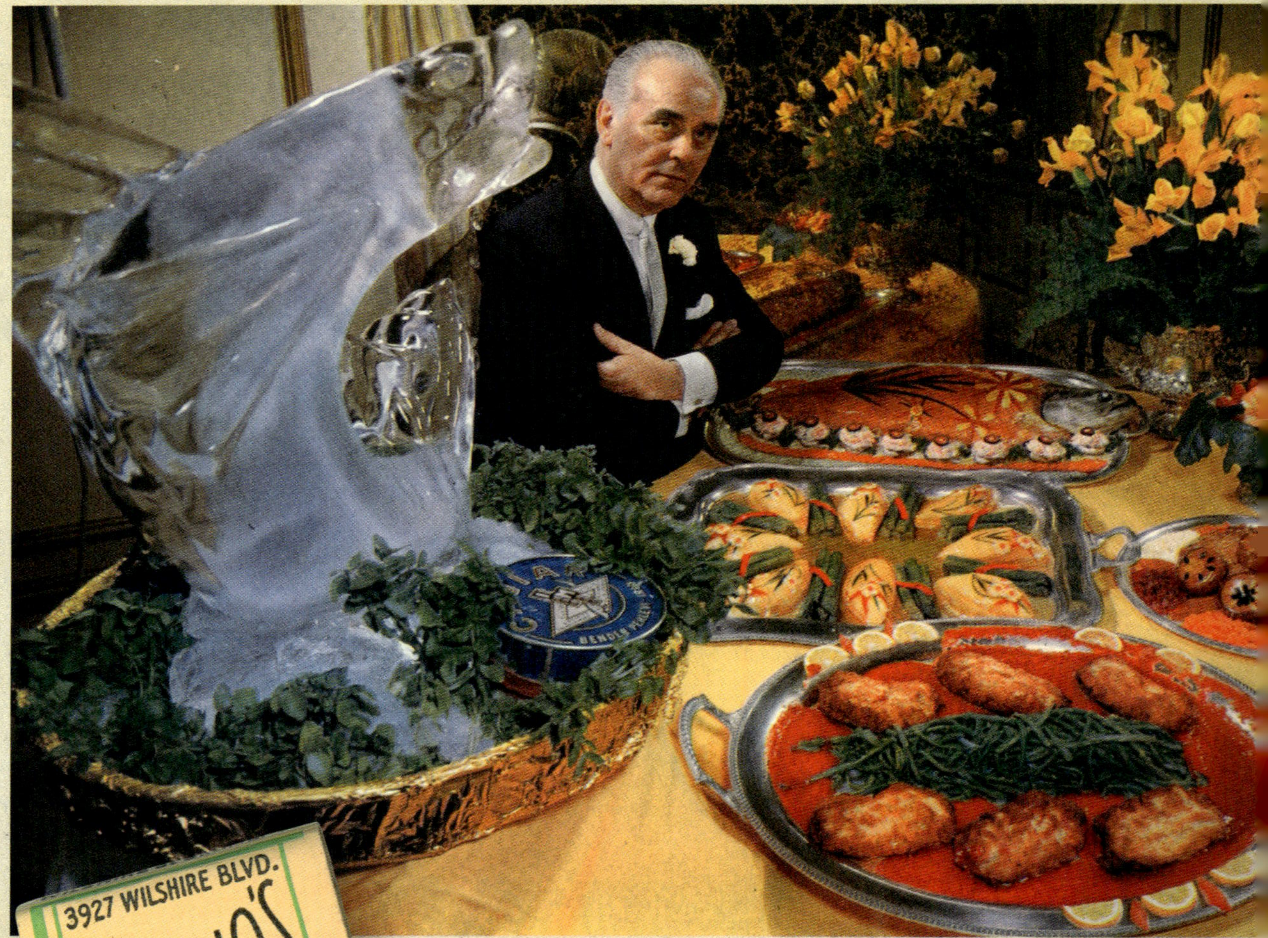

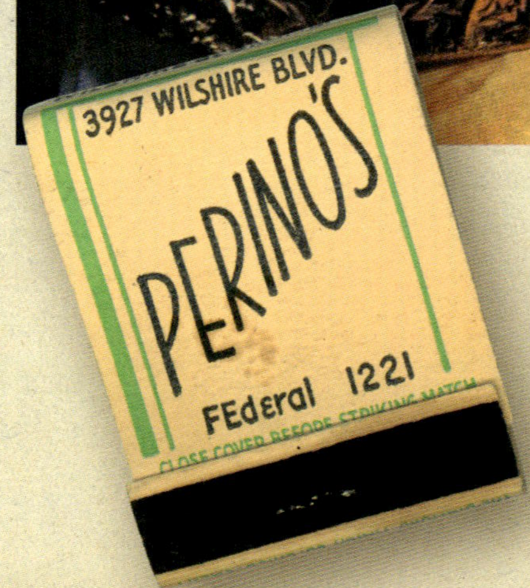

**ABOVE:** Perino's on Wilshire Boulevard was the finest continental-style fine dining restaurant in Los Angeles. From 1932 until 1969, Alexander Perino ensured perfection in service, atmosphere, and cuisine.

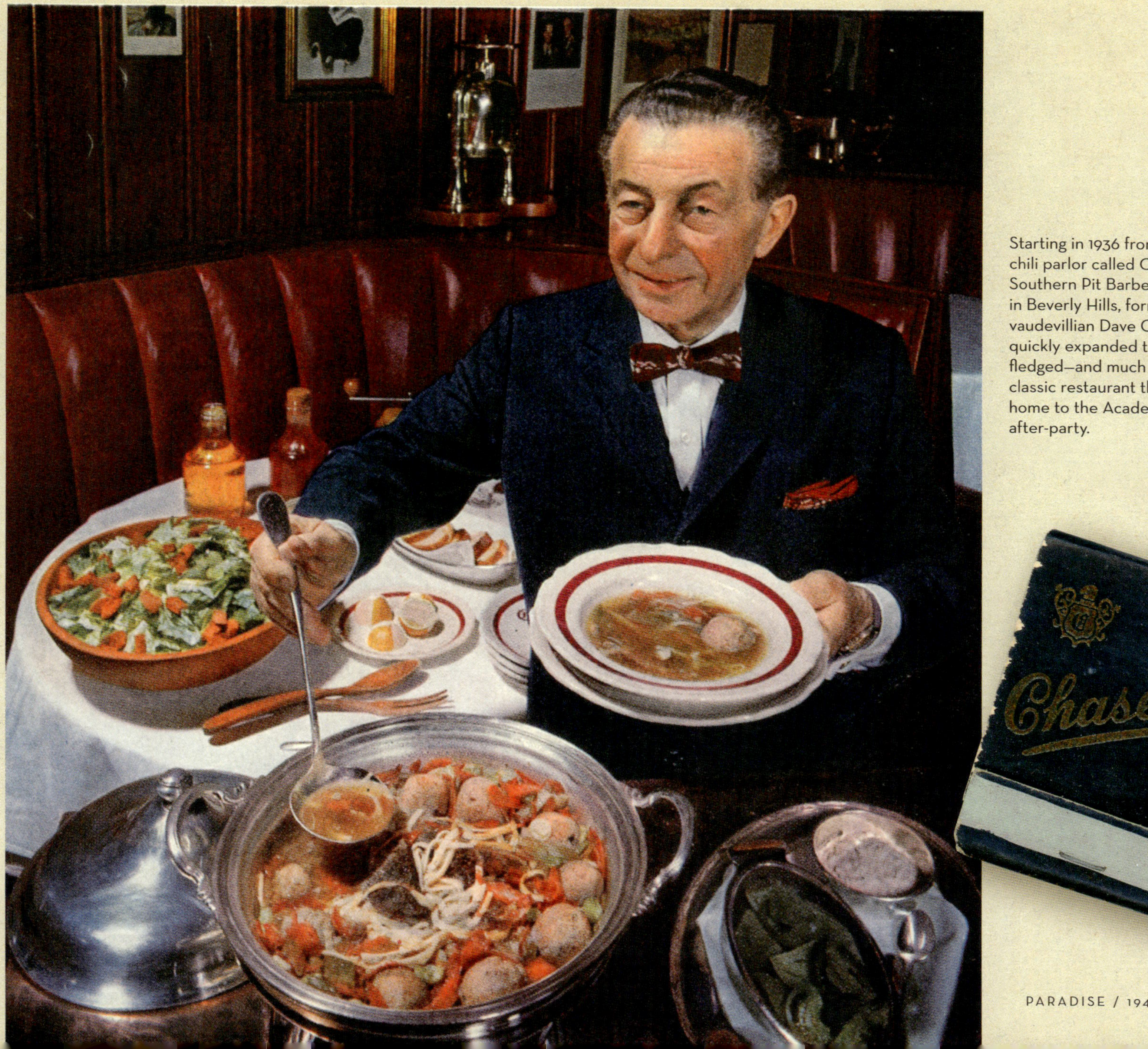

Starting in 1936 from a tiny chili parlor called Chasen's Southern Pit Barbecue in Beverly Hills, former vaudevillian Dave Chasen quickly expanded to a full-fledged—and much beloved—classic restaurant that became home to the Academy Awards after-party.

Mad men and women dining in 1964 atop Westwood's Kirkeby Center.

**ABOVE:** Enjoy the Pagoda Delight cocktail at Golden Pagoda, a neon palace in Chinatown.

**RIGHT:** Courtesy rickshaw service at the Islander featuring "romantic foods of Polynesia" and "strangely haunting beverages."

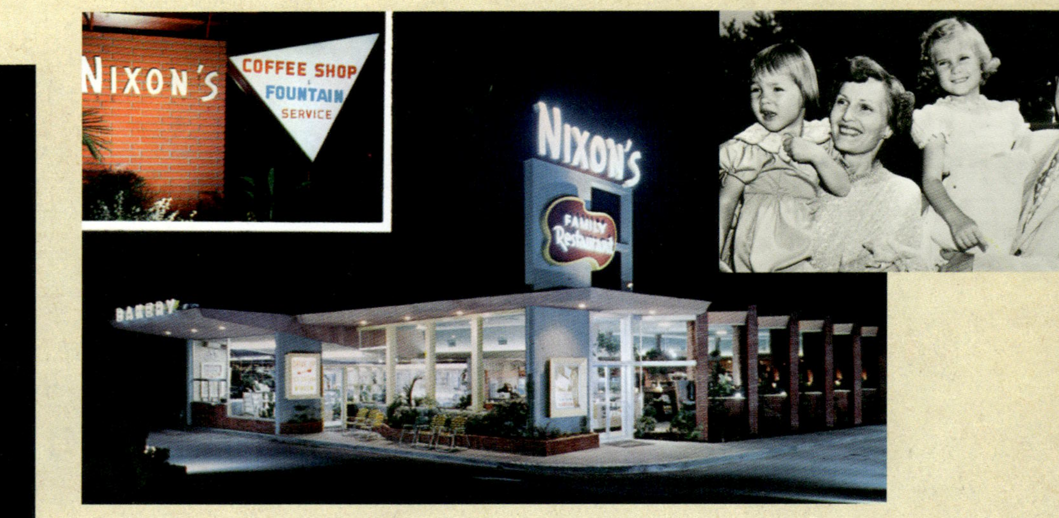


**ABOVE:** Richard Nixon and family in 1952, when he was running for vice president. Tricky Dick's younger brother, Donald, ran Nixon's Family Restaurant—"Home of the Nixon Burger"—in their hometown of Whittier.

**RIGHT:** "For gracious Dining . . . it's ONTRA Cafeteria." At one time, cafeterias were extremely popular in Southern California.

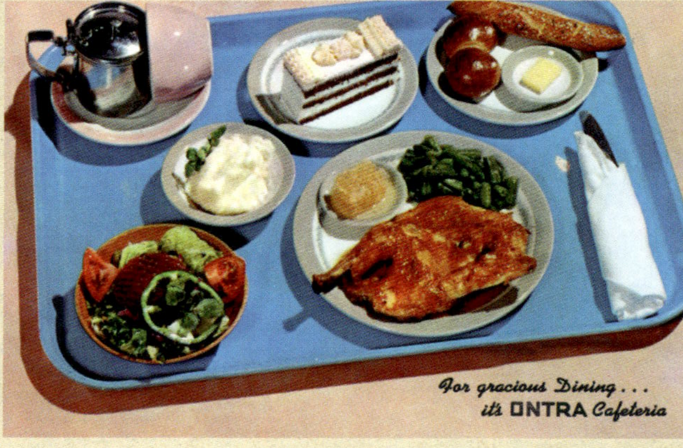


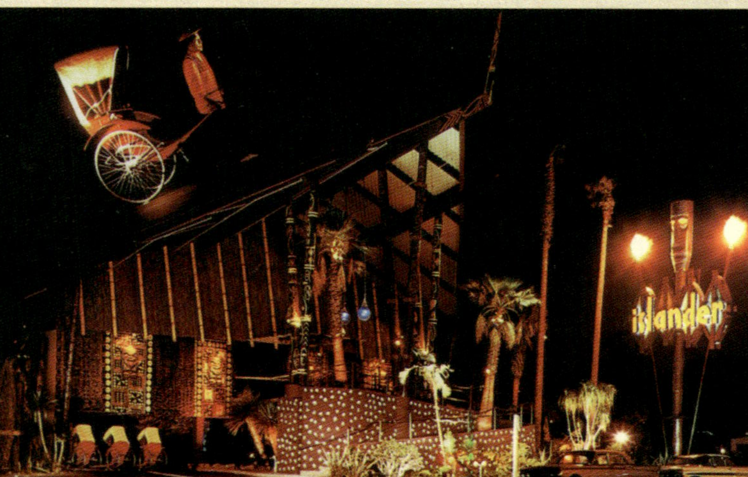

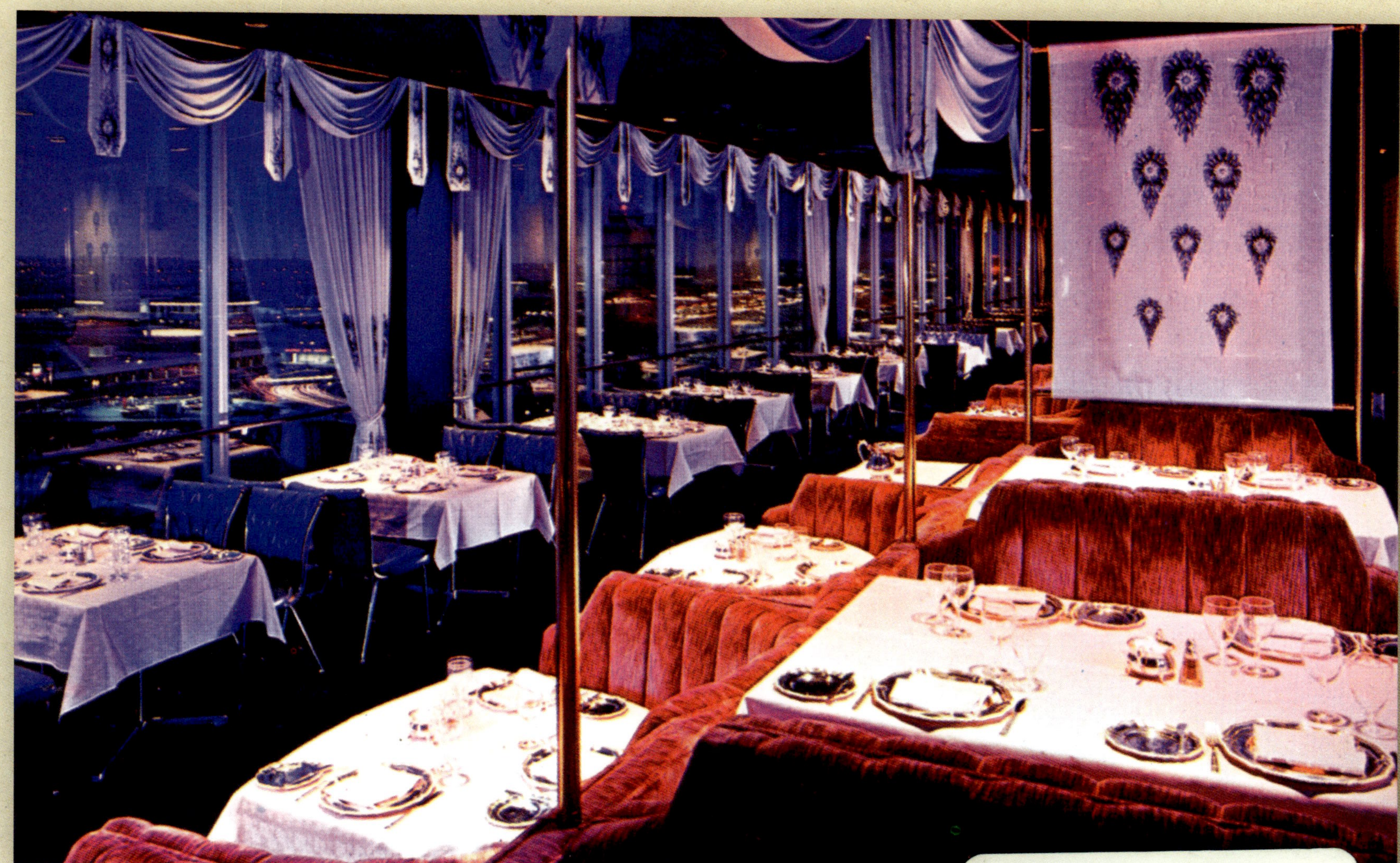

Burgundy and purple velvet (!) at the International Hotel's Penthouse Restaurant next to LAX, "featuring flambé specialties on sterling silver settings"

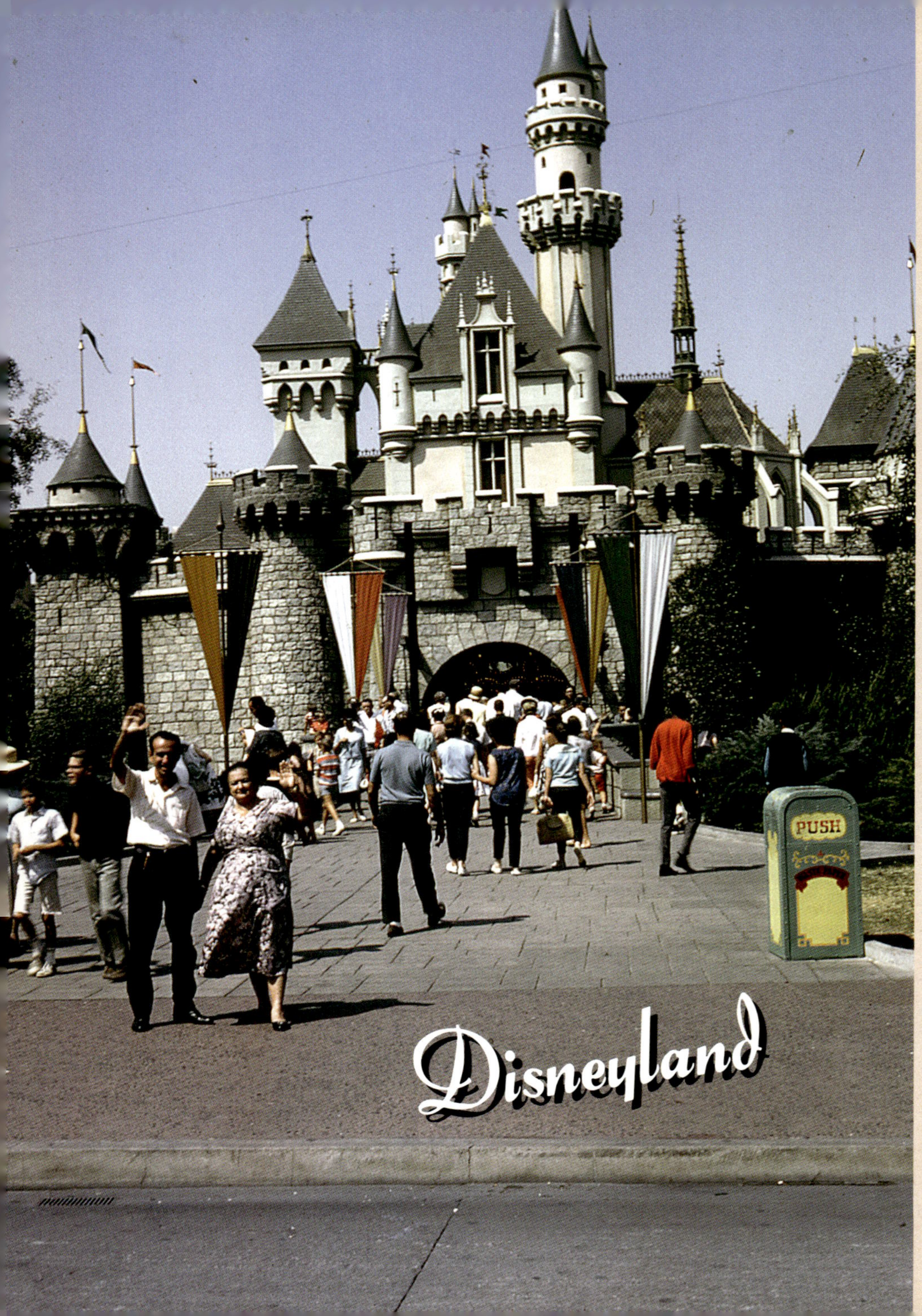

# Disneyland

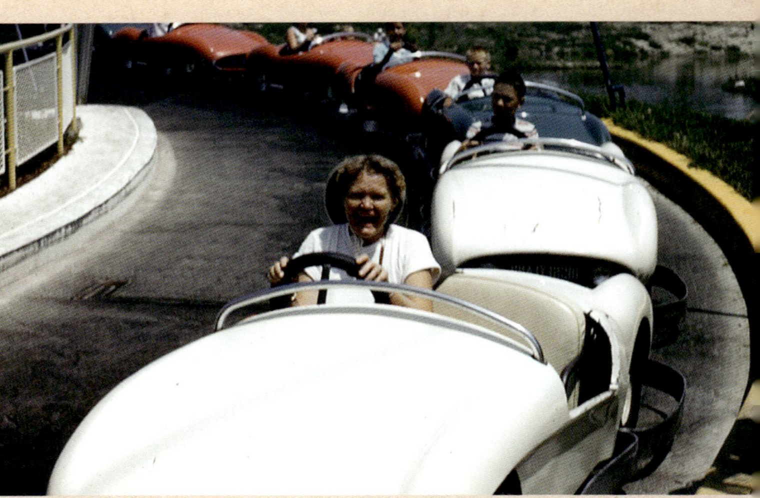

**LEFT:** Knowing that they would probably never see their children again, Hans and Helga waved a final good-bye as they were ushered off into "The Castle."

**ABOVE:** The only car Aunt Gert's allowed to drive since her DUI.

**BELOW:** Big Al fortified with two pens, a notepad, sunglasses, and a pack of smokes on the chilling Dumbo ride.

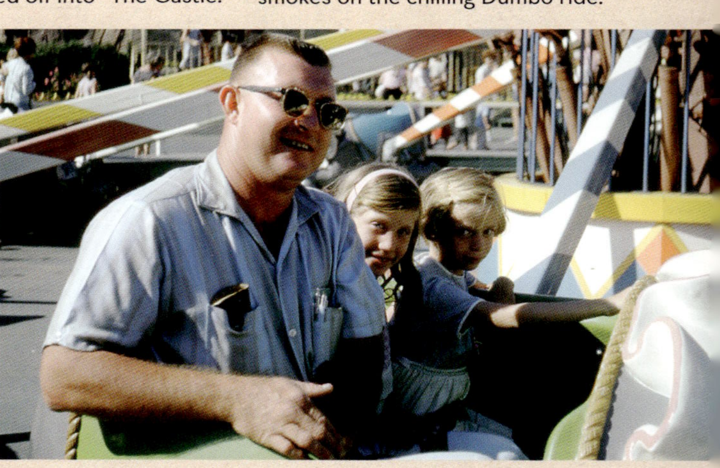

In 1955, Walt Disney fulfilled his dream of building an entirely new type of amusement park. He and his designers created a self-contained world of imaginary lands—Fantasyland, Adventureland, Frontierland, and Tomorrowland—surrounded

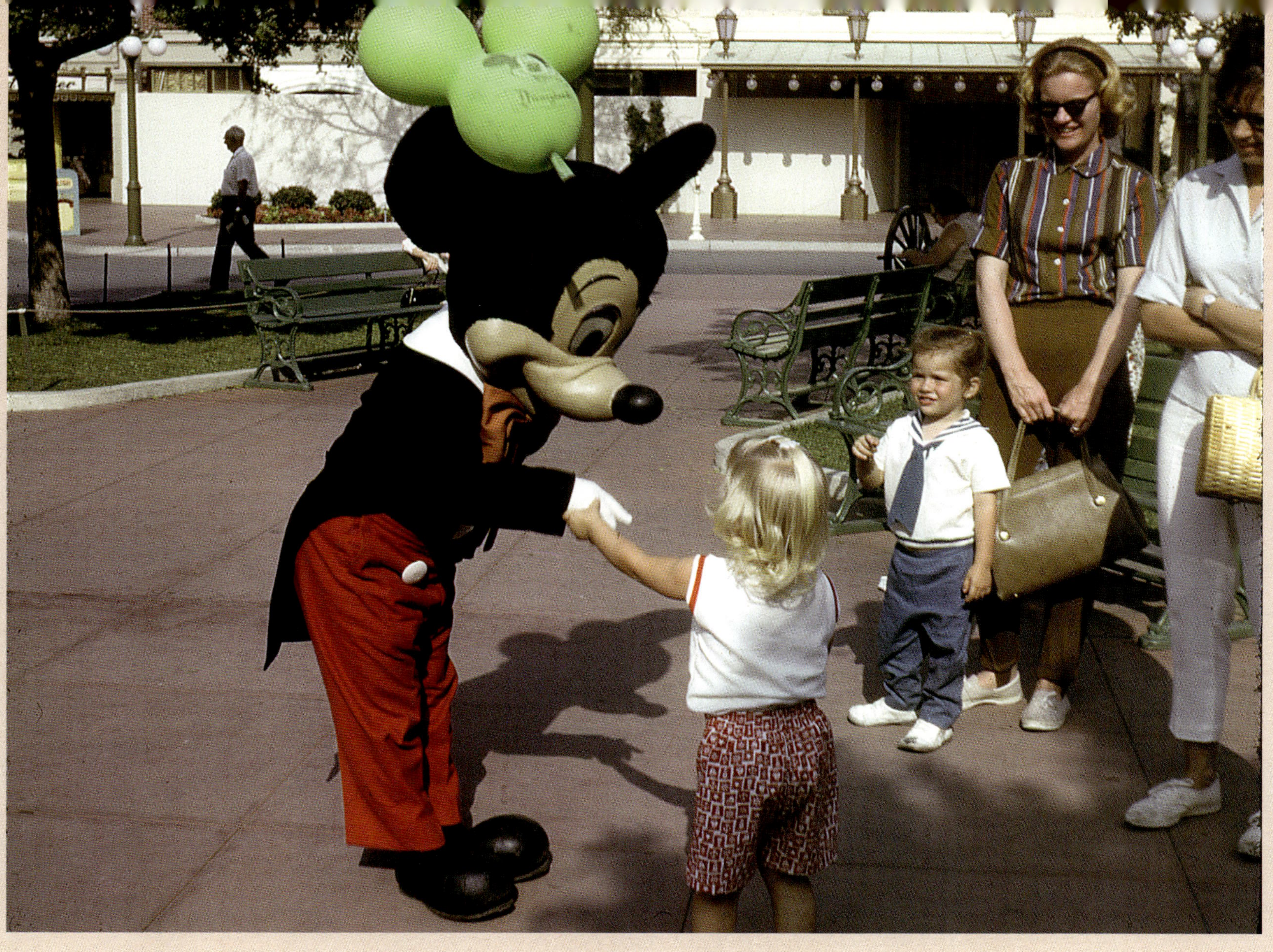

by citrus groves only 30 minutes from Los Angeles. Characters from Disney cartoons and films wandered the park with its Sleeping Beauty castle and Matterhorn, Tom Sawyer Island, Main Street, U.S.A., and Rocket to the Moon. Disneyland was a spectacular hit, sparking childhood imaginations while enchanting ticket-buying parents, who returned with their kids year after year as the park evolved.

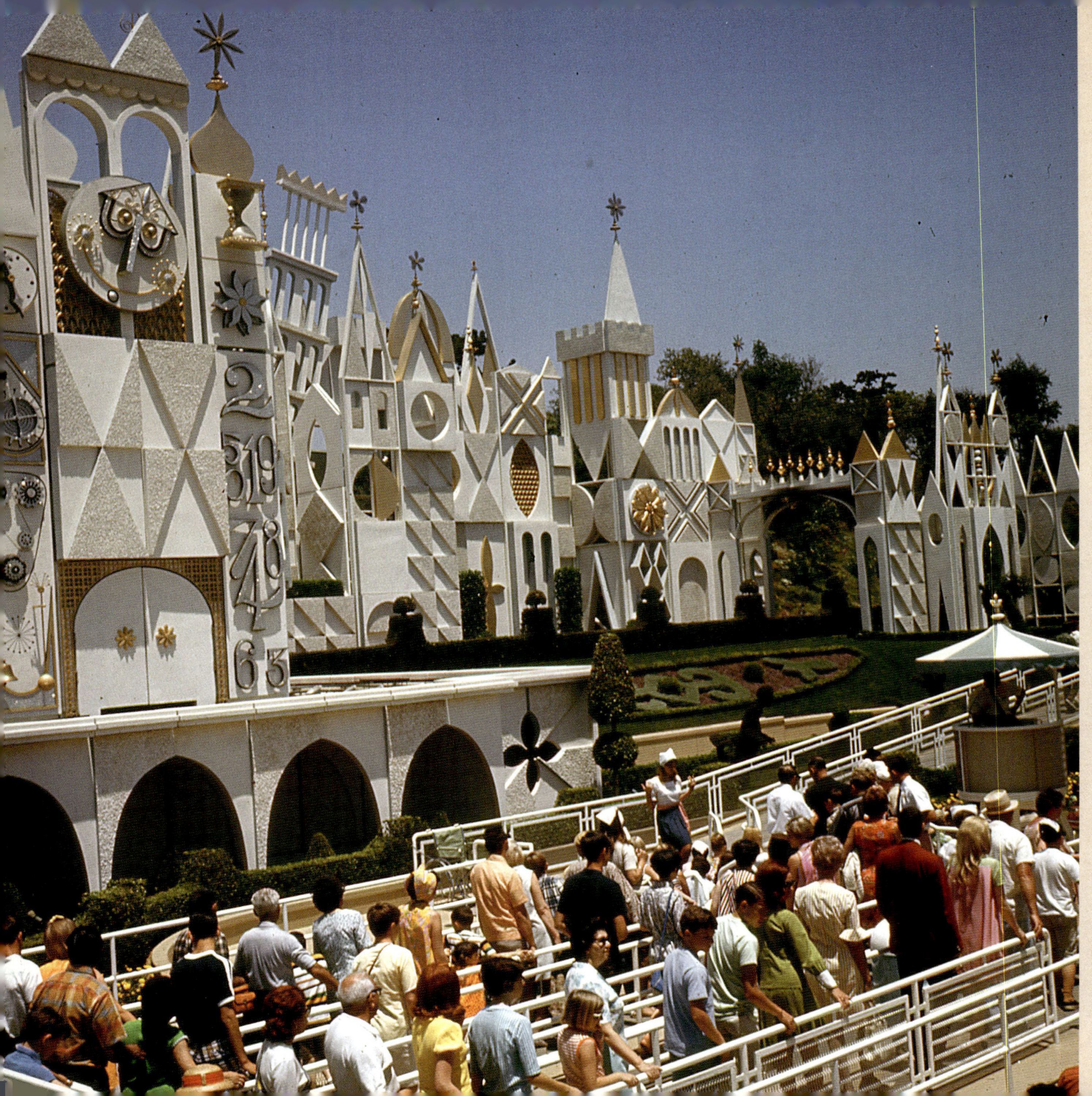

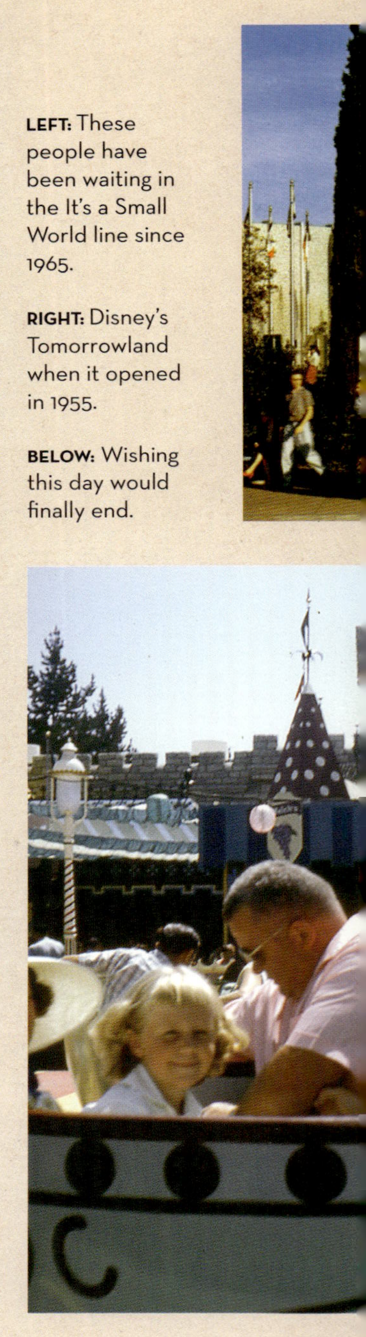

**LEFT:** These people have been waiting in the It's a Small World line since 1965.

**RIGHT:** Disney's Tomorrowland when it opened in 1955.

**BELOW:** Wishing this day would finally end.

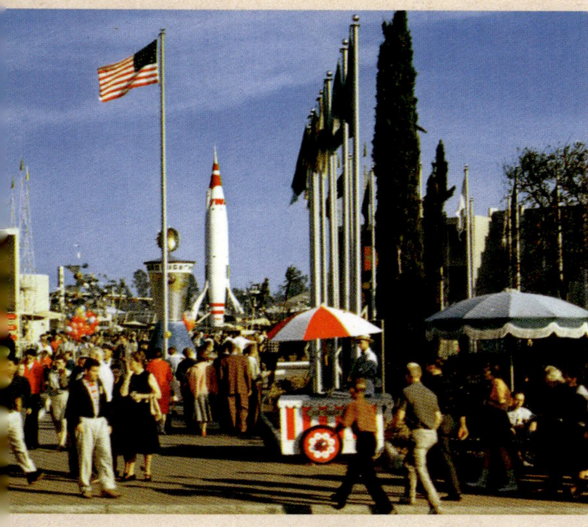

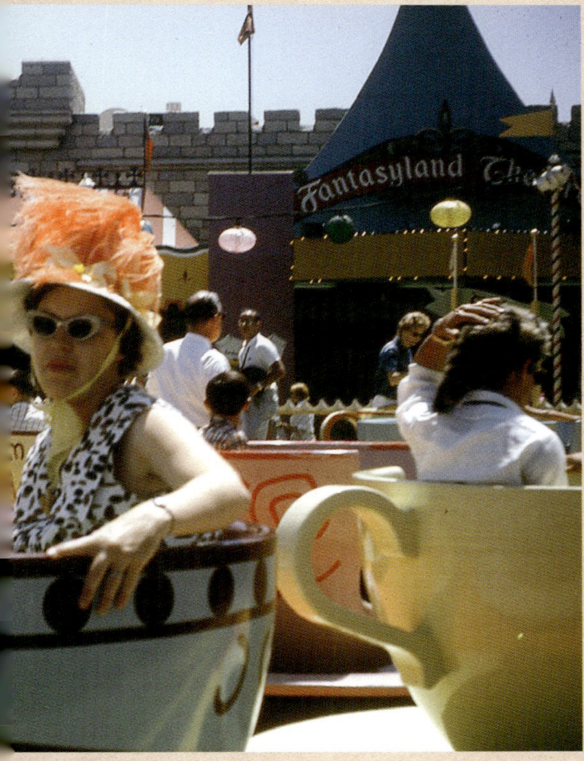

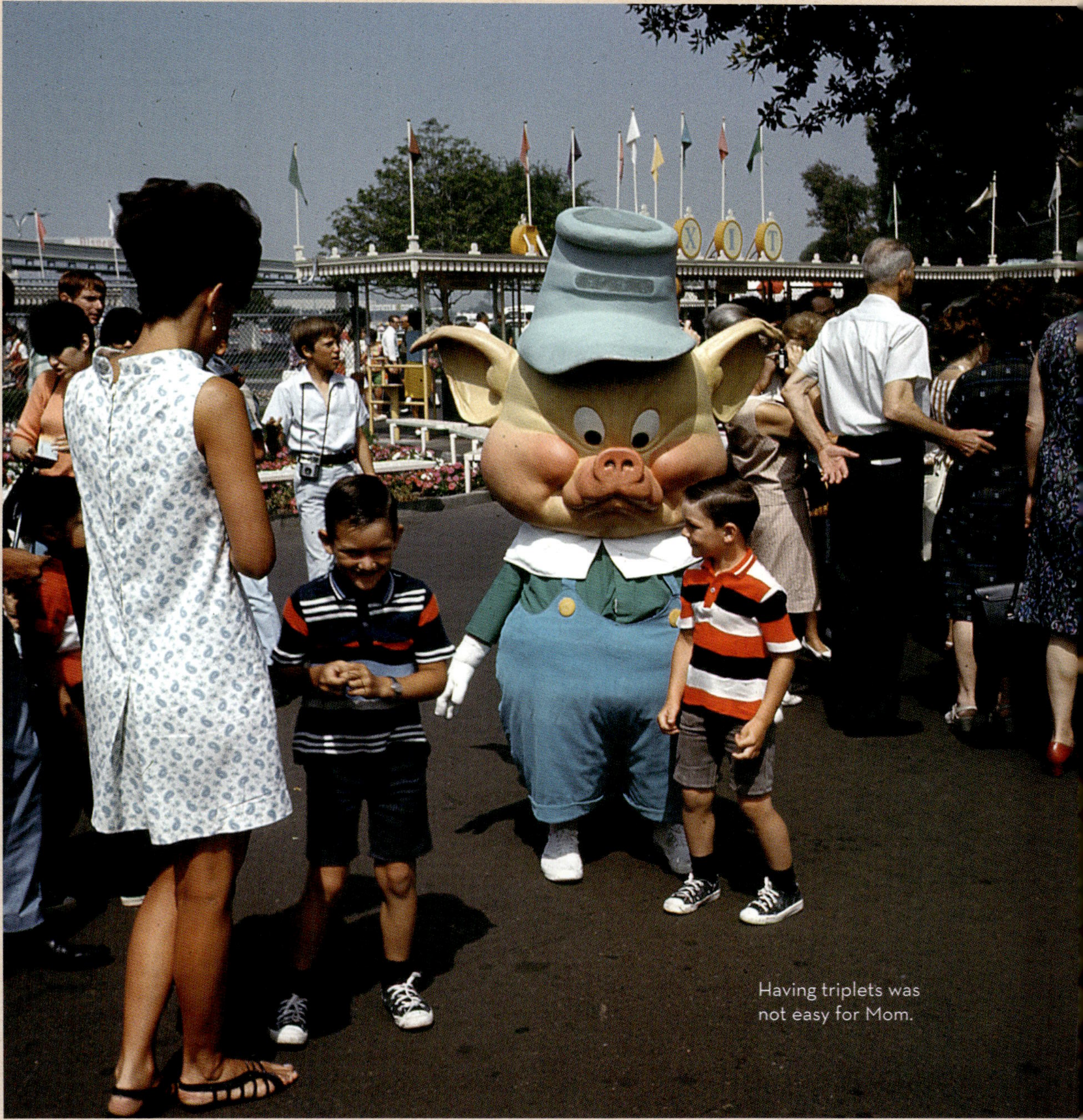

Having triplets was not easy for Mom.

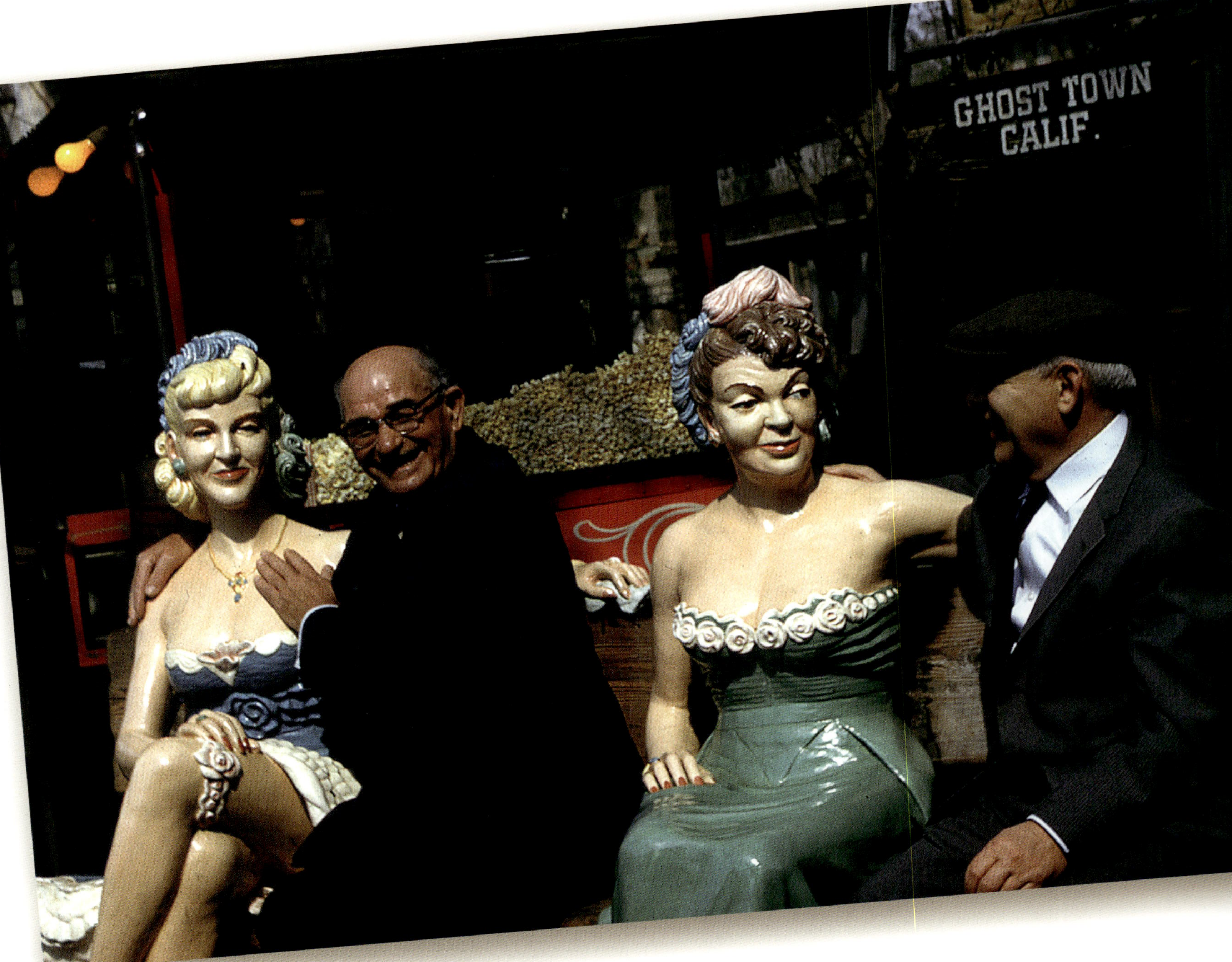
GHOST TOWN
CALIF.

Before Disneyland dominated the theme-park industry here, others vied for tourist dollars—Pacific Ocean Park in Santa Monica, Santa's Village near Lake Arrowhead, Marineland of the Pacific on the Palos Verdes Peninsula, and Knott's Berry Farm in Orange County. Of these Knott's became, like Six Flags, a realm of roller coasters and waterslides. Santa's Village reopened in 2016 as "SkyPark at Santa's Village."

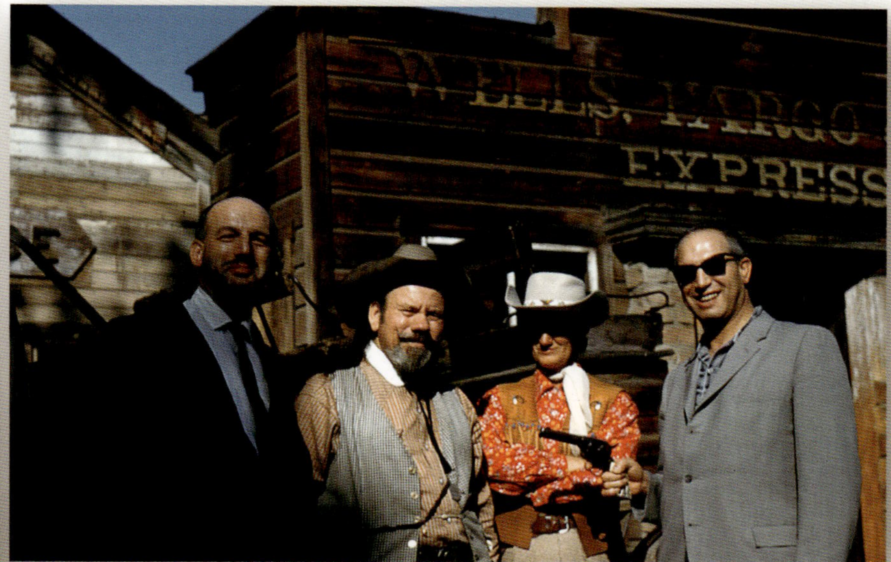


**LEFT:** A bit of excitement for the old duffers at Knott's Berry Farm.

**ABOVE:** This wise guy brought his own gun to Knott's.

**BELOW:** Olga (center) is always the life of the party.

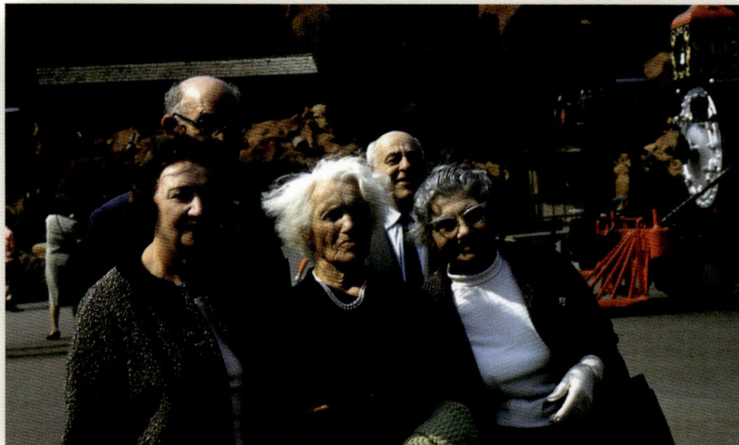

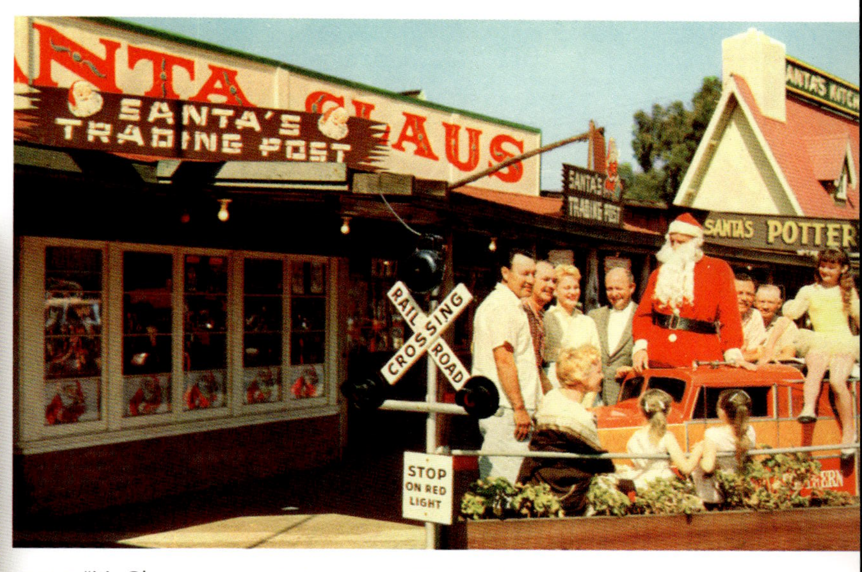


**ABOVE:** "It's Christmastime 365 days of the year at SANTA CLAUS, CALIFORNIA," near Santa Barbara.

**BELOW:** Marge wears a Santa's Village version of a camouflage dress.

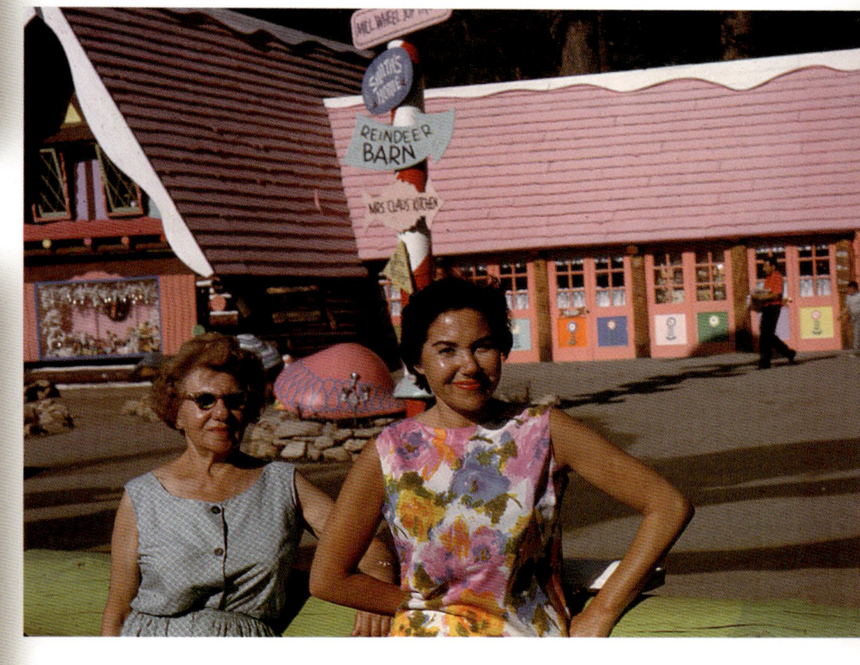

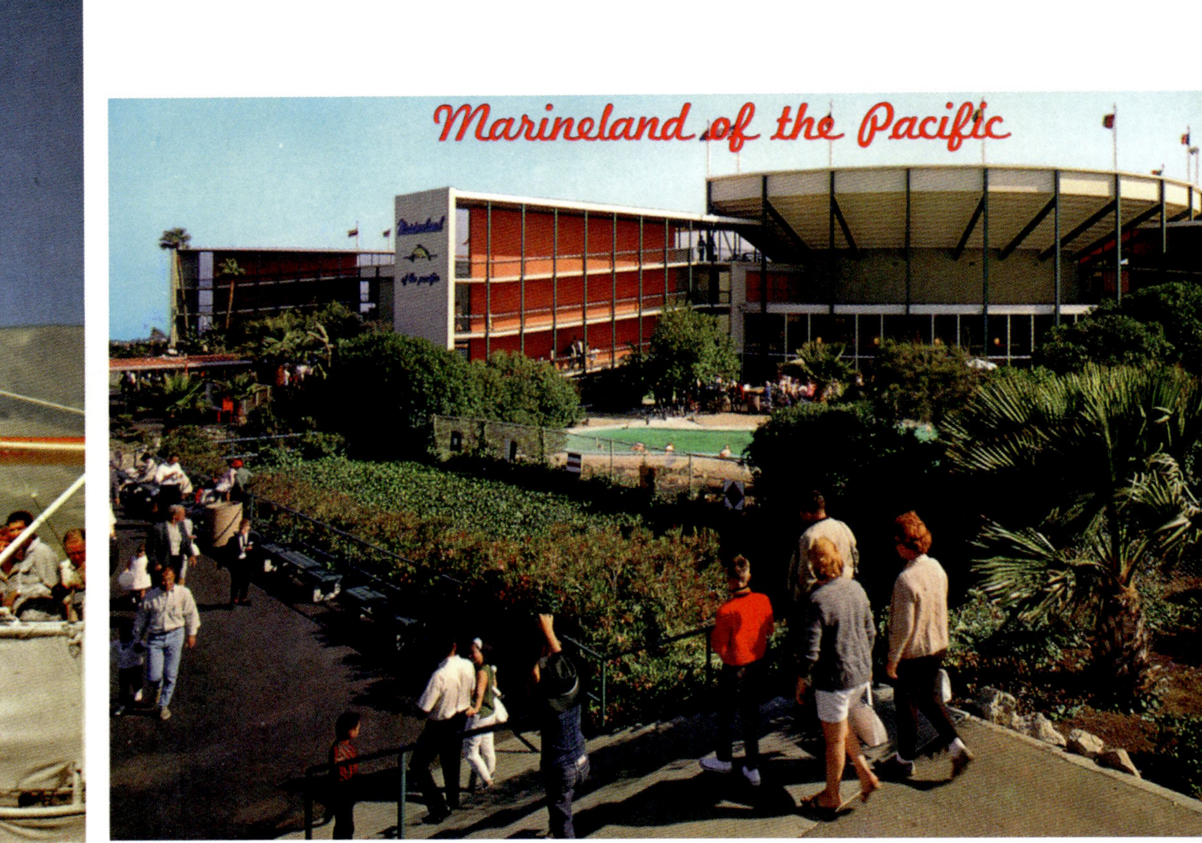


**FACING:** Traversing a rickety bridge to South Sea Island at Pacific Ocean Park in Santa Monica, with its waterfall that pours into the Pacific.

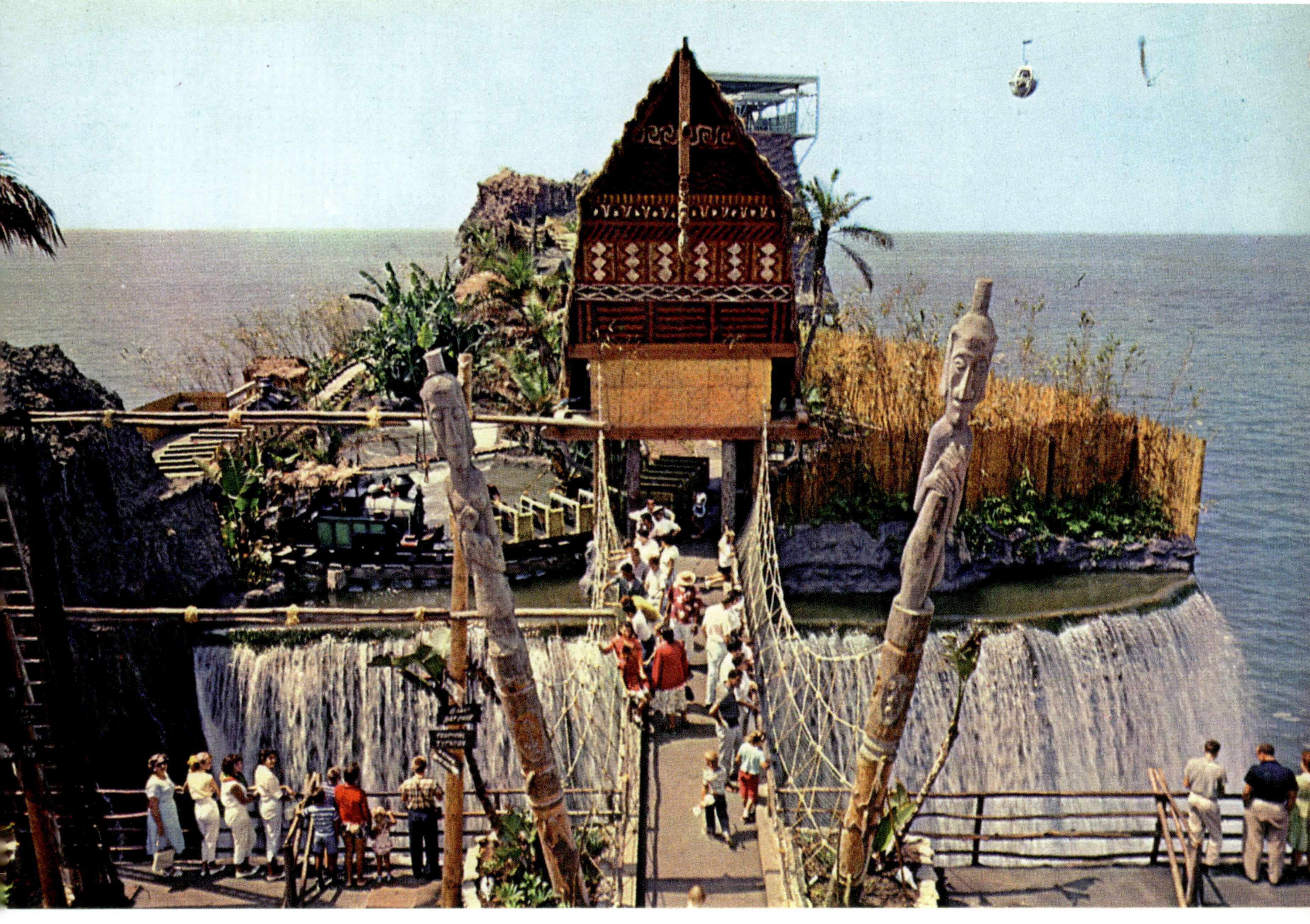

# DODGER STADIUM - Baseball at Its Exciting Best

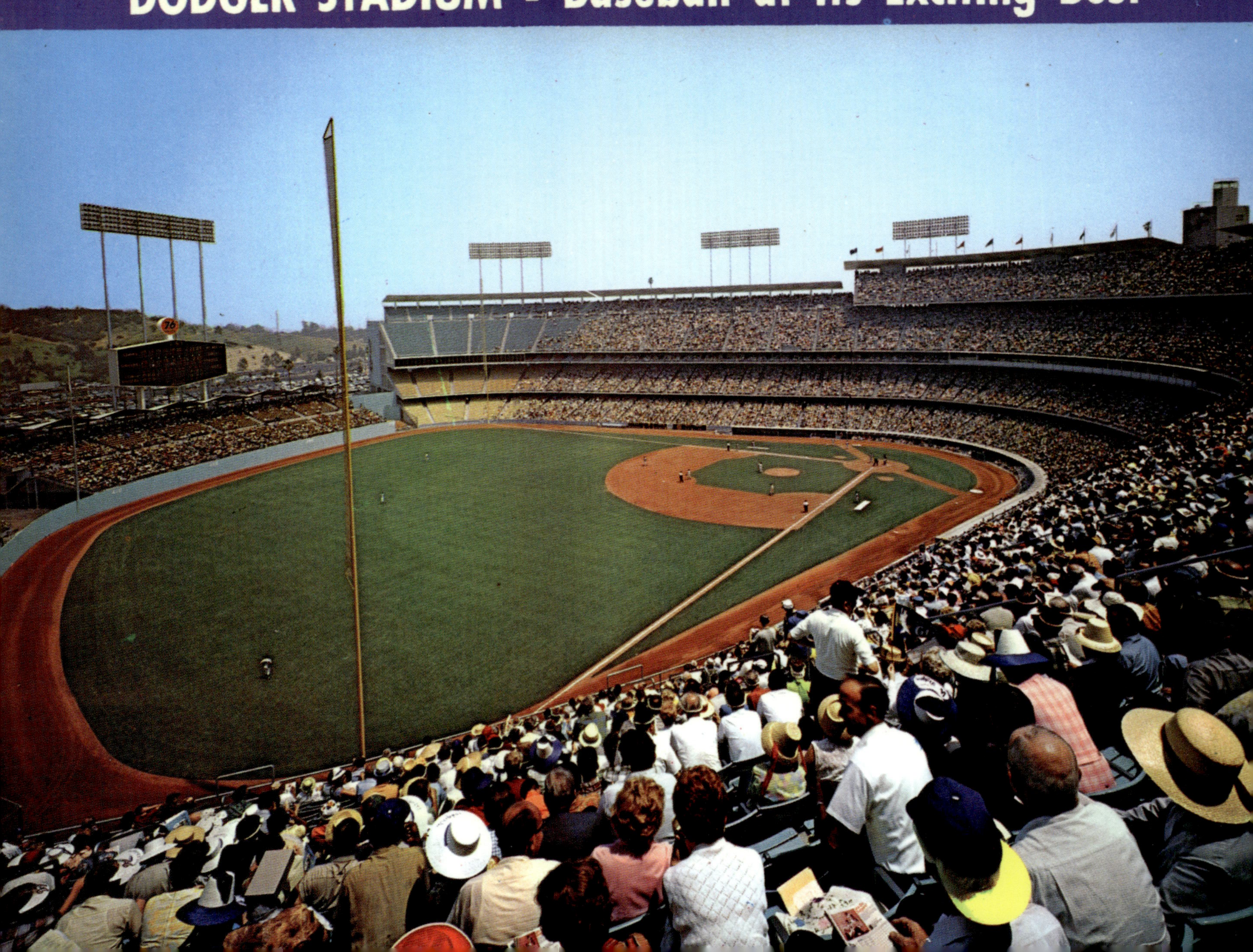

**FACING:** Dodger Stadium opened in 1962 to host the Brooklyn team that relocated to Los Angeles in 1958.

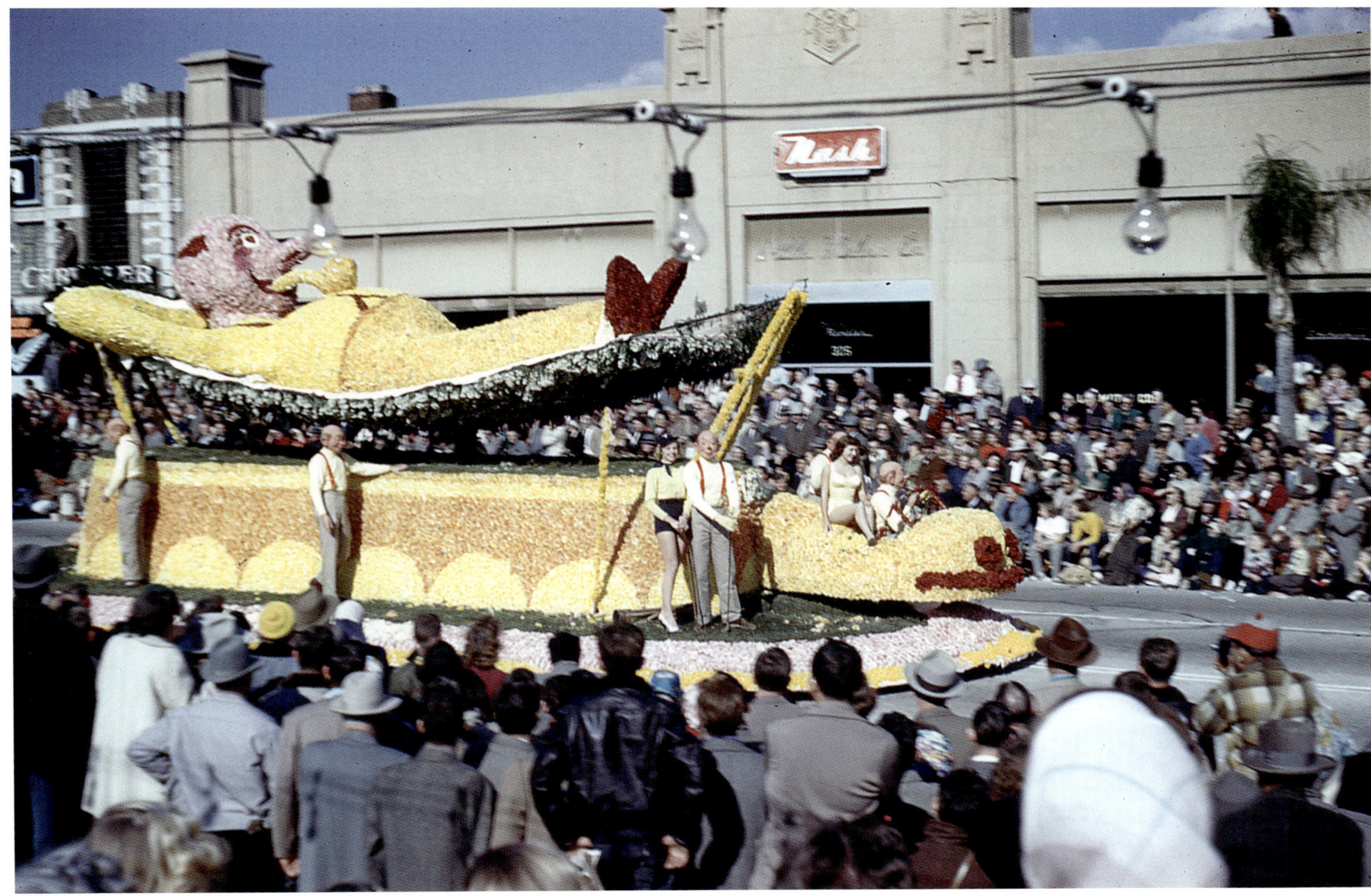


Scary clowns from outer space—and their babes—atop this peculiar float in the 1952 Pasadena Rose Parade.

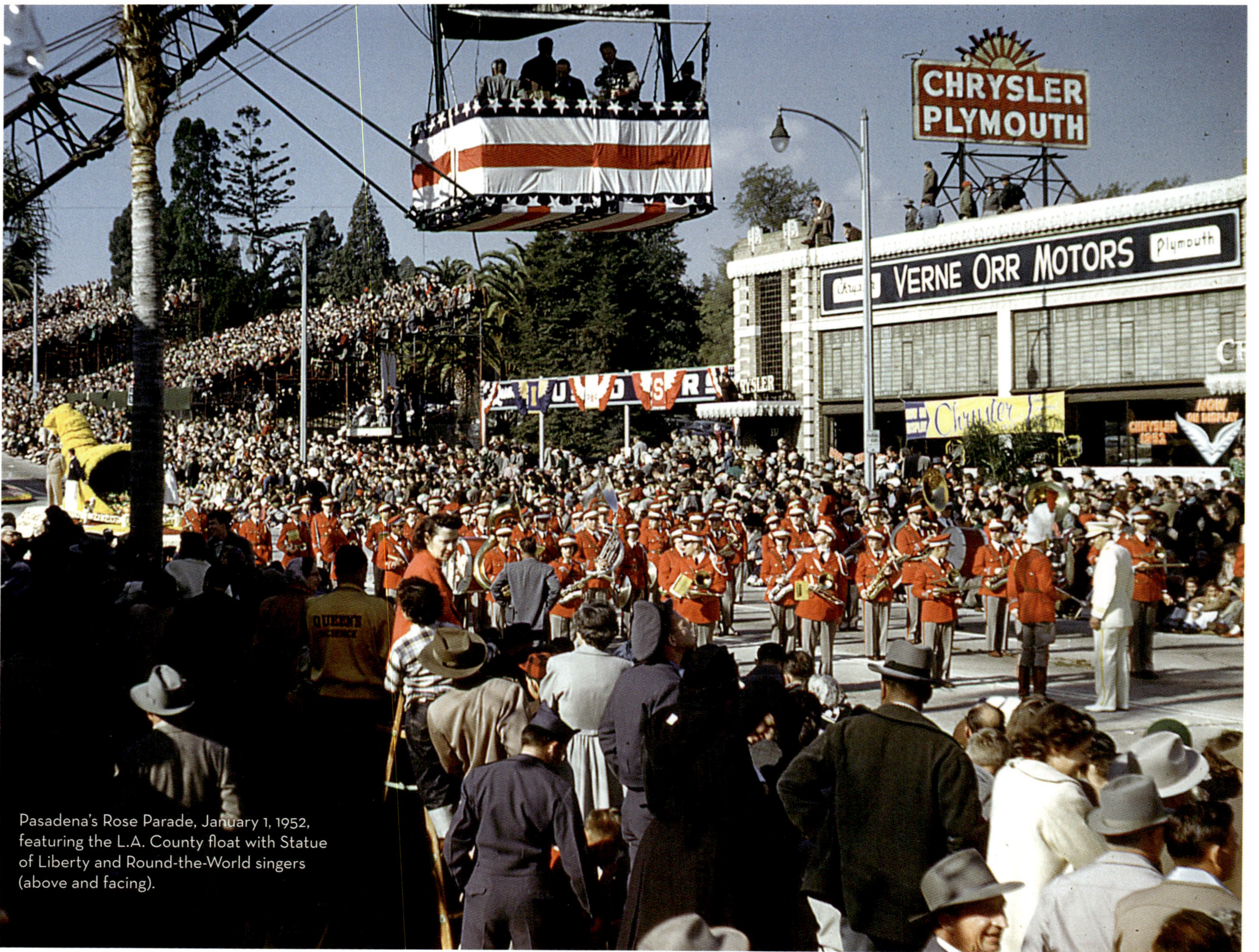


Pasadena's Rose Parade, January 1, 1952, featuring the L.A. County float with Statue of Liberty and Round-the-World singers (above and facing).

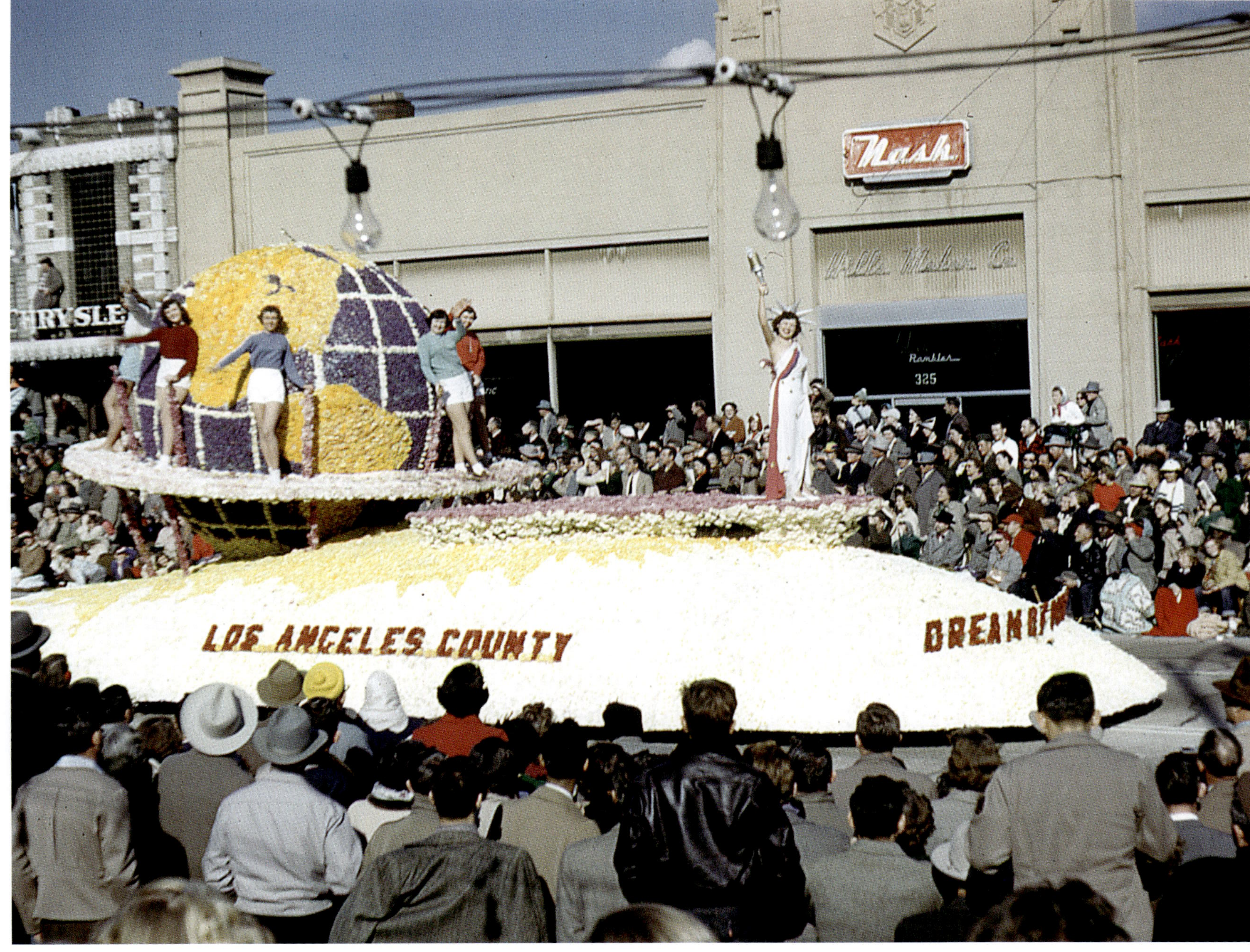
Nash
Rambler
325
LOS ANGELES COUNTY

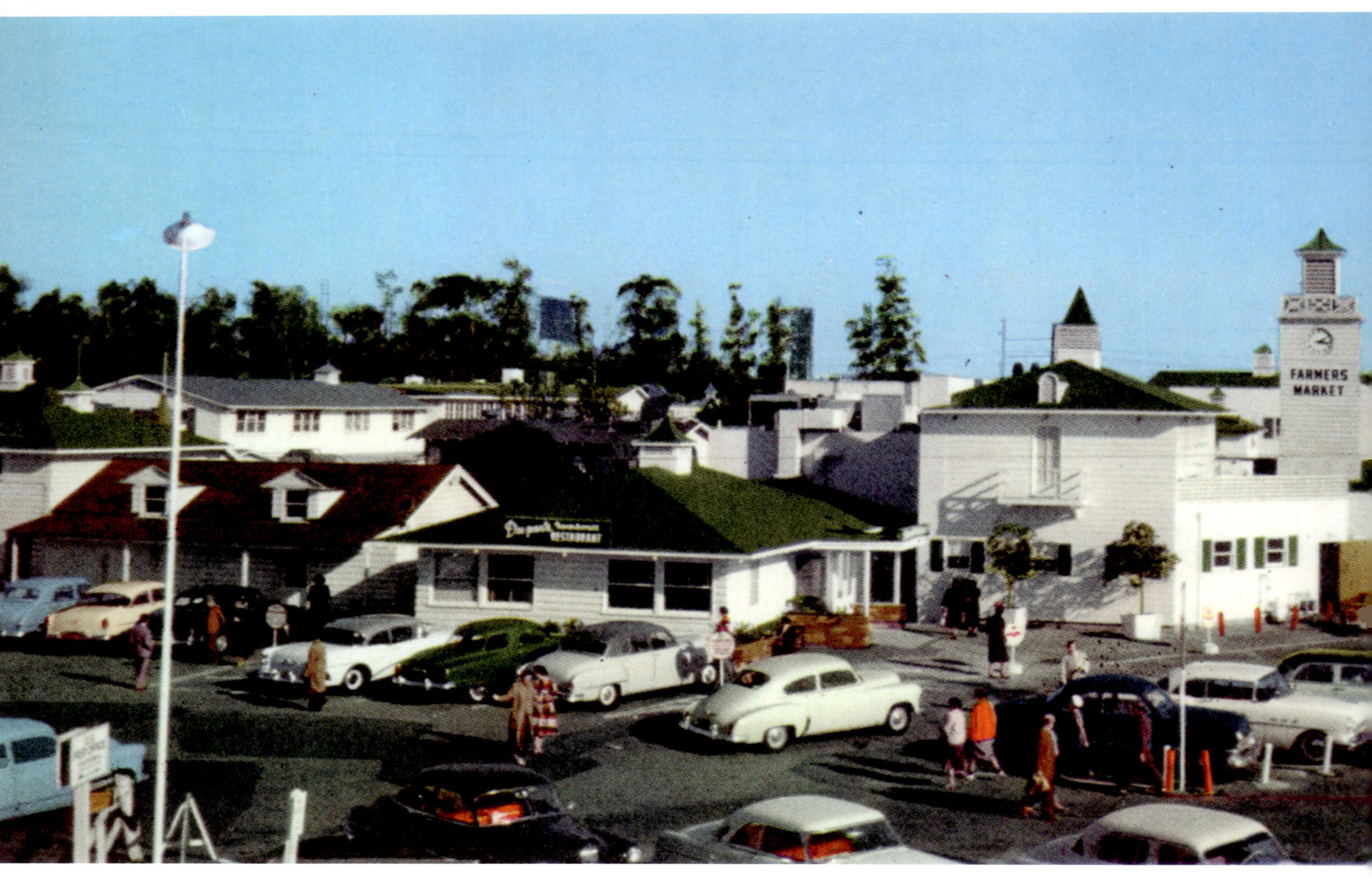


Farmers Market in the 1950s, before being consumed by The Grove shopping center.

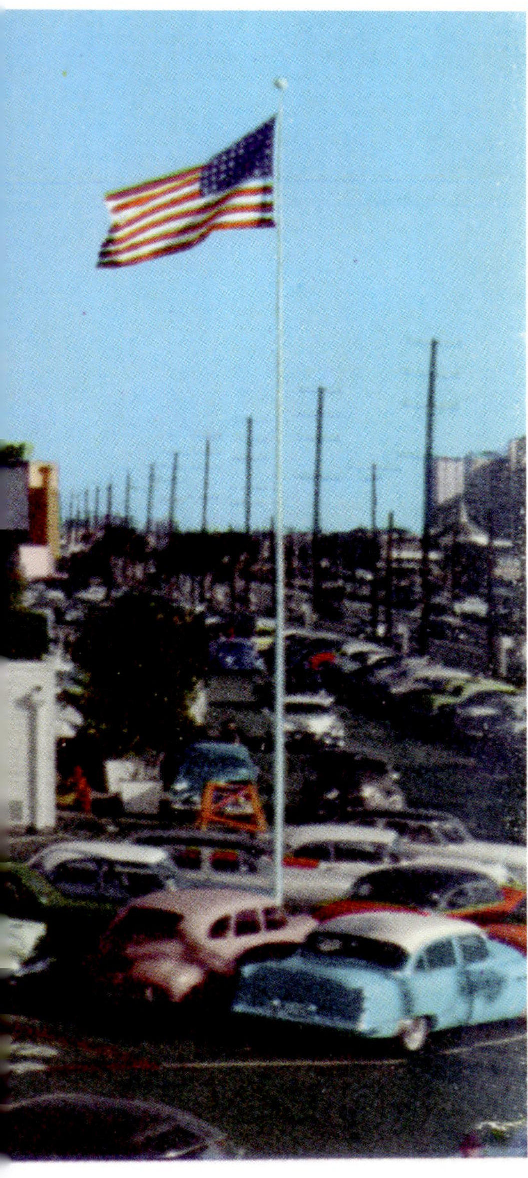

**RIGHT:** From 1921 to 1954, Simon Rodia built his Watts Towers, a magnificent example of outsider art made of rebar, wire mesh, and concrete embedded with colored tiles, bottles, mirrors, and seashells. The tallest tower reaches 99 feet in height.

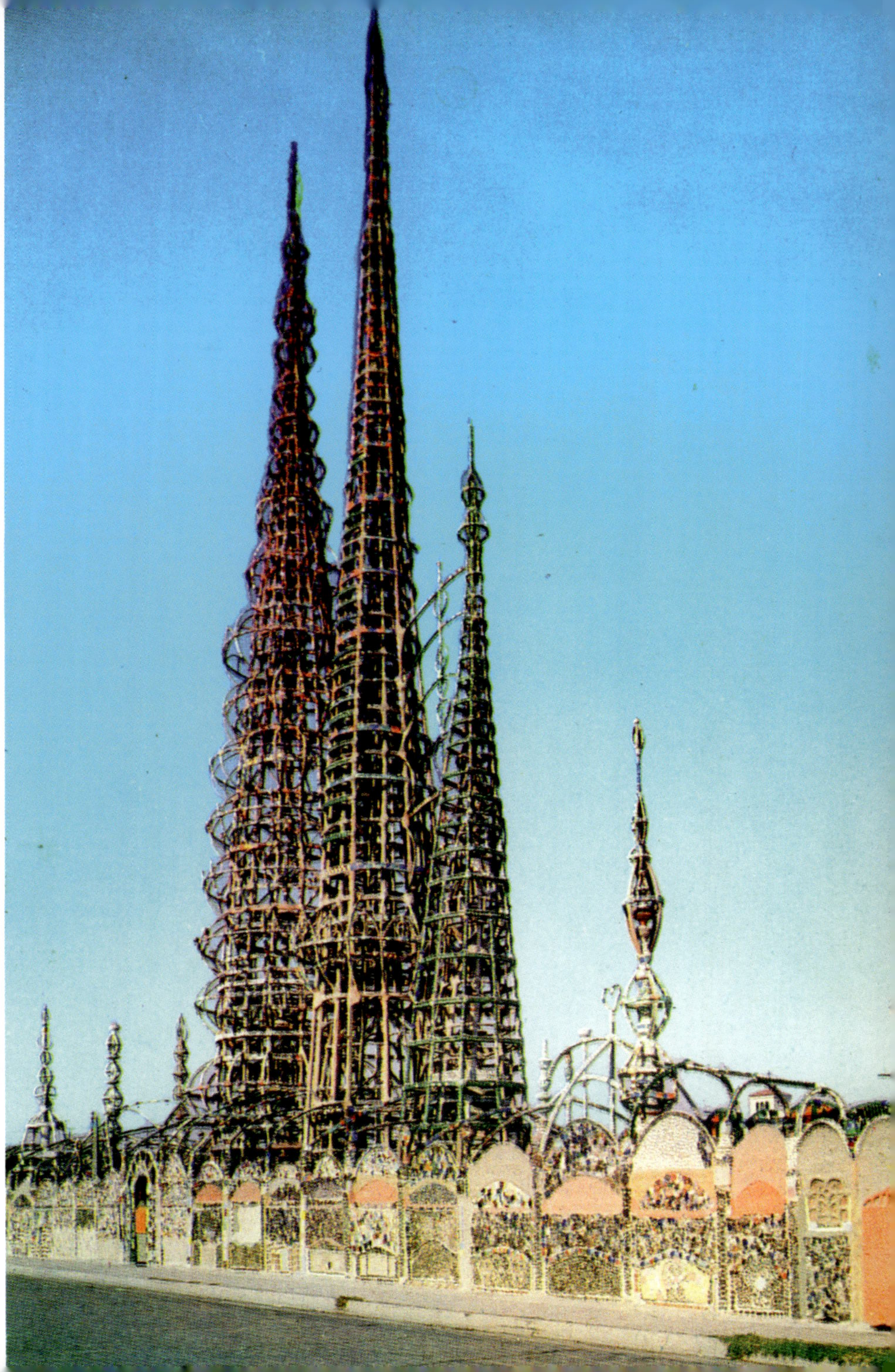

By 1965, the vision of transforming a dusty pueblo into the City of the Future had been realized. It was a horizontal city, a city of freeways and suburbs, aerospace and Hollywood, surf culture and bowling alleys, fine dining and fast food. It was also a segregated city with an occupying police force that engendered resentment and anger, leading to uprisings in Watts that year, and across the city 27 years later. 1965 was on the cusp of a new era that would witness decades of struggle and seemingly intractable challenges, from the decline of aerospace and manufacturing to the waning of downtown. Yet, with the recent rebirth of downtown and many of the city's historic neighborhoods, Los Angeles continues to transform itself—becoming the new, progressive, multicultural City of the Future.

**RIGHT:** 1955's *Rebel Without a Cause* with James Dean made Griffith Observatory world famous.

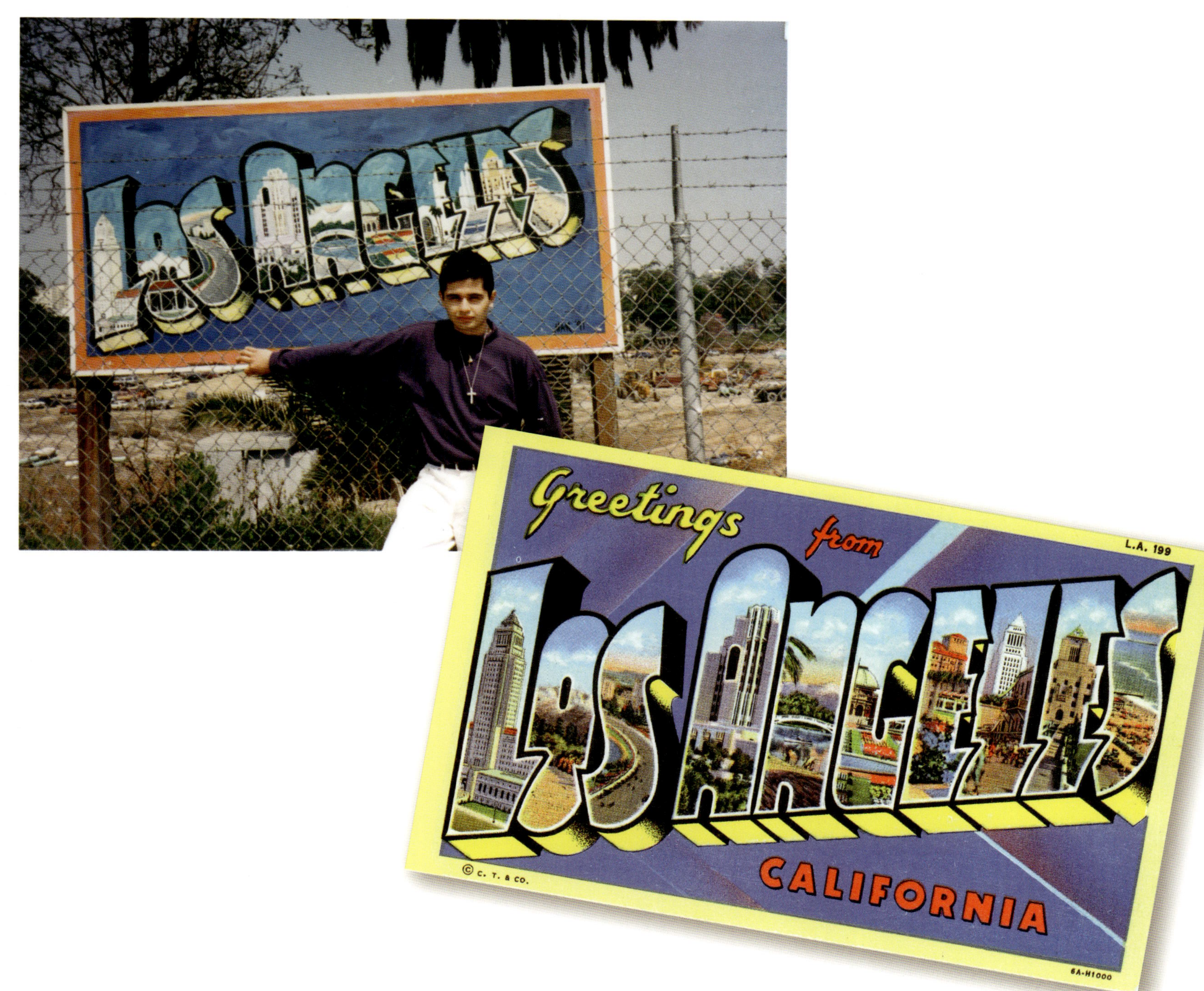
LOS ANGELES
Greetings from
L.A. 199
LOS ANGELES
CALIFORNIA
© C. T. & CO.
6A-H1000

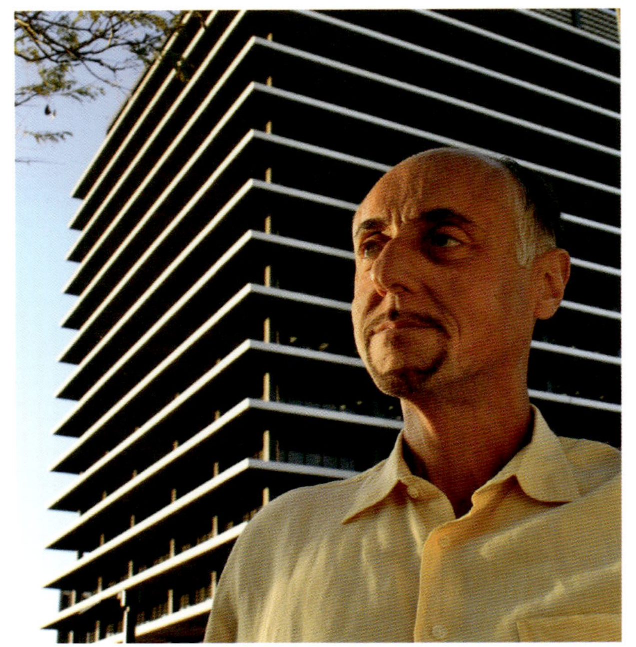

# About the Author

Historian Peter Moruzzi was born in Concord, Massachusetts, and raised in Hawaii. He graduated from the University of California at Berkeley and later attended the American Film Institute in Los Angeles. In 1999 he founded the Palm Springs Modern Committee, an architectural preservation group. Moruzzi is the author of *Havana Before Castro: When Cuba Was a Tropical Playground*, *Palm Springs Holiday: A Vintage Tour from Palm Springs to the Salton Sea*, *Classic Dining: Discovering America's Finest Mid-Century Restaurants*, and *Palm Springs Paradise: Vintage Photographs from America's Desert Playground*.

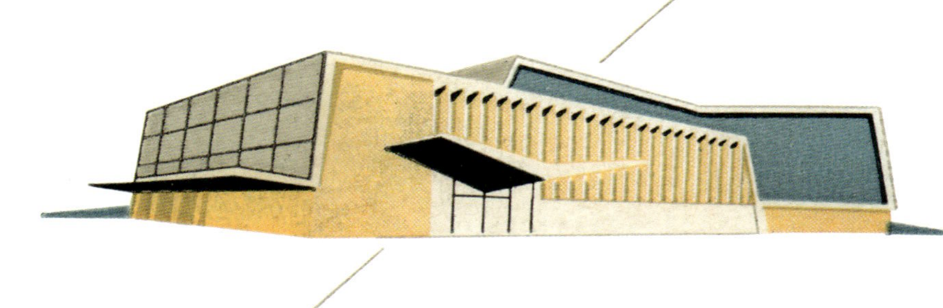

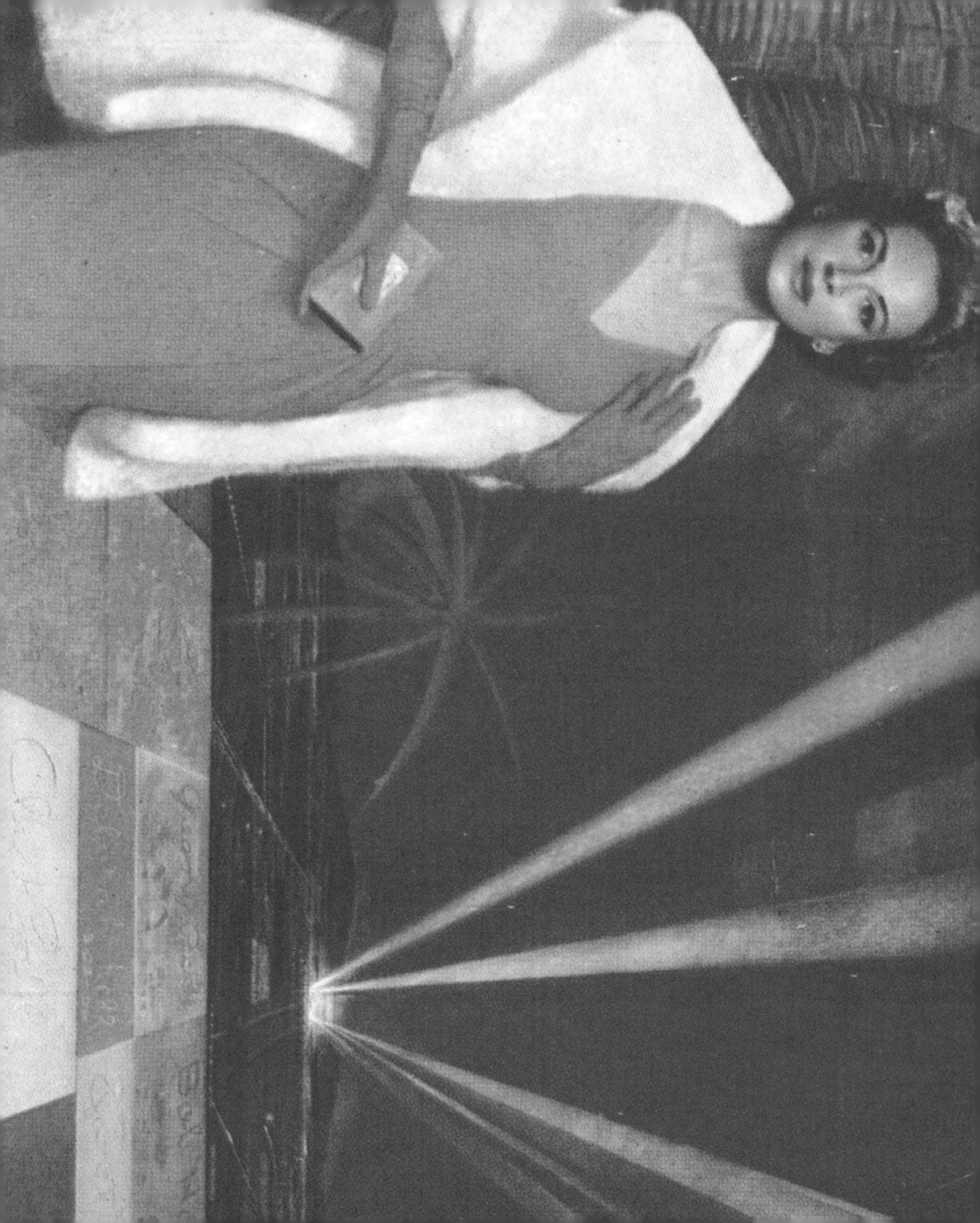

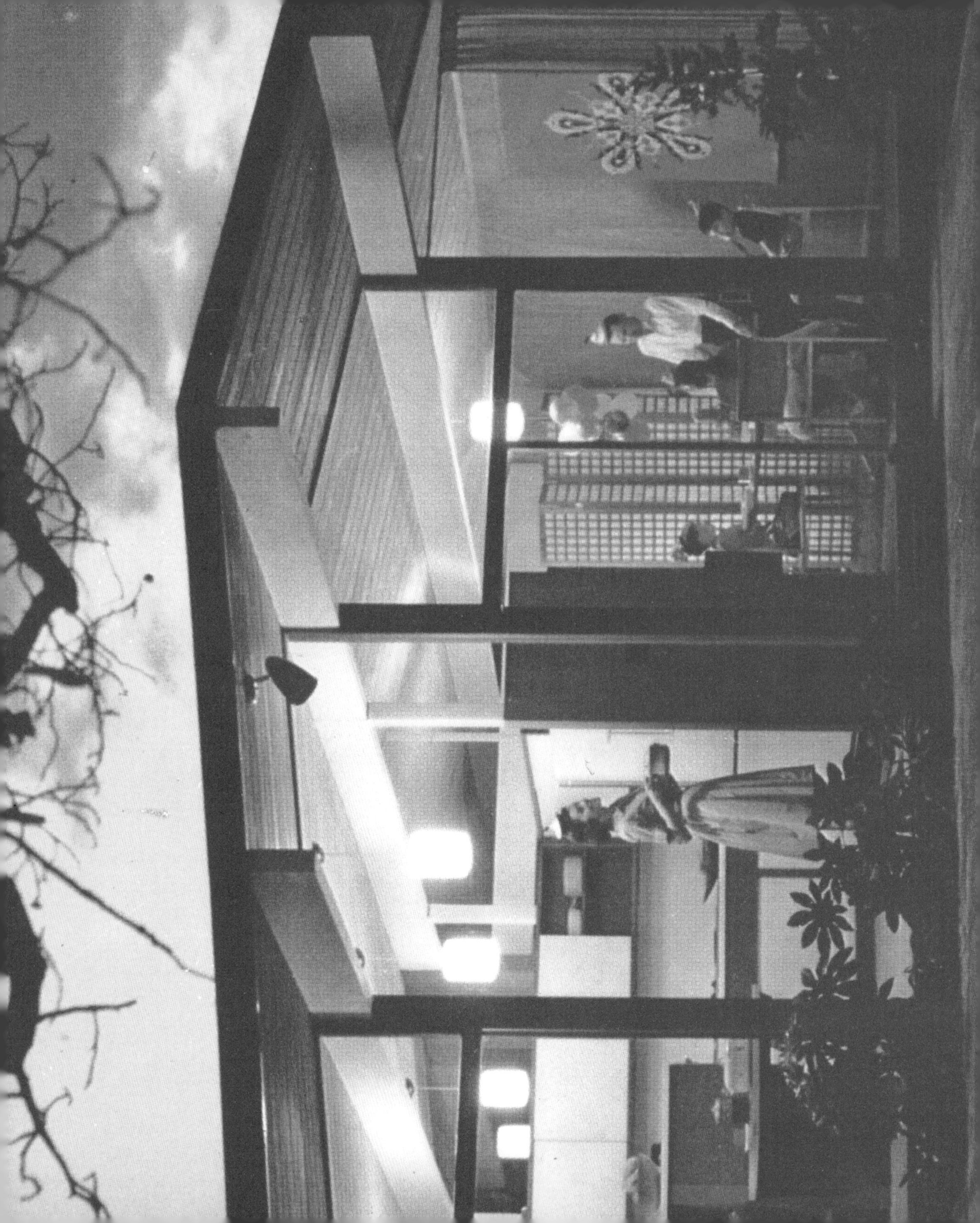